The Ultimate Guide to
Asheville & the Western
North Carolina Mountains
Including Hendersonville and
more than 50 other Mountain Cities and Towns

Expanded Third Edition

Written and Illustrated by
Lee James Pantas

Foreword by
Rick Boyer

R.Brent and Company
Asheville, North Carolina
RBrent.com

The Ultimate Guide to Asheville & the Western North Carolina Mountains: Including Hendersonville and more than 50 other Mountain Cities and Towns: Third Edition. Copyright © 1998–2006 by Lee James Pantas.

Foreword copyright © 1998, 2000, 2006 by Rick Boyer

Published in Asheville, North Carolina
by R. Brent and Company
P.O. Box 7055
Asheville, NC 28802-7055
828-350-9898
rbrent.com

Editor and publisher: *Robbin Brent Whittington*
Consulting editor: *Libby Riker*
Original cover design: *Gayle Graham*
Third edition cover design: *jb graphics, Asheville, North Carolina*
Compositor: *Electronic Publishing Services, Inc., Jonesborough, Tennessee*
Illustrations: *Lee James Pantas*

Library of Congress Data

Pantas, Lee James
    the ultimate guide to asheville & the western north carolina mountains: including hendersonville and more than 50 other mountain cities and towns—3rd ed.
        p.   cm.
    ISBN-13: 978-0-9678061-0-5
    ISBN-10: 0-9678061-0-0
        (Previously published by WorldComm®, ISBN 1-56664-129-2, 1st ed.,
        ISBN 1-57090-105-8, 2nd ed.)
        1. Asheville Region (NC)—Guidebooks 2. Blue Ridge Mountains—
    Guidebooks 3. Great Smoky Mountains National Park (NC and TN)—
    Guidebooks 4. Hendersonville Region (NC)—Guidebooks
        I. Title
    Third Edition   2006930057 LCCN

14 13 12 11 10 09 08 07 06   1 2 3 4 5

Printed in the United States of America.

Lee James Pantas may be contacted at 828-779-1569 or leepantas@bellsouth.net for ordering information. Visa and MasterCard accepted. This book is also available for order online at www.ashevilleguidebook.com.

Contents

Section One: Getting Acquainted   1

Section Two: The Best of
Asheville, Hendersonville & Flat Rock   43

Contents

Section Three: Asheville, All-America City   145

Contents

LEE JAMES PANTAS 1992

List of Maps

Foreword by Rick Boyer

Why I Live in the "Land of the Sky"

The Today Show, 1982:

On our fourth and final day in New York's NBC studios at Rockefeller Center promoting our new book, *Places Rated Almanac,* Jane Pauley leaned over and asked me the question:

"Okay Mr. Boyer—after doing all this research, after compiling this huge almanac based on facts, figures, and government data—what American city would you relocate to if you had a choice?"

Although I should have been expecting a question like this, I admit it took me somewhat off guard. As we filed out to the studio stage from the "green room" that morning, we were told that between eight and twelve million people would be watching. Now I had been asked to *personally choose* the one metro area in the U.S. out of 330 that had emerged as my *favorite city,* a place I would move to the next day if given the chance.

Where to start, given the fact that I had only a few seconds to come up with an answer? I knew it would not be a major city; I have always loved the countryside and knew that any population center I chose would be small to medium sized, and within an easy drive of farms and wilderness.

Although born and raised in the Middle West, I was sick and tired of the long, cold winters and hot humid summers in that region. Now, having lived in New England (Concord, Massachusetts) for a decade, I found the place charming, but the climate no better. I wanted a more southerly place. But not in the Deep South, where the heat and humidity would stifle me. The semitropical climates of Florida and Southern California, while attractive to so many people, never appealed to me; a place needs some cold weather, I reasoned, not just for variety but for hardiness. Also, places with "paradise climates" like San Diego and Honolulu, where the weather shows hardly any fluctuation from season to season, may be great for people suffering from aching joints, but I knew from experience, both researched and personal, that such monotonous climates have a long-term depressant effect on those confined to them.

The deserts and mountains of the West? Yes, they had always enthralled me. Their scenery and openness were spectacular, and their climates vigorous yet comfortable. Also, the major cities of the region, from Denver and Salt Lake to Boise and Albuquerque, were on the whole quite livable. Still, there was the inevitable drawback of isolation. How and when would I ever get to see my friends and family living like Jeremiah Johnson?

Then somewhere from the back of my mind—sifting through the endless lists and tables that my co-author and I had examined during the past four years, leapt a name. A name of a place small enough that many people outside the region had not heard of it. "I think I would move to Asheville, North Carolina," I answered.

And, less than seven months later, I did.

Basically stated, the reasons were simple: Asheville is not too far north nor too far south. It is in the eastern half of the country, but so far west in the coastal state of North Carolina that it lies directly south of Akron, Ohio. Nestled in a broad valley 2,200 feet high between the Blue Ridge and Smoky Mountains, it is shielded from the cold polar air masses that sweep down from Canada in the winter months, and likewise sheltered from most of the hot, humid air that moves inland from the Gulf and the Atlantic during the summer.

In Chicago, where I grew up, the finest season (the *only* fine season) is the fall. Too bad it only lasts two weeks. In Asheville, fall lasts at least ten weeks: the second half of September, all of October and November, and usually the first half of December. Spring begins on the Ides of March and lasts 'til June. The summers, from June until mid-September, have warm days and cool nights. For the most part, air conditioning—especially after seven in the evening—is not needed here. Nor are window screens, because there are no mosquitoes!

Although *Places Rated Almanac* is an extremely thorough publication, there was no section in it that "rated" beauty. Therefore, while I was relatively confident that I had made a good choice, *I had never actually seen the place. All my judgments had been made from printed data, not a personal visit.*

Uh oh ...

So it was with some apprehension that I boarded the plane in Boston for Asheville to enjoy a paid week (courtesy of the Asheville Chamber of Commerce) in the city that I had chosen on national television as the most livable in the country, but that I had never visited. The chamber put us up in the Grove Park Inn, an historic resort hotel that was destined to triple in size within a decade after "word got out" about Asheville. My co-author and I gave out interviews and spiels in mid-April, when the dogwood blossoms speckled the mountainsides, and mountain warblers sang on every branch (it was still snowing in Boston.) A time, as Thomas Wolfe writes in *Look Homeward Angel:*

"...when all the woods are a tender, smokey blur, and birds no bigger than a budding leaf dart through the singing trees...and when the mountain boy brings water to his kinsman laying fence, and as the wind snakes through the grasses hears far in the valley below the long wail of the whistle, and the faint clangor of the bell; and the blue great cup of the hills seems closer, nearer..."

There's a lot more we all like about Asheville: The Biltmore Estate south of town—the grandest, most exquisite chateau ever built, not on the banks of the Loire, but in the valley of the French Broad. The town's architecture, both in her city buildings and her majestic homes set on wide, sycamore-lined avenues. The native mountain people, taciturn at first, funny and kind after a time, and true to their word as a mountain oak.

And always remember this: Every January, there are always three or four days where you can play golf in a sweater...

—Rick Boyer, 2000

Introduction

I t is hoped that *The Ultimate Guide to Asheville & the Western North Carolina Mountains* will be just that. A complete resource for you as you visit our area, one that will allow you to make an informed decision as to what you wish to see and do during your stay. Besides being comprehensive in scope and highly factual as any good guidebook should be, *The Ultimate Guide* is unique in that it is filled with pen and ink illustrations that accompany the text. These highly detailed illustrations should also help you to make the right choices for your visit. A picture *can be* worth a thousand words!

I have tried to organize the material in the book into logical sections to help you in thinking about what to do. Section One, "Getting Acquainted," will provide you with an overview as well as vital and useful information to make your stay a successful one. Section Two, "The Best of Asheville, Hendersonville & Flat Rock," not only presents my personal selections and favorites but also covers topics of interest to all visitors, from accommodations and restaurants to art and crafts galleries to outdoor recreation. As a longtime resident who lives and works in this area, I am very confident in providing this vital information and very comfortable in making any recommendations, since these come from my firsthand knowledge. Sections Three and Four present the major attractions and things to see and do in "Asheville, All-America City" and "Hendersonville & Flat Rock." Section Five presents the major attractions in all of "Western North Carolina," realizing that you may wish to stay in Asheville or Hendersonville and venture out into the surrounding mountains on day trips.

I have tried to include in this guidebook everything that would be of interest to visitors. Many of the attractions and features included are very popular and well advertised. Some however are not as well known but just as worthy. It is hoped that my experience of living and working in the Asheville and Hendersonville area has enabled me to do it right, so to speak—to write a guidebook that really is thorough and accurate, not just one that provides superficial or limited information from the perspective of a nonnative.

One of the most delightful surprises along the way, and one I hope you will discover for yourself, is the wonderful friendliness of the many people who work at the places highlighted in *The Ultimate Guide to Asheville & the Western North*

Carolina Mountains. There is such a thing as "Southern Hospitality!" The people of the mountains, those whose families have lived here for generations and those who have just arrived, are the true treasures. There are truly beautiful and inspiring places to visit in the mountains, but the folks who greet you at the door make it all the better.

—Lee James Pantas, 2000

About the Author

Lee James Pantas, originally from Greenwich, Connecticut, has lived in the Asheville area since 1989. He has a Master's degree in Ecology from the University of Vermont, and has worked as a research scientist, military officer, lecturer, parapsychologist, marketing director, painter and illustrator in Vermont, Georgia, the orient, Brazil, Colorado, Connecticut and North Carolina. He is active in youth track and field and coaches hurdles for A.C. Reynolds High School as well as the Asheville Lightning Junior Olympics Team.

Well-known throughout North Carolina for his award-winning, exquisitely detailed pen and ink drawings, Mr. Pantas has completed more than 2,000 private and corporate commissions. Distinguished clients include Former President and Mrs. George Bush, Governor and Mrs. James B. Hunt Jr., United States Ambassador and White House Chief of Staff of Protocol Joseph Verner Reed, Mr. and Mrs. Ben Holden, George Sanders, and the Estate of Guy Lombardo. He has also completed drawings for more than 200 bed and breakfasts and inns, and more than 300 churches and synagogues. He is one of the few area artists with permission from the Biltmore Company to publish and market prints of his original pen and ink drawings of Biltmore Estate.

Mr. Pantas is also known for his imaginative visionary and fantasy paintings. His work has been exhibited in New York City, San Francisco and Washington, D.C., and locally in Blue Spiral 1, Broadway Arts and Seven Sisters Gallery, among others, and is found in many private collections. He is currently at work on a ten-year project "Liza's Reef," a series of paintings of an imaginary coral reef located near an imaginary island in the South Pacific. The goal of the project is to raise funds for selected environmental organizations and orphanages in the South Pacific. The project website is www.lizasreef.com.

He lives just outside of Asheville in a mountain valley in Fairview with his wife, Elizabeth.

Correspondence should be directed to:

Lee James Pantas
Cherry Orchard Studio
18 Garren Mountain Lane   828-779-1569
Fairview, NC 28730   leepantas@bellsouth.net

Acknowledgements

I am greatly indebted to the many people who offered their time and knowledge and helped to make this book a reality. Many thanks to the management and staff at the various agencies, attractions and other listings in this book for their valuable assistance and input. I am especially grateful to Dini Pickering, Diane LeBeau, Liz Calhoun, Barbara O'Neil, Elizabeth Sims, Marinda Williams and Kathleen Morris of Biltmore Estate; Charlie C. Lytle and Reginna Swimmer of Harrah's Cherokee Casino; Jennifer F. Martin, John H. Horton and Diane Jones of the North Carolina State Preservation Office; Harry Weiss of the Preservation Society of Asheville and Buncombe County; Melody Heltman and Gabby Snyder of the Hendersonville/Flat Rock Visitors Information Center; Angie Chandler, Helen Calloway, Bill Turner, and Angie Briggs of the Asheville Area Chamber of Commerce Visitor Center; Maggie O'Conner of the Historic Resources Commission; Stephen Hill, Susan Weatherford and Ted Mitchell of the Thomas Wolfe Memorial; Maggie Schlubach and David Tomsky of the Grove Park Inn Resort; Rhonda Horton of the Woodfield Inn; Grace Pless, Sara Bissette, and all of the other dedicated volunteers of the Asheville Urban Trail; Susan Michel-Robertson of the Richmond Hill Inn; Gail Gomez of High Country Guild; Roann Bishop of the Historic Johnson Farm; Sherry Masters of the Grovewood Gallery; Cae Gibson of the Flat Rock Playhouse; Joey Moore of the Asheville Arts Alliance; Donna Garrison of the N.C. Department of Transportation; Dick Stanland of Historic Flat Rock Inc.; Weston Utter of the Western North Carolina Nature Center; Patricia R. Crisco and David W. Blynt of the Buncombe County Parks & Recreation Department; Roxanne J. Royer of Office Depot; Sondra McCrary of ARCO Blueprinters; Terry Clevenger of the Asheville Downtown Association; Lisa Smith and Gwen Chalker of the Asheville Convention and Visitors Bureau; Richard Mathews of the Albermarle Park Association; Jerry and Nancy Marstall of The Blue Book; Joan S. Baity of the Old Wilkes Jail Museum; Pam Herrington of The Cove; Mary Alice Murphy of Christmount; Laura Rathbone of Lake Junaluska Assembly; Jim Danielson of Ridgecrest; John Paul Thomas of YMCA Blue Ridge Assembly; Mike Small of UNCA; and Liz Gress of Lutheridge.

Other professionals to whom I am indebted include Lauren Abernathy, Connie Backlund, Harry Bothwell, Bill Bornstein, Irby Brinson, Katherine Caldwell,

Wayne Caldwell, Lee Creech, Carol Donnelly, Cheryl Fowler, Jessica Gosnell, Leona Haney, Tom Hardy, Larry Harmon, Carl Hill, Hosey Horton, Dr. Jack Jones, Joy Jones, Elaine McPherson, Rev. Edward Meeks, Judy and Neil Meyer, Mary Alice Nard, David Olson, Marvin Owings, David Ross, Norm Sanders, Dick Shahan, Chris Smith, David Tate and Barbara Turman.

A special thank you for their encouragement and advice to Annie Ager, Bill and Kathy Agrella, Rem and Isabel Behrer, Larry and Yolanda Bopp, Joe and Bobbi Costy, Greg and Carla Filapelli, Mike and Chris Grier, Mary Herold, Charlotte Harrell, Marge Kavanaugh, John and Agnes Laughter, Roddy Lee, Daniel Lewis, Marilyn and Dick Marino, Elizabeth McAfee, Jane McNeil, Tom and L.J. McPherson, Erich and Liz Pearson, Myra Ramsay, and Phil and Rene Thompson.

I am also grateful to Jim Curwen of the Asheville Track Club for his information about the Track Club and especially for the Kimberly Avenue run; to Mickie Booth, for her wonderful exposition on the Asheville Urban Trail; and to my assistant Kiki Cook for her encouragement and help.

I am thankful to Ralph Roberts, publisher of Alexander Books, for allowing me the opportunity to bring this book to print in the first and second editions, and to Barbara Blood, Gayle Graham, Susan Parker, Vanessa Razzano, Pat Roberts, and Vivian Terrell of Alexander Books for advice and assistance.

A special word of thanks to my mother-in-law, Hazel Nading, and to Art and Martha Nading, Vincent and Maryjean Pantas, Lynne and Bob Boie, and Louise Lea Nading.

I would also like to especially thank both Liza Schillo for her encouragement and review of the Grove Park Inn Resort & Spa, and Robbin Brent, of R. Brent & Company, for her invaluable guidance and support in bringing the third edition to life.

Finally I would like to thank my wife Elizabeth, my son Daniel, and my daughter Susanna for their patience, love and support.

**This book is dedicated in loving memory of my parents
Leo and Alberta Pantas**

Icons, Abbreviations & Symbols Used in This Guide

NRHP   Listed in the National Register of Historic Places

NHL   National Historic Landmark

LHL   Local Historic Landmark

SEE   Sends you to another section of the guide for more information.

Restaurant Price Guide

$	Under $10
$$	$10-$20
$$$	$20-$30
$$$$	Over $30

The typical price for an evening meal for one person, excluding taxes, gratuity, and drinks.

Section One
Getting Acquainted

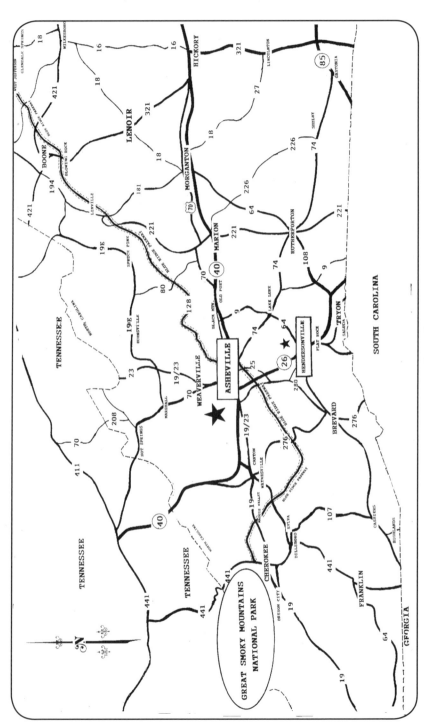

Western North Carolina

Chapter One
Getting Started

Once you arrive in either Asheville or Hendersonville, your very first stop should be the visitor centers in each city. Both centers are geared completely to help make the most of your visit. There you will find friendly and informed staff eager to help, a complete array of brochures and tourist-oriented publications, and complimentary maps. Both centers are centrally located and easy to find. (Additional WNC Chambers & Visitor Centers are listed in Section Five Chapter 4)

Chambers of Commerce/Visitor Centers
Asheville

Located just off Interstate 240 as it passes through downtown Asheville, the Asheville Area Chamber of Commerce Visitor Center is conveniently accessible to visitors to Asheville. The friendly and knowledgeable staff stand ready to assist with information, brochures, maps and recommendations for your visit to Asheville. The visitor center serves more than 150,000 people annually, providing a host of valuable information about the area. The center also has racks of brochures featuring publications on attractions and businesses located in Asheville and Western North Carolina. Visitor counselors are also on hand to help visitors with special needs, and a phone is available to make hotel reservations. In addition, the center also has a gift shop where you may purchase notecards, prints, gifts and souvenir items characteristic of the mountains.

For 100 years, the Asheville Area Chamber of Commerce has been creating win-win opportunities for Asheville's diverse and vital community. The Asheville Chamber works on many fronts to bolster the local business climate by working to bring new businesses to the area, helping existing companies expand and improving education in the area. Although the chamber is in the tenth largest city in North Carolina, it is the third largest chamber in the state.

Within the visitor center is the Asheville Area Chamber of Commerce Convention and Visitors Bureau, a chamber organization dedicated to arranging accommodations and help with convention planning for groups large and small. No matter what you request in planning a gathering or convention in Asheville, they

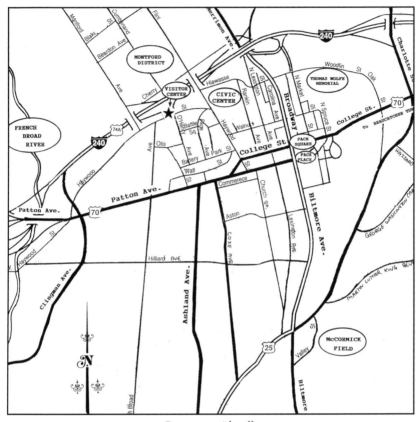

Downtown Asheville

will be able to help. They have current listings of all companies and individuals in the area whose businesses cater to conventions, as well as a complete knowledge of local accommodations.

Address: Asheville Area Chamber of Commerce Visitor Center, 36 Montford Ave., Asheville, NC 28801

Telephone: Visitor Center: 258-6100 or (800) 257-1300
Convention & Visitor Center: 258-6102 or (800) 257-5583
Chamber of Commerce Main Number: 258-6101
Hotline/Membership/Event Information: 253-8125
Communications/Public Affairs: 258-6131
Community Development: 258-6118
Economic Development: 258-6117
Executive Office: 258-6124
Finance: 258-6132
Member Services: 258-6114
Small Business Enterprise: 258-6116

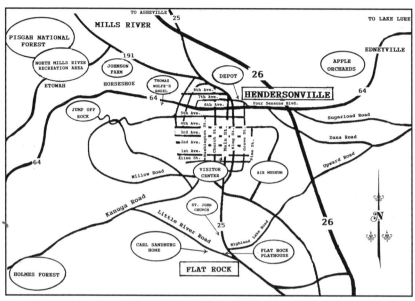

Hendersonville & Flat Rock

Websites: www.ashevillechamber.org (Chamber of Commerce)
www.ci.asheville.nc.us (City of Asheville)

Email: asheville@ashevillechamber.org

Hours: Open year-round, except Thanksgiving, Christmas and New Year's Day. Mon.-Sun.: 8:30 a.m.-5:30 p.m.

Directions: From I-240 East, take Montford Ave. Exit off I-240 west. Turn left onto Montford Ave. and then left onto Haywood St. From I-240 West, take Civic Center Exit and make a right onto Haywood St.

Hendersonville & Flat Rock

For more than 100 years, visitors have been welcomed to the mountain area of Hendersonville and Flat Rock. Today the same is still true, and the Visitors Information Center in the heart of the downtown historic district welcomes travelers from across the country and around the world.

Hendersonville Visitor Center

The friendly staff and volunteers welcome visitors to Hendersonville and Flat Rock with an invitation to stay and play. Offerings run from antique shopping to trout fishing and in between there's golf, historic sites, off-Broadway shows, sightseeing in the Pisgah National Forest or on the Blue Ridge Parkway. The information center offers maps, publications and hundreds of brochures to accommodate every interest.

Located on South Main Street, the visitors center is also the site of several festivals throughout the year. In early May the renewal of spring is celebrated with the Garden Jubilee Festival. During Labor Day weekend, one of North Carolina's most outstanding festivals takes place—The NC Apple Festival. This great, fun-filled event takes place in downtown Hendersonville and the surrounding area and features entertainment, crafts, food vendors, sporting events, and activities for the kids. The festival's theme is the apple harvest (Henderson County is one of America's major apple producing regions), and each year thousands of visitors attend the festivities. During the summer season, the Visitor Center also sponsors Music on Main Street, a concert series on the Historic Courthouse lawn located on Main Street, and "Sunday Melodies in the Park" at the Jackson Park amphitheater.

Many concerts, shows and festivities take place in the area during the year. Tickets for most of the events, along with tickets for Biltmore Estate, whitewater rafting and Chimney Rock Park are available to visitors.

The center's parking facility can accommodate car, RV and bus parking. Travelers are encouraged to park and explore the downtown area.

The Visitor Center prints and distributes a number of brochures and pamphlets that are of interest to visitors. "Home for the Holidays (WNC)" is a calendar of events brochure that lists activities happening throughout Western North Carolina during the months of November and December; and "Home for the Holidays (Hendersonville and Flat Rock)" is a calendar of events brochure that lists over 75 events taking place in Hendersonville and Flat Rock during November and December. Call (800) 828-4244 in October for these free brochures. "Mountain Seasons Vacation Planner," a publication of the visitors center, features attractions and activities in the area. This is a must-have magazine to receive either before a trip or to pick up at the visitors center. The publication contains current information about accommodations, restaurants, shopping, outdoor activities, historical sites and entertainment. The "Mountain Seasons Vacation Planner" is available at the center, or through the mail. Write to or call the Henderson County Travel and Tourism Visitors and Information Center, P.O. Box 721, Hendersonville, NC 28973 to receive your free copy.

Address: Hendersonville and Flat Rock Visitors Information Center, 201 South Main St., Hendersonville, NC 28792
Telephone: 693-9708 or (800) 828-4244
FAX: 697-4996
Website: www.historichendersonville.org

Hours: 9 a.m.-5 p.m. Monday-Friday; 10 a.m.-5 p.m. Saturday and Sunday; closed weekends Christmas through Easter

Directions: Take exit 18B off I-26. Travel south on Hwy. 64 about 2½ miles. Turn left onto Main St. and continue eight blocks.

Other Important Hendersonville Area Resources:

City of Hendersonville: 697-3084, (888) 870-8401, City Hall: 697-3000, www. cityofhendersonville.org

Henderson County: 697-4720

Greater Hendersonville Chamber of Commerce: 330 North King St., Hendersonville, NC 28792, 692-1413, FAX 693-8802, www.hendersonvillechamber.org

Town of Laurel Park: (Located in Henderson County and west of downtown Hendersonville) 693-4840

City of Fletcher: (Located north of downtown Hendersonville and south of Asheville) 687-3895

Black Mountain-Swannanoa

Located just fifteen miles east of Asheville on Interstate 40 in the charming mountain city of Black Mountain, the Black Mountain-Swannanoa Chamber of Commerce Visitors Center should be your first stop when you visit this part of Buncombe County. If you come to Asheville, chances are you might also visit Black Mountain, and if you do, a stop at the Visitors Center there will go a long way to making your trip a successful one. The folks at the Center stand ready to help you plan your day and assist you with brochures, free literature, and knowledgeable suggestions.

Black Mountain, with a resident township population of 10,000 and at an elevation of 2,400 feet, is know as "The Front Porch of Western North Carolina," one of the hallmarks of Black Mountain is the magnificent view of the surrounding mountains, including Mount Mitchell, the highest peak east of the Mississippi River. Famous for its arts & crafts and its antiques, Black Mountain overflows with many top quality art & craft galleries, antique and specialty shops, bookstores, and furniture stores. The epicenter of this wonderful eclectic mix of stores is the Cherry Street district, crowned by the world-class Seven Sisters Gallery and the historic Old Depot and Town Hardware and General Store.

In the Swannanoa Valley, where Black Mountain is located, there are eight religious conference centers, the largest concentration of centers in the world! Here you will find the following centers: In The Oaks (Episcopal), Montreat (Presbyterian Church USA), Ridgecrest (Southern Baptist), Christmount Christian Assembly (Christian Church), Blue Ridge Assembly (YMCA), Cragmont Assembly (Freewill Baptist Church), Camp Dorothy Walls (AME Zion), and The Cove (Billy Graham Training Center). This area is also the home to two four-year colleges: Warren Wilson College, in Swannanoa, and Montreat College, in Montreat just north of Black Mountain. Famous residents include Evangelist Billy Graham, former NBA star Brad Dougherty, and Minnesota Vikings quarterback Brad Johnson.

The Swannanoa Valley has been a coveted spot for hundreds of years. The Cherokee Indians guarded the mountainous ridges while would-be settlers from what is now Old Fort looked westward towards the game-filled forests. The Cherokee boundary was moved farther west in the late 1780s and settlers rapidly rushed through the Swannanoa Gap into the coves to establish homesteads along the many creeks and rivers. By 1850, there was a turnpike up the mountains from the east, but one so steep that wheels on the wagons had to be larger on one side to make the journey up and then switched to the other side to make the journey down. In 1879, the railroad arrived and changed things forever. Black Mountain has been known as a tourist destination and a wonderful place to vacation and live ever since.

Address:	Black Mountain-Swannanoa Chamber of Commerce Visitors Center, 201 East State St., Black Mountain, NC 28711
Telephone:	669-2300, (800) 669-2301
FAX:	669-1407
E-mail:	bmchamber@juno.com
Website:	www.blackmountain.org
Hours:	9 a.m.-4:30 p.m. Monday-Friday; 9 a.m.-1 p.m. Saturday
Directions:	From Asheville, take I-40 east 15 miles to Exit 64. Turn left onto NC Hwy. 9 to the intersection of State St. Turn right and the center will be on your left.

Climate

The mountains surrounding Asheville and Hendersonville serve as a moderating influence from extreme conditions. Major snow storms are rare and annual precipitation is around 50 inches and average annual snowfall is about 15 inches. The mountains serve to keep the area cool also during the summer months, and with their higher elevations are usually 10 to 15 degrees cooler than the lowlands of the Carolinas and Georgia.

Spring in the Appalachians is a wondrous time, with mild days and nights. Wildflowers are blooming in abundance and all chance of snow has virtually disappeared by April. Summer brings more humidity and heat, although nothing like what the lowlands experience. Late afternoon thunderstorms are common and August usually brings a few weeks when it is hot enough for air conditioning. Temperatures can reach over 90 degrees in Asheville and Hendersonville. Such extremes are rare, however, at elevations over 4,000 feet. Winter doesn't make its presence shown until after Christmas, and January and February can be very cold with temperatures dipping down below 20 degrees occasionally. Light snows and ice storms occur frequently, although the snow rarely stays on the ground for more than a few days. Big snowfalls can occur. The Blizzard of '93 dumped three feet of snow on the ground in less than 24 hours!

Autumn Glory

One of the most beautiful seasons in the mountains is autumn, when the colorful display of fall foliage spreads throughout the mountains. The peaks and valleys take on deep shades of crimson, brilliant orange, translucent yellow and earth brown every fall during September and October.

Every year millions of visitors return to the mountains to admire this natural pageant of beauty, and one of the major routes is the Blue Ridge Parkway with its unbroken vistas and towering mountain peaks.

The fall foliage usually reaches its peak in October, but the intensity of color and peak for each area is also determined by elevation. The higher elevations come into color first, followed by the lower ranges. Views from the Parkway can show you various stages of this transformation, with full color above you on the higher peaks and lush green in the valleys far below.

Chapter Two
Getting Around

Asheville is located at the junction of Interstates 26 and 40, with an I-240 connector that passes through the downtown district. Hendersonville is located to the south of Asheville off Interstate 26. The Blue Ridge Parkway also passes through the Asheville/Hendersonville area with a number of accesses.

Landing in Asheville

Asheville Regional Airport: (828) 684-2226, www.flyavl.com. The main gateway to the area is the Asheville Regional Airport, 15 miles south of downtown Asheville on I-26. This airport is serviced daily by major carriers with connections to all major cities. The airport has an 8,000-foot runway and modern navigational aids, including a windshear detection system. Facilities are also provided for corporate and private aircraft. The airport also has a Welcome Center that provides information, brochures, maps and souvenirs to visitors. Other highlights include a full service travel agency, remodeled ground-level commuter passenger concourse, expanded restaurant and bar, and a resurfaced runway. If you are coming into Asheville or Hendersonville via air travel, be sure and stop in at the Asheville Regional Airport Welcome Center, conveniently located in the airport terminal. This great little shop has free brochures, books, magazines and guides, newspapers, and craft items. They are open from 9 a.m. to 7 p.m. daily (telephone 687-9446).

Airlines in Asheville

Continental: (800) 525-0280, www.continental.com
Delta: (800) 221-1212, www.delta.com
Northwest Airlines: (800) 225-2525, www.nwa.com
United: (800) 241-6522, www.united.com
U.S. Airways: (800) 428-4322, www.usairways.com

Landing in Hendersonville

Hendersonville Airport: (828) 693-1897. This airport serves the Hendersonville area, has a 3,200-foot lighted runway, and provides charter service to larger airports. Located on Shepherd Street near the Blue Ridge Community College, the airport provides charter air service, flight school, and plane maintenance.

Bus Travel
Asheville
Asheville Transit: Located at 360 West Haywood St., provides bus service for Asheville. 253-5691

Greyhound-Trailways Bus Lines: Located at 2 Tunnel Rd. in Asheville, provides passenger service (253-5353) and package express (253-8451). (800) 231-2222

Young Transportation/Graylines: Located at 843 Riverside Dr., provides passenger service and charters. 258-0084 or (800) 622-5444

Travel Professionals Inc. Tourservice: 498 Swannanoa River Rd., Asheville. 298-3438

Emma Bus Lines Inc.: 1 Stoner Rd., charter buses. 274-5719

Runion Fun Tours: Charter buses. 669-5937

Hendersonville/Flat Rock
Greyhound-Trailways Bus Lines: Located at 350 7th Ave. in Hendersonville. Provides passenger service. 693-1201

Limousines
Asheville
Airport Ground Transportation: (Airport Transportation) 681-0051

All American Limousine: 667-9935

Carolina Limousine: 258-2526

Sky Shuttle Service: (Airport Transportation) 253-0006

Special Occasions: 274-6629

Hendersonville/Flat Rock
All American Limousine: 667-9935

Carolina Limousine: 258-2526

Dal Kawa Limousines: 692-7519

Elite Limousine: 890-2424

Taxi Service
Asheville
A Red Cab Co.: 232-1112

Beaver Lake Cab Co.: 252-1913

Candler Taxi (Candler, NC): 670-5565

Jolly Taxi Co.: 253-1411

New Blue Bird Taxi: 258-8331

Yellow Cab Co.: 253-3311

Your Cab II: 259-9904

Hendersonville/Flat Rock
A Cab: 698-2324
Apple Cab: 696-1583
Carolina Taxi: 693-3221
Checker Cab Co.: 692-2424

Car Rental
Asheville
Affordable Car Rental: 684-3811
Alamo Rent-a-Car: (800) 327-9633
Avis: (800) 831-2847
Budget Car & Truck Rental: 684-2272, 684-2273, 299-7381
Enterprise Rent-a-Car: (800) 325-8007, 251-0065
Hertz: (800) 654-3131 or 684-6455
National Car Rental: 684-8572, 254-7283
Rent a Wreck: 684-3811

Hendersonville/Flat Rock
Avis: (800) 831-2847
Budget Car & Truck Rental: 684-2272
Enterprise Rent-a-Car: (800) 736-8222
Hertz: (800) 654-3131 or 684-6455
U-Save Auto Rental: 696-2200

Driving Tips
Though relatively small, if you choose to drive in Asheville, you may find the street system a bit confusing at first. All streets are named rather than numbered, and as the city has evolved, some streets have become split into unconnected sections. Two important examples are Patton Avenue and Broadway.

Patton Avenue is split into a downtown section and a West Asheville section. The Smokey Park Bridge, which is actually part of I-240, runs between the two halves.

Heading north out of downtown, Broadway seemingly becomes Merrimon Avenue. One block west at the same point, Lexington Avenue heading north becomes Broadway. Most places listed in this guide with Patton Avenue or Broadway addresses are on the downtown extensions of these roads, but you would be wise to call ahead for directions to be sure. Also, like most city centers, Asheville's downtown has several one-way streets.

One other navigational oddity is how one gets to I-26 from most areas of Asheville. Even though I-26 runs east out of Asheville, you will usually take I-240 or I-40 *west* to access it because I-26 begins at the juncture of I-240 and I-40 on the far west side of Asheville.

The most direct route, though certainly not the fastest, between Hendersonville and Asheville is US 25. This non-interstate-grade thoroughfare changes names several times between and even within the two cities, being called Spartanburg Highway on the Flat Rock side, then Asheville Highway in Hendersonville, changing to Hendersonville Highway halfway to Asheville, briefly turning into Hendersonville Road, becoming Biltmore Avenue once reaching Asheville, then turning into the downtown section of Broadway, and finally becoming Merrimon Avenue leaving downtown headed north. I-26 is a much better route between these two cities with much less congestion and isn't hampered by US 25's many traffic lights. But as several of the addresses in this guide are on its various sections, you should be familiar with the different names to avoid confusion.

Chapter Three
A Wealth of Information

I n addition to this extensive guide, visitors may still wish to get specialty or more up-to-the-minute information on events, activities, news, etc. This section covers the wealth of information available through various publications, organizations, and businesses.

Newspapers & Magazines

Asheville Citizen-Times: The region's largest circulation daily newspaper. 14 O'Henry Ave., Asheville, NC 28801; 252-5611, (800) 800-4204. www.citizentimes.com

Hendersonville Times-News: Hendersonville's daily newspaper. 1717 Four Seasons Blvd, Hendersonville, NC 28792; 692-0505. www.hendersonville news.com

In addition to the daily papers, there are a number of other publications available that feature information on current attractions, restaurants, art gallery exhibitions and outdoor recreation activities.

Appalachian Voice: Bi-monthly newspaper published by Appalachian Voices, a nonprofit grass roots organization. Articles of general interest about the mountains, with focus on the environment. 703 W. King St., Suite 105, Boone, NC 28607. www.appvoices.org

Blue Ridge Outdoors: Monthly free publication covering all outdoor sports in the southern mountains. (434) 817-2755. www.blueridgeoutdoors.com

Bold Life: Monthly free magazine featuring Hendersonville and Asheville area dining, art, music, people and culture. 105 S. Main St., Hendersonville, NC 28792; 692-3230. www.boldlife.com

The Blue Ridge Parkway Directory: A free directory to sites and attractions along the Parkway. Blue Ridge Parkway Association, P.O. Box 453, Asheville, NC 28802.

Downtown—The Heart of Asheville: Published seasonally, this free paper highlights things to do and see in downtown Asheville. Asheville Downtown Association, P.O. Box 7148, Asheville, NC 28802; 251-9973.

Fairview Town Crier: A free monthly. This not-for-profit newspaper offers news and events about Fairview, a mountain community just south of Asheville. P.O. Box 1862, Fairview, NC 28730. www.fairviewtowncrier.com

Fun Things To Do in the Mountains: A not-for-profit newspaper publication that comes out nine times a year. Subscriptions are $17.95 annually, but individual issues are free at visitor centers. Visitor Publications, P.O. Box 35, Waynesville, NC 28786; 456-7577.

The Laurel of Asheville: Monthly free magazine focusing on the arts and culture of the Asheville area. 1 West Pack Square, BB&T Building, Suite G-145, Asheville, NC 28801; 670-7503. www.thelaurelofasheville.com

Mountain Xpress: A free weekly independent news, arts, and events newspaper for Western North Carolina. Excellent entertainment coverage, local commentary. P.O. Box 144, Asheville, NC 28802; 251-1333.

Rapid River: Monthly free arts and culture magazine serving Asheville and Western North Carolina. 70 Woodfin Place, Suite 212, Asheville, NC 28801; 258-3752. www.rapidriver.org

Take Five: A weekly tabloid insert in the *Asheville Citizen-Times* on Thursdays. It features a complete theater and events listing, articles and reviews. (SEE *Asheville Citizen-Times* listing above for contact information)

This Week of Western North Carolina: A weekly magazine published for the visitor, area newcomer and local residents. Includes restaurants, shows, galleries and current events in Asheville, Hendersonville and Western North Carolina. Mountain Meadow Publications, P.O. Box 1513, Asheville, NC 28802; 253-9299.

The Town Tooter: A free weekly shopper serving Buncombe, Henderson, Transylvania and Polk counties. Lists events, happenings of local interest and dining. 475 South Church St., Hendersonville, NC 28792; 692-7550. www. towntooter.com

Chamber of Commerce Publications

The following publications are available for purchase through the mail or at the Visitor Center.

Asheville

    Asheville—A View From the Top
    Asheville Fact Book
    Buncombe County Retail Report
    Community Profile
    Industrial Directory
    Major Employers Directory
    Membership Directory and Buyers Guide
    Newcomers Guide

These publications may be ordered from the Asheville Area Chamber of Commerce, Attn: Research Dept., P.O. Box 1010, Asheville, NC 28802; 258-6137.

Hendersonville
Hendersonville Information Guide
Hendersonville Magazine
Hendersonville County/City Map
Demographics
Industrial Directory
Membership and Civic Club Directory
Mountain Seasons Planner

These publications may be ordered from The Greater Hendersonville Chamber of Commerce, 330 North King St., Hendersonville, NC 28792; 692-1413.

Bookstores
A number of area bookstores carry books by local authors and books of regional interest. These are listed below, followed by a complete listing of all area bookstores.

Asheville Regional Titles & Guidebooks
Atlantic Books: 15 Broadway, 255-7654

Accent on Books: 854 Merrimon Ave., (800) 482-7964, 252-6255 (www.accent onbooks.com). Full-service bookstore. Regional titles.

Barnes & Noble: 89 S. Tunnel Rd., 296-9330 (www.barnesandnoble.com).

B. Dalton Bookseller, Asheville Mall Store: 3 S. Tunnel Rd., 298-7711.

Books-A-Million: 136 S. Tunnel Rd., 299-4165 (www.booksamillion.com). Large selection of regional books and guidebooks.

Common Ground Distributors Warehouse: 115 Fairview Rd., 274-5575.

Malaprop's Bookstore: 55 Haywood St., 254-6734, (800) 441-9829 (www. malaprops.com). Large selection of regional books. Fascinating and innovative bookstore. Art exhibitions and coffeehouse also.

Waldenbooks: 800 Brevard Rd., Biltmore Square Mall, 665-1066. Large selection of regional titles and guidebooks.

Other Asheville Specialty Book Stores
Book Rack: 485 Hendersonville Rd., 274-5050 (Used paperbacks)

Captain's Bookshelf: 31 Page Ave., 253-6631 (Used, rare)

Carpenter's Shop: Innsbruck Mall, Tunnel Rd., 252-3500 (Christian)

Christian Bookstore: 824 Haywood Rd., 253-8358 (Christian)

The Compleat Naturalist: 2 Biltmore Plaza, Biltmore Village, 274-5430 (Nature guidebooks)

Downtown Books & News: 76 N. Lexington Ave., 253-8654 (New and used books, magazines, and newspapers)

Family Christian Bookstore: 85 Tunnel Rd., 252-3500 (Christian)

Jenny's Book Exchange: 1 Fletcher Plaza, Fletcher, 684-7906 (Used)

Lifeway Christian Store: River Hills Center, 298-2101 (Christian)

Nine Choirs Catholic Books: 474½ Haywood Rd., 254-5905 (Christian)
Once Upon a Time: 7 All Souls Crescent, 274-8788 (Children's)
Paperback Palace: 1240 Brevard Rd., 665-0404 (Used)
Pastimes: 175 Weaverville Hwy., 253-0506 (Comics)
Patti's Book Swap: 1569 Patton Ave., 258-0652 (Used)
Rainbow's End: 10 N. Spruce St., 285-0005 (Gay/Lesbian)
Readers Corner: 31 Montford Ave., 285-8805 (Used)
Shepherd's Door: Turtle Creek Shopping Center, 274-3353 (Christian)
Sparrow's Nest: 1202 Patton Ave., 258-2665 (Christian)

Hendersonville Regional Titles & Guidebooks
Mountain Lore: 408 N. Main St., 693-5096. Regional guidebooks and books
about Western North Carolina. Full service bookstore.
Waldenbooks: 1800 Four Seasons Blvd, Blue Ridge Mall, 692-4957. Large selection of regional titles and guidebooks.

Other Hendersonville Specialty Book Stores
Book Exchange: Old Post Office Building, Flat Rock, 693-8311 (Used)
Crystal Visions: U.S. Hwy. 25, Naples, 687-1193 (Metaphysical)
The Open Door: 1800 Four Seasons Blvd., 698-1383 (Christian)
Yesterday's Thoughts: 2024-G Asheville Hwy., 697-2329 (Used)

Other Important & Useful Information
The following is an alphabetical listing of organizations, topics and information
that will help you during your visit.

AAA (American Automobile Association)
The AAA Carolinas Office is located at 660 Merrimon Ave., Asheville, NC
28804, 253-5376. Emergency Road Service, (800) 222-4357 for members. In
Hendersonville, AAA Carolinas is at 136 S. King St., Hendersonville, NC 28792,
697-8778.

Antiques, Asheville
Asheville is a shopping mecca for antique lovers from all over the world. Here
they can stroll through antique shops conveniently grouped in two different parts
of town (Lexington Avenue District and Biltmore Village) or visit often larger
antique "malls" sprinkled throughout the city. Visitors can also attend auctions
that sell "country" items on up to top-of-the-line pieces.

Additionally, Asheville is home to the Annual Grove Park Inn Arts & Crafts
Conference and Antique Show held the third weekend in February. This three-day
show is a major stop for serious antique collectors and involves tours, seminars,
discussion groups, books and antiques for sale. Contact the Grove Park Inn Resort
at 252-5611, 254-1912, or (800) 438-5800 for more information.

The following are some of Asheville's antique retailers:

Antique Market Gallery: 52 Broadway, 259-9977
Antique Tobacco Barn: 75 Swannanoa River Rd.
Archive Antiques: 57 Broadway, 254-4568
Arts and Crafts Mission Accomplished: 100 Edwin Pl., 225-9816
Asheville Antiques Mall: 43 Rankin Ave., 253-3634
Biltmore Antique Mall: 30-C Bryson St., 255-0053
Biltmore Station Antiques & Collectibles: 130 Swannanoa River Rd., 250-0229
Catskill Antique Company: 24 N. Lexington Ave., 251-2611
Chatsworth Art & Antiques: 54 N. Lexington Ave., 252-6004
Cottage Walk: 6 All Souls Crescent, 277-9066
Deluxe Retro-Modern: 602 Haywood Rd., 251-9074
Farmer's Tobacco Warehouse of Asheville: 75 Swannanoa River Rd., 252-7291
Fireside Antiques & Interiors: 30 All Souls Crescent, 274-5977
George's Place: 31 Glendale Ave., 254-5663
The Gilded Lily: 1 Battery Park Ave., 236-0006
King-Thomasson Antiques: 65-A Biltmore Ave., 252-1565
Kress Gallery: 59 College St., 250-0500
Lexington Park Antiques: 65 W. Walnut St., 253-3070
Lorraine's Antiques: 26 Battery Park Ave., 251-1771
Magnolia Beauregard's: 52 Broadway, 251-5253
Manor Antiques: 3½ All Souls Crescent, 274-7779
Riverside Antique Mall: 794 Riverside Dr., 225-0772
Stuf Antiques: 52 Broadway, 254-4054
United Surplus of America: 121 Sweeten Creek Rd., 277-5880
Village Antiques: 755 Biltmore Ave., 252-5090
West Asheville Antiques: 3 Louisiana Ave., 252-8040

Antiques, Hendersonville

Antiques & Decorative Arts: 305 S. Church St., 697-6930
Antiques Etc.: 147 4th Ave. West, 696-8255
Jane Asher Antiques: 344 N. Main St., 698-0018
Autumn Leaves Antique Mall: 2550 Chimney Rock Rd., 692-2404
Calico Gallery: 317 N. Main St., 697-2551
Eldorado Architectural & Antiques: 419 S. King St., 696-2595
Granny's Attic: 135 5th Ave. West, 696-8531
Hendersonville Antiques Mall: 670 Spartanburg Hwy., 692-5125
Home Again Used Furniture: 6342 Hendersonville Rd., 651-9296
JRD's Classics & Collectibles: 226 N. Main St., 698-0075
Main Street Curio: 240 N. Main St., 698-3805
Mehri & Company: 502 N. Main St., 693-0887
Nancy Roth Antiques: 127 4th Ave. West, 697-7555
Needful Things: 10 Francis Rd., 696-8745
The Old Man: 119 S. Main St., 698-4900

Piggy's & Harry's: 102 Duncan Hill Rd., 692-1995
Scotties Jewelry & Fine Art: 314 N. Main St., 692-1350
Shelley's Auction Gallery: 429 N. Main St., 698-8485
Smiley's Antique Mall: US 25, Fletcher, 684-3515
Tippy's A Touch of Charleston: 342 N. Main St., 697-3230
Trader's Junction: 706 Brooklyn Ave., 697-1664
Village Green Antique Mall: 424 N. Main St., 692-9057

Area Codes

Western North Carolina, including Asheville, Hendersonville and Flat Rock, uses area code 828. Unless indicated otherwise, this is the area code needed for all telephone numbers in this book.

Asheville City Government

The city of Asheville is governed by Asheville city council, and consists of a mayor and five council members chosen in a nonpartisan election every two years. The city council sets policies, adopts ordinances and sets the tax rate. The council-appointed city manager is the administrative head of the city, directly responsible for its day-to-day operations and its 900-plus employees. Asheville City Hall, 70 Court Plaza, P.O. Box 7148, Asheville, NC 28802; 251-1122. www.ci.asheville.nc.us

Asheville Symphony Orchestra

The Asheville Symphony Orchestra has been performing in Asheville for more than 30 years. They perform on Saturday nights once a month from September to April in the Thomas Wolfe Symphony Hall located in the Asheville Civic Center. An annual Holiday Pops Concert is held during the Christmas season and a May Pops Concert is held each spring. For current concert schedule listings, call 254-7046. www.ashevillesymphony.org

Baseball

Historic McCormick Field is home to the Asheville Tourists, Single A Minor League farm team of the Colorado Rockies. Schedules are available at all sporting goods stores, or you may call 258-0428 or visit www.theashevilletourists.com. Most games are played at night, starting at 7:05 p.m. Sunday games begin at 5:05 p.m. McCormick Field is located at 30 Buchanan Place. (SEE Section Three, Chapter 2)

Better Business Bureau

The BBB of Asheville-Western North Carolina is located at 1200 BB&T Building, Asheville, NC 28801. 253-2392, (800) 452-2882

Camps in the Area
For girls:
Camp Glen Arden: (ages 7-17) P.O. Box 7, Tuxedo, NC 28784, 692-8362
Camp Green Cove: (ages 8-17) P.O. Box 38, Tuxedo, NC 28784, (800) 688-5789, 692-6355

Camp Greystone: (ages 7-17) P.O. Box 68, Tuxedo, NC 28784, 693-3182

Camp Hollymont: (ages 6-16) 475 Lake Eden Rd., Black Mountain, NC 28711, www.hollymont.com

Camp Pinnacle for Girls: (ages 7-16) Route 13, Box 100, Hendersonville, NC 28739, (800) 336-6992, 692-2677

Camp Pisgah: (ages 7-17) Pisgah Girl Scout Council, P.O. Box 8249, Asheville, NC 28814, 862-4435

Camp Ton-A-Wandah: (ages 6-15) Route 13, Box 75, Hendersonville, NC 28739, 692-4251

Camp Merri-Mac for Girls: (ages 6-16) 1229 Montreat Rd., Black Mountain, NC 28711, 669-8766

For boys:

Camp Arrowhead for Boys: P.O. Box 248, Tuxedo, NC 28784, 692-1123

Camp Mondamin: (ages 7-17) P.O. Box 8, Tuxedo, NC 28784, (800) 688-5789, 693-7446

Camp Pinnacle for Boys: (ages 7-16) 4080 Little River Rd., Hendersonville NC 28739, (800) 336-6992, 692-2677

Camp Rockmont: (ages 7-16) 375 Lake Eden Rd., Black Mountain, NC 28711, 686-3885

Elks Camp for Boys: (ages 8-14) Gap Creek Rd., Tuxedo, NC 28784, 692-3568

Falling Creek: (ages 6-15) P.O. Box 98, Tuxedo, NC 28784, 692-0262

Timberlake for Boys: (ages 6-14) Montreat Rd., Black Mountain, 28711, 669-8766

For girls and boys:

Bonclarken Adventure Camp: (junior high 13-15; senior high 16-18) 500 Pine Dr., Flat Rock, NC 28731, 692-2223

Bonclarken Music-Drama Camp: (ages 8-12) 500 Pine Dr., Flat Rock, NC 28731, 692-2223

Camp Blue Star: (ages 7-17) P.O. Box 1029, Hendersonville, NC 28793, 692-3591

Camp Bonclarken: (ages 8-12) 500 Pine Dr., Flat Rock, NC 28731, 692-2223

Camp Highlander: (ages 7-16) 42 Dalton Rd., Horse Shoe, NC 28742, 891-7721

Camp Joy/Bonclarken: (mentally and physically handicapped) 500 Pine Dr., Flat Rock, NC 28731, 692-2223

Camp Judea: (ages 8-12, 13-16) Route 9, Box 395, Hendersonville, NC 28739, 685-8841

Camp Kanuga: (ages 8-17) Postal Drawer 250, Hendersonville, NC 28793, 692-9136

Camp Lurecrest: P.O. Box 400, Lake Lure, NC 28793, 625-4673

Camp Tekoa: P.O. Box 160, Hendersonville, NC 28793, 692-6516

Camp Wayfarer: (ages 6-17, 6-14 day camp) P.O. Box 850, Flat Rock, NC 28731, 696-9000

Camp Pinewood: (ages 6-16) 300 Orr's Camp Rd., Hendersonville, NC 28739, 692-6239

The Cove Youth Camp: (ages 9-15) Located at The Cove Retreat Center, Asheville, (800) 950-2092, www.thecove.org

Henderson County YMCA Summer Day Camp: (ages 6-12) 810 6th Ave. West, Hendersonville, NC 28739, 692-5774

Ridgecrest Summer Camps: P.O. Box 278, Ridgecrest, NC 28770, 669-8051

Wildlife Camp of the National Wildlife Federation: (ages 8-13) P.O. Box 2860, Hendersonville, NC 28793, (800) 245-5484

Dance

The professional dance community in Asheville includes a number of groups that often perform together for special performances. Asheville is also visited by a number of touring troupes, and "Folkmoot," an international dance and folk festival, is held every year in nearby Waynesville. (SEE Section Two, Chapter 3 for Festivals) Ballroom dancing is also popular in Asheville, and every year the Grove Park Inn Resort hosts prestigious ballroom dancing competitions, including the Heritage Classic Dance Sport Championships. Listed below are some of the area's dance troupes, schools and organizations:

Asheville:

Asheville Academy of Ballet & Contemporary Dance: 4 Lynwood Rd., Asheville, NC 28804, 258-1028 (ballet, contemporary)

Asheville Center of Performing Arts: 9 W. Walnut St., Asheville, NC 28801, 258-3377 (ballet, modern, tap, jazz, preschool, acrobatics) Home of Asheville Civic Ballet.

Asheville Dance Theatre: 800 Fairview Rd., Asheville, NC 28803, 298-0258 (jazz, tap, ballet)

Blue Ridge Dance Center: New Bridge Shopping Center, Asheville, NC 28804, 253-9108 (ballroom)

Center Stage Dance Studio: 7 Long Shoals Rd., Asheville, NC, 654-7010 (all styles)

CoMotion Dance Center: 1145 Tunnel Rd., Asheville, NC, 299-4676

Dance Lovers USA: 658-2242 (ballroom)

A Dancer's Place: 14 Patton Ave., Asheville, NC 28801, 253-1434 (dance supplies)

Fabiana's Dance: 10 Beechwood Rd., Asheville, NC, 296-9856 (cabaret-style and belly dance)

Fairview Center for Dance: 1334-A Charlotte Hwy., Fairview, 628-7888 (ballet, jazz, tap, clogging)

Fletcher School of Dance: 177 Patton Ave., Asheville, NC 28801, 252-4761 (ballet, modern, tap, jazz, preschool, acrobatics)

In His Steps Dance Ministry: 2 Sulphur Springs Rd., Asheville, NC, 285-0360

Just for Kicks: 6 Long Shoals Rd., Asheville, NC, 654-8110 (dance supplies)

Kinderdance of Asheville: 250-0063 (children's dance, gymnastics)

New Studio of Dance and Asheville Contemporary Dance Theatre: 20 Commerce St., Asheville, NC 28801, 254-2621 (ballet, modern, jazz, tap, fencing)

Miss Kellie's Dance Studio: Royal Pines Plaza, Arden, NC 28803, 684-7999 (creative movement, preschool, jazz, tap, ballet)

Steppin' Out: 2 Sulphur Springs Rd., Asheville, NC 28806, 253-1302 (tap, jazz, ballet, gymnastics, line)

Victor Dru International Inc.: 1220 Bee Tree Rd., Asheville, NC 28778, 299-8856

Hendersonville:

Balance Pointe: 506½ North Main St., Hendersonville, NC 28792, 698-1967 (classical ballet, modern and pilates)

Dance ETC: 615 Greenville Hwy., Hendersonville, NC 28792, 696-2806 (dancewear)

Merles Dance Place: 126 West Blue Ridge Rd., Flat Rock, NC 28731, 692-4907 (tap, jazz ballet, tumbling for children-adult)

Pat's School of Dance: 1256 N. Main St., Hendersonville, NC 28792, 692-2905 (tap, jazz, ballet, acrobatics, pointe, adult)

Studio L Dance School: 1311 East 7th Ave., Hendersonville, NC 28792, 697-1980 (ballet, pointe, jazz, tap, lyrica for preschool to adult)

Vagabond School of the Drama: 2661 Greenville Hwy., Flat Rock, NC, 696-8835

Emergencies

Fire, Police & Ambulance: dial 911

Asheville Police Department Information Center: 259-9039

Biltmore Forest Police Department: 274-0822

Black Mountain Police Department: (emergency calls) 669-8072

Buncombe County Sheriff's Department: (non-emergency) 277-3131

Fletcher Police Patrol: 687-7922

Hendersonville Police Department General Business: 697-3025 (www.blueridge.cc.nc.us/hpd/)

Montreat Police Department: 669-8072

NC State Highway Patrol: 298-4252

Woodfin Police Department: 253-4889

Weaverville Police Department: 645-5700

Other Emergency Numbers:

Buncombe County Emergency Management: 255-5638

Bureau of Alcohol, Tobacco and Firearms (ATF): (704) 344-6125

Call Before You Dig: (800) 632-4949

Carolinas Poison Center: (800) 848-6946 (Charlotte)

Civil Air Patrol: 687-2875
CSX Transportation Police Department: (800) 232-0144
Drug Helpline: (800) 378-4435
Federal Tax Information: (800) 829-1040
First Call for Help: 252-4357 (Links people with services)
Mission St. Joseph Health Line: 255-3000, (800) 321-6877
Missing Children Information Clearing House: (888) 356-4774
NC Center for Missing Persons: (800) 522-5437
Norfolk Southern Railroad Police: (800) 453-2530
Oil & Toxic Chemical Spills: (800) 424-8802 (voice/TTY)
Pardee Hospital's Ask-A-Nurse: 697-2829
Poison Center of WNC: 255-4490
Rape Crisis Center of Asheville: 255-7576
State Bureau of Investigation (SBI): 654-8901
State Highway Patrol: 298-4252
Teen Crisis Hotline: (800) 367-7287
U.S. Marshall: 271-4652
U.S. Secret Service: (704) 523-9583 (Charlotte)

Flat Rock Village Government
Incorporated Village of Flat Rock: P.O. Box 1173, Flat Rock, NC 28731,
   697-8100

Governor's Western Office
   The governor of North Carolina has a Western North Carolina office at 46
Haywood St., Asheville, NC 28801, and a residence for use during visits on Town
Mountain Road. The office phone number is 251-6160.

Hospitals in Western North Carolina
Avery County:
   Cannon Memorial Hospital, Linville; 737-7000
   Sloop Memorial Hospital, Crossnore; 733-9231
Buncombe County:
   Mission+St. Joseph's Health System, Asheville; 509 Biltmore Ave., 255-4000;
      also 428 Biltmore Ave., 255-3100
   V.A. Medical Center, Asheville; 1100 Tunnel Rd., 298-7911
Burke County: Grace Hospital, Morganton; 2201 S. Sterling St. (Hwy. 18),
   438-2000
Cherokee County:
   District Memorial Hospital, Andrews; Whitaker Ln., 321-1200
   Murphy Medical Center, Murphy; 2002 Hwy. 64 East, 837-8300
Haywood County: Haywood Regional Medical Center, Clyde; 90 Hospital Dr.,
   456-7311 or (800) 834-1729

Henderson County:
Pardee Hospital, Hendersonville; 715 Fleming St., 696-1000
Park Ridge Hospital, Fletcher; 681-2141
Macon County: Angel Hospital, Franklin; 197 Riverview St., 524-8411
McDowell County: The McDowell Hospital, Marion; 100 Rankin Dr., 659-5000
Polk County: St. Luke's Hospital, Columbus; 220 Hospital Dr., 894-3311
Jackson County: Harris Regional Hospital, Sylva; 59 Hospital Rd., 586-7000
Rutherford County: Rutherford Hospital, Rutherfordton; 308 S. Ridgecrest Ave., 286-5000
Swain County: Swain County Hospital, Bryson City; 45 Plateau St., 488-2155
Transylvania County: Transylvania Community Hospital, Brevard; Hospital Dr., 844-9111
Yancey County: Yancey Community Medical Center, Burnsville; 320 Pensacola Rd., 682-6136

Health and Fitness

Asheville:
Asheville Health & Fitness: 237 Sardis Rd., 665-2007
Asheville Racquet Club: 200 Racquet Club Rd., 274-3361
Biltmore Racquet Club: 711 Biltmore Ave., 253-5555
Curves for Women: 3749 Sweeten Creek Rd., 651-8543
        8 Regent Park Blvd., 258-5288
Grove Park Inn Resort & Spa: 290 Macon Ave., 252-2711
        (SEE review in Section Three, Chapter 6)
Ladies Workout Express: 802 Fairview Rd., 298-4667
        1854 Hendersonville Rd., 274-0770
Mountain View Health Spa: 121 Laurel Cove Rd., Candler, 665-7388
Southeastern Fitness & Rehabilitation: 59 Turtle Creek Rd., 274-2188
Spa Health Club: 30 Westgate Parkway, 254-4946
Vision Sports Fitness Centers: 9 Kenilworth Knoll, 252-0222
World Gym: 780 Hendersonville Rd., 277-8588
YMCA of Western North Carolina: 252-4726
YWCA: 185 South French Broad Ave., 254-7206

Hendersonville:
The Body Shop Fitness Center: 2314 Asheville Hwy., Hendersonville, 692-7902
        580 Upward Rd., Flat Rock, 999-9999
Bodywize Fitness Center: 2113 Spartanburg Hwy., East Flat Rock, 698-9406
Curves for Women: 500 South Allen Rd., Flat Rock, 698-2600
Excel Fitness Center: 3754 Brevard Rd., 890-4049
Fitness First: 2111 Asheville Hwy., 696-3416
Health Enhancement Medical Institute: 1749 Brevard Rd., 698-8233

Hendersonville Racquet Club: 88 Oak Creek Ln., 693-0040
Professional Fitness Center: 306 Ramble Hill Ln., 693-8096
The Pump House: 602 Old Spartanburg Hwy., 698-9447

Hendersonville City Government

The Hendersonville city government is run by a mayor and a council of four. Council members and the mayor are elected from the city at large for a period of four years. City offices are located at 145 5th Ave. East, Hendersonville, NC 28792. 697-3000

Horse Shows

Asheville boasts one of the best agricultural centers in the U.S. The Western North Carolina Agricultural Center hosts some of the top horse shows in the Southeast. Call 687-1414 for current listings or to receive their calendar. (SEE Section Three, Chapter 2) The famous Foothills Equestrian Nature Center (FENCE) is located in Tryon, about an hour's drive from Asheville. This center schedules major horse shows of all types. (SEE Section Five, Chapter 2)

Legal Organizations

North Carolina State Bar Lawyers Referral Service: (800) 662-7660
North Carolina Bar Association, 28th Judicial District: (Buncombe County Chapter) 252-5733

Libraries

Asheville: Asheville/Buncombe Library System: The main library, Pack Memorial, is located next to the Civic Center at 67 Haywood St. Hours: 10 a.m. to 9 p.m. Monday-Thursday; 10 a.m. to 6 p.m. Friday and Saturday; and 2 to 6 p.m. Sundays (September-May only). 255-5209

Branches:

Black Mountain Branch: 105 Dougherty St., Black Mountain, 669-2652
East Asheville Branch: 902 Tunnel Rd., Asheville, 298-1889
Enka-Candler Branch: 1404 Sand Hill Rd., Candler, 667-8153
Fairview Branch: 1 Taylor Rd., Fairview, 628-5837
Law Library: 60 Court Plaza, Asheville, 250-4734
Leicester Branch: 1561 Alexander Rd., Leicester, 683-8867
North Asheville Branch: 37 Larchmont Dr., Asheville, 251-4991
Pack Memorial Library: 67 Haywood St., Downtown Asheville, 255-5203
South Asheville (Oakley) Branch: 749 Fairview Rd., Asheville, 274-1007
South Buncombe Branch: 260 Overlook Rd., Asheville, 684-1827
Swannanoa Branch: 101 West Charleston St., Swannanoa, 686-5516
Weaverville Branch: Main & Pine Sts., Weaverville, 645-3592
West Asheville Branch: 924 Haywood St., Asheville, 251-4990

Hendersonville: The Henderson County Public Library is located at 301 N. Washington St. Hours: 9 a.m. to 9 p.m. Monday-Thursday; 9 a.m. to 6 p.m. Friday and Saturday; closed Sunday. 697-4725

Branches:
Etowah: 891-6577
Fletcher: 687-1218
Tuxedo-Green River: 697-4969

Merchants Associations
Asheville Merchants Association: P.O. Box 1600, Asheville, NC 28802, 251-4147
Hendersonville Merchants Association: 400 North Main St., Hendersonville, NC 28792, 692-4179

Mountain Dancing
Every Saturday night during July, August, and September, "Shindig on the Green" takes place at the City/County Plaza in downtown Asheville. Drop by for some fine singing, mountain square dancing, clogging, and picnicking. No charge. www.folkheritage.org

Movie Theaters
Asheville:
Asheville Pizza and Brewing Company: (one screen), 675 Merrimon Ave., 236-2799. All shows $2. Second-run Hollywood and independent films. Pizza and micro-brews available in theater or adjoining restaurant.
Beaucatcher Cinemas: (eight screens), South Tunnel Rd. across from Asheville Mall, 298-1234. First-run Hollywood films.
Biltmore Square: (six screens), I-26 at Brevard Rd., Biltmore Square Mall, 665-7776. First-run Hollywood films.
Carmike 10: (ten screens), 2994 Swannanoa River Rd., down from Asheville Mall, 298-4452. First-run Hollywood films.
Fine Arts Theater: (two screens), 36 Biltmore Ave., 232-1536. First-run independent, foreign, cutting edge and classic films.
Hollywood Cinema 14: (fourteen screens), 1640 Hendersonville Hwy., 274-9500. First-run Hollywood films.

Hendersonville:
Four Seasons Cinemas: (four screens), 1300 East 7th Ave., 693-8989. First-run Hollywood films.
Hendersonville Film Society: Blue Ridge Mall, Four Seasons Blvd., 697-7310. First-run foreign and independent films with screenings Sundays at 3 p.m. and Mondays at 3 and 7 p.m. Call for film information.
Skyland Arts Cinema: (one screen), 38 North Main St., 697-2463. First-run foreign, independent and classic films.

National Weather Service

For current weather information, call 864-848-3859.

Newspapers

Asheville Citizen-Times: P.O. Box 2090, Asheville, NC 28802, 252-5611 or (800) 800-4204

Hendersonville Times-News: P.O. Box 490, Hendersonville, NC 28793, 692-0505

Quality Forward

Quality Forward is a nonprofit organization of concerned volunteers dedicated to creating a clean and green Buncombe County. Since 1976, Quality Forward has promoted proper waster disposal, recycling, as well as pedestrian and planting efforts through grassroots activities, school programs, and public awareness. P.O. Box 22, Asheville, NC 28802; 29 Page Ave., Asheville, NC 28801, 254-1776, FAX: (828) 253-5427, E-mail: info@qualityforward.org, www.qualityforward.org/about.html

Radio Stations

AM Stations:

WWNC/570	Asheville (Country) 253-3835
WESC/660	Greenville, SC (Country) (864) 242-4660
WTZY/880	Asheville (News-talk) 281-1049, 255-1906
WPTL/920	Canton (Country, NC Sports)
WKYK/940	Burnsville (Country, NBC News)
WWIT/970	Canton (Oldies Rock)
WFGW/1010	Black Mountain (Christian) 669-8477
WSKY/1230	Asheville (Christian) 251-2000
WISE/1310	Asheville (Nostalgic Pop) 253-1310
WTZK/1350	Black Mountain (Talk) 669-3880
WKJV/1380	Asheville (Christian) 252-1380
WHCC/1400	Waynesville (Country, Sports)
WHKP/1450	Hendersonville (Easy Listening, Talk) 693-9061
WHBK/1460	Marshall, (Southern Gospel, News, Sports)
WTZQ/1600	Hendersonville (Adult Standards, CNN News) 697-1506

FM Stations:

WCQS/88.1	Asheville (Public Radio) 253-6875
WNCW/88.7	Spindale (Public Radio) 287-8000
WLFA/91.3	Asheville (Religious)
WESC/92.5	Greenville, SC (Country) (864) 242-4660
WTPT/93.3	Forest City (Alternative Rock)
WFBC/93.7	Greenville, SC (Top 40) (864) 271-9200
WXRC/95.7	Charlotte (Rock)

WZLS/96.5	Biltmore Forest (Rock) 277-0011
WSPA/98.9	Spartanburg (Light Rock) 253-9999
WKSF/99.9	Asheville (Modern Country) 257-2700, 253-3835
WMYI/102.5	Greenville, SC (Soft Rock) (864) 235-1025
WMXF/104.3	Old Fort (Rock, Hip Hop) 240-1043
WQNS/104.9	Asheville (Classic Rock) 281-1049
WMIT/106.9	Black Mountain (Religious) 669-8477

Real Estate

Asheville:

For information regarding real estate in the Asheville area, contact the Asheville Board of Realtors/MLS, 209 E. Chestnut St., Asheville, NC 28801 (255-8505). The Board of Realtors also publishes two excellent magazines: *The Real Estate Weekly,* which is distributed free to over 350 rack locations in Buncombe, Henderson, Madison and Haywood counties, and *The Real Estate Monthly,* which is distributed free to over 200 rack locations in Buncombe and Madison counties. *Real Estate Weekly* has advertising and property listings of members of the Asheville Board of Realtors. *Real Estate Monthly* also has advertising and property listings of members but is a color magazine format. You may obtain a copy of either by writing to Real Estate Publications, 209 E. Chestnut St., Asheville, NC 28801 or by calling 255-8505. The Homebuilders Association of Greater Asheville can also supply you with information regarding member builders and contractors. They are located at 34 N. Ann Street, Asheville, NC 28801 (254-8677).

Hendersonville/Flat Rock:

For information regarding real estate in the Hendersonville/Flat Rock area, contact: Hendersonville Board of Realtors, 316 East 1st Ave., Hendersonville, NC 28792 (693-9642). A useful publication available free is *Homes and Land of Hendersonville.* Copies may be obtained at the Visitor Center. Additional information about the area can be obtained by contacting the Hendersonville/Flat Rock Area Visitors Information Center. They are eager to assist people interested in moving to the mountains.

Road Conditions

Driving conditions in Asheville and the surrounding region are provided as a service by WLOS Channel 13 in Asheville. Also, call the Road Info Line at 684-1999, extension 1302. This line is updated by the State Highway Patrol. Additionally, WHKP offers "Weather Fone" service at 692-1450.

Senior Services

American Association of Retired Persons (AARP): 601 E St. NW, Washington, D.C. 20049, (202) 434-2277. Its Purchase Privilege Program secures discounts for members on lodging, car rentals and sightseeing. AARP is a strong national association with many benefits for senior citizens.

Buncombe County Council on Aging: 50 South French Broad Ave., Asheville, NC 28801, 258-8027.

Buncombe County Department of Social Services: 40 Coxe Ave., Asheville, NC 28801, 250-5500.

Harvest House: 205 Kenilworth Rd., Asheville, NC 28803, 252-6021.

Henderson County Council on Aging: 304 Chadwick Ave., Hendersonville, NC 28792, 692-4203.

Henderson County Department of Social Services: 246 2nd Ave. East, Hendersonville, NC 28792, 697-5500.

Land of Sky Regional Council: 25 Heritage Dr., Asheville, NC 28806, 251-6622.

The North Carolina Center for Creative Retirement: The University of North Carolina at Asheville, Asheville NC 28804, 251-6140. The purpose of this organization is to advance the quality of life for retirees and pre-retirees by providing many valuable resources and opportunities for older residents.

Opportunity House: 1411 Asheville Hwy., Hendersonville, NC 28791, 692-0575. A multifaceted center for senior citizens in the Hendersonville area. Opportunity House provides arts and crafts classes, bridge, sports, lectures, exercise classes, college courses in connection with Blue Ridge Community College, trips, dinners, dances and more.

Senior Friendships of Henderson County: www.seniorfriendships.com

Shipping Stuff Home

One of the dilemmas occasionally facing travelers is getting some of the purchases they make shipped home. Most gift shops and retail stores do not ship, and most of us don't carry shipping supplies with us on vacation. The solution is to have someone else do it. In both Asheville and Hendersonville, there are a number of places that will do the job from start to finish—professionals who will not only ship your newfound treasures, but also package them in such a way that they arrive intact. These shipping stores are:

Asheville:

Andy's Pak-N-Post: Innsbruck Mall, 85 Tunnel Rd., 253-0065
Postnet Shipping: 129 Bleachery Blvd., 298-1211
QPS Quality Pack & Ship: 4 Long Shoals Rd., 654-7770
The UPS Store: 1854 Hendersonville Rd., 277-7445
              825-C Merrimon Ave., 252-6930
              1070 Tunnel Rd., 299-8988

Hendersonville:

The Home Office: 1734 Brevard Rd., 692-7701
Mail Box & Pack: Old Wal-Mart Plaza, 224 Thompson St., 693-1700
Parcel Service East: 102 Duncan Hill Rd., 693-6204
Postnet: 677 Spartanburg Hwy., 692-4549
The UPS Store: 172 Highlands Square Dr., 697-5623

Television Stations
WLOS TV 13: (www.wlos13.com) ABC affiliate based in Asheville offering the best coverage of the mountain area.

Tours/Touring
A number of self-guided tours of historic districts are offered in this book:
The Asheville Urban Trail: SEE Section Three, Chapter 5
Historic Asheville: SEE Section Three, Chapter 4
Historic Hendersonville: SEE Section Four, Chapter 3
Historic Flat Rock: SEE Section Four, Chapter 4

Additionally, the following companies offer tour services:

Asheville Blue Ridge Tours: (www.ashevilleblueridgetour.com) 275-5765, FAX 255-7590. Provides individual, couple, and small group transport and guided tours in Asheville and the Southern Blue Ridge mountains of Western North Carolina. They also offer three-hour tours of the area at $25 per person, visiting historic sites, arts & crafts galleries and shops, gardens, the farmer's market, and other attractions. Available by reservation.

Asheville Historic Trolley Tours: (www.ashevilletrolleytours.com) 667-3600. Narrated tours on vintage trolleys covering all major points of interest in Asheville.

Young Tours: 843 Riverside Dr., Asheville, NC 28804; 258-0084 or 800-622-5444. Asheville's oldest tour service offers customized visits to Western North Carolina, Canada and the United States. They can also arrange a motor coach tour of Asheville for groups. Prices vary depending upon group size, coach size and length of tour. Call for rates.

Travel Agencies
Asheville:
AAA Travel Agency: 660 Merrimon Ave., 253-5376
American Express Travel Service Representative: Wilcox World Travel and Tours, BB&T Building
Beacon Travel Service: 200 Ashland Ave., 252-2431
Fugazy Travel: 1550 Hendersonville Rd., 274-2555; 788 Merrimon Ave., 253-2555
Perry Travel Agency: 2270 Hendersonville Rd., 687-8200
Travelink Inc.: 46 Haywood St., 252-8484
Wilcox World Travel and Tours: BB&T Building, 254-0746. www.wilcox travel.com

Hendersonville:
AAA Carolinas: 136 South King St., 697-8778
Educational Travel Consultants: 2876 Middleton Vista, 693-0412
Fifth Avenue Travel: 1504 5th Ave. West, 696-8200
Fugazy Travel: 404 S. Main St., 693-0701
General Travel Agency: 117 West Barnwell St., 692-4294

Wilcox World Travel and Tours: 140 S. Church St., 693-0393; E-mail: hendersonville@pobox.com

Visitor Centers in Western North Carolina

(SEE also Section Five, Chapter 4 "Western North Carolina Cities and Towns")

Asheville: 36 Montford Ave., P.O. Box 1010, Asheville, NC 28802; 258-6100 or (800) 257-1300, FAX: 251-0926; www.ashevillechamber.org

Beech Mountain: 403A Beech Mountain Parkway., Beech Mountain, NC 28604; 387-9283, (800) 468-5506; www.beechmountain.com

Black Mountain: 201 E. State St., Black Mountain, NC 28711; 669-2300, FAX 669-1407. www.blackmountain.org

Blowing Rock: 1038 Main St., Blowing Rock, NC 28605; 295-7851, (800)295-7851; www.blowingrock.com

Boone: 208 Howard St., Boone, NC 28607; 264-2225, (800) 852-9506, FAX: 264-6644; www.boonechamber.com

Brevard: 35 W. Main St., Brevard, NC 28712; 883-3700, (800) 648-4523, FAX: 883-8550; www.visitwaterfalls.com

Bryson City: 16 Everett St., Bryson City, NC 28713; 488-3681, (800) 867-9246; www.greatsmokies.com

Burnsville: 106 W. Main St., Burnsville, NC 28714; 682-7413, (800) 948-1632, FAX: 682-6599; www.yanceychamber.org

Cashiers: P.O. Box 238, Cashiers, NC 28717; 743-5191, FAX: 743-9446; www.cashiersnorthcarolina.org

Cherokee: Main St. (P.O. Box 460), Cherokee, NC 28719; 497-9195, (800) 438-1601, FAX: 497-3220. www.cherokee-nc.com

Chimney Rock: P.O. Box 32, Chimney Rock, NC 28720; 625-2725; www.hickorynutgorge.com

Franklin: 425 Porter St., Franklin, NC 28734; 524-3161, (800) 336-7829, FAX: 369-7516; www.franklin-chamber.org

Hayesville: Business Hwy. 64, P.O. Box 88, Hayesville, NC 28904; 389-3704, FAX: 389-1033. www.claycounty-nc-chamber.com

Hendersonville: 201 S. Main St., Hendersonville, NC 28792; 693-9708, (800) 828-4244, FAX: 697-4996. www.hendersonvillechamber.org

Hickory: 470 Hwy. 70 SW (P.O. Box 1828), Hickory, NC 28603; 328-6111, FAX: 328-1175; www.catawbachamber.org

Highlands: 396 Oak St. (P.O. Box 404), Highlands, NC 28741; 526-2112, FAX: 526-0268; www.highlandschamber.org

Maggie Valley: 2487 Soco Rd. (P.O. Box 87), Maggie Valley, NC 28751; 926-1686, (800) 624-4431, FAX: 926-9398. www.smokeymountains.net

Marion: 629 Tate St., Marion, NC 28752; 652-4240, FAX: 659-9620; www.mcdowellnc.org

Morganton: 110 E. Meeting St., Morganton, NC 28680; 437-3021, FAX: 437-1613. www.burkecounty.org

Murphy: 115 U.S. Hwy. 64 W., Murphy, NC 28906; 837-2242, FAX: 837-6012; www.cherokeecountychamber.com

North Wilkesboro: 717 Main St., North Wilkesboro, NC 28659; (336) 838-8662, FAX: (336) 838-3728; www.wilkesnc.org

Robbinsville: P.O. Box 1206, Robbinsville, NC 28771; 479-3790, (800) 470-3790; www.grahamcountytravel.com

Spruce Pine: Route 1, Box 796, Spruce Pine, NC 28777; 765-9483, (800) 227-3912, FAX: 765-0202; www.mitchell-county.com

Sylva: 116 Central St., Sylva, NC 28779; 586-2155, (800) 962-1911, FAX: 586-4887; www.mountainlovers.com

Tryon: 401 N. Trade St., Tryon, NC 28782, 859-6236, FAX: 859-2301; www.polkchamber.org

Waynesville: 14 Walnut St., Waynesville, NC 28786; 456-3021, FAX: 452-7265. www.haywood-nc.com

West Jefferson: 6 N. Jefferson Ave. (P.O. Box 31), West Jefferson, NC 28694; (336) 246-9550, (888) 343-2743, FAX: (336) 246-8671; www.ashe chamber.com

In addition to the Visitor Centers listed above, the following telephone numbers can be called for full-color brochures. Websites can be accessed for additional regional information. (SEE also Section Five, Chapter 4 for Western North Carolina Cities and Towns.)

Asheville: 1-800-354-9015; Websites: www.ashevillechamber.org (Chamber of Commerce); www.ci.asheville.nc.us (City of Asheville)

Northern Mountains: 1-800-438-7500, www.highcountryhost.com

Central Mountains: 1-800-807-3391, www.ncblueridge.com

Southern Mountains (Great Smoky Mountains): 1-800-432-4678, www.smoky mtnhost.com

Maggie Valley/Waynesville: 1-800-334-9036, www.smokeymountains.net

Cherokee Indian Reservation: 1-800-438-1601, www.cherokee-nc.com

North Carolina: 1-800-VISIT NC, www.visitnc.com

Western North Carolina Counties & Elevations

Avery	Newland 3,589 feet
Buncombe	Asheville 2,216 feet
Burke	Morganton 1,182 feet
Cherokee	Murphy 1,535 feet
Clay	Hayesville 1,893 feet
Graham	Robbinsville 2,150 feet
Haywood	Waynesville 2,635 feet
Henderson	Hendersonville 2,146 feet
Jackson	Sylva 2,047
Macon	Franklin 2,113 feet
Madison	Marshall 1,650 feet

McDowell	Marion 1,437 feet
Mitchell	Bakersville 2,550 feet
Polk	Columbus 1,145 feet
Rutherford	Rutherfordton 1,096 feet
Swain	Bryson City 1,736 feet
Transylvania	Brevard 2,230 feet
Yancey	Burnsville 2,817 feet

Western North Carolina Independent Informational Websites

A number of websites not affiliated with Chambers of Commerce or Visitor Centers present a wealth of valuable and useful information about Asheville, Hendersonville, and Western North Carolina in general. Many of these sites are online guides; some offer virtual tours; and most have extensive links to other sites of interest. The table on the following page contains a list great websites for information on Asheville, Hendersonville, and Western North Carolina.

The homepage for *The Ultimate Guide to Asheville & the Western North Carolina Mountains,* www.ashevilleguidebook.com, has one of the most exhaustive link indexes to be found concerning the area. The site's "Link Treasury" lists over 250 related websites and is updated regularly to remain current.

Asheville Citizen-Times	
Mountain Travel Guide	www.carolinamountains.com
Asheville.com	www.asheville.com
Asheville-NC.com	http://asheville-nc.com/
Hendersonville.com	www.hendersonville.com
Just Asheville	www.ashevilleusa.com
Mountain Area	
Information Network	www.main.nc.us
NCNatural.com	www.ncnatural.com

Yoga

Asheville:
ACK Institute Yoga: 180 Merrimon Ave., 255-1914
Asheville Yoga Center: 239 S. Liberty St., 254-0380
Awakening Heart: 3 Walden Ridge, 684-1084
Lighten Up Yoga & Healing Arts Center: 60 Biltmore Ave., 254-7756
Namaste Yoga & Healing Center: 57 Broadway, 253-6985
One Center Yoga: 120 Coxe Ave. Ste 3A, 225-1904

Hendersonville:
Samadhi Yoga Center: 142 Joel Wright Dr., 698-9642
The Yoga Studio at Highland Lake Inn: 618 Sunset, 891-4313

Chapter Four
Making the Move

If you are considering a move to the Asheville or Hendersonville areas, the following listings should prove to be helpful in planning and making the move. Your best resources are the Asheville Area Chamber of Commerce and the Hendersonville Chamber of Commerce. (SEE also Section One, Chapter 3)

If you are planning to relocate to Western North Carolina and want someone who really knows the mountains, please consider having me help you. I am a realtor with Appalachian Realty who works only with buyers and who specializes in gated, golf, retirement and recreational communities. As a guidebook author, I am extremely familiar with what is available and have helped many clients find a home in the mountains. For more information about my real estate services, please visit my guidebook website: www.ashevilleguidebook.com, or call me at 828-779-1569.

Asheville Relocation Resources
Asheville Area Chamber of Commerce
Address: 36 Montford Ave., Asheville, NC 28801
P.O. Box 1010, Asheville, NC 28802
Telephone: (800) 257-1300
Website: www.ashevillechamber.org/relocation.htm
FAX: 251-0926
Publications: Newcomer's Guide
Membership Directory
Industrial Directory
To Order: 258-6101, xtn. 555

Asheville Board of Realtors/MLS
Address: 209 East Chestnut St., Asheville, NC 28801
Telephone: 255-8505
Publication: The Real Estate Weekly (Free)

General Real Estate Websites
Asheville Board of Realtors: www.ashevillebdrealtors.com

Realtor.com/Asheville: www.realtor.com/asheville/
Realtor.com/Hendersonville: www.realtor.com/hendersonville/

Hendersonville Relocation Resources
Hendersonville & Flat Rock Area Visitors Information Center
Address: 201 South Main St., Hendersonville, NC 28792
Telephone: (800) 828-4244
FAX: 697-4996
Website: www.historichendersonville.org
Publication: Mountain Seasons Vacation Planner (Free)

Hendersonville Chamber of Commerce
Address: 330 N. King St., Hendersonville, NC 28792
Telephone: 692-1413
FAX: 693-8802
Website: www.hendersonvillechamber.org
Publication: General Brochure (Free, this brochure lists the variety of publications available from the chamber.)

Hendersonville Board of Realtors
Address: 316 East 1st Ave., Hendersonville, NC 28792
Telephone: 693-9642
Publication: Homes and Land of Hendersonville (Free)

Employment Resources
North Carolina Employment Security Commission
Address: 48 Grove St., Asheville, NC 28801
Telephone: 251-6200

Mountain Area JobLink Career Center
Address: 40 Coxe Ave., Suite G-040, Asheville, NC 28801 P.O. Box 729, Asheville, NC 28802
Telephone: 250-4761

Senior Organizations
Senior Friendships
The organizational objectives are to introduce newcomers of Henderson County to their community, to meet new people and establish friendships, to support worthy causes in the community and to encourage participation in club and community activities. Club activities include bridge games, bowling, social supper club and dining out, games, golf, poker, singles group, Christmas Dinner Dance and travel slides and video group. PO Box 2828, Hendersonville, NC 28793. 891-4399. www.seniorfriendships.com

Welcome Club of Hendersonville

The Welcome Club of Hendersonville has the objectives of introducing new members to the Hendersonville area, providing helpful information and supporting local charities by various fundraising efforts. They welcome all persons new (and not so new). Members meet new friends by attending general meetings, holiday get-togethers, and by joining any of their many activity groups, which include gardening, book clubs, lunch groups, day trips, bridge and evening social groups. For information call 698-5744.

The North Carolina Center for Creative Retirement

The NCCCR is a department of the University of North Carolina at Asheville and has the threefold purpose of promoting lifelong learning, leadership and community service. Located in a 20,000 square-foot facility on the UNCA campus, the center is an excellent senior resource. 116 Rhoades Hall, CP 2420, UNCA, One University Heights, Asheville, NC 28804. 251-6140. www.unca.edu/ncccr

Additional Resources

Driver's License Offices

Asheville: 600 Tunnel Rd., Asheville, NC 28805; 298-4544
1624 Patton Ave., Asheville, NC 28806; 251-6065
Hendersonville: 139 Baystone Ave., Hendersonville, NC 28791; 692-6915

Motor Vehicle Registration

Asheville: 137 Smoky Park Hwy., Asheville, NC 28806, 667-2104; 16D
Innsbruck Mall, 85 Tunnel Rd., Asheville, NC 28805; 252-8526
Hendersonville: 200 N. Grove St., Hendersonville, NC 28791; 697-4970

Voter Registration

Asheville: Register at any Buncombe County branch library, or Buncombe County Board of Elections, Courthouse Annex, Asheville, NC 28801, 250-4200
Hendersonville: Henderson County Elections Board, 100 King St., Hendersonville, NC 28792; 697-4970

Local Governments

Buncombe County:

Buncombe County has a full-time county manager and an elected board of commissioners. Each municipality within Buncombe County has an elected mayor, a city or town council, plus an employed city or town manger who handles day-to-day administrative duties.

Buncombe County	255-5650
Asheville	258-3223

Biltmore Forest	274-0824
Black Mountain	669-8732
Montreat	669-8002
Weaverville	645-7116
Woodfin	253-4887

Henderson County:

Henderson County has a full-time county manager and an elected board of five commissioners. Each municipality within Henderson County has an elected mayor, a city or town council, plus an employed city or town manager who handles day-to-day administrative duties.

Henderson County	697-4809
Fletcher	687-3985
Hendersonville	697-3000
Flat Rock	697-8100
Laurel Park	693-4840

Property Taxes

For details on valuations and listings, call the County Assessor's Office. For details on bills and payments, call the County Tax Collector's Office.

Asheville:

Buncombe County Assessor	255-5511
Buncombe County Tax Collector	255-5511

Hendersonville:

Henderson County Assessor	697-4870
Henderson County Tax Collector	697-5595

Utilities

Buncombe County:

Carolina Power & Light	258-1010
Bell South	780-2355
Public Service Co. of NC	253-1821 (natural gas)
Water/Sewer, Asheville	258-0161
Water/Sewer, Black Mtn.	669-8250
Water/Sewer, Woodfin	253-5551

Hendersonville:

Duke Power	697-3400
Bell South	780-2355
Public Service Co. of NC	692-0511 (natural gas)
Water/Sewer	697-7779, 697-3052
Sanitation	697-3084

Chapter Five
Environmental Issues in Western North Carolina

Paradise is not without its problems, and even though it would seem at first glance that there are really no environmental concerns in the beautiful mountains of Western North Carolina, there are a couple of issues that have just about everyone who lives here worried. Tops on the list is the air quality problem that occurs primarily in the summer. On certain days even the most remote mountains and valleys, especially in the Great Smokies, have smog that rivals even Los Angeles and other urban centers. The primary culprits are the coal-fired power plants in the Midwest, which spew nitrous oxides and sulfur dioxides into the atmosphere, which are then carried by the prevailing west to east air currents and deposited to our area. A secondary cause, of course, is the fossil fuel driven vehicles that we all use. The battle to stop this pollution from the Midwest plants is being fought on a national level, with North Carolina legislators (and those of adjoining states that are similarly affected) in the forefront of the war. This problem is directly related to a much larger and more ominous issue facing our planet—global warming, which is caused by release of greenhouse gases, some of the very ones that are creating the local air quality problems in the mountains.

Other issues are also acid deposition from acid rain in the higher mountain forests. This issue is clearly related to the air pollution problem stemming from the outdated and inefficient coal-fired power plants. Western North Carolina mountains are some of the most biologically diverse temperate forests in the world. Clear cuttings, pollution and sprawling developments are wiping out species and habitats at an alarming rate. While most developers are sensitive to the environment in their developments, the gradual loss of habitat from so many new such projects springing up all over the mountains is having a negative effect on many plant and animal species.

Western North Carolina Environmental Organizations

This list includes organizations that are actively working to preserve the environment in the Western North Carolina mountains and other parts of America.

ECO—Environmental & Conservation Organization

ECO is dedicated to preserving the natural heritage of Henderson County and the mountain region through education, recreation, service and civic action. Their guiding statement is to take care of your own backyard. Seeking to think globally and act locally, they work to preserve and protect our streams and wetlands, wildlife and natural habitats, air, and trees—the environment that sustains us all. 119 3rd Ave., Hendersonville, 692-0385, www.eco-wnc.org

Liza's Reef

An art- and science-based resource portal website dedicated to the protection and conservation of coral reefs, other oceanic environments and rain forests. Liza's Reef is also involved in supporting local WNC environmental organizations in their efforts to protect the Western North Carolina mountains. 779-1569, www.lizasreef.com

RiverLink

RiverLink is a regional nonprofit spearheading the economic and environmental revitalization of the French Broad River and its tributaries as a place to work, live and play. RiverLink was born in 1987 of simultaneous efforts to address water quality concerns throughout the French Broad River basin, expand public opportunities for access and recreation, and spearhead the economic revitalization of Asheville's dilapidated riverfront district. As expressed in their mission statement, they focus on related issues that directly impact the environmental health of our region's rivers and streams and the growth and sustainability of our economy. 70 Woodfin Place, Asheville, 225-0760, www.riverlink.org

Southern Appalachian Biodiversity Project

SABP is a nonprofit regional organization dedicated to empowering citizens to appreciate, defend, and restore the native biodiversity of the Southeast. SABP seeks permanent protection for the region's public lands and sustainable management of private lands. The group pursues its goals through public education, legal advocacy, and grassroots organizing. Battery Park Ave., Asheville, 258-2667, www.sabp.net

Southern Alliance for Clean Energy

SACE is a nonprofit, nonpartisan organization that promotes responsible energy choices that solve global warming problems and ensure clean, safe, and healthy communities throughout the Southeast. SACE has programs throughout the southeastern United States, including Alabama, Florida, Georgia, Kentucky, Mississippi, North Carolina, South Carolina, and Tennessee. Asheville, 254-6776, www.cleanenergy.org

Southern Appalachian Forest Coalition

SAFC is a nonprofit organization formed in 1994 whose objective are to create a unified and compelling regional conservation vision for the 21st century; to achieve greater representation in Washington, DC; and to strengthen grassroots groups with the tools and leadership needed to protect the forests at the local level. It is now comprised of 22 of the best conservation groups spanning the six states of Alabama, Georgia, South Carolina, North Carolina, Tennessee, and Virginia. 46 Haywood St., Asheville, 252-9223, www.safc.org

The Southern Appalachian Highlands Conservancy

Founded in 1974 as a nonprofit charitable organization, the SAHC's mission is to conserve unique plant and animal habitats, clean water, and scenic beauty of the mountains of North Carolina and Tennessee for the benefit of present and future generations. The Conservancy works with individuals and local communities to identify, preserve, and manage the region's important lands. It has helped ensure the protection of more than 21,000 acres throughout the mountain region. 34 Wall St., Suite 802, Asheville, 253-0095, www.appalachian.org

Western North Carolina Alliance

The Western North Carolina Alliance is a grassroots organization that aims to promote a sense of stewardship and caring for the natural environment. Their primary goal is to protect and to preserve our natural land, water and air resources through education and public participation in policy decisions at all levels of business and government. They have chapters throughout Western North Carolina that mobilize Task Forces for rapid involvement around specific environmental issues. 70 Woodfin Place, Asheville, 258-8737, www.wnca.org

Western North Carolina Green Building Council

WNCGBC is a nonprofit organization whose mission is to promote environmentally sustainable and health-conscious building practices through community education. Their main goal is to educate homeowners, builders and architects on the benefits of green building practices. PO Box 17026, Asheville, 232-5080, www.wncgbc.org

Western North Carolina Nature Center

The Western North Carolina Nature Center is the premier nature center in Western North Carolina. Their mission is to increase public awareness and understanding of all aspects of the natural environment of Western North Carolina through hands-on and sensory experiences. An outstanding 42-acre center, the Nature Center receives over 100,000 visitors a year and features indigenous wildlife and plant life native to the Southern Appalachian Mountains. 75 Gashes Creek Rd., Asheville, 298-5600, www.wildwnc.org

Section Two
The Best of Asheville, Hendersonville & Flat Rock

Chapter One
Author's Choice Accommodations

B oth Asheville and Hendersonville have a wide variety and number of accommodations, from world-class resort hotels to budget motels. A select list of recommended accommodations is given below. Those recommended are established businesses and are on lists published by the two visitor centers in Asheville and Hendersonville. I am personally familiar with these accommodations and feel confident in recommending them. Those selected are the cream of the crop and are listed to provide you with the best choices, unbiased by any affiliation with any establishment or organization.

For more information on the complete range of accommodations available, contact the appropriate visitor center:

Asheville Chamber of Commerce Visitor Center: 258-6100
Hendersonville Area Visitors Information Center: 693-9708

An excellent alternative to the hotels and motels are the area's many bed & breakfasts. Each is unique in style, furnishings and decorations, and as a rule guest rooms are lovingly and individually theme decorated. Often they are furnished with period pieces, antiques and high quality furniture. B&B guest rooms are often among the most tasteful and elegant in an area. The ambience of these restored historic houses, more often than not in quiet residential neighborhoods or country settings, is hard to match. Another plus, which is often overlooked when seeking accommodations, are the wonderful breakfasts that are usually served in bed & breakfasts.

The season of the year has a lot to do with accommodation availability. Summer and the fall leaf season in October are by far the most crowded and busiest times of the year. Also, the weekend around Bele Chere Festival, and Christmas and New Year weekends are all high-volume times. Reservations for these weekends can be hard to find if not booked in advance.

There are a number of reservation services in the Western North Carolina area that will give accommodation referrals to help you find a place to stay. This book contains *all* of the best accommodations locally, but if you are looking farther afield to other areas of WNC, these services and their websites can be a great resource.

Carolina Mornings, Inc.: Cabin reservation services for Asheville and Western North Carolina. Phone: (800) 770-9055; FAX: (919) 929-9055; www. carolinamornings.com

Internet Accommodation Resources

Bed & Breakfast Inns ONLINE (www.bbonline.com) is a great online resource for travelers looking for B&Bs and country inns. Currently, more than 2,500 B&Bs are represented on their website nationally. For bed and breakfasts in Western North Carolina, visit their website and log onto the North Carolina directory (www.bbonline.com/nc/). Over 75 are listed, with each property represented with color pictures, descriptions, and contact information. Many of the select B&Bs presented in this book are also listed on this site.

For Asheville area lodging, visit the Asheville Bed & Breakfast Association website (www.bbonline.com/nc). Henderson County's Blue Ridge Escapes website (www.bbonline.com/nc/hendersonville) can help you find accommodations in Hendersonville.

Prices

Lodging prices quoted in this guide are for double occupancy during the summer season (June-August). In most cases a range is given. Prices are subject to change.

Asheville's Grand Hotels, Country Inns & Lodges

Forest Manor Inn: Charming 21-unit, three-diamond AAA rate motel featuring cottage-style buildings, homelike ambience, landscaped grounds, heated pool, rooms with king, queen or double beds, cable TV, AC and continental breakfast. Close to Biltmore Estate. 866 Hendersonville Rd., Asheville, NC 28803; 274-3531 or (800) 866-3036; $89-169.

Grove Park Inn Resort & Spa (NRHP): Superlative world-class resort hotel. Four-diamond and many other awards. 510 rooms, sports center, indoor and outdoor pools, 18-hole championship golf course. Opened in 2001, the hotel's world-famous spa is one of the finest in the world and features lush gardens, waterfalls and a wide range of treatments. SEE Section Three, Chapter 6 "The Grove Park Inn Resort & Spa" for a review of the spa and for more information about this extraordinary hotel. 290 Macon Ave., Asheville, NC 28804; (800) 438-5800 or 252-2711, FAX: 252-6102; $180-595. www.groveparkinn.com

Haywood Park Hotel (NRHP): Four-diamond hotel in the heart of downtown. 33 rooms, all suites, Jacuzzis. Continental breakfast delivered to suite daily. One Battery Park Ave., Asheville, NC 28801, (800) 228-2522 or 252-2522; $155-295.

The Inn at Wintersun: Located in the countryside in Fairview, just southeast of Asheville. The Inn at Wintersun is an elegant country inn situated on 80 acres. Spacious rooms, beautifully appointed with fine furnishing, designer fabrics, lush linen and down comforters. Champagne receptions and gourmet breakfasts are compliments of the Inn. One Wintersun Lane, Fairview, NC 28730; 628-7890, (888) 628-1628, FAX: 628-7891; $190-338. www.innatwintersun.com

Inn on Biltmore Estate: A truly world class deluxe inn with over 200 rooms located on Biltmore Estate grounds, near the Biltmore Estate Winery. Spectacular mountain vistas from porches, balconies, and guest rooms. An experience in the graciousness of America's resorts at the turn of the century offering guests the opportunity to experience the same hospitality George Vanderbilt extended to his family and friends when they visited Biltmore Estate in the 1890s. Inn has a variety of function and meeting spaces. Guest rooms ranging from deluxe to suites as well as on site dining for breakfast, lunch, and dinner. Library, lobby bar, and a swimming pool nestled on adjacent grounds. Four-star rating by both Mobil Travel Guide and AAA. One Antler Ridge Rd., Asheville, NC 28801; (800) 624-1575, 225-1600, Group Sales: 255-1147 or 255-1148; $206-2,000, many packages available. www.biltmore.com

Princess Anne Hotel (NRHP): Sophistication and grace describe this little gem of a historic hotel. The lovingly restored Princess Anne is characterized by its timeless, classic 1920s appeal with modern luxury and conveniences. The hotel, recently reopened, still retains its original ambience and charm. Each two-room suite is individually designed, with amenities that include LCD TV, high-speed Internet access, micro kitchens and private bedrooms. 301 E. Chestnut St., Asheville, NC 28801; (866) 552-0986, 258-0986; $125. www.princessannehotel.com

Renaissance Asheville Hotel: Downtown next to Thomas Wolfe Memorial. 281 mountain-view rooms within walking distance of 40 restaurants and more than 150 shops. One Thomas Wolfe Plaza, Asheville, NC 28801; (800) 333-3333 or 252-8211; $139-175.

Richmond Hill Inn (NRHP): Four-diamond historic country inn. 36 luxurious rooms, cozy croquet cottages or the new garden pavilion rooms. Two restaurants—Gabrielle's and the Arbor Grill. 87 Richmond Hill Dr., Asheville, NC 28806; (888) 742-4536 or 252-7313; weekdays $155-325, weekends $175-425. www.richmondhillinn.com (SEE also Section Three, Chapter 4)

National Chain Hotels & Motels, Asheville

Asheville Courtyard by Marriott: 1997 Gold Award-winning hotel, 78 deluxe rooms with in-room coffee makers, ironing boards and irons. Indoor pool and fitness facility. Deluxe breakfast. Just east of downtown off Tunnel Rd. One Buckstone Pl., Asheville, NC 28805; 281-0041 or (800) 321-2211; $119-159.

Baymont Inn: Located only four blocks from Biltmore Estate, this new facility (1999) offers complimentary breakfast, an indoor swimming pool and spa, smoking and nonsmoking rooms, in-room coffee makers, and a fitness center. Single, double, king, business leisure suite, and whirlpool equipped rooms are available. 204 Hendersonville Rd., Asheville, NC 28803; 274-2022 or (800) 301-0200; $79-119. www.baymontinn.com

Best Western Asheville Biltmore: Features coffee makers in all 150 interior-corridor rooms. Restaurant and lounge. 22 Woodfin St., Asheville, NC 28801; 253-1851; $89-140.

Best Western Asheville Biltmore East: Pet-friendly. 90 spacious and beautifully decorated rooms. Rated three diamonds by AAA. Outdoor heated pool, king and queen beds and free continental breakfast. East Asheville. 501 Tunnel Rd., Asheville, NC 28805; 298-5562; $52-99.

Best Western Asheville Biltmore West: Full-service hotel with 225 rooms, indoor and outdoor pools, spacious atrium area, and workout facilities. Mountain Brook Café located on premises. 275 Smoky Park Hwy., Asheville, NC 28806; 667-4501 or (800) 925-5486; $89-109.

Biltmore Howard Johnson: Pet-friendly. Near Biltmore Estate entrance in historic Biltmore Village. Rated four stars, is newly refurbished, and offers queen- and king-size beds. The hotel has a courtyard with outdoor pool, full-service restaurant; bed and breakfast plans available. 190 Hendersonville Rd., Asheville, NC 28803; 274-2300 or (800) 446-4656; $69-179.

Biltmore Sleep Inn: Pet-friendly. Near Biltmore Estate entrance in historic Biltmore Village. Offers 64 rooms; queen and double rooms available. Free coffee bar each morning. 117 Hendersonville Rd., Asheville, NC 28803; 277-1800; $100 & up. www.biltmorefarms.com/sleep.html

Comfort Inn Asheville Airport: Pet-friendly. 58 rooms, free continental breakfast, cable TV/HBO, pool, exercise room, near airport south of Asheville. 15 Rockwood Rd., Arden, NC 28704; 687-9199 or (800) 228-5150; $69-149.

Comfort Inn River Ridge: Pet-friendly. 177 rooms, whirlpool suites, spectacular mountain views, walking, jogging course. East Asheville. 800 Fairview Rd., Asheville, NC 28803; 298-9141; $79-159.

Comfort Inn West: 64 rooms, all queen- and king-size beds with twelve king suites. Fitness room and free continental breakfast. 15 Crowell Rd., Asheville, NC 28806; 665-6500; $59-159.

Comfort Suites: Pet-friendly. 125 rooms, outdoor heated pool. Southwest Asheville, near Biltmore Square Mall. 890 Brevard Rd., Asheville, NC 28806; 665-4000.

Country Inn Suites: New facility with 57 beautifully appointed guest rooms and suites. Country theme throughout. All rooms with 25-inch TV, HBO, ESPN and expanded cable, and telephone with voice mail and dataport. Suites include microwave, refrigerator, and wet bar. Whirlpool suites available. Complimentary continental breakfast, free USA Today, in-room coffee maker, hair dryer, ironing board, heated outdoor pool, and exercise room. Located in West Asheville near the Biltmore Square Mall. 845 Brevard Rd., Asheville, NC 28806; 670-9000 or (800) 456-4000; $65-129. www.countryinns.com

Crowne Plaza Resort: Country setting with golf course close to downtown. 280 rooms & suites, indoor and outdoor tennis facilities and outdoor pools. One Holiday Inn Dr., Asheville, NC 28806; 254-3211 or (800) 733-3211; $98-250. www.sunspree.com

Days Inn Airport: Pet-friendly. 116 rooms, outdoor pool, continental breakfast, cable TV, HBO, located near Asheville airport. 183 Underwood Rd., Fletcher, NC 28732; 684-2281 or (800) 329-7466; $39-120.

Days Inn Asheville Mall: Pet-friendly. 120 rooms, outdoor heated pool, complimentary breakfast bar, close to Tunnel Road restaurants. 201 Tunnel Rd., Asheville, NC 28805; 252-4000 or (800) 329-7466; $39-120.

Days Inn East: Pet-friendly. 125 guest rooms, swimming pool, Zhao Feng Garden Chinese Restaurant, free movie channel. Exit 55 on I-40, 1500 Tunnel Rd., Asheville, NC 28805; 298-5140; $39-120.

Days Inn North: Pet-friendly. 60 rooms, outdoor pool, free continental breakfast, Jacuzzi suites, children stay free. Five miles north of downtown. 3 Reynolds Mtn. Rd., Asheville, NC 28804; 645-9191; $39-120.

Days Inn West: Pet-friendly. 122 guest rooms, cable TV and HBO. Free continental breakfast. Truck and RV parking. Exit 37 on I-40. 2551 Smoky Park Hwy., Candler, NC 28715; 667-9321; $39-120.

Double Tree Biltmore Hotel: Next to Biltmore Estate entrance. A full-service property with 160 rooms including 20 suites and two restaurants: The Biltmore Dairy Bar and TGI Friday. 115 Hendersonville Rd., Asheville, NC 28803; 274-1800 or (800) 222-TREE; $199-219. www.doubletree.com

Extended Stay America: 101 rooms, each with a queen-size bed, recliner, cable TV, voicemail with free local calls and computer dataport. Each room also has a kitchen with refrigerator, range, microwave, coffee maker, utensils and tableware. Just east of downtown. 6 Kenilworth Knoll Rd., Asheville, NC 28805; 253-3483; $300 weekly or $66 nightly.

Fairfield Inn Asheville: Continental breakfast, indoor pool, Jacuzzi, fitness center, free local calls, airport shuttle, three conference rooms, HBO and ESPN. Exit 9, I-26. 31 Airport Park Rd., Fletcher, NC 28732; 684-1144; $65-89. www.fairfieldinn.com/avlnc/

Hampton Inn Biltmore Square: Deluxe continental breakfast, indoor pool, whirlpool spa, sauna and meeting space for 20. Southwest Asheville, near Biltmore Square Mall. 1 Rocky Ridge Rd., Asheville, NC 28806; 667-2022; $74-179.

Hampton Inn Tunnel Road: New hotel, convenient to I-240, downtown and 40-plus restaurants. Continental breakfast, indoor pool, whirlpool spa, sauna and meeting space for 20. 204 Tunnel Rd., Asheville, NC 28805; 255-9220; $74-179.

Hampton Inn & Suites: New facility, lovely building, outdoor pool, indoor and outdoor whirlpools, and fitness center. Exit 9 off I-26, near airport. 18 Rockwood Rd., Fletcher, NC 28732; 687-0806 or (800) 426-7866; $74-179.

Holiday Inn Airport: Newly renovated, indoor heated pool, fitness room, sauna, Horsefeather's Restaurant and Christy's Cafe. Near airport south of Asheville. 550 New Airport Rd., Fletcher, NC 28732; 684-1213 or (800) HOLIDAY; $75-139.

Holiday Inn Blue Ridge Parkway: Pet-friendly. Newly renovated inn, 111 guest rooms, mountain views. Full-service restaurant, outdoor swimming pool. 1450 Tunnel Rd., Asheville, NC 28805; 298-5611 or (800) HOLIDAY; $73-150.

Holiday Inn Express Biltmore Estate: 72 rooms, outdoor swimming pool, wheelchair-accessible, complimentary continental breakfast. 234 Hendersonville Rd., Asheville, NC 28803; 274-0101 or (800) HOLIDAY; $69-159.

Holiday Inn Express Hotel & Suites: Near Biltmore Square Mall. New Hotel and suites in 1998, 108 rooms, free continental breakfast, indoor spa, fitness center, and business center. 1 Wedgefield Dr., Asheville, NC 28806; 665-6519 or (800) HOLIDAY. $60-$140.

Marriott Residence Inn: Pet-friendly. Studio, one- or two-bedroom suites, fully equipped kitchens, living areas, bath(s) and vanity. Indoor pool, whirlpool spa, Sports Court and fitness room. Near Biltmore Estate in hospital district. 701 Biltmore Ave., Asheville, NC 28803; 281-3361 or (800) 331-3131; call for rates. www.asheville.com/residenceinn/

Ramada Limited: A courtyard-style inn. Free continental breakfast served each morning. Free in-room coffee. Facilities include heated swimming pool, sauna, exercise room and spa. Arthur's Restaurant on site. Just east of downtown. 180 Tunnel Rd., Asheville, NC 28805; 254-7451; $58-99.

Ramada Plaza Hotel West: Pet-friendly. 156 rooms, restaurant, room service, lounge, indoor/outdoor pool, Jacuzzi, sauna, fitness center, gift shop, valet/laundry service. Exit 44 off I-40, 435 Smoky Park Hwy., Asheville NC 28806; 665-2161 or (800) 678-2161; $68-119.

Red Roof Inn Asheville West: Pet-friendly. One- and two-bedrooms with outside entrance, multilevel with elevator. Wheelchair-accessible rooms on all levels. Nonsmoking rooms available. Free Showtime, CNN and ESPN. Free local calls, Fax service, modem hookup in some rooms. Kids stay free; small pets welcome. West Asheville. 16 Crowell Rd., Asheville, NC 28806; 667-9803 or (800) THE ROOF; $50-100.

Quality Inn Asheville: Pet-friendly. 117-room hotel with meeting space for up to 75 people, indoor pool, Jacuzzi, workout area and free continental breakfast. Shuttle van with free airport transportation. Suites available, free local calls. South Asheville. 1 Skyland Dr., Arden, NC 28704; 684-6688 or (800) 222-2222; $59-100.

Sleep Inn Biltmore West: New hotel, 74 rooms, complimentary continental breakfast, voice mail, free HBO, computer dataports. I-40 Exit 44. 1918 Old Haywood Rd., Asheville, NC 28806; 670-7600 or (800) 62-SLEEP; $60-151.

Asheville's Bed & Breakfasts

Abbington Green Bed & Breakfast Inn (NRHP): Colonial Revival-style home with romantic English flavor that includes antique furnishings, fine rugs, piano, library and fireplaces. Listed in the National Register of Historic Places as the Wythe Peyton House after a prominent Asheville resident whose family owned the house for more than 40 years. Richard Sharp Smith designed it and an award-winning renovation has restored it to its former glory. Prize-winning English gardens surround the inn. Inside, the stylish guestrooms are named after parks and gardens around London. Each room has a private bath and canopy-draped bed. The charming Eaton Square Carriage House suite has a living and dining area, two separate bedrooms and a full kitchen. Located in the Montford Historic District. 46 Cumberland Circle, Asheville, NC 28801; 251-2454; $125-325. www.abbingtongreen.com

Aberdeen Inn: Six guest rooms and cottages, all with private baths, four with fireplaces. Children over 12 welcome. Pleasant neighborhood. Hot tub, full gourmet breakfast. 64 Linden Ave., Asheville, NC 28801; 254-9336; $110-140. www.aberdeeninn.com

Acorn Cottage Bed & Breakfast: An English country bed & breakfast that features queen-size beds, fine linens and private baths. A 1925 vintage granite home that has maple hardwood floors and a stone fireplace. A full breakfast is served daily and features orange french toast and apple and cheddar quiche served with freshly baked breads, fruit and coffee or tea. 25 St. Dunstans Circle, Asheville, NC 28803; 253-0609; $90-120. www.acorncottagebnb.com

Albemarle Inn (NRHP): The Albemarle Inn, an elegant Greek Revival mansion, is located in the beautiful residential Grove Park section of Asheville. An exquisite carved oak staircase with a unique balcony dominates the main parlor. The Inn's eleven exceptionally spacious period rooms offer private baths with claw-foot tubs, fine linens and fresh flowers. A massive stone veranda overlooks nearly an acre of landscaped grounds with award-winning gardens. A full gourmet candle-light breakfast and afternoon refreshments complete the elegant experience. The mansion was built in 1907 as the private residence of Dr. Carl Reynolds, a prominent local physician. Since its sale in 1920, the residence has housed the

Albemarle Inn, 86 Edgemont Road

Grove Park School for Boys and Girls, the Plonck School for Young Women and has been operated as a boarding house. In 1943, the Hungarian composer Bela Bartok lived in the home as a boarder. Inspired by the birds singing outside of his third-floor room, Bartok composed his third piano concerto, known as "The Asheville Concerto" or "The Concerto of the Birds." The mansion has been operated as a bed and breakfast inn since 1980. 86 Edgemont Road, Asheville, NC 28801; 255-0027. $165-320. www.albemarleinn.com

Applewood Manor Inn (NRHP): A Colonial Revival-style house on almost two acres of secluded lawn and shade trees. Full gourmet breakfast and bicycles provided to guests. Located in the Montford Historic District. 62 Cumberland Cir., Asheville, NC 28801; 254-2244 or (800) 442-2197; $105-130. www.applewoodmanor.com (SEE illustration, Section Three, Chapter 4)

Beaufort House Bed & Breakfast Inn (NRHP): A grand Queen Anne mansion, features wood-burning fireplaces, two-person Jacuzzis, fitness facility and mountain views. The house has a lovely gingerbread porch, with beautifully landscaped grounds that include tea gardens. A unique Victorian bed & breakfast. Popular afternoon tea offered on outdoor porch. 61 North Liberty St., Asheville, NC 28801; 254-8334 or (800) 261-2221; $135-285. www.beauforthouse.com

A Bed of Roses (NRHP): Situated on a quiet, tree-lined street in the historic Montford district of Asheville, A Bed of Roses was built at the end of the Victorian era by Oliver Davis Revell and meticulously renovated in 2002. Enjoy the comfort of the tastefully decorated 1897 Queen Anne house with its shaded porch and tended gardens. Many of the guest rooms have fireplaces and private baths including Jacuzzi-style tubs. 135 Cumberland Ave., Asheville, NC 28801; 258-8700 or (800) 471-4182. www.abedofroses.com

A Bed of Roses, 135 Cumberland Avenue

Bent Creek Lodge: Bent Creek Lodge is a rustic mountain retreat surrounded by acres of woods and miles of trails and located less than one mile from the North Carolina Arboretum. Built in 1999, the Lodge is an ideal base for biking, hiking, canoeing, and exploring the Asheville area. Features gourmet breakfasts and intimate dinners for guests only. Amenities include a great room with stone fireplace, pool table, spacious decks, and six comfortably appointed guest rooms with private baths and air conditioning. 10 Parkway Crescent, Arden NC 28704; 654-9040; $110-179. www.bentcreeknc.com

Biltmore Village Inn: Located in historic Biltmore Village, this lovely B&B is the closest to Biltmore Estate. 119 Dodge St.; 274-8707; $150-295. www.biltmorevillageinn.com

Black Walnut Bed & Breakfast Inn (NRHP): A finely preserved Shingle-style home, was built in 1899 by Richard Sharp Smith and restored into a bed & breakfast in 1992. The Black Walnut Inn has four guest rooms in the main house and two separate rooms in a garden cottage. All rooms include private baths and are decorated with a blend of antiques and fine traditional furniture. A full hot breakfast is served daily in the formal dining room. In Montford Historic District. 288 Montford Ave., Asheville, NC 28801; 254-3878 or (800) 381-3878; $155-250. www.blackwalnut.com

Blake House Inn: Located in a restored, circa 1847, Italianate-Gothic style mansion. Originally, the home of wealthy, lowland rice plantation owners; now serving as a distinctive B&B. The Blake House Inn has five well-appointed guest rooms, each with private bath, sitting area, fine linens, cable TV, and telephone with dataport. 150 Royal Pines Dr., Arden, NC 28704; 681-5227 or (888) 353-5227; $155-185. www.blakehouse.com

Carolina Bed & Breakfast (NRHP): A turn-of-the-century restoration located in the Montford district, this historic house has seven rooms with fireplaces, private baths, and air-conditioning. The rooms are decorated with a blend of antiques and collectibles. Porches and gardens complement the gracious interior. 177 Cumberland Ave., Asheville, NC 28801; 254-3608; $115-200. www.carolinabb.com

Cedar Crest Victorian Inn (NRHP): One of the largest and most opulent residences surviving from Asheville's 1890s boom period, is an 1890 Queen Anne mansion featuring elegant interiors created by Vanderbilt's craftsmen. Romantic guest suites, rooms and beautiful grounds. One of three accommodations in Asheville to be awarded AAA's Four Diamond rating. 674 Biltmore Ave., Asheville, NC 28803; 252-1389 or (800) 252-0310. $150-$300.

Chestnut Street Inn (NRHP): A superbly restored Colonial Revival bed & breakfast located in the Chestnut Hill Historic District. The entire grounds are designated a "Treasure Tree" preserve. The inn has been lovingly restored and has some of the most elegant interior woodwork to be found in Asheville. Eclectic furnishings with great porches and all rooms have private baths. Private suite also available. Afternoon tea and breakfast are served on antique china. 176

The Colby House & Cottage, 230 Pearson Drive, Asheville

East Chestnut St., Asheville, NC 28801, 285-0705 or (800) 894-2955; $135-250. www.chestnutstreetinn.com (SEE illustration, Section Three, Chapter 4)

The Colby House & Cottage (NRHP): Located in the Montford Historic District, this elegant home offers four guest rooms, queen size beds, fine linens, and private baths. Full breakfast and evening refreshments are served on fine china, crystal, and silver service. The landscaped grounds have flower and rock gardens, a koi pond, and patio. Rated three-diamond AAA, A+ excellent ABBA. 230 Pearson Dr., Asheville, NC 28801; 253-5644 or (800) 982-2118; $150-250. www.colbyhouse.com

Corner Oak Manor Bed & Breakfast: A 1920 English Tudor residence in a quiet neighborhood. Renovated and decorated with oak antiques, arts and hand-crafted items. Features a full gourmet breakfast, living room fireplace with baby grand piano and an outdoor deck with Jacuzzi. 53 St. Dunstans Rd., Asheville, NC 28803; 253-3525 or (888) 633-3525; $125-135, $175 for cottage.

Cumberland Falls Bed & Breakfast Inn (NRHP): Turn-of-the-century home located in Montford Historic District. Grounds are landscaped with water-falls, koi ponds, and gardens. The inn features quilted maple woodwork and solarium. Guest rooms have wood or gas-burning fireplaces and two-person Jacuzzi tubs surrounded by marble. Fresh pastries, flowers, and robes in rooms, turndown service with chocolates, massage, and concierge service. Gourmet breakfasts served outdoors, weather permitting, overlooking the waterfalls and gardens. All rooms have CD player, TV/VCR, and telephone. AARP. AAA Three Diamond Award. Special midweek packages. 254 Cumberland Ave., Asheville, NC 28801; 253-4085 or (888) 743-2557; $120-250.

The Corner Oak Manor Bed & Breakfast, 53 St. Dunstans Road, Asheville

Flint Street Inns (NRHP): Two side-by-side distinguished early 20th century homes located in the Montford District. Eight guest rooms with queen size beds and private baths, some with fireplaces and claw-foot tubs. Generous Southern-style breakfast. 100 & 116 Flint St., Asheville, NC 28801; 253-6723 or (800) 234-8172; $85-130. www.flintstreetinns.com

A Hill House Bed & Breakfast Inn (NRHP): Seated on an acre of beautiful gardens and century-old trees, the original tin roof still graces this 1885 Grand Victorian. Recently restored and decorated in an eclectic mix of antiques and unique pieces, the varied accommodations include AC, VCR, phone, fax, in-room coffee maker, private Jacuzzi tub and fireplaces. 120 Hillside St., Asheville, NC 28801; 232-0345 or (800) 379-0002, Fax: 255-9855; $99-250, midweek and off-season special rates, cottage with kitchen available. www.hillbb.com

The 1900 Inn on Montford (NRHP): A turn-of-the-century Richard Sharp Smith-designed English country cottage, is furnished with period antiques from 1730 to 1910, oriental rugs and an extensive collection of antique maps. Full breakfast also served daily. Five large and comfortable guest rooms have private in-suite baths, fireplaces, and queen-sized poster beds. In Montford Historic District. 296 Montford Ave., Asheville, NC 28801; 254-9569 or (800) 254-9569; $165-345. www.innonmontford.com

The Lion & the Rose (NRHP): A Queen Anne/Georgian-style home, was built around 1898. Lovely antique-filled suites and private rooms complete with fresh flowers, linens and turndown service with chocolates on your pillow! Gourmet breakfast served daily in the sunny dining room and in the afternoon, tea on the verandas or in the parlors. In Montford Historic District. 276 Montford Ave., Asheville, NC 28801; 255-7673 or (800) 546-6988; $155-195. www.lion-rose.com

A Hill House Bed & Breakfast Inn, 120 Hillside Street, Asheville

North Lodge Bed & Breakfast (NRHP): A lovingly restored 1904 stone and
cedar shingle home with private baths and TV in every room. Antiques and
contemporary furnishings. Deluxe hot breakfast. No smoking. 84 Oakland
Rd., Asheville, NC 28801; 252-6433; $100-160. www.northlodge.com

The Old Reynolds Mansion (NRHP): An antebellum mansion with breathtaking
mountain views. Offers ten guest rooms plus a cottage suite, verandas, fireplaces,
and a pool. The Old Reynolds Mansion is one of Asheville's few remaining brick
homes that predates the Civil War. Set in a stunning location on a Reynolds
Mountain knoll surrounded by acres of trees. 100 Reynolds Hghts., Asheville,
NC 28804; 254-0496; $100-175. www.oldreynoldsmansion.com

North Lodge Bed & Breakfast, 84 Oakland Road, Asheville

Owl's Nest Inn and Engadine Cabins (NRHP): A unique 1885 Victorian house restored and modernized, has been awarded three stars by AAA and Mobil Travel. Country setting with wraparound porches, patios and walking paths in fields and meadows with breathtaking mountain views. Five spacious guest rooms, private baths, fireplaces, and AC. Full breakfast served daily. 2630 Smoky Park Hwy., Candler, NC 28715; 665-8325 or (800) 665-8868; $135-225. www.engadineinn.com

Owl's Nest Inn and Engadine Cabins, 2630 Smoky Park Hwy., Candler

Pinecrest Bed & Breakfast: 1905 English Tudor-style home with matching front towers. Located in Montford Historic District. Believed to be a Richard Sharp Smith designed house, having his signature pebbledash exterior. Situated on an acre of lush grounds and woods. Two elegant parlors, each with fireplace. Rooms have queen size or antique twin beds. Gourmet breakfast served in formal dining room on fine china and crystal with heirloom silver. 249 Cumberland Ave., Asheville, NC 28801; 281-4275 or (888) 811-3053; $125-200. www.pinecrestbb.com

Sourwood Inn: Located 10 miles from downtown Asheville, Sourwood Inn has 12 guest rooms with wood-burning fireplaces, balconies, and baths. Also available is the charming Sassafras Cabin. Located near the Blue Ridge Parkway in the mountains surrounding Asheville, Sourwood Inn has two miles of walking trails and offers a unique experience of the mountains that city bed and breakfasts can't. 810 Elk Mountain Scenic Hwy., Asheville, NC 28804; 255-0690; $150-180. www.sourwoodinn.com

Sweet Biscuit Inn: 1915 Colonial Revival house with rich decorative details throughout, including 11-foot ceilings, tiger oak floors, dramatic formal staircase, and a comfortable full length porch. 3 spacious guest rooms and carriage house with private baths. Located in Kenilworth neighborhood of East Asheville. Casual comfort and unpretentious sophistication are the hallmarks of this sweet and charming B&B. Expect multicolored Fiestaware, whimsical decorations, and elegant simple touches of nature. Children welcomed. 77 Kenilworth Rd., Asheville, NC 28803; 250-0170; $105-165. www.sweetbiscuitinn.com

1889 White Gate Inn & Cottage (NRHP): One of Asheville's premier bed & breakfasts, the historic White Gate Inn & Cottage is conveniently located near downtown Asheville. Romance, elegance and tranquility perfectly describe the ambience of this New England-style inn. Sumptuous breakfasts, luxurious spa suites and award-winning gardens, complete with cascading waterfalls and koi ponds, are just part of what make this B&B special. And if that isn't enough, they have a wonderful greenhouse for guests to visit, home to the extraordinary orchid collection of one of the inn's owners, Ralph Coffey. Hundreds of prize orchids and other fragrant seasonal flowers offer an attraction for guests that is hard to match. 173 East Chestnut St., Asheville, NC 28801; 253-2553 or (800) 485-3045; $170-215, Suite $285-315, Cottage $240-295. www.whitegate.net

The Wright Inn & Carriage House (NRHP): One of the finest examples of Queen Anne architecture in Asheville, has eight distinctive bedrooms and a luxurious suite with fireplace. All rooms have private baths, cable TV and telephones. The three-bedroom Carriage House is ideal for groups or families. Full breakfast and afternoon tea served daily in the inn. In Montford Historic District. 235 Pearson Dr., Asheville, NC 28801; 251-0789 or (800) 552-5724; $140-245, carriage house $325. www.wrightinn.com

Asheville's Cabins, Cottages & Chalets

Mountain Springs Cabins & Chalets: Three Diamond AAA rating. Outstanding country cabins with fireplaces overlooking a rushing mountain stream. Nestled on 30 landscaped, parklike acres just off the Blue Ridge Parkway and 10 minutes west of Asheville. Breathtaking views, a really special place to stay. 151 Pisgah Hwy., Candler, NC 28715 (P.O. Box 6922, Asheville, NC 28816); 665-1004, FAX: 667-1581; $100-145. www.mtnsprings.com (SEE illustration on the following page)

The Pines Cottages: AAA recommended. Offers 15 cottages and cabins 1.5 miles north of Asheville. All with kitchens, some with fireplaces and cable TV. Children welcome. 346 Weaverville Hwy., Asheville, NC 28804, 645-9661 or (888) 818-6477; $55-165. www.ashevillepines.com

Pisgah View Ranch: 19 miles southwest of Asheville at the base of Mount Pisgah. 42 cottage rooms with private baths. Famous family style country dining (three meals a day included). Nightly entertainment, swimming, tennis, hiking and horseback riding. Route 1, Candler, NC 28715; 667-9100; $55-110. www.pisgahviewranch.com (SEE also illustration "Pisgah National Forest," Section Five, Chapter 1)

Willow Winds/Woodland Gardens: Homes for rent in a 20-acre forest that features nature trails, lake and waterfalls. Near Biltmore Estate and Blue Ridge

Mountain Springs Cabins & Chalets, 151 Pisgah Hwy., Candler

Parkway. Complete kitchens, cable TV/VCR, washer/dryer, stone fireplaces and decks. 39 Stockwood Rd. Extension, Asheville, NC 28803; 277-3948 or (800) 235-2474; $885-1,360 per week. www.willowwinds.com

Hendersonville/Flat Rock's Grand Hotels, Country Inns & Lodges

Copper Crest Inn at Osceloa Lake: Historic 1908 inn with nine fireplaces located on a 40-acre lake with kayaks and beachfront for relaxation. 90-room resort with pool, tennis courts, Jacuzzi & claw-foot tubs, fast access DSL and wireless connections, buffet breakfast daily, beautiful gardens and courtyards with gazeboes, fountains and trellises. Osceloa Rd., Hendersonville, NC 28793; 692-2544 or (866) 80-CREST. $99-$215. www.coppercrestresort.com.

Echo Mountain Inn: Historic inn with great views. Built in 1896 on Echo Mountain, the inn offers one or two bedroom apartments, rooms with mountain views and fireplaces, private bath, cable TV and telephones. Restaurant, swimming pool and shuffleboard. 2849 Laurel Park Hwy., Hendersonville, NC 28739; 693-9626 or (888) 324-6466; $75-115. www.echoinn.com

Etowah Valley Country Club & Golf Lodge: Spacious air-conditioned lodge rooms, double beds, private baths, screened balcony, telephone and cable TV. Early bird coffee and pastries outside lodge. Other package rates include breakfast, dinner, golf and croquet. Just west of Hendersonville. 450 Brickyard Rd., Etowah, NC 28729; 891-7022 or (800) 451-8174; $89-109. www.etowahvalley.com

Highland Lake Inn: Offers accommodations in the inn, cabins or cottages. Located on scenic Highland Lake. Award-winning dining, outdoor pool, walking trails, organic gardens. P.O. Box 1026, Highland Lake Rd., Flat Rock, NC 28731; 693-3868 or (800) 762-1376; Inn: $139-239, Cottages: $209-369, Cabins: $119-169. www.hlinn.com

Inn on Church Street: Downtown inn built in 1921. Casual elegance, with room themes ranging from Oriental to Americana. Each room equipped with data-port access, cable television, voice mail and air conditioning. Daily gourmet breakfast, afternoon social, fresh baked cookies and turndown service with handmade chocolates also. 201 3rd Ave. West, Hendersonville, NC 28739; 693-3258 or (800) 330-3836. $129-$225. www.innonchurch.com

Lake Lure Inn (NRHP): Located on beautiful nearby Lake Lure, the historic 50-room Lake Lure Inn has been host to presidents, writers, and movie stars during its history. Member of Historic Hotels of America and the International Association of Conference Centers. Hwy. 42-74A (P.O. Box Ten), Lake Lure, NC 28746; 625-2525; $109-139. www.lakelureinn.com

Woodfield Inn (NRHP): A historic 1852 country inn near Flat Rock Playhouse and Carl Sandburg home. Authentic bedrooms, wine room, parlor and dining rooms all restored to their original elegance. Many of the Victorian bedrooms offer private baths, fireplaces, and French doors leading to sweeping verandas. Parklike setting on 28 acres. Tennis courts, gazebo, formal English garden, seven acres of walking trails, and entertainment facilities. Fine mountain and continental cuisine. Popular wedding setting. 2901 Greenville Hwy., P.O. Box 98, Flat Rock, NC 28731; 693-6016 or (800) 533-6016; $107-199. www.woodfieldinn.com (SEE illustration, Section Four, Chapter 4)

National Chain Hotels & Motels, Hendersonville/Flat Rock

Best Western Henderson Inn: Pet friendly, 100 rooms, outdoor pool, free continental breakfast. Located just east of Hendersonville. 105 Sugarloaf Rd., Hendersonville, NC 28792; 692-0521 or (800) 528-1234; $69-89.

Comfort Inn: Pet-friendly. Gold Award winner. Jacuzzi rooms with micro-refrigerators. Outdoor hot tub and pool. Deluxe continental breakfast. East Hendersonville, Exit 18A off I-26. 206 Mitchell Dr., Hendersonville, NC 28792; 693-8800 or (800) 882-3843; $59-139.

Days Inn: Free continental breakfast, cable color TV with complimentary HBO & ESPN. 102 Mitchell Dr., Hendersonville, NC 28792; 697-5999 or (800) DAYS INN. $56-$109.

Hampton Inn: 117 spacious rooms, two suites. Health Club privileges, cable and HBO. Free deluxe continental breakfast. Swimming pool. East Hendersonville, Exit 18A off I-26. 155 Sugarloaf Rd., Hendersonville, NC 28792; 697-2333 or (800) 426-7866; $72-160.

Holiday Inn Express: Spacious rooms, fireplaces, king-sized beds in five large theme-decorated rooms. Free continental breakfast, indoor swimming pool and exercise room. East Flat Rock, Exit 22 off I-26. 111 Commercial Boulevard, Flat Rock, NC 28731; 698-8899 or (800) 465-4329; $60-135.

Mountain Inn & Suites: Sixty-eight rooms, fitness center, free continental breakfast. 755 Upward Rd., Flat Rock, NC 28731; 692-7772; $55-$135.

Ramada Limited: 53 rooms, free continental breakfast. 150 Sugarloaf Rd., Hendersonville, NC 28792; 697-0006 or (800) 272-6232; $58-99.

Red Roof Inn: King rooms with whirlpool, free HBO, dataport phones. 240 Mitchell Dr., Hendersonville, NC 28792; 697-1223. $69-$130.

Quality Inn & Suites: Hendersonville's only full-service hotel, features domed atrium and indoor heated pool, sauna and whirlpool. Restaurant and lounge. East Hendersonville, Exit 18A of I-26. 201 Sugarloaf Rd., Hendersonville, NC 28792; 692-7231 or (800) 228-5151; $49-100 includes meals.

Hendersonville/Flat Rock's Bed & Breakfasts

Apple Inn: Mountain views and delicious home-cooked breakfast. Each room in this charming home is named after an apple variety. Parklike secluded grounds with hammocks, rockers and lawn games. House built circa 1900. 1005 White Pine Dr., Hendersonville, NC 28739; 693-0107 or (800) 615-6611; $109-149. www.appleinn.com

Claddagh Inn (NRHP): A historic bed & breakfast, has been lovingly restored. Built between 1888 and 1906, the Claddagh Inn has 14 lovely guest rooms, all uniquely decorated. Each has a private bath, AC, telephone and TV. A full home-cooked breakfast is served every morning in the inn's large, comfortable dining room. 755 N. Main St., Hendersonville, NC 28792; 697-7778 or (800) 225-4700; $99-169. www.claddaghinn.com

Elizabeth Leigh Inn: Elegant bed and breakfast in historic 1893 residence. Four suites with king-size beds, private baths and fireplaces. 908 5th Ave. West, Hendersonville NC 28792; 698-9707; $150-198. www.elizabethleighinn.com

Flat Rock Inn Bed & Breakfast (NRHP): Victorian elegance in the country. Four theme-decorated guest rooms, each furnished to take you back to a bygone era. The inn was built in 1888 as a private residence and has been wonderfully restored. Breakfast is served family style in one of two dining rooms and is varied every day. Country buttermilk biscuits, local jams and jellies, Belgium walnut waffles, eggs Benedict and cherry blintzes are regular items. 2810 Greenville Hwy., Flat Rock, NC 28731; 696-3273 or (800) 266-3996; $95-150. www.bbhost.com/flatrockinn

Little Man Lodge: Located in nearby Tuxedo. Lodge with 5 large rooms, private baths, 600 acres of private woodland with trails and waterfalls. Dock on nearby Lake Summit and lakeside cabins. 692-3241 or (866) 692-3241; $100-$125. www.littlemanlodge.com

Mary Mills Coxe Inn (NRHP): Great B&B in the wonderfully restored historic Mary Mills Coxe House, located half way between Hendersonville and Flat Rock. Antiques and period furnishings complement the authentic restoration. Seven rooms. One suite incorporating a bedroom, sitting room, and antique bath. Full breakfast served in the Mary Mills Coxe Inn Restaurant. 1210

Melange Bed & Breakfast, 1230 5th Ave. West, Hendersonville

Greenville Hwy., Hendersonville, NC 28792; 692-5900 or (800) 230-6541; $90-195. www.marymillscoxeinn.com

Melange Bed & Breakfast: Newly restored with European flair and charm, is a unique bed & breakfast with a refined atmosphere and museum-quality art and sculpture, oriental rugs, Mediterranean porches, crystal chandeliers and antique furnishings. Formal rooms, enchanting gardens, 4 large guest rooms and a two-room suite that feature either solid brass, old plantation oak or French canopy beds, boudoir style wall coverings and private baths. AC in all rooms, two rooms with Jacuzzis. A gourmet breakfast is served during summer in the Rose Garden and on covered porches and in winter in the formal dining room. 1230 5th Ave. West, Hendersonville, NC 28739; 697-5253 or (800) 303-5253; $119-195. www.melangebb.com

RoseTree Bed & Breakfast: Turn-of-the-century mission style country home set on six acres in Flat Rock. Named for the many Rhododendrons on the property. Beautifully kept grounds with old-fashioned roses, peonies, columbine, sunflowers, and other flowers. A full country breakfast served each morning. House has great wraparound porch complete with rockers. Two two-room suites, eight fireplaces, hardwood floors, and country/mission style furnishings. 1 Boxwood Dr., Flat Rock, NC 28731; 698-8912 or (800) 672-1993; $160 & up; www.bbonline.com/nc/rosetree/

Waverly Inn (NRHP): An elegant bed & breakfast established in 1898 that is famous for Southern breakfasts. Fourteen unique guest rooms and one suite, each with private bath, are named for native wildflowers. Special features include four-poster canopy beds, brass beds, claw-foot bathtubs, and pedestal sinks. 783 N. Main St., Hendersonville, NC 28792; 693-9193 or (800) 537-8195, FAX: 692-1010 or (800) 537-8195; $149-225 (winter specials available). www.waverlyinn.com (SEE illustration, Section Four, Chapter 4)

Hendersonville/Flat Rock's Cottages

The Beehive Cottages: Twelve furnished cottages in the Edneyville section of Henderson County (just east of Hendersonville). Newly remodeled, the cottages are located on an 86-acre farm in the heart of apple growing country. Beehive Rd., Rt. 2 Box 357, Hendersonville, NC 28792 (call for directions); 685-7702; $75-100.

The Cottages of Flat Rock: 14 immaculate one- and two-bedroom cottages nestled on 2.5 acres. Each cottage has a private front porch with rocking chairs overlooking a one acre parklike setting complete with gazebo and quiet stream. Laundry on grounds. 1511 Greenville Hwy., Hendersonville, NC 28792; 693-8805; $75-125. www.thecottagesofflatrock.com

Edgewater Inn Mountain Lake Cottages: Located on Osceola Lake, has offered lakeside cottages for more than 50 years. Country atmosphere close to town. Newly remodeled, cable TV, AC, fully equipped kitchens. Fishing and walking by lake. 801 N. Lakeside Dr., Hendersonville, NC 28739; 692-6269 or (800) 692-6269; $75-85, also weekly and monthly rates. www.mountainlakecottage.com

Lakemont Cottages: Located in Flat Rock, Lakemont Cottages features 14 individually decorated units that each sleep from two to six guests. All cottages are furnished, with separate bedrooms, air conditioning, heat, fully equipped kitchens and cable TV. Most have enclosed porches. No pets. 100 Lakemont Drive, Flat Rock, NC 28731; 693-5174; $60-110. www.lakemontcottages.com

Rose Cottages: On six shady acres away from the road, offers a casual, relaxed atmosphere just minutes from downtown Hendersonville and Flat Rock. Large and small studio cottages with kitchenettes and cable TV. 1418 Greenville Hwy., Hendersonville, NC 28792; 693-7577 or (888) 817-7229; $75-95. www.rosecottagesnc.com

Villa Capri Cottages: 19 cottages situated on two landscaped acres in a residential setting. 920 Greenville Hwy., Hendersonville, NC 28792; 692-7660; $50-100. www.villacapri.net

Rose Cottages, 1418 Greenville Hwy., Hendersonville

Chapter Two
Author's Choice Dining

T he choice of restaurants in the Asheville, Hendersonville and Flat Rock area can be overwhelming. Restaurants of all types and quality abound, and in order to make your vacation in Asheville as enjoyable as possible, I have included a list of recommended dining establishments. The ones selected are all locally owned, although Asheville and Henderson have many fine chain restaurants. I have elected not to include these since you are probably familiar with them already. However, if that is your choice for dining, the section of Tunnel Road beginning at Beaucatcher Tunnel in Asheville has more than 20 chain restaurants, all within one mile. The lineup includes Joe's Crab Shack, Lone Star Steakhouse and Saloon, Don Pablo's Mexican Kitchen, Outback Steakhouse, Applebee's, Olive Garden Italian Restaurant, Red Lobster, Waffle House, Carrabba's Italian Grill, O'Charley's Restaurant & Lounge, Roadhouse Grill, IHOP Restaurant, and Chili's Grill & Bar.

Reservations are always a good idea and those restaurants that require reservations are so noted. Dress is only mentioned when a jacket, or a jacket and tie, is required. Hours of operation are listed, but these frequently change, so I recommend that you call ahead to confirm if possible.

Area residents may wish to consider the locally owned Discover Dining program. Membership in the program can introduce a wide variety of area dining and lodging establishments, some of WNC's most beautiful attractions, area health and fitness providers, recreation activities, theater, music, art, and local businesses—and save you money at the same time. All of the Asheville and Hendersonville establishments covered in this program are presented in this book. For more information, call (800) 763-1458 or 298-3719 or write to Discover Dining at 28 Cedar Trail, Asheville, NC 28803.

I am personally familiar with all of the fine restaurants listed on the following pages and am delighted to be able to recommend them to you as among the very best Asheville and Hendersonville have to offer. Since restaurants can come and go, please visit my book's web site—ashevilleguidebook.com—for the most up-to-date restaurant listings.

Pricing Guide

Menu changes affect the pricing of the restaurants listed; however, in an attempt to help you make choices, a basic pricing guide is provided for some idea as to what you can expect to pay for an evening meal for one person, excluding sales tax, gratuity, drinks and dessert.

$ under $10
$$ $10-20
$$$ $20-30
$$$$ over $30

Asheville Fine Dining

Biltmore Estate Restaurants (SEE Section Three, Chapter 3 Biltmore Estate) Biltmore Estate has three superb restaurants on their premises: the elegant Deerpark ($$), the Stable Cafe ($) for casual dining, and The Bistro ($$) for continental cuisine. To access these fine restaurants, however, one must purchase a pass to the Estate. Plan to eat at one of these restaurants during the course of your visit.

Blue Ridge Dining Room at the Grove Park Inn Resort ($$): Southern Heritage cuisine including shrimp and grits and other southern classics. Enclosed terrace dining with a wonderful sunset view. Grove Park Inn Resort & Spa, 290 Macon Ave., 252-2711. Reservations recommended. Breakfast: 6:30-11 a.m.; Sunday Brunch: 10 a.m.-2 p.m. Dinner: 3-9:30 pm.

Cafe on the Square ($$): High ceilings and great windows provide wonderful views of Pack Square. Traditional American cuisine with a lighter California fare, with an emphasis on grilled meats and fish, fresh produce, pasta and specialty sauces. Outdoor dining on the brick courtyard also. A really unique dining spot! 1 Biltmore Ave., 251-5565. Reservations suggested. Lunch 11:30 a.m.-4 p.m. Dinner: 5-close. Open Sunday nights. www.cafeonthesquare.com

Cottonwood Café ($$): Excellent cosmopolitan cuisine, best described as "global fusion." Dishes from New Zealand Rack of Lamb to classic American fare. 1930s decor. 122 College St., 281-0710. Lunch: Monday-Saturday 11 a.m.-3:30 p.m. Dinner: Monday-Thursday 4:30-9:30 p.m.; Friday-Saturday 4:30-10 p.m.

Fig ($$): Traditional French bistro cuisine. Menu changes regularly so they can offer fresh and local ingredients. Located in Biltmore Village. 18 Brook St., 277-0889. Lunch: Monday-Saturday 11 a.m.-2 p.m., Sunday 10 a.m.-3 p.m. Dinner: Monday-Saturday 5-10 p.m.., Sunday 5-10 p.m.

Gabrielle's at Richmond Hill ($$$$): Gabrielle's is a nationally recognized restaurant located in the mansion at Richmond Hill Inn. They serve continental cuisine with a Southern flair in one of two dining rooms. The mansion's formal dining room, with its rich cherry paneling and three-tiered chandelier, has the stately Victorian ambience of the 1890s. The food presentation mirrors the quality of the menu. Gabrielle's is an elegant and sublime dining experience. Richmond Hill Inn, 87 Richmond Hill Dr., 252-7313. Reservations recommended, jacket required. Dinner: 6-10 p.m.; closed Tuesday and Wednesday. www.richmondhillinn.com/dining.html

The Greenery ($$): The Greenery features original and classic cuisine in a warm, inviting setting of antique table sets and soft candlelight. Superb recipes of mountain trout, Maryland crab cakes, prime choice steaks and duck complemented by an award-winning wine list. 148 Tunnel Rd., 253-2809. Reservations suggested. Dinner: nightly after 5 p.m.

Grove Park Inn's Sunset Terrace ($$): One of the most beautiful places for dining anywhere in Asheville is the Sunset Terrace at the historic Grove Park Inn. Here you can enjoy the outdoors (weather permitting), have an elegant dinner and experience a magnificent view of the lights of Asheville as darkness falls. Grove Park Inn, 290 Macon Ave., 252-2711. Dinner: 6-9 p.m.

Grovewood Cafe ($$): Features regional and classic cuisine with a Southern flare. Located in a cozy cottage setting within walking distance to the Grove Park Inn Resort. 111 Grovewood Rd., 258-8956. Open Monday-Sunday for lunch and dinner. Lunch: 11 a.m.-2:30 p.m. Dinner: 5-8:30 p.m.

Horizons ($$$): One of the few area restaurants to be awarded the prestigious DiRoNA Award given by members of the Distinguished Restaurants of North America. Extraordinary plate preparation and service. Known for its innovative, classic cuisine and extensive wine list. Grove Park Inn, 290 Macon Ave., 252-2711; reservations required, jacket and tie. Dinner: 6:30-9:30 p.m.

La Caterina Trattoria ($$): Superb authentic cuisine in an informal, relaxed atmosphere like the small restaurants found in small Italian villages. 254-1148. Reservations suggested. Monday-Friday—Lunch: 11:30 a.m.-2 p.m. Dinner: 5-9 p.m. (Closed Monday for lunch.) Saturday and Sunday—Lunch: noon-3 p.m. Dinner: 5-9 p.m.

The Marketplace & Cafe Oggi ($$): Exquisite continental cuisine in the historic district of downtown Asheville. 20 Wall St., 252-4162. Reservations suggested. Dinner: 5:30-9 p.m.

Orchards ($$): Located in the Renaissance Asheville Hotel. Casual, upscale, pleasant country cuisine. Signature dish is Fried Green Tomatoes with goat cheese and two sauces (black bean or red). One Thomas Wolfe Plaza, 252-8211. Breakfast, lunch, and dinner. Dinner: Sunday-Thursday 5-10 p.m.; Friday-Saturday 5-11 p.m.

Southside Cafe ($$): Unpretentious fine dining in a refined setting. American cuisine with fresh seafood dishes. 1800 Hendersonville Rd., 274-4413. Dinner reservations suggested. Lunch: 11 a.m.-2:30 p.m. Monday-Saturday, Sunday Brunch: 9 a.m.-2 p.m. Dinner: 5-9 p.m. Monday-Thursday, 5-10 p.m. Friday-Saturday.

Table ($$): American cuisine with focus toward seasonal, organic and local ingredients, and an obsession with freshness. Lunch: 11:30 a.m.-2:30 p.m. Dinner: 5:30 p.m.–until. Saturday and Sunday brunch: 9:30 a.m.-3 p.m. Closed Tuesdays.

Trillium—A Bistro ($$): Creative American cuisine with an artistic flair. Located on Highway 74A in the Reynolds district. 4 Olde Eastwood Blvd., 299-0470. Breakfast: 8-10:30 a.m. Lunch: 11 a.m.-3 p.m. Dinner: 5:30-10 p.m.

Usual Suspects ($$): Casual, fun restaurant located on the north side of town offering an eclectic and exotic selection of seasonal dishes. Menu changes every two months. Full bar, laid back atmosphere. 791 Merrimon Ave., 350-8181. 5:30 p.m.-2 a.m., 7 days a week.

Vincenzo's ($$): Chic and trendy restaurant, yet warm and friendly. Offering the finest in Northern Italian and continental cuisine. 10 North Market St., 254-4698. Reservations suggested. Lunch: 11:30 a.m.-2 p.m. Monday-Friday. Dinner: 5:30-11 p.m. daily.

Wildflower Restaurant ($$): Fine dining in a refined atmosphere. Updated classic cuisine to contemporary American fare. Candlelit European-style dining room. 900 Hendersonville Rd., 277-1010. Reservations accepted. Lunch: 11 a.m.-2 p.m. Dinner: 5-9 p.m.

Zambra ($$): Spanish, Portugese and Moroccan cuisine served in an exotic European setting. Like taking a trip to Spain for dinner. Not to be missed. 85 Walnut St., 232-1060. Dinner: Monday-Thursday 5:30-9 p.m.; Friday-Saturday 5:30-10 p.m.; Sun 5:30-9 p.m. Lounge service menu starts an hour earlier.

Asheville Family Dining

Angelo's Family Restaurant ($): Located in beautiful Fairview, about 30 minutes from downtown. Excellent country cooking with Greek flair. Family oriented. Great stop for lunch on your way to Lake Lure and the Chimney Rock area. 1226 Hwy. 74A, 628-4031. Open 11 a.m.-9 p.m.

Biltmore Depot Restaurant ($): Grilled seafood, chicken, burgers, sandwiches and soups. Located in the original Biltmore Railroad Depot. 30 Lodge Street, 277-7651. Open 11 a.m.-9 p.m. every day.

Cornerstone Restaurant ($): Family-oriented restaurant with a wide variety of cuisine, from simple sandwiches to shrimp pastas and steak. 102 Tunnel Rd., 236-0201. 6:30 a.m.-10 p.m. seven days a week.

DJ's Café & Diner ($): A cool family restaurant located in a chrome silver diner that is a tribute to the beautiful, bright and shiny diners of yesteryear. The authentic '50s decor, including the Wurlitzer jukebox, add to the nostalgic atmosphere. And the food is good! Located in the Reynolds district. 230 Highway 74A, 299-8883. Monday-Thursday 6:30 a.m.-9 p.m.; Friday-Saturday 6:30 a.m.-10 p.m.; Sunday 7:30 a.m.-9 p.m.

Frank's Roman Pizza ($): Great pizza, pastas, subs and salads. Casual and relaxed. 90 South Tunnel Rd., Asheville, 298-5855 or 85 Weaverville Hwy., 645-2910. Monday-Sunday 11 a.m.-9 p.m.

Little Pigs B-B-Q ($): An institution in Asheville for more than 35 years. If it's BBQ you want, this is the place! Four locations: 384 McDowell St. (254-4253), 1916 Hendersonville Rd. (277-7188), 901 Smoky Park Hwy. (670-9155), and 100 Merrimon Ave. (253-4633). Open 10:30 a.m.-8:30 p.m.; closed Sunday.

Michael's ($$): Located in the Arden section of Asheville, Michael's specializes in steaks, seafood and gourmet pizza. Full bar. 3 Glen Bridge Rd., Arden,

684-5991. Monday-Thursday 11 a.m.-9 p.m.; Friday-Saturday 11 .m.-10 p.m.; Sunday noon-6 p.m.

Moose Cafe ($): Features award-winning country food served with a smile at a reasonable price. Located at the Farmer's Market, 570 Brevard Rd., 255-0920 and at 3 Glen Bridge Rd., 684-1119. Breakfast, lunch, and dinner. Monday-Saturday 7 a.m.-8:30 p.m. Sunday 7 a.m.-8 p.m.

Picnics Restaurant and Bake Shop ($): Award-winning homestyle cooking. Great wood-roasted chicken! Picnic baskets prepared. 371 Merrimon Ave., 258-2858. Tuesday-Saturday 11:30 a.m.-8 p.m.

Pisgah Inn ($$): About an hour's ride south on the Blue Ridge Parkway, the Pisgah Inn is often shrouded in mists. Really high up in the clouds, the restaurant at the inn is a special dining experience. Wonderful relaxed atmosphere and great views out over the green valleys and rolling mountains. Southern menu with fresh mountain trout a specialty. Open March 31 to November 2. Milepost 408, Blue Ridge Parkway at Mount Pisgah, 235-8228. Breakfast: 7:30-10:30 a.m. Lunch: 11:30 a.m.-4 p.m. Dinner: 5-9 p.m.

Pisgah View Ranch ($$): About 45 minutes south of Asheville out in the country and off the beaten path, this restaurant is famous for its wonderful home cooking and generous portions. Fried chicken, country ham and tables full of side dishes. This is Southern country dining at its best. The real thing! Davis Creek Rd., Candler, 667-9100. Reservations. Seating for dinner at 5:30 and 7:15 p.m.

Trevi ($$): Great little Italian restaurant. Specialties include Fried Calamari, Canneloni and Tuscan Herb Crusted Tenderloin. 2 Hendersonville Rd., Asheville, 281-1400. Lunch: Monday-Saturday 11:30 a.m.-2:30 p.m.; Sputino: Saturday only 2:30-5 p.m. Dinner: Monday-Saturday 5-10 p.m.; Sunday 5-9 p.m.

Asheville Cafeterias

J&S Cafeterias ($): Since 1984, outstanding quality cafeterias. Pleasant decor, friendly service and expansive selection. 3 locations: River Ridge Mall 800 Fairview Rd., 298-0507; 645 New Airport Rd., 684-3512; 900 Smoky Park Hwy. (Westridge Market Place in Enka), 665-1911. Breakfast (Fairview Rd. location only): 6:30-10 a.m. Lunch: 10:45 a.m.-2:15 p.m. Dinner: 3:45-8:30 p.m. (summer), 3:45-8 p.m. (winter).

Asheville Seafood Restaurants

Beaver Lake Seafood and Steak Restaurant ($$): Casual dining and excellent seafood reminiscent of the beach restaurants all along the Southern coast. 1435 Merrimon Ave., 252-4343. Tuesday-Thursday 11 a.m.-9 p.m.; Friday 11 a.m.-9:30 p.m.; Saturday 3-9:30 p.m.; Sunday 11:30 a.m.-8 p.m.

Bistro 1896 ($$): Seafood with altitude is their slogan! Excellent selection and a great setting on historic Pack Square. 7 Pack Square, 251-1300. Lunch: Monday-Saturday 11:30 a.m.-4 p.m.; Dinner: Monday-Saturday 5-10 p.m.

The Boathouse at Lake Julian ($$): Asheville's only waterfront dining experience. Fresh seafood, steaks and innovative low country cuisine. 65 Long Shoals Rd., 687-4141. Dinner: nightly from 4:30 p.m. on. Sunday brunch: 10:30 a.m.-2 p.m.

The Lobster Trap ($$): Located downtown on Patton Avenue, offering fresh seafood and n oyster bar. 35 Patton Ave., 250-0505. Dinner: seven nights a week, from 5 p.m. on.

Magnolia's Raw Bar & Grill ($$): Casual raw bar and grill, European-style outdoor patio and an elegant dining room, the Magnolia Room. Three different and unique dining rooms in one restaurant. Home of the fresh oyster! 26 Walnut St., 251-5211. Lunch: Monday-Friday 11:30 a.m.-2:30 p.m. Dinner: Monday-Saturday 5-10 p.m. Closed Sunday.

Asheville Overseas & Exotic

Anntony's Caribbean Café ($): Authentic dishes from the islands! One Page Ave., Suite 129, Historic Grove Arcade Building, 255-9620. Monday-Thursday 11:30 a.m.-9 p.m.; Friday-Saturday 11:30 a.m.-10 p.m.; Sunday 11:30 a.m.-3 p.m.

Apollo Flame Bistro ($): Award winning restaurant serving Greek and Mediterranean specialties. 485 Hendersonville Rd., 274-3582. Monday-Saturday 11 a.m.-10 p.m.

Asaka ($$): Authentic Japanese cuisine and sushi served in comfortable surroundings. 801 Biltmore Ave., 250-9301. Lunch and dinner: 11 a.m.-10 p.m., 7 days a week.

Asian Grill ($$): Excellent selection of Chinese, Japanese and Thai delicacies prepared "New York Style." Wonderful interior and service. Another of the author's favorites. 1851 Hendersonville Rd., 277-1558. 11 a.m.-11 p.m. daily.

Black Forest Restaurant ($$): Authentic German and Northern Italian cuisine, steaks, and seafood. All dishes are scratchmade. Fireside lounge with all permits. Seven distinctive dining rooms. 2155 Hendersonville Rd., Skyland, 687-7980. Reservations suggested, Dinner: Monday-Saturday 5-10 p.m.; Lunch: Monday-Friday 11:30 a.m.-2:30 p.m.; open Sunday 11 a.m.-8:30 p.m.

Café Pacific ($$): Gourmet American fusion cuisine. 1378 Hendersonville Rd., 277-0108, Dinner: Monday-Thursday 5-9 p.m.; Friday-Saturday 5-10 p.m. Closed Sunday.

Cancun Mexican Restaurant & Cantina ($$): Wide selection of traditional Mexican foods from nachos, quesadillas, and chimichangas to burritos and chalupas. Full bar. 1201 Patton Ave., 232-0057. Monday-Thursday 11 a.m.-10 p.m.; Friday 11 a.m.-11 p.m.; Saturday noon-11 pm, Sunday noon-9 p.m.

China Palace ($$): Excellent Chinese food with additional Asian specialties. Vegetarian available. No MSG. Beer, wine, liquor permits. 4 South Tunnel Rd., 298-7098. Lunch: Monday-Friday 11:30 a.m.-2:30 p.m. Dinner: Monday-Thursday 5-10 p.m.; Friday 5-10:30 p.m. Open Saturday noon-10:30 p.m.; Sunday noon-9 p.m.

Doc Chey's Noodle House ($): Affordable, large portions of fresh Pan-Asian cuisine. Seating outside on Pack Square. 37 Biltmore Ave., 252-8220. Sunday-Thursday 11:30 a.m.-10 p.m.; Friday-Saturday 11:30 a.m.-11 p.m.

East Buffet ($): Buffet-style Oriental dining. Over 100 items offered. 125 Tunnel Rd., 253-9899, Monday-Thursday 11 a.m.-9:30 p.m.; Friday-Saturday 11 a.m.-10 p.m.; Sunday 11:30 a.m.-9:30 p.m.

Eddie Spaghetti ($): Spaghetti and more, including pizzas, subs, soups and homemade Italian food. Wine and beer. 1378 Hendersonville Rd., 277-9300. Monday-Saturday 11 a.m.-9:45 p.m.

El Chapala Mexican Restaurant ($$): Authentic Mexican cuisine—burritos, tacos, enchiladas, tamales and great margaritas. 868 Merrimon Ave., 258-0899; and 282 Smoky Park Hwy., 665-0430. Dinner: Monday-Friday 5-10 p.m. Open Saturday and Sunday noon-10 p.m.

Flying Frog ($$): Indian, Italian, Caribbean, French and Cajun specialties. 76 Haywood St., 254-9411. Sunday-Thursday 5:30-9:30 p.m.; Friday-Saturday 5:30-10:30 p.m. Closed Tuesday.

Guadalajara Mexican Restaurant ($$): Authentic Mexican cuisine. Full menu including quesadillas, nachos Mexicanos, vegetarian dishes, fajitas and more. 4 South Tunnel Rd., Asheville, 298-0702. Lunch: 11 a.m.-2:30 p.m. Dinner: Monday-Friday 5-10 p.m.; Saturday noon-10 p.m.; Sunday noon-9 p.m.

Hannah Flanagan's Pub & Eatery ($$): A little bit of Ireland in the mountains. Full menu that ranges from sandwiches to Irish stew and shepherd's pie. 27 Biltmore Ave., 252-1922. Monday-Saturday 11:30 a.m.-2 a.m.; Sunday noon-midnight. www.hannahflanagans.com

Heiwa Shokudo ($$): A charming little Japanese restaurant that is another favorite of mine. Authentic Japanese cuisine. Tempura, teriyaki, sukiyaki, vegetarian dishes and more. 87 North Lexington Ave., 254-7761. Tuesday-Saturday 5:30-9 p.m.

Jae Restaurant & Bar ($$): Thai cuisine. Fresh sushi, home-baked breads, savory soups and full bar. 70 Westgate Shopping Center, 281-4155. Monday-Friday 11:30 a.m.-9 p.m.; Saturday 11:30 a.m.-10 p.m.; Sunday noon-9 p.m.

Jerusalem Garden Cafe ($): Middle Eastern restaurant featuring gyros, kabobs, and many other ethnic dishes. Belly dancing: weekends at 7 p.m. 78 Patton Ave., 254-0255. Open 8:30 a.m.-5 p.m. Monday-Friday; 11:30 a.m.-4 p.m. Saturday.

John Henry's ($$): Intimate bistro setting featuring Charleston-style cuisine with an emphasis on fresh seafood. 57 Haywood St., 255-0010. Reservations suggested. Lunch: Monday-Saturday 11 a.m.-2:30 p.m. Dinner: Monday-Saturday 5:30 p.m.-till. Sunday brunch: 11 a.m.-2:30 p.m.

La Paz Cantina Restaurante ($$): Gourmet Mexican food served in a casual atmosphere. Located in Biltmore Village. Features indoor and patio seating. Great Margaritas. 10 Biltmore Pl., 277-8779. Monday-Thursday 11 a.m.-10 p.m.; Friday-Saturday 11 a.m.-11 p.m.

The Laughing Seed ($): Great vegetarian restaurant. Casual atmosphere and sumptuous vegetarian delicacies! 40 Wall St., 252-3445. Monday-Saturday 11:30 a.m.-9 p.m.; Sunday 10 a.m.-8 p.m. www.laughingseed.com

Left Bank ($$): Small, intimate, and romantic restaurant offering an eclectic cosmopolitan menu. Relaxed atmosphere with local art and murals creating a unique décor. Menu presents a wide variety from grilled Jamaican shrimp to breast of duckling with a wild berry sauce. 90 Patton Ave., 251-5552. Tuesday-Thursday 5-10 p.m.; Friday-Saturday 5-10:30 p.m.

The Noodle Shop ($): Authentic Chinese cooking is offered in this charming little restaurant located on Pack Square downtown. Noodle and rice dishes are the main attractions with a wide range of Chinese cooking styles from Szechwan to Shandong. Generous portions. Best noodle dishes by far in Asheville. 3 Pack Square, 250-9898. Lunch: Tuesday-Friday 11:30 a.m.-2:30 p.m. Dinner: Monday-Thursday 5-9:30 p.m.; Friday 5-10:30 p.m.; Saturday noon-10:30 p.m.

Poncho's La Casita Restaurante ($): Famous for its frozen margaritas, Poncho's specializes in "California-style" Mexican dishes with milder seasonings and liberal use of cheese. 505 Tunnel Rd. (US-70), 298-2578. Lunch and dinner: daily 11 a.m.-9:30 p.m.

Province 620 Restaurant ($$): Mediterranean cuisine with seafood and pasta specialties. 620 Hendersonville Rd., 277-0355. 11 a.m.-10 p.m., seven days a week.

Rezaz Restaurant ($$): Eclectic Mediterranean cuisine in sleek, contemporary setting. 28 Hendersonville Rd. (in Biltmore Village), 277-1510. Lunch: Monday-Saturday: 11:30 a.m.-2 p.m. Dinner: Monday-Friday 5:30 -9 p.m., Saturday 5- 10 p.m. www.rezaz.com

Salsa ($): Wonderful blend of Cuban-Caribbean and Mexican cuisine. Innovative and distinctive food that includes such dishes as trout tacos and Mandingo burritos. 6 Patton Ave., 252-9805. Open Monday-Thursday 5-9:30 p.m.; Friday-Saturday 5-10 p.m.

Savoy Cucina Italiana ($$): Refined Italian cuisine. Excellent pasta and seafood. 641 Merrimon Ave., 253-1077. Open Monday-Thursday 5-9:30 p.m.; Friday-Sunday 5-10 p.m.

Sorrento D'Italia Restaurant ($$): A true slice of Italy in Asheville. Sorrento's offers great Italian cuisine in a warm and welcoming atmosphere. The focus is on the food of Tuscany and Emilia Romagna, with great specialty dishes that include Linguini Vere and wonderful desserts. 875 Tunnel Rd., 299-1928. Tuesday-Thursday and Sunday 5-9 p.m.; Friday-Saturday 5 p.m.-closing.

Spirits on the River ($$): Native American cuisine in a small restaurant overlooking the Swannanoa River. 571 Swannanoa River Rd., 299-1404. Reservations suggested. Open Tuesday 5-9 p.m.; Wednesday-Thursday noon-9 p.m.; Friday-Saturday noon-10 p.m.; Sunday noon-9 p.m.

Three Brothers Restaurant ($$): An Asheville landmark since 1959, Three Brothers is Greek food at its best. Souvlakia, spanakopita and wonderful baklava. 183 Haywood St., 253-4971. Monday-Friday 11 a.m.-10 p.m.; Saturday 4-10 p.m.

Wanpen Thai Restaurant ($$): Traditional Thai cuisine in a relaxed setting. 2292 Hendersonville Rd., 684-2777. Monday-Friday. Lunch: 11:30 a.m.-2:30 p.m. Dinner: 5-10 p.m.

Yoshida Japanese Steakhouse ($$): Japanese cuisine. A fun restaurant with food cooked hibachi-style by chefs at your table. 4 Regent Park Blvd., 252-5903. Monday-Thursday 4:30-10 p.m.; Friday-Saturday 4:30-10:30 p.m.; Sunday noon-8 p.m.

Zen Sushi ($$): Japanese cuisine and sushi bar. High-quality fresh sushi and sashimi. 640 Merrimon Ave., 225-6033. Open seven days a week, 11:30 a.m.-10:30 p.m.

Asheville Cafes & Grills

Back Yard Burgers ($): Great hamburgers charbroiled just like you'd grill them in the backyard! 705 Merrimon Ave., 255-7767, and 1055 Patton Ave., 255-8075. Monday-Saturday 10 a.m.-10 p.m.; Sunday 10 a.m.-9 p.m.

Battery Park Café ($-$$): Casual dining with emphasis on regional fare. 22 Battery Park Ave., 253-2158. Tuesday-Wednesday 11 a.m.-4 p.m., Thursday 11 a.m.-9 p.m., Saturday 10:30 a.m.-10 p.m., Sunday 10:30 a.m.-9 p.m.

Biltmore Dairy Bar ($): Serving lunch and dinner since 1957. Features Biltmore ice cream, shakes, sodas, and more. 115 Hendersonville Rd., Biltmore Village, 274-1501. Daily 10:30 a.m.-10 p.m. www.biltmorefarms.com/dairy.html

Boston Pizza ($): Excellent Pizza and Italian-American dishes. 501 Merrimon Ave., 252-9474. Open noon-11 p.m. daily.

Bruegger's Bagel Bakery ($): Excellent bagel chain, takeout or dine-in. Creative bagel sandwiches. Three Asheville locations: 1950 Hendersonville Rd. (684-8599), 671 Merrimon Ave. (254-1560), 160 Hendersonville Rd. (277-1070). Monday-Saturday 6:30 a.m.-5:30 p.m.; Sunday 7 a.m.-4 p.m.

Candy's Café and Courtyard ($$): Featuring classic French and Cajun cuisine, live music and a delightful outdoor courtyard. 12 Biltmore Ave., 255-0371. Reservations accepted. Lunch: 11:30 a.m.-2 p.m. Dinner 5-10 p.m. Sunday brunch: 11:30 a.m.-2:30 p.m.

Charlotte Street Grill & Pub ($): Affordable dining in charming Victorian room or European "Public House" atmosphere of English pub. Burgers, pastas, steaks and more. 157 Charlotte St., 253-5348 (grill), 252-2948 (pub). Open seven days a week.

Chelsea's and The Village Tea Room ($): Take some quiet time and enjoy lunch beginning at 11:30 a.m., and then experience a traditional English tea beginning at 3:30 p.m. A charming restaurant! 6 Boston Way, Biltmore Village, 274-0701.

City Bakery Café: Cafe and bakery located just down from Pack Square that serves pastries and breads along with their coffee. Great place for breakfast as well. They also have a second smaller location at 88 Charlotte St. Open 7 a.m. to 7 p.m., seven days a week. 60 Biltmore Ave., 252-4426.

Early Girl Eatery ($$): Located in the historic Wall Street section, the Early Girl Eatery offers healthy, made-from-scratch cuisine with a regional emphasis. 8 Wall Street, 259-9292. Breakfast: Monday-Friday 7:30-11:30 a.m. Lunch: Monday-Friday 11:45 a.m.-3 p.m. Dinner: Thursday-Saturday 5:30-10 p.m. Sunday brunch: 9 a.m.-3 p.m.

Laurie's Catering Gourmet-to-Go ($): Primarily a gourmet catering service, they offer wonderful takeout, and have a few seats available for lunch. More of a deli setting than a restaurant, they are included here because of the absolutely superb quality of the food. 67 Biltmore Ave., 252-1500. Open Monday-Friday 10 a.m.-6 p.m.; Saturday 10 a.m.-4 p.m. www.laureysyum.com

Loretta's ($): Great spot for lunches. Back-to-basics sandwiches, featuring fresh bread and homemade soups. 27 Patton Ave., 253-3747. Monday-Friday 9 a.m.-3 p.m.

Marco's Pizzeria ($): One of the best pizzerias around. Wide range of pies. 640 Merrimon Ave., 285-0709. Tuesday-Thursday 11 a.m.-9:30 p.m.; Friday-Saturday 11 a.m.-9:45 p.m.; Sunday noon-9 p.m.

Mellow Mushroom ($): Great pizza and hoagies served in a colorful retro-dellic setting. The kids will love this place. 50 Broadway (downtown), 236-9800. Monday-Thursday 11 a.m.-11:30 p.m.; Friday-Saturday 11 a.m.-12:30 a.m.; Sunday noon-10:30 p.m. Full bar open slightly later. www.mellowmushroom.com

Northside Sports Bar & Grill ($): One of Asheville's best sports bar-and-grills. 853 Merrimon Ave., 254-2349. Open Monday-Friday 4 p.m.-2 a.m.; Saturday-Sunday noon-2 a.m.

Old Europe ($): Scrumptious Old World tortes, cakes, cookies. Also breakfast and light lunches. 41 N. Lexington Ave., 252-0001. Open Monday-Thursday 9 a.m.-10 p.m.; Friday and Saturday 9 a.m.-midnight; Sunday 11:30 a.m.-6 p.m.

Paris Bakery & Tearoom ($): Authentic French bakery offering light lunches and great desserts. 301 Merrimon Ave., 252-2315. Open daily for lunch.

Rio Burrito ($): Cozy downtown storefront that serves only burritos. A wide innovative selection of variations. 11 Broadway, 253-2422. Monday-Friday 11:30 a.m.-7:30 p.m.

Rosetta's Kitchen ($): A fun, eclectic cafe serving vegan and vegetarian home cooking. 116 Lexington Ave., 232-0738. Lunch: 11:30 a.m.-3 p.m.

Souper Sandwich ($): Specializing in great lunches that include freshly baked muffins and pastries, scratch-made soups, fresh salads, and award-winning sandwiches. 46 Haywood St., 285-0003. Open Monday-Friday 8 a.m.-5 p.m.; Saturday 10 a.m.-5 p.m.

Tupelo Honey Café ($): Elegant southern cuisine. 12 College St., 255-4863. Tuesday-Sunday 9 a.m.-3 p.m.; Friday-Saturday 5:30 p.m.-3 a.m.

Two Guys Hoagies ($): One of the best sandwich and sub shops in Asheville. 132 Charlotte St., 254-9955. Open Monday-Saturday 10:30 a.m.-9 p.m.

Urban Burrito ($): Wide selection of California-style burritos, as well as great salsas. Voted best burritos of WNC. Four locations: 640 Merrimon Ave.,

(251-1921); 1865A Hendersonville Rd., 129 Bleachery Blvd., 1341 Parkwood Rd. Monday-Saturday 11 a.m.-10 p.m.; Sunday noon-10 p.m.

Viva Europa Marketplace and Deli ($): Located at the entrance to the historic Montford district, Viva Europa offers specialty sandwiches and a full deli menu. 102 Montford Ave., 281-1777. Breakfast, lunch and dinner: Monday-Friday 7:30 a.m.-10 p.m.; Saturday-Sunday 10 a.m.-10 p.m.

West End Bakery ($): Soups, salads, sandwiches, desserts and baked goods are the hallmarks of this great little neighborhood bakery. Located in West Asheville. 757 Haywood St., 252-9378.

Westville Pub ($): Casual dining in a non-smoking pub atmosphere located in West Asheville. Wide variety of homemade food including sandwiches, wraps, quesadillas, soups and lasagna. 777 Haywood Rd., 225-9782. Sunday-Thursday 4 p.m.-1 a.m.; Friday-Saturday 4 p.m.-2 a.m.

Asheville Coffeehouses

City Bakery Café: Cafe and bakery located just down from Pack Square that serves pastries and breads along with their coffee. Great place for breakfast as well. They also have a second smaller location at 88 Charlotte St. 60 Biltmore Ave., 252-4426. Open 7 a.m. to 7 p.m., seven days a week.

Dripolator Coffeehouse: Superb coffeehouse located just down from Pack Square. Wide selection of coffee and espresso, and open for lunch. 144 Biltmore Ave., 252-0021.

Gold Hill Espresso and Fine Teas: Specializing in cappuccino, latte and espresso. A comfortable and welcoming place to relax. 67 Haywood St., 254-3800. Monday-Friday: 7:30 a.m.-7:00 p.m.; Saturday 8:30 a.m.-7 p.m.; Sunday 9 a.m.-2 p.m.

Kismet Café and Coffeehouse: Located in Biltmore Village, Kismet also offers lunches and a wide selection of gourmet coffees, teas and pastries. Refined, English atmosphere. 1 Boston Way, 277-0098.

Malaprop's Bookstore Café ($): Located downtown on Haywood Street in a great local bookstore, Malaprop's. Offering a wide variety of coffees and teas as well as soups, sandwiches and light lunches. Live music Friday and Saturday evenings. 55 Haywood St., 254-6734. Monday-Thursday 8 a.m.-9 p.m.; Friday-Saturday 8 a.m.-10 p.m.; Sunday 8 a.m.-7 p.m. www.malaprops.com

Old Europe: One of the author's favorites. Wonderful refined atmosphere and they also offer seating outside on the sidewalk. A great place for coffee anytime. They also serve lunch on the weekend. 41 N. Lexington Ave., 252-0001.

Port City Java: Started in Wilmington, NC. Three locations: 870 Merrimon Ave., 255-3881; Westridge Shopping Plaza, 670-5595; and the Super Walmart Shopping Plaza, 298-9651.

Starbucks: A number of locations in Asheville, including 40 All Souls Crescent in Biltmore Village, 277-3248 and 62 Charlotte St., 225-3753.

World Coffee Café: Serving fair-trade and eco-friendly coffee in an exotic atmosphere. Outdoor seating in a wonderful section of Asheville and the only balcony seating for a coffeehouse in town. 18 Battery Park Ave.

Hendersonville/Flat Rock Fine Dining

Echo Mountain Inn ($$): Innovative gourmet casual dining. Cuisine with a continental flair. 2849 Laurel Park Hwy., 693-9626, (800) 324-6466. Reservations suggested. Dinner: Tuesday-Friday 5-9 p.m.

Expressions ($$): Creative upscale dining. Mobil three-star rated. 114 North Main St., Hendersonville, 693-8516. Reservations suggested. Lunch: Monday-Friday 11:30 a.m.-2 p.m. Dinner: Monday-Saturday 6-9 p.m.

Harvest Moon ($$): Fresh farm produce prepared seasonally. Wide selection of vegetarian dishes also. 502 N. Main St., 696-8804. Tuesday-Friday 8 a.m.-9 p.m.; Sunday 8 a.m.-3 p.m. Closed Monday.

Kelsey's Restaurant & Lounge ($$): Since 1985, fresh steaks, seafood, chicken, pasta and salads. 850 Spartanburg Hwy., Hendersonville, 693-6688. Monday-Thursday 11 a.m.-10 p.m.; Friday-Saturday 11 a.m.-11 p.m.; Sunday 9:30 a.m.-10 p.m.

Mary Mills Coxe Inn Restaurant ($$$): Located in the historic Mary Mills Coxe House. Two intimate colonial dining rooms. International cuisine with emphasis on fresh-cut, top-quality foods. 1210 Greenville Hwy., 692-0908, 692-5900. Reservations required. Open Tuesday-Saturday 5 p.m.-8 p.m.; Sunday brunch starts at 11 a.m.

Season's at the Highland Lake Inn ($$-$$$): Fine dining in a casual country setting. Restaurant is located on the grounds of the Highland Lake Inn in Flat Rock. An award-winning restaurant that gets most of its vegetables from its own gardens. Highland Lake Rd., Flat Rock, 696-9094. Breakfast: 7:30-9:30 a.m. Lunch: 11:30 a.m.-2:30 p.m. Dinner: 5-9 p.m. Sunday brunch buffet: 10:30 a.m.-2 p.m. Sunday dinner: 5:30-8 p.m.

Woodfield Inn Restaurant ($$$): Four-course dining in the historic Woodfield Inn located in Flat Rock. Entrees include blackened filet of salmon, seared halibut and scallops, roast breast of duck and tenderloin of beef Oscar. 2901 Greenville Hwy., Flat Rock, 693-6016. Reservations required. Wednesday-Friday 5-9 p.m.; Sunday brunch: 11 a.m.-2 p.m.

Hendersonville Family Dining

Binion's Roadhouse ($$): Country style and casual. 1565 Four Seasons Boulevard, Hendersonville, 693-0492. Sunday-Thursday 11 a.m.-10 p.m.; Friday-Saturday 11 a.m.-11 p.m.

Fireside Restaurant & Pancake Inn ($): Great breakfasts served in this family-owned business. Homemade bread and breakfast served all day. 295 Sugarloaf Rd., Hendersonville, 697-1004. Breakfast and lunch: open seven days a week, 6:30 a.m.-2:30 p.m.

Main Street Pizza and Pasta ($): Family-oriented restaurant serving American and Italian dishes in a casual setting. 300 S. Main St., Hendersonville, 692-2202. Sunday-Thursday 10:30 a.m.-10 p.m.; Friday-Saturday 10:30 a.m.-11 p.m.

McGuffey's Restaurant ($$): A great family restaurant and very kid-friendly. Wide selection from nationally recognized menu. White Tablecloth Sunday

Brunch. 1800 Four Seasons Boulevard, Hendersonville, 697-0556. Open Monday-Thursday 11 a.m.-11 p.m.; Friday-Saturday 11 a.m.-midnight; Sunday 10:30 a.m.-10 p.m.

Mills River Restaurant ($): Just north of Hendersonville. Family style country restaurant. Intersection of highways 191 and 280, 4201 Haywood Rd., Mills River, 891-4039. Open 6 a.m.-9 p.m. daily.

The Peddler Steakhouse ($$): Excellent steaks and American cuisine. 1225 Spartanburg Hwy., 693-7999. Monday-Thursday 5-9 p.m.; Friday-Saturday 5-10 p.m.

Hendersonville Seafood Restaurants

Charleston Grill ($$): Low country cuisine, specializing in seafood. 342 N. Main St., 697-6252. Reservations suggested. Lunch: Monday-Saturday 11 a.m.-3:45 p.m. Dinner: Monday-Saturday 3:45-9 p.m. Sunday brunch: noon-3 p.m.

Hendersonville Overseas & Exotic

Asian Grill ($$): Excellent selection of Chinese, Japanese, and Thai delicacies prepared "New York Style." Wonderful interior and service. Buffet and takeout. 807 Spartanburg Hwy., 698-7501. Open Sunday-Thursday 11 a.m.-10 p.m.; Friday-Saturday 11 a.m.-11 p.m.

China Garden ($$): Chinese cuisine. 825 Spartanburg Hwy., Hendersonville, 698-0880. Monday-Thursday 11 a.m.-10 p.m.; Friday-Saturday 11 a.m.-11 p.m.; Sunday 10 a.m.-10 p.m.

China Grill ($$): Oriental cuisine, lunch and dinner. 2111 Asheville Hwy., Hendersonville, 698-0031. 11 a.m.-11 p.m. seven days a week.

Cypress Cellar ($$): Authentic South Louisiana cuisine. Gumbo, jambalaya and red beans & rice. Beer, wine, liquor permits. 321-C North Main St., Hendersonville, 698-1005. Tuesday-Thursday 11 a.m.-9 p.m.; Friday-Saturday 11 a.m.-10 p.m.

The Gypsy Cab Company ($$): Urban cuisine, a mixed blend of Latin, Mediterranean, Cajun and other cultures. 111 S. Main St., Hendersonville, 698-5598. Lunch and dinner: Tuesday-Sunday 11:30 a.m.-9:00 p.m.

Hannah Flanagan's Pub & Eatery ($$): A little bit of Ireland in the mountains. Full menu that ranges from sandwiches to Irish stew and shepherd's pie. Children's menu. Featuring authentic fish and chips every Friday. 300 N. Main St., 696-1665. Monday-Wednesday 11 a.m.-1 a.m.; Thursday-Saturday 11 a.m.-2 a.m.; Sunday 11 a.m.-midnight.

Haus Heidelberg ($$): Real German cuisine and deli takeout. Specializing in German beer. 630 Greenville Hwy., Hendersonville, 693-8227. Lunch: 11:30 a.m.-2:30 p.m. Dinner: Tuesday-Saturday 5-9 p.m.; Sunday noon-9 p.m.

New York Burrito ($): Extensive selection of exotic burritos. 343 N. Main St., Hendersonville, 694-1492. Lunch and dinner: Monday-Saturday 11 a.m.-7 p.m.

Pro's Italian Dining ($$): Full course traditional Italian dinners, pizza with beer, wine, and liquor available. 805 Spartanburg Hwy., 692-8366. Lunch: Monday-Friday 11 a.m.-2 p.m. Dinner: Monday-Friday 4-9 p.m.; Saturday-Sunday 4:30-10 p.m.

Samovar Café ($): Middle Eastern dishes. Lunch only. 121 E Barnwell St., 692-5981. Monday-Saturday 11 a.m.-4 p.m.; Sunday 11 a.m.-3 p.m.

Sinbad Restaurant ($$): Mediterranean cuisine served in the historic Reese House. Delicately prepared seafood, lamb specialties, steaks, pasta, traditional Middle Eastern favorites: baba, hommus, falafel, kabobs, grape leaves, curry and more. 202 S. Washington St., Hendersonville, 696-2039. Lunch: 11:30 a.m.-2:30 p.m. Dinner: 5:30-"until." www.sinbadrestaurant.com

Yoshida Japanese Steakhouse ($$): Japanese cuisine. 707 Greenville Hwy, 696-8484. Dinner: Monday-Saturday 4:30-9:30 p.m.; Sunday noon-8 p.m.

Hendersonville Cafes, Coffeehouses & Grills

Black Bear Coffee Co. ($): Superb coffee and refreshments. 318 N. Main St., Hendersonville, 692-6333, $. September-May: Monday-Friday 8 a.m.-6 p.m.; Saturday 9 a.m.-6 p.m.; Sunday 11 a.m.-5 p.m. Summer: Monday-Friday 8 a.m.-9 p.m.; Saturday 9 a.m.-9 p.m.; Sunday 11 a.m.-5 p.m.

Café on the Veranda ($): Located in one of Hendersonville's most unique stores, A Day in the Country. 130 Sugarloaf Rd., 692-0393. Monday-Saturday 11 a.m.-7 p.m.; Sunday 11 a.m.-7 p.m.

Dean's Deli ($): Terrific deli located in historic Flat Rock. Sandwiches, pasta, specialty dishes. 2770 Greenville Highway, Flat Rock, 692-5770. Monday-Friday 10 a.m.-5 p.m.; Saturday 10 a.m.-3 p.m.

Dixie Diner ($): Really great breakfasts. Lunch specials. 1724 Brevard Rd., 697-5025. Tuesday-Sunday 6 a.m.-2 p.m.

McFarland Bake Shop ($): A great old-fashioned bakery; the best in Hendersonville. Excellent sandwiches as well. Not to be missed! 309 N. Main St., Hendersonville, 693-4256. Open Tuesday-Saturday 7 a.m.-5:30 p.m.

Mike's on Main Street ($): An old-fashioned ice cream parlor that serves soup, sandwiches and breakfast. Like stepping back into the 1920s! 303 N. Main St., Hendersonville, 698-1616. Monday-Saturday 7:30 a.m.-5 p.m.; Sunday noon-5 p.m.

The Park—Deli & Café ($): Complete breakfast menu, authentic deli sandwiches, homemade soups, oven deserts, and more. Unique and original establishment known for its omelets and original lunch menu. Over 60 feet of wall murals, full bar, and great cooking make this deli special. 437 N. Main St., 696-3663. Breakfast: Tuesday-Saturday 7:30-10 a.m. Lunch: Monday-Saturday 11 a.m.-3 p.m. Dinner: Monday-Saturday 5:30-close. Sunday brunch: 10 a.m.-2 p.m.

Patelli's Pizza ($): Great pizza and sandwiches. 1328 Asheville Hwy., 693-0665. Daily 10 a.m.-10 p.m.

Three Chopt ($): An excellent sandwich shop located downtown. Luncheon only. 103 Third Ave., Hendersonville, 692-0228. Open Monday-Saturday 11 a.m.-2:30 p.m.

Chapter Three
Festivals & Events

A sheville, Hendersonville and Flat Rock have festivals throughout the year. Most of these occur annually, during the same month each year. Listed below are some of the major festivals and events. For a complete listing, or for exact dates, contact the appropriate visitor center. They can also supply you with yearly calendar of events booklets.

Asheville Chamber of Commerce Visitor Center: 258-6100
Hendersonville Area Visitors Information Center: 693-9708

For a monthly listing of events and happenings in Asheville, visit the Asheville Chamber of Commerce website (www.ashevillechamber.org/calendar5.htm). This site not only lists the major annual events listed in this guide but also lists smaller, non-annual happenings.

January
First Night Asheville: Sponsored by Mission St. Joseph's Hospital, First Night Asheville is an alcohol-free New Year's Eve party with entertainment venues all over the city. A spectacular grand finale celebration is complete with downtown fireworks. Tickets are $6 per person and admit the holder to all of the entertainment sites. Tickets are available at participating area stores including Food Lion, Malaprop's, and Pack Place. Call 259-5800 for more information (or visit www.asheville.com/firstnight/). First Night Asheville is a special celebration for the whole family.

All That Jazz Weekend at Grove Park Inn Resort (Asheville): The inn hosts a fabulous lineup of entertainers and events, all jazz-related. (252-2711)

Big Band Dance Weekend at the Grove Park Inn Resort (Asheville): Big band entertainment and dancing at the legendary grand hotel. (252-2711)

March
Heritage Classic DanceSport Championships at the Grove Park Inn Resort (Asheville): One of the nation's premier dancesport events. Competition in five dance styles: American Smooth, International Ballroom, American Rhythm, International Latin and Theatre Arts. (252-2711)

St. Patrick's Festival (Asheville): An annual St. Patrick's street festival held downtown in the Market Street district. (258-6101)

April

Historic Johnson Farm Festival (Hendersonville): Farm animals, arts and crafts at the Johnson farm. There is also a charity auction, tours and demonstrations of farm activities. Bring the kids! (891-6585)

Festival of Flowers at the Biltmore Estate (Asheville): A celebration that highlights the spring blooming of flowers at Biltmore Estate. Guided tours through the gardens alive with color from more than 50,000 tulips, azaleas, flowering shrubs and much more. Live music and other special events. Ongoing April through May. (800 543-2961)

May

Spring Herb Festival (Asheville): The largest herb festival in the Southeast. More than 50 herb vendors marketing herbs, herb plants and herb products. Held at the Western North Carolina Farmers Market. (253-1691)

Great Smoky Mountain Trout Festival (Waynesville): A one-day festival of music, crafts, educational programs and fishing demonstrations. A festival all about trout and trout fishing in the mountains. (456-3021)

Jubilee Arts Festival (Hendersonville): Arts and crafts and festivities on Main Street. (693-9708)

Carl Sandburg Folk Music Festival (Flat Rock): Held at the Carl Sandburg home in Flat Rock. Day-long festival of poetry readings, folk music, house tours and a dairy goat program. (693-4178)

Tell It in the Mountains Festival (Asheville): A festival celebrating the ancient art of storytelling held in several downtown Asheville locations. (259-5306)

Lake Eden Arts Festival (Black Mountain): Located at a mountain retreat, Camp Rockmont, the festival features music from dozens of national and regionally known musicians as well as crafts, storytelling, drumming, dancing and a healing arts tent. (686-8742) www.theleaf.com

Ramp Convention (Waynesville): The day-long heritage event honors the mountain onion and garlic relative known as a "ramp," a tasty yet odoriferous vegetable! (456-8691)

Mountain Sports Festival (Asheville): Focus is on outdoor sports, including mountain biking, rock climbing, triathlon, road and trail races and much more. www.mountainsportsfestival.com

Mountain Renaissance Adventure Faire (Asheville): Entertainment and fun times of old. Held on the campus of A.B. Tech. www.refnnfaire.org

June

Riverfest at the French Broad River (Asheville): Riverfest is a festival celebrating the French Broad River. Events include Riverlink Bridge party, triathalon and arts and crafts. Held at French Broad River Park. (250-4260)

A Day at the Races (Asheville): A fun family event held at French Broad River Park. Zany boat races, including Riverlink Raft Race, Mayor's Cup and Anything That Floats Boat Parade. (250-4260)

Blue Ridge Barbecue Festival (Tryon): Two days of BBQ competitions from over 50 top BBQ-cooking teams. Music, games, foothills craft fair, and of course, BBQ. (859-6236) www.blueridgebbqfestival.com

Brevard Music Festival (Brevard): Held at the Brevard Music Center, this famous festival features over 70 different concerts, from symphony orchestra to Broadway musicals. www.brevardmusic.org

Singing on the Mountain (Grandfather Mountain): Annual gospel music festival. (733-2013)

July

Fabulous 4th Celebration (Hendersonville): Held at Jackson Park. Fireworks and festivities. (697-4884)

Fourth of July Celebration (Asheville): Traditional Fourth celebration with fireworks. Held at City/County Plaza. (259-5800)

Bele Chere Festival (Asheville): A community celebration in downtown Asheville. One of the greatest street festivals in America. Not to be missed! (259-5800) www.belechere.com (SEE Section Two, Chapter 4 "Bele Chere")

Grandfather Mountain Annual Highland Games (Grandfather Mountain): Scottish athletes and musicians share their heritage from bagpipes and Celtic music to border collies and sheep herding at the largest gathering of Scottish clans in North America. ((800) 468-7325, 733-2013)

Shindig on the Green (Asheville): Held every Saturday night on the green at City/County Plaza. Bluegrass music, dancing, clogging. Held during July, August and September. (258-6107) www.exploreasheville.com/music

Folkmoot USA (Waynesville): Folk festival with international dancers and musicians performing their countries' traditional folk dances. www.folkmoot.com

August

Mountain Dance and Folk Festival (Asheville): The oldest festival in America. For more than 70 years, a celebration of traditional mountain music and dance. Held at various venues in Asheville. (626-FOLK, 258-6107)

Mrs. John Forest Memorial Sidewalk Show (Hendersonville): Held on Main Street. A top-quality art show. (696-7926)

Village Art & Craft Fair (Asheville): Excellent outdoor arts and crafts show held in Biltmore Village. (274-2831)

Goombay Festival (Asheville): A street festival in the historic black business district in downtown Asheville. A celebration of African-Caribbean culture. (252-4614)

Sourwood Festival (Black Mountain): All the best in crafts, dancing, music, food and games. www.blackmountain.org/festivals

September

Apple Festival (Hendersonville): Another not-to-be-missed festival. A celebration of apples and the fall season. (696-7756, 693-4146)

Mountain Heritage Day (Cullowee): For over 20 years, a showcase of old-time music, dance, crafts, food, and more. (227-7272)

North Carolina Mountain State Fair (Asheville): Great state fair held at the Western North Carolina Agricultural Center. Rides, farm animals and great food. For the whole family. (687-1414) www.mountainstatefair.com

Kituwah (Asheville): A celebration of the art and culture of American Indians. Held at the Civic Center. Native American arts and crafts, exhibits, traditional dancing and more. (254-0072)

Riverrun International Film Festival (Brevard): The mountains' only film festival. Held on the Brevard College campus and in Brevard venues. (862-3618)

October

Asheville Greek Festival (Asheville): A celebration of Greek culture, dance and food. Held at City/County Plaza. (259-5800, 253-3754)

Craft Fair of the Southern Highland Craft Guild (Asheville): Held at the Civic Center. Traditional mountain crafts shown by the world famous Southern Highland Craft Guild members. (298-7928)

Thomas Wolfe Festival (Asheville): A festival about the life of the Asheville-born author Thomas Wolfe. Walking tours, concerts, plays, Wolfe workshops, road race and other events centered on Wolfe's life. (253-8304)

Great Smokies Craft Brewers Invitational Bluegrass Festival (Asheville): One-day celebration of the Southeastern brewing scene with more than 30 brewers participating. Live music and entertainment. (281-3910)

Lake Eden Arts Festival (Black Mountain): Located at a mountain retreat, Camp Rockmont, the festival features music from dozens of national and regionally known musicians as well as crafts, storytelling, drumming, dancing and a healing arts tent. (686-8742)

Woolly Worm Festival (Banner Elk): The stripes on the winner of the woolly worm race will be inspected by the town elders. Brown signals a mild winter, black predicts severe weather. Nonstop music, food, crafts, and children's rides. (800 972-2183)

Oktoberfest (Asheville): Held at the Grove Park Inn Resort. Plenty of German food, music and beer to go around. (252-2711)

Bascar Lamar Lunsford Festival/Madison County Heritage Festival (Mars Hill): This old-time hoedown includes Appalachian music, dance, crafts, food and storytelling. (689-9351)

Michaelmas at Biltmore Estate (Asheville): Ongoing country-like fair held primarily in the estate's Italian Garden from October 1-29. Recalls the popular English tradition of celebrating Michaelmas. Events include demonstrations of blacksmithing, wool weaving, handling of farm equipment, jazz concerts and a grape stomp. (274-6333)

Black Mountain Music Festival (Flat Rock): Held at Mills River's scenic Deerfields. A weekend of music featuring nationally known acts. (281-3382)

November

Christmas Parade (Asheville): Held traditionally the day before Thanksgiving in downtown Asheville. (251-4147)

Premiere Celebration of Light Up Your Holidays (Asheville): Christmas carols, vendors, fireworks. Traditionally held just before Thanksgiving to usher in the Christmas season. Held at City/County Plaza. (254-0072)

Light Up Your Holidays (Asheville): The Light Up Your Holidays festival began as a cooperative effort between the City of Asheville, the Community Arts Council, and the Asheville Area Chamber of Commerce. It is a community-wide celebration with six weeks of holiday happenings throughout the city. Hundreds of thousands of white lights adorn area trees, homes, and businesses. From mid-November at the Premiere Celebration through the popular First Night Asheville celebration on New Year's Eve, the Light Up Your Holidays Festival has something for everyone. An official holiday calendar of events is published yearly by the Asheville Citizen-Times and are usually available at the Asheville Area Chamber of Commerce's Visitor Center. (258-6100, 800 257-1300)

December

A Victorian Christmas at Smith-McDowell House (Asheville): Christmas decorations throughout the house recreate the Victorian era when Christmas carols and trees were first introduced to America. Ongoing during December. (253-9231)

Christmas at Biltmore House (Asheville): Biltmore House is especially memorable during the Christmas season. During Candlelight Christmas Evenings, Biltmore's doors open to a world of crackling fires, festive music performances, glittering trees and the warm glow of hundreds of candles illuminating the richly decorated rooms. Ongoing during December. (274-6333)

A Dickens Christmas in Biltmore Village (Asheville): Ongoing Christmas festivities in picturesque Biltmore Village during the month of December. (274-8788)

Christmas at Vance Birthplace (Weaverville): Ongoing candlelight tours. Relive Christmas during the 1830s at the birthplace of Zebulon Vance, North Carolina's Civil War-era governor. (645-6706)

Chapter Four
Bele Chere

One of the most outstanding street festivals in America, Bele Chere attracts more than 300,000 people each year. Bele Chere, which roughly translates as "beautiful living," always begins with a parade on Friday at noon with the festival continuing through Sunday until 6 p.m. Bele Chere is usually held on the last weekend in July.

Variety is the festival's primary focus as the downtown streets of Asheville are filled with music, dance, arts and crafts, souvenirs, hundreds of food vendors, and attractions for young and old alike. Music lovers will be amazed by the wide selection, with over 100 free performances on eight outdoor stages as well as indoor performances at many private facilities. The talent ranges from popular local performers to nationally known showcase artists. Besides the great music, special events include a 5K all-comers road race, a bicycle race, lacrosse and soccer tournaments, basketball 3-on-3 tournaments, and a $50,000 half-court basketball shot contest. Also included are games, street dances, a human maze, fountain raft rides, and a great Children's Funland. For teenagers, there is "The ZONE," which includes laser tag, bungee run, jousting, fast pitch, and Jacob's Ladder. In the evenings, dances are hosted by local DJs playing the most popular music. Seniors are welcome at Bele Chere too, and a Senior Oasis is always set up as a quiet place to sit and relax.

Arts and crafts are in abundance at Bele Chere, with the emphasis on mountain crafts. Baskets, pottery, furniture, suncatchers, weaving and more are displayed in colorful tents alongside more contemporary art and sculpture throughout Bele Chere. There is also a special section reserved only for juried arts and crafts. This is where you will find the "best in show." The author also has a booth at Bele Chere every year. Look for the white tent with the two flags and the sign "Cherry Orchard Studio." Stop by and say "Hi!"

One of the greatest attractions of Bele Chere is of course the food. Concentrated around Pack Square, hundreds of food vendors set up shop. There you will find gourmet restaurants offering full course meals next to homemade barbecue and Greek souvlaki. The array is staggering and you will have a hard time choosing. Traditional mountain cuisine, Greek, Italian, Scottish, Chinese, Thai, Mexican,

French, and other international offerings all tempt hungry festival-goers. Beer is also served at Bele Chere, with proper ID, on Friday and Saturday. Sunday is designated as alcohol-free.

Hours for the festival may vary slightly but are usually noon-11 p.m. on Friday, 10 a.m.-11 p.m. on Saturday, and noon-6 p.m. on Sunday. Information booths are located throughout the festival at Pack Square, Pritchard Park, and at the intersection of College and Spruce streets. Also, look for roving "info-tendants." They'll be on street corners and in other high traffic areas wearing official Bele Chere Staff festival shirts. First Aid is available at Pritchard Park and in the Children's Funland area.

Parking is available downtown at city parking decks adjacent to the Civic Center, on Rankin Avenue, Wall Street, Pack Place, and the BB&T building. Several surface lots are also open for parking; a special events parking fee will apply in most cases. Free handicapped parking is available in the Renaissance Asheville Hotel parking lot off Woodfin Street and in the Rankin Garage parking area.

If you are a visitor to Asheville for Bele Chere, I recommend that you park in one of the two easily accessed outlying parking areas and take the shuttle buses that run approximately every 20 minutes. Cost is $2 per person. Each day, shuttle service begins one hour before the festival starts until one hour past regular festival hours. There are two shuttle loops. The first is the East Loop, which runs between River Ridge Shopping Center and the corner of Oak and College streets in downtown. River Ridge Shopping Center is easily accessed by taking I-240 to Exit 8 and heading east on Fairview Rd. The shopping center will be on the left. The second shuttle is the West Loop, which runs between Westgate Shopping Center and the corner of Patton and Coxe avenues. Westgate Shopping center is the first exit off of Patton Avenue as you travel west from downtown over the Smoky Park Bridge.

ATM machines are located throughout downtown at the following locations: BB&T Building, 1 West Pack Square (across from the Vance Monument); First Citizens Bank, 108 Patton Avenue (a few blocks west on Patton from Pritchard Park); Bank of America, 162 College Street (near the east entrance to the festival near the Children's Funland); Wachovia Bank on the corner of Haywood Street across from Pritchard Park; and the Civic Center up the hill from Wachovia on Haywood Street.

If you are planning to attend Bele Chere, please keep in mind that accommodations in Asheville fill up every year, so make your reservations early in the year. For more information about Bele Chere, or if you would like to be a vendor, contact their office at 259-5800. Bele Chere also has a website which posts dates, times, and all the latest festival news and information (www.belechere.com).

Chapter Five
Author's Favorites

No guidebook would be complete without a list of the author's personal favorite places and attractions. It is with real confidence that I have included my favorites in hopes that it will help you in making your decisions about what to see and do while visiting our mountains. In some ways making this list was difficult because of the many wonderful and historic attractions. In truth, anything included in this book is noteworthy and worth visiting. However, recommendations do help, so here goes!

Man-Made Awesome Majesty
Biltmore Estate: An absolute stunner. Not to be missed. Breathtaking gardens and grounds. (SEE Section Three, Chapter 3)

Grove Park Inn Resort & Spa: Monumental building. Great ambience. Wonderful special events and facilities. (SEE Section Three, Chapter 4)

Historical Treasures
Carl Sandburg House: Not to be missed. The goat farm is enchanting. (SEE Section Four, Chapter 2)

Thomas Wolfe Memorial: A fascinating time capsule. Superb restoration. (SEE Section Three, Chapter 2)

Smith-McDowell House: A historic gem. Wonderful at Christmas in its Victorian finery. (SEE Section Three, Chapter 2)

Thomas Wolfe Angel Statue: In Oakdale Cemetery in Hendersonville. Worth the trip. Take a close-up look. (SEE Section Four, Chapter 3)

Architectural Masterpieces
Asheville City Building: An Art Deco stunner. Great colors and detail. (SEE Section Three, Chapter 4)

Basilica of St. Lawrence, D.M.: Wonderful stained glass. Make time to take the self-guided art and architecture tour. (SEE Section Three, Chapter 4)

Cathedral of All Souls: Inside and out, this elegant church is truly inspirational. The most beautiful building in Asheville. (SEE Section Three, Chapter 4)

St. Mary's Parish, Grove Park: A treasure of a building in an historic neighborhood. (SEE Section Three, Chapter 4)

S&W Cafeteria Building: Another Art Deco triumph. (SEE Section Three, Chapter 4)

Your Kids Will Thank You!

Western North Carolina Nature Center: Animals from otters to cougars and more. A must! (SEE Section Three, Chapter 2)

Pack Place Education, Arts & Science Center: The Health Adventure is especially terrific for kids. Fascinating stuff for all ages. (SEE Section Three, Chapter 2)

Pisgah National Forest: A perfect day trip in the summer. Take a picnic lunch. Visit Looking Glass Falls, Sliding Rock's natural waterslide, and the National Forest Fish Hatchery to let the kids feed the huge trout. Finish up at the Forest Discovery Center at the Cradle of Forestry. (SEE Section Five, Chapter 1)

Sweet Treats

The Chocolate Fetish: 36 Haywood Street, Asheville. Handmade truffles rated "America's best" by the Los Angeles Times. They're right!

The Hop Ice Cream Shop: 507 Merrimon Avenue, Asheville. Great ice cream. The Hop is an Art Deco 1950 gas station converted into a drive-through ice cream parlor. Unique!

Festivals

Bele Chere in Asheville: One of the best street festivals in America! (SEE Section Two, Chapter 4)

Apple Festival in Hendersonville: Small-town friendliness and wonderful mountain culture. (SEE Section Two, Chapter 3)

Unbelievable Views/Natural Wonders

Chimney Rock Park: This place will take your breath away. Take a good pair of walking shoes and go on a clear day. (SEE Section Five, Chapter 1)

Blue Ridge Parkway: Head out in any direction. Be sure to take a picnic lunch. (SEE Section Five, Chapter 1)

Looking Glass Falls: Pisgah National Forest. Unforgettable. (SEE Section Five, Chapter 1)

Gardener's Delights

Formal Flower Gardens at Biltmore Estate: World-class. Especially wonderful in April-May during the Festival of Flowers. Will leave you dazzled. (SEE Section Three, Chapter 3)

North Carolina Arboretum: Extraordinary gardens and educational center. Inspirational. (SEE Section Three, Chapter 2)

Botanical Gardens at Asheville: Charming in-town parklike gardens. (SEE Section Three, Chapter 2)

Chapter Six
Great Things To Do With Kids

A trip to Western North Carolina doesn't have to be a bore for the kids. Scattered throughout all the beautiful sights that thrill adults but can turn children cranky are a plethora of "fun" things that will bring smiles to the faces of kids and kids-at-heart alike.

Asheville

Western North Carolina Nature Center: Animals of all types, Appalachian nature exhibits, and much more. (SEE Section Three, Chapter 2)

Pack Place Education, Arts & Science Center: Art, science, exhibits, Health Adventure. (SEE Section Three, Chapter 2)

Pisgah National Forest: Plan day trip and include stops at Looking Glass Falls, Sliding Rock, State Fish Hatchery and Cradle of Forestry. (See Chapter 8 of this section, "Waterfalls & Trout!")

Folk Art Center: Art and craft exhibits, craft demonstrations. (Section Three, Chapter 2)

North Carolina Arboretum: Wonderful gardens and botanical exhibits. (Section Three, Chapter 2)

McCormick Field: Asheville Tourists baseball games. (Section Three, Chapter 2)

Biltmore Estate: Educational, awe-inspiring and fascinating (for older kids). (Section Three, Chapter 3)

Zebulon B. Vance Birthplace: Pioneer history exhibits and demonstrations. (Section Five, Chapter 2)

Lake Julian District Park: Swimming, fishing, boating and picnic area. (Section Three, Chapter 9)

Asheville Parks: Outdoor sports, playgrounds. (Section Three, Chapter 9)

Waterfalls: Great natural attractions. (Section Five, Chapter 1)

Blue Ridge Parkway: Many educational and interesting attractions near Asheville. Picnics, hiking. (Section Five, Chapter 1)

French Broad River Park: Picnic area, hiking, fishing. (SEE Section Three, Chapter 8)

Hendersonville/Flat Rock

Carl Sandburg Home: Historical exhibits, goat farm, hiking trails. (Section Four, Chapter 2)

Historic Johnson Farm: Farm animals, exhibits, farm history. (SEE Section Four, Chapter 2)

Holmes Educational Forest: Trails, nature center, exhibits, picnic areas. (Section Four, Chapter 2)

Lake Lure: Swimming, fishing, wonderful boat tour of lake. (Section Five, Chapter 1)

Chimney Rock Park: Spectacular hiking trails, nature center. (Section Five, Chapter 1)

Hendersonville Area Parks: Outdoor sports, playgrounds, cookouts. (Section Four, Chapter 7)

Chapter Seven
Planning a Gourmet Picnic

Awonderful way to highlight a day trip into the surrounding mountains, no matter what your itinerary or destination, is to bring along a picnic lunch. This is particularly true if your exploring takes you on the Blue Ridge Parkway or deep into one of the national forests. Restaurants are few and far between, and besides, what could be better than eating a picnic lunch beside a wilderness waterfall or from a rocky overlook perched high above the green valleys below? If this idea appeals to you, then you are in luck, because not only does Western North Carolina have an unlimited supply of really great picnic spots, but there are four stores in Asheville within minutes of each other where you can purchase the ingredients for an unforgettable picnic lunch. They are located on Biltmore Avenue just as you leave Pack Square heading south. Park your car near any of the stores.

Laurie's Catering Gourmet-to-Go: A full-service catering company which also offers gourmet foods to go. This is the place to go for your picnic entree and maybe a second dessert! 67 Biltmore Ave., 252-1500

Asheville Wine Market: Right next door. Extremely good selection of fine wines and quality beers. 65 Biltmore Ave., 253-0060

French Broad Food Co-op: Just down the street is an outstanding organic grocery. Fresh vegetables, fruit, cheese, crackers and more. 90 Biltmore Ave., 255-7650

If your wish to have your picnic lunch prepared, both Laurie's Catering Gourmet-to-Go (252-1500) and Picnics (258-2858) prepare baskets to go. See their listings in Chapter 2 of this section.

Chapter Eight
Great Itineraries

For visitors new to an area, planning some day trips or itineraries can be a challenge, especially in an area as rich in interesting things to do as Asheville, Hendersonville and Flat Rock. Considering the size and scope of the whole Western North Carolina mountains, the task can seem overwhelming. In an attempt to make your visit easier, I have presented below a number of itineraries, both local and farther afield, from which you can choose.

Downtown Asheville

The best way to experience downtown Asheville is by walking the Urban Trail. This self-guided tour takes a few hours and follows thematic markers. A wonderful way to see the city. (SEE Section Three, Chapter 5)

Historic Asheville

If you are interested in history and especially architecture, then there are a number of self-guided tours by car that you might be interested in doing. These self-guided tours visit four of Asheville's eleven Historic Districts and highlight all of the interesting and really important buildings and sites. The four are Montford, Chestnut Hill, Grove Park and Biltmore Village. (SEE Section Three, Chapter 4)

Historic Hendersonville

A self-guided tour by car of historic Hendersonville. (SEE Section Four, Chapter 3)

Historic Flat Rock

Self-guided tour by car of historic Flat Rock. (SEE Section Four, Chapter 4)

Biltmore Estate

A visit to Biltmore Estate is one of the high points of any visit to Asheville and highly recommended. You will want to allow a minimum of half a day to see the grounds and estate as well as allowing time to eat at one of the Biltmore Estate's

View of Craggy Gardens off the Blue Ridge Parkway at milepost 364

three fine restaurants. Afterwards, be sure and take some time to visit the historic Biltmore Village just outside the estate entrance. (SEE Section Three, Chapter 3)

High Country Adventure

For this tour, allow a whole day. Start off by packing a gourmet picnic (SEE Section Two, Chapter 7) and heading east on the Blue Ridge Parkway. Your first stop will be the Folk Art Center (SEE Section Three, Chapter 2) just east of Asheville at milepost 382; then continue north to Craggy Gardens at milepost 364. Here you will find nature trails, native rhododendron and magnificent views. Continue on to Mount Mitchell State Park at milepost 355 (SEE Section Five, Chapter 1) and hike the short distance to the tower on the summit. Mount Mitchell will be a great place to picnic. After lunch continue up the parkway to Grandfather Mountain at milepost 305. (SEE Section Five, Chapter 1) After visiting Grandfather, if you have time, there are a couple of excellent options. You can visit Linville Caverns (SEE Section Five, Chapter 1) or take in Tweetsie Railroad. (SEE Section Five, Chapter 2) Return to Asheville by Highway 19 East through Burnsville.

The Land of the Cherokee

Allow one full day for this outing that will take you two hours west to Cherokee Indian Reservation. (SEE Section Five, Chapter 2) Take I-40 west from Asheville and get off at Exit 27. Follow 19/23 & 74 to Cherokee. At Cherokee you will want to visit the Oconaluftee Indian Village, the Mountain Farm Museum and the Cherokee Indian Museum. During the afternoon you may wish to drive south on U.S. 441 about 14 miles to Dillsboro and take a ride on the Great Smoky Mountains Railway. (SEE Section Five, Chapter 2)

Waterfalls & Trout!

This day trip is a great one for kids. Be sure and bring a picnic lunch. You will be visiting the Pisgah District of the Pisgah National Forest and seeing some spectacular waterfalls. Take the Blue Ridge Parkway south and stop at the Pisgah Inn for some wonderful views of the mountains. Just beyond, get on 276 south and follow this into the forest. Stop at the Cradle of Forestry and visit the Forest Discovery Center. (SEE Section Five, Chapter 2) Continue on and turn right on Forest Road 445 to the Fish Hatchery. The kids will really love this. They can hand-feed monster trout! After the fish hatchery, continue on to Sliding Rock, where they can put on their bathing suits and slide down a wonderful natural waterslide. After Sliding Rock, the nearby Looking Glass Falls is the perfect place for a picnic lunch. If you have time you may wish to see other waterfalls in the area (SEE Section Five, Chapter 1) or return to Asheville by way of Highway 280.

Last of the Mohicans

This day trip is also a great one for kids. It will take you from an historic site in Asheville to the exact spot where the famous trail scene in "The Last of the Mohicans" was filmed. Begin your tour in Asheville by taking Charlotte Street to #265, The Manor. This impressive historic building (SEE Section Three, Chapter 4) was where the headquarters scene in the movie "Last of the Mohicans" was filmed. Cast members of an earlier movie, "The Swan," including Grace Kelly, also stayed here while filming. After visiting the Manor, return by way of Charlotte Street and get on I-240 east. Get off at exit 9 (Bat Cave, Lake Lure) and take Scenic Byway 74A through beautiful Fairview to Hickory Nut Gap. While passing through Hickory Nut Gap, you will see the historic Sherrill's Inn. (SEE Section Three, Chapter 4) Continue on 74A through Bat Cave (so named for the numerous bat caves in the area) and down into Chimney Rock. This will be your major destination (SEE Section Five, Chapter 1) and at Chimney Rock you will be able to hike the wonderful trails with their unbelievable views. One of the trails, the Cliff Trail, takes you to the exact spot where the climactic fight between Chingachgook and Magua took place in the "The Last of the Mohicans."

After Chimney Rock, which will take you two-three hours, return to your car and journey on 74A to Lake Lure. At the beginning of the lake is a public beach where the kids can swim. Finish out the day with a wonderful boat tour of Lake Lure. (SEE Section Five, Chapter 1) Lake

Chimney Rock Park

Connemara, former home of poet Carl Sandburg, located in Flat Rock

Lure is one of the most beautiful man-made lakes in the world and this boat ride is a real treat. The boats are operated by Lake Lure Tours and are located at the Lake Lure Marina on Highway 64/74A.

Return to Asheville by taking 74A west from Lake Lure through Chimney Rock and then turning left on Highway 64 towards Hendersonville. This will take you through some lovely apple growing sections (See Section Four, Chapter 7) and to I-26, which you will take north to Asheville.

Famous Authors

If the lives of famous writers interest you, this is the day trip for you. Begin by visiting the Thomas Wolfe Memorial (SEE Section Three, Chapter 2) in the morning. After touring the historic boyhood home of Thomas Wolfe, travel to nearby Riverside Cemetery in the Montford Historic District, where Wolfe and author O. Henry (William Sidney Porter) are buried. (SEE Section Three, Chapter 4) From the Wolfe memorial get on I-240 heading west and get off at the next exit, Montford. Take Montford Avenue north into the Montford area and turn left onto Cullowee Street. Turn right onto Pearson Drive and then left onto Birch Street to the cemetery. After visiting the grave sites (refer to cemetery map in Riverside Cemetery section), drive to the famous Grove Park Inn Resort (SEE Section Three, Chapter 4) for lunch by retracing your steps to I-240 and going east to the Charlotte Street exit. Take Charlotte Street to Macon Avenue and then to the hotel. Many famous authors, including F. Scott Fitzgerald and his wife, Zelda, have stayed at this historic resort. After lunch, travel to Hendersonville via I-240 west and I-26 south. Take exit 18 off I-26 onto 64 west. Follow 64 west to just beyond Hendersonville. Look for Oakdale Cemetery on your left and the State Historic Highway Marker indicating the Thomas Wolfe Angel. (SEE Section Four, Chapter 4) You may park your car and get out and visit this lovely statue which Wolfe immortalized in his famous novel *Look Homeward Angel*. After viewing the statue return to Hendersonville by way of 64 east. Turn right on Main Street (Highway 25 south) and follow this through Hendersonville to Flat Rock, a few miles south. In Flat Rock, you will pass by the famous Flat Rock Playhouse (SEE Section Four, Chapter 2), where the dramatic works of legendary authors are performed every summer. Turn right onto Little River Road just beyond the playhouse and visit the home of poet Carl Sandburg, "Connemara." After touring the home and seeing the grounds, return to Asheville by Highway 25 north through Hendersonville and then on I-26.

The Craft Heritage Trails of Western North Carolina

Western North Carolina, and especially Asheville, is famous for its crafts, both traditional mountain crafts and contemporary. A very popular book, available at most bookstores as well as the Asheville and Hendersonville visitor centers, is The Craft Heritage Trails of Western North Carolina. This superb guidebook offers seven driving trips of varying lengths with over 400 stops listed. If you're interested in crafts, this book and its tours are for you. Published by HandMade in America, 67 North Market Street, Asheville, NC 28801 (252-0121 or 800-331-4154). (SEE Section Two, Chapter 11, Craft Galleries, and Section One, Chapter 3, Bookstores)

Chapter Nine
Places of Worship

S hould you wish to attend church while visiting the mountains, a listing of religious denominations and their phone numbers is included for your convenience. Asheville has nearly 300 religious institutions with the Baptist Church (100 churches) and Methodist Church (60 churches) being the two largest denominations. This is a very abbreviated list. Check the telephone book when you get here for additional worship opportunities. (SEE also Section Five, Chapter 3 on Retreat Centers in Western North Carolina)

Asheville
Assembly of God: (Pentecostal) 254-5519
African Methodist Episcopal: 253-5191
Baha'i Faith: 251-1051
Beth Ha Tephila Congregation: 253-4911
Beth Israel Synagogue Conservative: 252-8431
Christian Church: (Disciples of Christ) 252-1503
Church of Christ: 274-2829
Church of God in Christ: 252-2164
Church of God: 252-8529
Church of God of Prophecy: 252-3303
Church of Jesus Christ Latter-Day Saints: 684-2895
Church of the Nazarene: 253-2095
Christian and Missionary Alliance: 253-2784
Christian Science: 252-1787
Episcopal Church: 274-2681
Evangelical Presbyterian: 299-4909
First Baptist Church: 252-4781
Full Gospel: 274-7678
Greek Orthodox: 253-3754
Independent Baptist: 254-6816
Jehovah's Witnesses: 254-8401
Jubilee Community Church: 252-5335

Lutheran, ELCA: 253-0043
Lutheran, LCMS: 252-1795
Mennonite: 298-4487
Methodist: 253-3316
Presbyterian: 252-8872
Presbyterian Church America: 684-7221
Presbyterian Church USA: 253-1431
Quakers (Religious Society of Friends): 258-0974
Roman Catholic: 252-6042
Salvation Army: 253-4723
Seventh-Day Adventist: 274-2014
Trinity Episcopal Church: 253-9361
United Church of Christ: (Congregational) 252-8729
Unitarian Universalist Church: 254-6001
Wesleyan: 253-3980

Hendersonville/Flat Rock

Agudas Israel Congregation: 693-9838
AME Zion Church: 891-1732
Anglican Church: 891-7216
Assemblies of God: 687-2762
Christian and Missionary Alliance: 692-3814
Christian Science: 697-9774
Church of Christ: 692-0306
Church of God: 693-6909
Church of Jesus Christ Latter-Day Saints: 692-9997
Church of the Nazarene: 692-7746
Episcopal: 693-7458
First Baptist Church: 693-3493
Jehovah's Witnesses: 891-5922
Methodist: 693-4275
Pentecostal Holiness: 692-2942
Presbyterian: 693-8651
Roman Catholic: 693-6901
Salvation Army: 693-4181
Seventh Day Adventist: 692-2255
Unitarian Universalist Church: 693-3157
Wesleyan: 693-9787

Chapter Ten
Art Galleries

For a complete listing of all current exhibitions and ongoing art-related events, pick up a free copy of *Mountain Xpress* or *This Week of Western North Carolina.* The *Asheville Citizen-Times* also has current listings in "The Calendar" section of its Friday edition. *Carolina Arts,* a publication covering the arts in North and South Carolina, is an excellent newspaper that has in-depth coverage of the art scene in the two states. *Carolina Arts'* mailing address is P.O. Drawer 427, Bonneau, S.C. 29431. You may also order by phone at (803) 825-3408. Additionally, *Art Now Gallery Guide* (Southeast) reviews major exhibitions monthly for the Southeastern United States. Contact them at Art Now Inc., 97 Grayrock Rd., P.O. Box 5541, Clinton, NJ 08809, or call (908) 638-5255. This publication is available free in most of the larger galleries.

Asheville

Located in Asheville, The Arts Council is a nonprofit umbrella service organization that represents the interests of more than 100 cultural and arts related groups. An excellent resource for people interested in the artistic life of Asheville, the Council conducts an annual united campaign for cultural endeavors each spring, issues grants, and is in partnership with many vital community organizations to promote and support the arts. The Arts Council has been instrumental in the resurgence of downtown Asheville as a vibrant cultural center. 11 Biltmore Ave., Asheville, NC 28802; 258-0710

Other local organizations in Asheville that can help answer any questions you might have about the art scene in the area are the Asheville Art League (P.O. Box 744, Asheville 28802) and the Asheville Art Museum (253-3227).

Asheville has a wide range of art galleries and exhibition spaces, from funky neo-hippie stores to galleries that are as avant-garde as any in SOHO or the East Village. The best Asheville and Hendersonville have to offer, in the opinion of the author, a professional artist, are listed below:

Asheville Institutional Galleries

Asheville Art Museum at Pack Place: Ongoing exhibits of local and nationally known artists. The museum's permanent collection features 100 years worth of images, including those of America's acclaimed impressionists, regionalists and abstract artists. 2 South Pack Sq., 253-3227.

Arts Council Front Gallery: Various ongoing exhibits by local artists, 11 Biltmore Ave., 258-0710.

University of North Carolina Gallery: The University has two galleries located in Owen Hall, Second Floor Gallery and University Gallery, that have monthly exhibitions. UNCA, Owen Hall, One University Heights, 251-6559.

YMI Cultural Center: Exhibitions of art, sculpture and crafts with an emphasis on African-American culture. Pack Place Education, Arts & Science Center, 39 South Market St., 252-4614.

Asheville Commercial Galleries

16 Patton: Regional artists who work with oils and pastels. Also wood furniture and wood crafts. 16 Patton Ave., Asheville, 236-2889. www.16patton.com

American Folk Art & Antiques: Features the best in contemporary and antique folk art, pottery and fine American furniture. 64 Biltmore Ave., 251-1904. www.amerifolk.com

Artworks: Original work by area artists, prints, complete framing services. 32 Battery Park Ave., 252-8621.

Asheville Gallery of Art: Top quality original paintings by local artists. Cooperative artist-run gallery. 16 College St., 251-5796.

Blue Spiral 1: Features changing shows of sculptures and paintings. Oils, pastels, mixed media and watercolor. More than 11,000 square feet of gallery space. World-class gallery. 38 Biltmore Ave., 251-0202. www.bluespiral1.com

Frame Shoppe and Gallery: Large selection of poster prints and limited edition prints. Complete framing services. 1378 Hendersonville Rd., 274-3635.

Gallery Minerva: Fine art featuring landscapes, still life, sculpture and photography. Local and international artists. 12 Church St., Asheville, 255-8850.

Merrimon Gallery: Unique originals by local artists. Extensive collection of limited and open edition prints and graphics. Complete framing services. 365 Merrimon Ave., 252-6036.

Seven Sisters Gallery: Gallery exhibits work of local artists and fine quality crafts. 117 Cherry St., Black Mountain, 669-5107.

Village Galleries: Prints and fine art. 32 All Souls Crescent, 274-2424.

Working Hands Gallery: Large scale paintings, sculpture in stone, sand, metal and ice. 1429 U.S. 70, Swannanoa, 299-7711.

Hendersonville/Flat Rock

For a complete listing of all current exhibitions and ongoing art-related events, pick up a free local entertainment guide at the Hendersonville/Flat Rock Visitors

Information Center. The Hendersonville Times-News also has current listings in the "Preview Page" of the Friday edition. The following list includes some of the highly recommended local art galleries and exhibition spaces.

Hendersonville/Flat Rock Institutional Galleries

Art League of Henderson County Gallery: Monthly ongoing exhibits of original work by local guest artists. Located at Opportunity House, 1411 Asheville Hwy., 692-0575.

The Arts Council of Henderson County: Ongoing exhibits of national and regional artists. 538A North Main St., 693-8504. www.theartscenterofhc.com

Mountain Phoenix School for Art Gallery: Ongoing exhibits of regional and national artists. Mt. Phoenix is a professional art school. Singleton Centre, P.O. Box 1347, 2700 Greenville Hwy., Flat Rock, NC 28731, 696-3971.

Hendersonville/Flat Rock Commercial Galleries

Blue Ribbon Custom Frame Shop: Full-service custom framing. Local artists and prints. 234 North Main St., 693-7967.

Framing Arts: Regional artists and prints. Authorized Winn-Devon art group dealer. Custom framing. 119 Third Ave. West, 696-3818.

McCarter Gallery: Specializing in the beauty of nature, in paintings, giclees and prints. 411 N. Main St., Hendersonville, 698-7117.

The Portrait Source: Top quality portrait artists, 318 N. Main St., 692-7056.

Silver Fox Gallery: Arts for living. 3000 square feet of gallery space. Contemporary American craft and art, and interiors. 508 N. Main St., Hendersonville, 698-0601. www.silverfoxartgallery.com

Touchstone Gallery: Regional artists and sculptors. 318 North Main St., 692-2191.

Wickwire: Features some of WNC's finest artisans. Also collectibles. 330 N Main St., 692-6222.

Chapter Eleven
Craft Galleries

Considered to be one of the major craft areas in the country and home to HandMade in America, Asheville and the surrounding area have a staggering number of craft stores, galleries, gift shops, outlets and artisan studios open to the public. If you are seriously interested in crafts, one of the best places to start would be to pick up a copy of The Craft Heritage Trails of Western North Carolina, published by HandMade in America, at local bookstores or retail craft outlets. This is a guidebook dedicated to telling the story of the region's craft heritage and then lets you experience it firsthand through descriptions of seven driving loops of varying lengths with almost 400 stops of studios, galleries, historic inns and noteworthy restaurants. You may order a copy of this excellent book by calling HandMade in America at 252-0121 or (800) 331-4154, or writing to them at 67 Market Street, Asheville, NC 28801.

Asheville

Not to be missed in the immediate Asheville area are the craft galleries listed below. These are outstanding gallery spaces displaying top-quality works.

Asheville Institutional Craft Galleries

Allanstand Craft Shop at the Folk Art Center: One of Appalachia's oldest and best-known craft shops. Sells the work of more than 200 members of the Southern Highland Craft Guild. Milepost 382, Blue Ridge Parkway in Asheville, 298-7928.

Guild Crafts: Features the work of regional artists who are members of the Southern Highland Handicraft Guild. 930 Tunnel Rd., 298-7903.

North Carolina Homespun Museum: Exhibits and artifacts from the Biltmore Industries handweaving operation from 1901 to 1980. 111 Grovewood Rd., next to Grove Park Inn Resort, 253-7651.

Asheville Commercial Craft Galleries

Appalachian Craft Center: Traditional Appalachian crafts. 10 North Spruce St., 253-8499.

Ariel Gallery: A cooperative gallery featuring local artists exhibiting in clay, fiber, wood, glass and paper. 46 Haywood St., 236-2660. www.arielcraftgallery.com

A Touch of Glass: Stained glass, ready to buy or custom made to your design, 421 Haywood Rd., 258-2749.

Bellagio: Features exquisitely handcrafted jewelry and clothing. 5 Biltmore Plaza, Biltmore Village, 277-8100.

Candlertown Chairworks: Wonderful handcrafted chairs done in the traditional ways. 652 Hendersonville Rd., Asheville, 277-2654.

Chimera Designs: Exquisite jewelry crafted by Barbro Bengtson, one of North Carolina's most renowned silversmiths. Jewelry in all precious metals with gems and semiprecious stones. 90 Taylor Rd., Fairview, 628-4350.

Gallery of the Mountains: Wonderful selection of fine mountain crafts by regional artisans. Hand-dyed and handpainted silk vests, handwoven coats, wraps and scarves, pottery, woodwork and jewelry. Superb quality. Located in the Grove Park Inn, 290 Macon Ave., 254-2068.

Grovewood Gallery: A spacious shop displaying the work of some of the Southeast's finest craftspeople. Highest quality innovative work on display. A must-see gallery. 111 Grovewood Rd. next to the Grove Park Inn in the Homespun Shops, 253-7651. www.grovewood.com

Earth Guild: World-class fiber art supply house. Included here for that reason. Looms and instructors available for lessons. 33 Haywood St., 255-7818.

Interiors Marketplace: More than 80 shops offering furnishings and accessories for the home. Original crafts and art by local artists. 2 Hendersonville Rd., 253-2300.

Jewelry Design: Jewels That Dance: Exquisite handcrafted jewelry from gold, silver, diamonds and other precious gems and metals. 63 Haywood St., 254-5088.

Kress Antique Art & Craft Emporium: Original crafts and art by local artists and craftspeople as well as home furnishings and decorative accessories. 19 Patton Ave., 281-2252.

Kress II Gallery: Fine furniture, bronze statues, glass and art. 59 College St., Asheville, 250-0500.

New Morning Gallery: One of Asheville's premier craft galleries. Functional and sculptural pottery, fine art glass, furniture, jewelry and other handmade objects. 7 Boston Way, Biltmore Gallery, 274-2831.

Odyssey Gallery: Located in the River District, the Odyssey Gallery features pottery and works of art in clay and ceramics by national and regional artists. 242 Clingman Ave., Asheville, 285-9700.

Seven Sisters Gallery: A marvelous craft gallery. 117 Cherry Street, Black Mountain, 669-5107.

Woolworth Walk: Woolworth Walk is a multi-faceted collection of arts and crafts galleries and retail stores housed in the historic F.W. Woolworth & Co. building downtown. 25 Haywood St., 254-9234, www.woolworthwalk.com

Hendersonville/Flat Rock
Hendersonville/Flat Rock Commercial Galleries

A Day in the Country: A wonderfully eclectic gift shop and regional craft outlet. 130 Sugarloaf Rd., Hendersonville, 692-7914.

Brightwater Art Glass: Stained glass showcase and gallery. Custom glass work: doors, windows, sidelights, lamps, suncatchers and restorations. 342 North Main St., Hendersonville, 697-6842.

Crystal Carvings Glasswerks & Gallery: Original and custom glass art. 2852 Haywood Road, Hendersonville, 698-8997.

Four Seasons Crafters: Fifty member co-op with emphasis on cottage crafts. 516 N. Main St., 698-0016.

Hand in Hand Gallery: High-quality crafts by regional artists. Decorative porcelain pottery by David Voorhees and silver and gold jewelry by Molly Sharp. 2713 Greenville Hwy., Flat Rock, 697-7719.

Manual Woodworkers and Weavers: Locally manufactured crafts and award-winning afghans and weavings. Outlet store on Highway 74-A in nearby Gerton, 625-9523.

Narnia Studios: Local artists and crafters. 315 N. Main St., Hendersonville, 697-6393. www.narniastudios.com

South Main Emporium: Art, gifts, antiques, home accents, rugs. Local artists and crafters. 1197 Greenville Hwy., Hendersonville, 698-0565.

Sweet Memories: Traditional to contemporary pottery. High quality and extensive selection. Focus on regional crafts and jewelry. Distinctive collection of Southeastern art glass. 430 North Main St., Hendersonville, 692-8401.

Touchstone Gallery: Regional and nationally recognized craftspeople in all media. 318 North Main St., Hendersonville, 692-2191.

Chapter Twelve
Shopping, Flea Markets & Auctions

Asheville has a great range of shopping opportunities, from charming historic shopping districts to major malls. Downtown Asheville is a mix of art and craft galleries, specialty shops, bookstores and antique shops. Especially noteworthy is the historic Wall Street district, with its fascinating collection of shops. Biltmore Village is a historic district of specialty and gift shops, art and crafts galleries, men's and women's apparel stores and bookstores. Not to be missed!

Asheville Malls & Shopping Centers

Biltmore Square Mall: Southwest Asheville off I-26 has Profitt's, Dillard's, Belk and Goody's as anchor stores. This mall and the Asheville Mall are the two major malls in Asheville. Take Exit 2 off I-26.

Asheville Mall: East Asheville off Tunnel Road is anchored by Sears, Dillard, J.C. Penney, Montgomery Ward and Belk. Take Exit 7 off I-240.

River Ridge Market Place: East Asheville off I-240 is primarily factory outlet stores. Take Exit 8 off I-240.

Westgate Mall: 40 Westgate Plaza west of Asheville features Earth Fare natural foods grocery stores and specialty shops. Look for Westgate Mall signs off I-240 heading west out of Asheville.

Westridge Mall: Located on Highway 19/23 Smoky Park Highway in West Asheville has J&S Cafeteria and a Food Lion supermarket.

Innsbruck Mall: On Tunnel Road. Anchored by Office Depot and Ingle's supermarket. There is a Wal-Mart store next to this mall. Take Exit 6 off I-240.

Wal-Mart Plaza: On Hendersonville Road in South Asheville is anchored by Wal-Mart and specialty stores. There is also a Super Wal-Mart located on Swannanoa River Road.

Overlook Village: Located across from Asheville Mall and features Books-a-Million, Phar-Mor and T.J. Maxx. Next to Overlook Village is a K-Mart.

River Hills Shopping Center: Located on the corner of Wood Avenue and Swannanoa River Road. Just follow South Tunnel Road away from town and it will change names, becoming Wood Avenue after you cross over Swannanoa River Road. River Hills features Circuit City, Michael's Crafts, and Officemax.

Biltmore Parkway Center: On Hendersonville Road in South Asheville. Offers restaurants and is anchored by a Harris-Teeter grocery store.

Northland Shopping Center: On Merrimon Avenue features the Fresh Market and specialty shops.

Hendersonville/Flat Rock Malls & Shopping

The whole Main Street section in downtown Hendersonville is a great shopping district. Specialty shops, gift stores, card stores, galleries, craft outlets, antiques and much more. This pleasant street is unique not only for its rich collection of stores but also the beautiful flowers, benches, and shady trees.

The major mall in Hendersonville is the Blue Ridge Mall on Highway 64, which is anchored by J.C. Penney, Belk, and K-Mart.

Flea Markets

Smiley's Flea Market: Friday-Sunday, 7 a.m.-5 p.m. Located halfway between Asheville and Hendersonville. Antique Mall and small discount stores also located on the property. Free parking. 6785 Asheville Highway (US 25), Fletcher, 684-3532.

Auctions

Asheville has a lively auction scene as one would expect from a city known for its antiques and arts and crafts. Contact the auctions directly for more information, schedules and directions.

Brunk Auctions: Asheville's version of Sotheby's. Elegant and respected, and includes world-class antiques that go up for sale. 117 Tunnel Rd., Asheville. 254-6846. www.brunkauctions.com

Roger Rector Auctions: Out in the country in nearby Fairview. 82 Whitaker Rd., Fairview, 628-0791.

Tommy Tuten and Johnny Penland Auctions: Everything goes, even if it's for only $1. Coffee and hot dogs sold, and be sure to bring a chair. 6 p.m. every Friday, 155 Craven St., Asheville, 255-0455. www.tommytutenandjohnnypenlandauction.com

Wilson and Terry Auction Company: Focus is on mid-range of collectible pricing, from pottery to fine furniture. 1098 New Stock Rd., Asheville. 645-0695. www.wilsonandterryauctions.com

Richard Hatch Auctions: Hendersonville auctioneer. 3700 Asheville Hwy., Hendersonville, 696-3440.

Chapter Thirteen
Unique & Special Shops

The Asheville/Hendersonville area has a number of small shops that are so special that they, like the art and craft galleries, warrant a chapter of their own. These stores are totally unique and are found nowhere else. In a real way, their very presence reflects the vitality and creativity that has become a hallmark of this area.

Asheville Unique & Special Shops

A Far Away Place: This store is like visiting a museum, blending the feeling of a high-quality world cultural art gallery filled with sculptures, art, instruments and textiles from the world over. It also carries a large collection of world music, beautiful clothing for men and women, and a fascinating collection of ethnic jewelry. 11 Wall St. (downtown Asheville), 252-1891.

Baggie Goose: A charming gift shop in historic Biltmore Village. They specialize in personalized gifts and have personalized imprinting in the store. More stationery and invitations that anyone in Western North Carolina, including Cranes Paper. 3 Swan St. (Biltmore Village) 274-3333.

B.B. Barns: An inspiring store that all gardeners, hikers, and naturalists will love. A wide variety of gardening tools as well as hiking, bird watching, and outdoor equipment and supplies, making this store stand out. 3377 Sweeten Creek Rd., 650-7300.

Beads and Beyond: Unique beads and craft supplies from around the world and through the ages. An unbelievable collection of beads of all kinds. 35 Wall St. (downtown Asheville), 254-7927.

Chelsea's & The Village Tea Room: French and English antiques, imported gifts, fancy food items, tea sets. An elegant gift shop and English tearoom in Biltmore Village. 6 Boston Way (Biltmore Village), 274-4400.

Chevron Trading Post & Bead Company: One of Asheville's two great bead stores as well as unique gifts. 40 N. Lexington Ave., 236-2323.

The Chocolate Fetish: A tiny shop that makes truly wonderful chocolate truffles. Made by hand in the store from pure chocolate and whipping cream, they are best savored like fine cognac. More than 12 flavors, including bittersweet, semisweet, milk chocolate mint, toasted almond milk, Kahlua, Amaretto, and pungent Irish creme. Rated the best truffles in America by the *Los Angeles Times*. They are! 36 Haywood St. (downtown), 258-2353.

The Compleat Naturalist: Asheville's premier nature store. Guidebooks, outdoor equipment, clothing...This store has it all! If you love the outdoors, be sure to visit. 2 Biltmore Plaza (Biltmore Village), 274-5430, (800) 678-5430. www.completenaturalist.com

Enter the Earth: Gems, minerals and fossils. Located in the historic Grove Arcade Public Market. 1 Page Ave., Suite 124, 350-9222.

Enviro Depot: This interesting store has a little of everything, all of it environmentally friendly and produced with a concern for the planet. Gifts, toys, games, prints, and educational products. 18 Haywood St. (downtown Asheville), 252-9007.

Himalayas Import: Art, handicrafts, antiques and more from Nepal and Tibet. 6 Battery Park Ave., 255-0506.

Longstreet Old Maps & Prints: Over 20,000 unusual and rare maps and prints in all price ranges. 8 Biltmore Ave., 254-0081.

Mast General Store: Opened in 1999, this is the newest of the world-famous chain unique to North Carolina. Antique restoration sets the tone for this special store. Features traditional Mast Store provisions, gifts, clothing, and much more. 15 Biltmore Ave., 232-1883. www.mastgeneralstore.com/av.htm

Silver Armadillo: A unique showroom offering silver jewelry, gemstones, minerals, fossils, beads, findings and more. 40 Westgate Parkway (Westgate Shopping Center), 253-3020.

Wildbirds Unlimited: If you are interested in birds, this is the store for you. Everything imaginable related to wild birds. Supplies, feeders, birdwatching equipment, books, and more. Associated with Cornell University and staffed by certified bird specialists. 1997 Hendersonville Hwy., 687-9433.

Ten Thousand Villages—A Fair Trade Store: Experience the sights, sounds and texture of extraordinary creations handcrafted by skilled artisans from more than 30 countries. Fancy baskets, playful toys, bright batiks, artful jewelry, festive ceramics and plush sweaters. 10 College St. (downtown), 254-8374.

Hendersonville/Flat Rock Unique & Special Shops

A Day in the Country: An exceptional and eclectic gift shop that features gourmet foods, kitchen ware, locally made handicrafts and more. Victorian, Country and English Garden themes throughout the store. 130 Sugarloaf Rd., Hendersonville (near Exit 18A off I-26), 692-7914.

Bloomfield's Dishbarn: Set in a country barn, this store offers a combination of housewares, glasswares, gourmet cookware and bath accessories. Discounted dinnerware, collectibles such as Boyd Bears, garden pottery and local jams and jellies also. Route 4, Flat Rock (located near Exit 22 off I-26 and Upward Rd.), 693-3350.

Dancing Bear Toys Ltd.: Great toy store with two locations. 418 N. Main St. Hendersonville 693-4500; 144 Tunnel Rd., Asheville, 255-8697.

Forge Mountain Foods and Gifts: The only retail store for the world-famous Forge Mountain products. A country store brimming with fine Southern foods, with an emphasis on products from North Carolina. Memorable gifts, cookbooks and handicrafts. Their jams and jellies are the best! 1215 Greenville Hwy., Flat Rock (located between Hendersonville and Flat Rock), 692-9470. www.forgemountain.com

Foxfire Gallery and Kitchen Shop: High-quality home decor, pottery, gifts and a complete kitchen shop. 1735 Brevard Hwy., Hendersonville (located in Laurel Park Village on Hwy. 64 West going toward Brevard), 697-1005.

Honeysuckle Hollow: A delightfully magical antique and gift shop, romantically spirited. Exceptional quality. 512 North Main Street, Hendersonville, 697-2197.

Manual Woodworkers: Located between Bat Cave and Gerton, 3 miles west of Chimney Rock on Hwy. 74, this outstanding gift shop is the outlet for the world-famous Manual Woodworkers and Weavers. Charming country afghans, linens, and decorative accessories for home and garden. Hwy. 74, Bat Cave, 625-9523.

Mast General Store: One of the world-famous Mast Stores unique to North Carolina. An original Victorian facade and freshly oiled antique floors set the tone for this fabulous store. Features traditional Mast Store provisions, gifts, clothing and much more. 52 North Main St., Hendersonville, 696-1883.

The Pickity Place: Gift shop offering a wide selection of items, including tapestry, pillows, rugs, lace and foods. 423 N. Main St., 698-6999. www.pickityplace.com

Van's Chocolates: Chocolate, vanilla, and penuche fudge. Creams, caramels, turtles, toffee, nut clusters, meltaways, and cordials. All homemade! Visit from 10 a.m.-4 p.m. and you can watch the chocolates being made. 620 Greenville Hwy., Hendersonville, 697-2120.

The Wrinkled Egg: A most unusual art and garden shop, with a superb selection of art and gifts for people, home and garden. They are nationally known for exceptional summer camp surprise packages. 2710 U.S. Hwy 25, Flat Rock, 696-3998.

Chapter Fourteen
Nightlife

Downtown Asheville is one of the most alive and vibrant city centers in America, and the combination of great historic architecture, fine restaurants, coffeehouse, specialty stores, art galleries and nightclubs, pubs and cafes all add to the mix that has made Asheville an exciting nighttime destination. Listed below is a selection of the more established venues and places to check out. The author highly suggests that you also pick up a copy of the *Mountain Xpress*, Asheville's weekly free newspaper that is the absolute best source for current happenings in town—everything from concerts to movies to music. Sidewalk boxes that dispense the *Mountain Xpress* are everywhere. If you can't locate one, just call their office at 251-1333. Their office is located at 2 Wall St., Asheville.

The following is a selective sampling of the nightclubs and cafes offering live entertainment.

Asheville Microbreweries

Over the past ten years, a number of microbreweries have sprung up in the Asheville area, enough so that Asheville is gaining a reputation as a beer-lover's city! Four local breweries are turning out a wide selection of local ales and lagers and while most have focused on darker pale ales and bitters, some are now producing lighter varieties. The breweries are Highland Brewing Company (www.highlandbrewing.com), Asheville Pizza and Brewing Company (www.ashevillepizza.com), French Broad River Brewing, and Jack of the Wood (www.jackofthewood.com). Local Asheville watering holes for these great beers and ales are Barley's Taproom (www.barleys-taproom.com.asheville), 42 Biltmore Ave., 255-0504; Asheville Pizza and Brewing Company, 675 Merrimon Ave., 254-1281; Jack of the Wood, 95 Patton Ave., 252-5445; and The Bier Garden, 46 Haywood St., 285-0002. These establishments are covered in greater detail in this chapter.

Asheville

Asheville Pizza and Brewing Company: This nightclub not only features custom brews, live entertainments, and tons of dance floor space but also shows second-run Hollywood and independent films for only $2. 675 Merrimon Ave., 254-1281.

Barley's Taproom & Pizzeria: Asheville's most popular watering hole. Great selection of beer, including micro-brews, and wonderful pizzas. Entertainment Tuesday, Thursday, Saturday and Sunday with a blend of jazz, bluegrass and more. Billiard tables and dart boards available upstairs. 42 Biltmore Ave., 255-0504, no cover.

Grey Eagle Tavern & Music Hall: Formerly of Black Mountain, the relocated Grey Eagle has become one of Asheville's premier music halls. Situated in Asheville's vibrant French Broad River district, the Grey Eagle is known for presenting local and nationally known artists, making it a cornerstone of the Asheville music scene. 185 Clingman Ave., 232-5800. www.greyeaglemusic.com

Jack of the Wood: In addition to making their own unique beers and ales, Jack of the Wood offers a distinctively British-style pub atmosphere. They also feature fresh-baked breads and desserts. 95 Patton Ave., 252-5445. www.jackofthewood.com

Malaprop's Bookstore/Café: Wonderful cafe located downtown in the best private bookstore in Western North Carolina. Offers a wide variety of coffees, juice drinks, as well as beer and wine, soups, sandwiches and light lunches. If you love books and coffeehouses, this is the place for you. Live music (no cover charge) most Friday and Saturdays.

Orange Peel: Asheville's premier nightclub and entertainment venue. An amazing lineup of big-name talent, huge concert hall and room enough for almost 1,000. Most shows start early, are standing only and non-smoking. Beer and wine. 101 Biltmore Ave., 225-5851, Ticket hotline: (866) 468-7630 (toll-free). www.theorangepeel.net

Scandals: Mixed lesbian/gay with lively dancebar, and various areas to escape the madness of the dance floor. Asheville's premier lesbian/gay nightclub. 11 Grove St., Asheville, 252-2838. www.scandals-club.com

Westville Pub: Something happening seven evenings a week, including open mike nights. Non-smoking pub serving a light menu. 777 Haywood Rd., 225-9782.

Hendersonville

Hannah Flanagan's Irish Pub: More than 30 beers on tap, pub food and Irish dishes. Live music. 300 N. Main St., 696-1665.

Chapter Fifteen
Theatre

The theatre is alive and well in Western North Carolina, especially in the Asheville, Hendersonville and Flat Rock area. Big-city ensembles like The Acting Company, one of America's premier touring companies, regularly return each year. There is a strong local theatre, which ranges from innovative and cutting-edge performances by the Montford Park Players to the full-scale productions at the Diana Wortham Theatre. (SEE Section Three, Chapter 2 Pack Place Education, Arts & Science Center) You can even find Shakespeare in the summer from the Montford Park Players. For children, The Mockingbird Theatre regularly schedules performances for their benefit and interest. Asheville has an established theater in the Asheville Community Theatre (ACT), which regularly schedules award-winning shows. (SEE Section Three, Chapter 2)

Located in Flat Rock, the Flat Rock Playhouse has been rated one of the top ten summer theaters in the nation. Home to the Vagabond Players, this theater is a major attraction. (SEE Section Four, Chapter 2)

Flat Rock Playhouse, home of the Vagabond Players

For current performances and schedules, call the theater companies listed below:

Asheville

Asheville Community Theatre: 254-1320, www.ashevilletheatre.org
Diana Wortham Theatre: 257-4530
Montford Park Players: 254-5146, www.montfordparkplayers.com
Theatre UNCA: 232-2291

Hendersonville/Flat Rock

Flat Rock Playhouse: 693-0731
Hendersonville Little Theatre: 692-1082

Nearby

Lees-McRae Summer Theatre: Banner Elk, 898-8721
Southern Appalachian Repertory Theatre: Mars Hill, 689-1239
The Blowing Rock Stage Company: Blowing Rock, 295-9168

Chapter Sixteen
Outdoor Recreation

Western North Carolina abounds with numerous outdoor recreational opportunities, many of them rare in other areas but plentiful here. Whitewater rafting, trout fishing, llama trekking, mountain biking and mountain climbing are prime examples.

Both Asheville and Hendersonville have excellent city parks (SEE Section Three, Chapter 9 Asheville Parks; and Section Four, Chapter 7 Hendersonville Area Parks) that provide various outdoor sporting venues. The Buncombe County Parks and Recreation Department also manages a number of parks that are used for various outdoor and sporting activities. Aston Park Tennis Complex, Lake Julian District Park, Buncombe County Golf Course and various community swimming pools are all maintained by the Parks and Recreation Department. This organization is also sponsor for many senior activities as well as youth athletics, including softball and soccer leagues. They are also the organizers for Buncombe County Special Olympics. Their offices are at 205 College Street, Asheville, NC 28801; 255-5526.

Bicycling

Biking is a very popular recreation in the mountains. Scenic vistas and winding country and mountain roads make for some of the best bicycle touring in the world. Because of this fact, Asheville in the past has been one of the stops in the Tour Dupont, which used the Grove Park Inn Resort as race headquarters.

The premier bicycling club for Western North Carolina is the Blue Ridge Bicycle Club. They have meetings the 3rd Wednesday of every month. For more information, visit their website at www.blueridgebicycleclub.org.

Local bookstores and bicycle shops carry a guide to bicycling in the Asheville area. Titled *Road Bike Asheville,* this informative guide describes sixteen road-biking routes in and around Asheville that the Blue Ridge Bicycle Club sees as tops. Also ask for the Bike-Transportation Map developed by the Bikeways Task Force and the Blue Ridge Bicycle Club, which serves as an excellent resource for route planning.

A number of bicycle shops also rent bicycles and can give expert advice as to some scenic routes. Some of the better shops in the area are:

Hearn's Cycling and Fitness: 34 Broadway, Asheville, NC 28801; 253-4800.
Liberty Bicycles: 1378 Hendersonville Hwy., Asheville, NC 28803; 274-2453.
Pro Bikes: 793 Merrimon Ave., Asheville, NC 28804; 253-2800
The Bicycle Co.: 210 S. Washington St., Hendersonville, NC 28739; 696-1500.
Epic Cycles: Black Mountain; 669-5969.

Mountain Biking

The same shops listed above can give you advice as to mountain biking trails in the Asheville/Hendersonville area. Excellent off-road riding can be found in the nearby Pisgah District of the Pisgah National Forest. (SEE Section Five, Chapter 1) This section of the forest has more than 400 miles of trails. Check in at the Ranger Station Visitor Center 1½ miles west of NC 280 on U.S. 276 and pick up a copy of their trail map. The Bent Creek section of the forest is an especially popular riding area, as is the North Mills River Recreation Area and the Dupont State Forest near Hendersonville. (SEE Section Four, Chapter 7)

Two great websites devoted to mountain biking are The NC Mountain Biking Trails Authority (http://members.aol.com/NCMBA/Home.html) and the MTB WNC site (www.mtbikewnc.com).

Campgrounds & Camping

Listed below are some campgrounds and RV parks that are among the best in the area. These lists are followed by information about primitive camping facilities and sites. For RV owners, Ledford's RV and Marine located off I-26 halfway between Asheville and Hendersonville is a great resource for sales and service should you need help while visiting the mountains. 480 N. Rugby Rd., Hendersonville, 651-0007.

Asheville

French Broad River Campground: 1030 Old Marshall Hwy., Asheville, NC 28804; 658-0772
KOA Asheville-East Tanglewood: 102 Hwy. 70 East, Swannanoa, NC 28778: 686-3121
KOA Asheville-West: I-40 Exit 37 & Wiggins Rd., Candler, NC 28715; 665-7015, (800) 562-9015.

Blue Ridge Parkway

There are six campgrounds open to the public on the Parkway in North Carolina from May 1 through October or into early November, depending on weather conditions. Facilities are limited in winter. Fees are charged and length of stay may be limited. Camping is permitted only in designated campgrounds. Drinking water and comfort stations are provided; shower and laundry facilities are not.

Sites in each campground are designated for trailers but none is equipped for utility connections. Campgrounds have sanitary dumping stations. Each campsite has a table and fireplace. Limited supplies may be purchased at most Parkway gasoline stations and camp stores.

Milepost 241.1: Doughton Park
Milepost 297.1: Julian Price Memorial Park
Milepost 316.4: Linville Falls
Milepost 339.5: Crabtree Meadows
Milepost 408.6: Mount Pisgah
Milepost 418.8: Graveyard Fields

For further information, call the Parkway headquarters at 298-0398. (SEE also Section Five, Chapter 1)

Hendersonville/Flat Rock

Apple Valley Travel Park: 1 Apple Orchard Rd., Hendersonville, NC 28792; 685-8000

Jaymar Travel Park: Hwy. 64, Hendersonville, NC 28792; 685-3771

Lakewood R.V. Resort: 915 Ballenger Rd., Flat Rock, NC 28731; 697-9523, (888) 819-4200; www.lakewoodrvresort.com

Lazy Boy Travel Trailer Park: 110 Old Sunset Hill Rd., Hendersonville, NC 28792; 697-7165

Park Place R.V. Park: Allen Rd., Flat Rock, NC 28731; 693-3831

Phil & Ann's R.V.: 818 Tracy Grove Rd., Flat Rock, NC 28731; 696-9089, (800) 753-8373

Town Mountain Travel Park: 2030 Spartanburg Hwy., Hendersonville, NC 28792; 697-6696; www.townmountain.bizhosting.com

Twin Ponds R.V. Park: 24 Empire Ln., Flat Rock, NC 28731; 693-4018, 698-1617; www.nctwinponds.com

Pisgah National Forest

The Pisgah District of the Pisgah National Forest borders the Asheville/Hendersonville area. This magnificent forest is easily accessible from many points and offers wonderful camping facilities. Keep in mind that there are some rules governing camping in national forests. You can pitch your tent just about anywhere providing you are 100 feet or more from all water sources, at least 1,000 feet from the road and there are no signs prohibiting camping. Pets must be under control and on a leash when you are near people or a campground. For more information about camping in the forest, call 257-4200. (SEE also Section Five, Chapter 1)

Other popular camping areas in Western North Carolina are the Great Smoky Mountains National Park, the Nantahala National Forest and the Appalachian Trail. (SEE Section Five, Chapter 1)

Maps

Maps of the Nantahala and Pisgah National Forests, and other wilderness areas, can be ordered from the Cradle of Forestry in America Interpretive Association (CFAIA). Their address is CFAIA, 100 South Broad St., Brevard, NC 28712. (800) 660-0671. www.cradleofforestry.com.

National Forest Contacts

Forest Supervisor—National Forests in NC: 106 A Zillicoa Street, Asheville, NC 28801; 257-4200

Pisgah National Forest:

Appalachian Ranger District, French Broad Station: PO Box 128, Hot Springs, NC 28743; 622-3202

Appalachian Ranger District, Toecane Ranger Station: PO Box 128, Burnsville, NC 28714; 682-6146

Grandfather Ranger District: 109 East Lawing Lane, Nebo, NC 28761; 652-2144

Pisgah Ranger District: 1001 Pisgah Highway, Pisgah Forest, NC 28768; 877-3265

Nantahala National Forest:

Cheoah Ranger District: 1133 Massey Branch Road, Robbinsville, NC 28711; 479-6431

Highlands Ranger District: 2010 Flat Mountain Road, Highlands, NC 28741; 526-3765

Golf in the Mountains

Golf enthusiasts from all over challenge their skills on the area's many well known courses. The mild climate offers nearly four seasons on courses that range from wide river valleys and rolling terrains to fairways that pitch and roll to challenge even the most experienced golfer. Asheville's standout course is the prestigious Grove Park Inn Resort. Hendersonville's is the Etowah Valley Country Club and Golf Lodge.

An excellent resource for finding Western North Carolina golf clubs beyond the Asheville and Hendersonville area is the Great Smoky Mountain Golf Association. They can be reached through their website at www.greatsmokiesgolf.com; by writing then at P.O. Box 18556, Asheville, NC 28814; or calling 258-0123.

Asheville & Hendersonville Area Driving Ranges

Big D's Golf Range and Pro Shop: Exit 44 off I-40 in West Asheville. 20 Crowell Rd., 665-1817

Double Tee Golf & Batting Cages: South Asheville. 485 Brookside Camp Rd., 693-7420

Golf Augusta Driving Range: 640 Dana Rd., Hendersonville, 696-4005
Jake's Driving Range: Highway 25 North, Naples, 684-8086
Practice Tee & Golf Shop: East Asheville. 161 Azalea Rd. East, 298-0123

Asheville Area Golf Courses

Black Mountain Golf Club
Address: Ross St., Black Mountain, NC 28711
Telephone: 669-2710
Status: Semiprivate
Course: 18 holes, par 71 men and women; featuring the world's longest par 6 at 747 yards.

Broadmoor Golf Links
Address: 101 French Broad Ln., Fletcher, NC 28732
Telephone: 687-1500
Status: Public
Course: 18 holes, par 72 men and women

Brookwood Golf Club
Address: Mills Gap Rd., Asheville, NC 28704
Telephone: 684-6278
Status: Semiprivate
Course: 9 holes; par 35 men, 36 women

Buncombe County Golf Course
Address: 226 Fairway Dr., Asheville, NC 28805
Telephone: 298-1867
Status: Public
Course: 18 holes, par 72 men and women

Great Smokies Holiday Inn Sunspree Golf & Tennis
Address: 1 Holiday Inn Dr., Asheville, NC 28806
Telephone: 253-5874
Status: Resort/public
Course: 18 holes, par 70 men and women

The Grove Park Inn Resort & Spa
Address: 290 Macon Ave., Asheville, NC 28804
Telephone: 252-2711
Status: Resort/public
Course: 18 holes, par 71 men and women; National Landmark Hotel, championship course

Northwoods Golf Club
Address: 70 Old Beaverdam Creek Rd., Asheville, NC 28804
Telephone: 253-1659
Status: Public
Course: 9 holes, par 31 (more holes to be added, course opened 1999)

Reems Creek Golf Club
Address: 36 Pink Fox Cove Rd., Weaverville, NC 28787
Telephone: 645-4393
Status: Semiprivate
Course: 18 holes, par 72 men and women

Hendersonville/Flat Rock Area Golf Courses

Colony Lake Lure Golf Resort
Address: 201 Boulevard of the Mountains, Lake Lure, NC 28746
Telephone: 625-3000
Status: Resort/public
Course: Two 18-hole courses; par 72 men and women

Crooked Creek Golf Course
Address: Crooked Creek Rd., Hendersonville, NC 28739
Telephone: 692-2011
Status: Public
Course: 18 holes, par 70 men and women

Cummings Cove Golf & Country Club
Address: 3000 Cummings Rd., Hendersonville, NC 28739
Telephone: 891-9412, (800) 958-2905
Status: Resort/public
Course: 18 holes, par 70 men and women

Etowah Valley Country Club & Golf Lodge
Address: 450 Brickyard Rd., Etowah, NC 28739
Telephone: 891-7022, (800) 451-8174
Status: Resort/public
Course: South Course: 9 holes, par 36 men and women
West Course: 9 holes, par 36 men and women;
North Course: 9 holes, par 37 men and women

Etowah Valley Country Club & Golf Lodge, Hendersonville

Highland Lake Golf Club
- Address: 111 Highland Lake Rd., Flat Rock, NC 28731
- Telephone: 692-0143
- Status: Resort/public
- Course: 9 holes, par 35 men and women

Lake Lure Town Golf Course
- Address: Hwy. 64-74, Lake Lure, NC 28746
- Telephone: 625-4472
- Status: Public
- Course: 9 holes, par 36 men and women

Orchard Trace Golf Club
- Address: 942 Sugarloaf Rd., Hendersonville, NC 28792
- Telephone: 685-1006
- Status: Public
- Course: 18 holes, par 54 (3 each hole) men and women

Pine Links Golf Club
- Address: South Orchard Rd., Flat Rock, NC 28731
- Telephone: 693-0907
- Status: Public
- Course: 9 Holes, par 35

Golf Courses in WNC That You Can Play

The following is a comprehensive listing of all golf courses that allow public play. In this list are resorts and private clubs allowing pay per play.

Asheville Area:
Broadmoor Golf Links: (Asheville) 687-1500
Brookwood Golf Club: (Asheville) 684-6278
Black Mountain Golf Club: (Black Mountain) 669-2710
Buncombe Country Golf Course: (Asheville) 298-2867
Crowne Plaza Resort: (Asheville) 254-3211
High Vista Country Club at High Vista Falls: (Asheville) 891-8047, (888) 500-4233
Northwoods Golf Club of Asheville: 253-1659
Reems Creek Golf Club: (Weaverville) 645-3120
Springdale Country Club: (Canton) (800) 553-3027

Hendersonville Area:
Apple Valley: (Lake Lure) 652-2888
Bald Mountain: (Lake Lure) 625-9111
Cummings Cove: (Hendersonville) (800) 958-2905
Etowah Valley Country Club: (Etowah) 891-7022, 891-9412
Highland Lake Golf Course: (Flat Rock) 692-0143
Glen Cannon Country Club: (Brevard) 884-9160

Lake Lure Town Golf Course: (Lake Lure) 625-4472
Sherwood Forest Golf Course: (Brevard) 884-7825

West of Asheville:
Chatuge Shores Golf Club: (Hayesville) 389-8940
Cherokee Hills Golf & Country Club: (Murphy) (800) 334-3905
Iron Tree Golf Course: (Waynesville) 627-1933
Franklin Golf Course: (Franklin) 524-2288
Lake Junaluska Golf Course: (Lake Junaluska) 456-5777
Laurel Ridge Country Club: (Waynesville) (800) 433-7274
Mill Creek Country Club: (Franklin) (800) 533-3916
Mountain Harbour Golf Course: (Hayesville) (800) 577-4020
Sapphire Mountain Golf Club: (Sapphire) 743-1174

East of Asheville:
Blue Ridge Country Club: (Linville Falls) 756-7001
Boone Golf Club: (Boone) 264-8760
Brushy Mountain Golf Club: (Jefferson) (336) 982-4449, (800) 292-6274
Cleghorn Golf Club: (Rutherfordton) 286-9117
Granada Farms Country Club: (Granite Falls) 396-2313
Grassy Creek Golf & Country Club: (Spruce Pine) 765-7436
Greenstreet Mountain Golf Course: (Traphill) (336) 957-4422
Hawks Nest: (Seven Devils) 963-6561, (800) 822-4295
High Hampton Inn & Country Club: (Cashiers) 743-2450, (800) 334-2551
High Meadows Golf and Country Club: (Roaring Gap) (910) 363-2445
Jefferson Landing Club: (Jefferson) (336) 982-4449, (800) 292 6274
Lenoir Golf Club: (Lenoir) 754- 5093
Marion Lake Club: (Nebo) 524-6458
Meadowbrook Golf Club: (Rutherfordton) 863-2690
Mountain Aire Golf Club: (West Jefferson) (336) 877-4716
Mountain Glen Golf Club: (Newland) 733-5804
Mount Mitchell Golf Club: (Burnsville) 524-6458
Oak Valley: (Advance) (336) 940-2000
Olde Beau Golf & Country Club: (Roaring Gap) (800) 752-1634
Old Fort Golf Course: (Old Fort) 668-4256
Orchard Hills Golf Club: (Granite Falls) 728-3560
Quaker Meadows Golf Course: (Morganton) 437-2677
Silver Creek Plantation Golf Club: (Morganton) 584-6905
Somerset Country Club: (North Wilkesboro) (336) 667-9595
Sugar Mountain Municipal Course: (Sugar Mountain) 898-6464
Rock Creek Country Club: (North Wilkesboro) (336) 696-2146
Rutherfordton Golf Club: (Rutherfordton) 287-3406
Willow Creek: (Boone) 963-6865

Resorts (With Golf Courses That Allow Public Play)
Colony Lake Lure Golf Resort: (Lake Lure) (800) 260-1040
Eseeola Lodge: (Linville) (800) 742-6717, 733-4311
Etowah Valley Country Club: (Etowah) 891-7022, 891-9412
Crowne Plaza Resort: (Asheville) (800) 733-3211
Grove Park Inn Golf & Country Club: (Asheville) (800) 438-5800
High Hampton Inn & Country Club: (Cashiers) 743-2450, (800) 334-2551
Hounds Ear Club: (Blowing Rock) 963-4321
Jefferson Landing Club: (Jefferson) (336) 982-4449, (800) 292 6274
Lake Junaluska Golf Course: (Lake Junaluska) 456-5777
Maggie Valley Resort: (Maggie Valley) (800) 438-3861
Mount Mitchell Golf Club: (Burnsville) 524-6458
Olde Beau Golf & Country Club: (Roaring Gap) (800) 752-1634
Waynesville Country Club & Inn: (Waynesville) (800) 311-8230
Willow Valley Resort: (Boone) 963-6551
Wolf Laurel Resort: (Mars Hill) 689-4111

Hiking & Backpacking
The mountains and valleys around Asheville and Hendersonville are a hiker's paradise. Hundreds of thousands of visitors come to this region every year just to hike and to experience the countless trails that range from short day hikes to the world famous Appalachian Trail.

Because of the vast territory involved for possible hiking, some considerations should be made concerning planning and safety. For the most part, the Western North Carolina mountains are wilderness or semi-wilderness areas. That means there are a lot more trees and woods than people. Getting lost is a possibility if proper planning and cautions are not taken. In order to prevent any problems, you should always take the following precautions before venturing out into the woods on any hike that takes you away from civilization.

1. **Always check in at a ranger station or park headquarters** for the latest trail information before you leave. Trail conditions often change due to weather conditions and knowing about any changes in advance can prevent much aggravation later. In addition, rangers know the trails and can best advise you regarding which trails to take, length of hikes and so on.
2. **Always leave word with someone about where you're going,** when you plan to leave and when you plan to return. In the worst case, this will insure that you will be searched for should you not return at the designated time.
3. **Always take a trail map on your hike,** unless it is a short self-guided nature trail or similar trail. Know how to read the map. Check with a local forest ranger if you have any questions about the map and the trail you intend to hike.

Migration of the Monarch Butterflies

LEE JAMES PANTAS

A marvelous natural phenomenon, that can be seen, in the fall is the migration of the Monarch butterflies through the Western North Carolina mountain valleys as they make their way south from the mountains on their long pilgrimage to Mexico, where they spend the winter in the Sierra Madre mountains. Monarchs that emerge in late summer and autumn in the Western North Carolina mountains are different than their cousins born earlier in the summer as the shorter, cooler days of fall postpone the development of their reproductive organs. This, plus changes in light and temperature, perhaps along with other factors not yet understood, cues these butterflies to take to the skies, migrating hundreds and even thousands of miles across the continent to warmer wintering grounds. They are strong, fast fliers, reaching speeds of ten to thirty miles per hour. Along the way, they get nourishment from plants, fattening themselves for the coming winter. This migration usually takes place from August to October, reaching a peak usually the third week in September. An excellent viewing site is the Cherry Cove Overlook on the Blue Ridge Parkway seven miles south of Pisgah Inn.

4. **If at all possible, never hike alone.** An injury alone in the woods can be life-threatening without someone else to assist or go for help.
5. **Lock valuables in the trunk of your car** or take them with you.
6. **Be prepared! Do your homework before you even start out.** Talk to professional outfitters to insure that you have the right hiking shoes, equipment, food, first aid supplies and maps. Take plenty of food and water, and cold weather gear in the fall or spring. A cell phone is a great idea for emergencies.
7. **Never leave the trail.** Even experienced hikers can get lost by taking off-the-trail shortcuts.
8. **Do not drink the water in streams or springs.** Bacterial diseases can be contracted by drinking untreated "wild waters."

Hiking Trails Accessible From the Blue Ridge Parkway

Listed below are the hiking trails in North Carolina that can be accessed from the Blue Ridge Parkway. Keep in mind that Asheville is located around milepost 380 and getting to milepost 260, for example, 100 miles on the parkway, will take a good three hours driving time.

Milepost	Trail	Mileage*	Difficulty
217.5	Cumberland Knob Trail (ideal lazy-day walk)	0.5	Easy
217.5	Gully Creek Trail (rewarding loop that meanders by stream)	2.0	Strenuous
218.6	Fox Hunters Paradise Trail (view)	0.2	Easy
230.1	Little Glade Millpond (easy loop stroll around pond)	0.4	Easy
238.5	Cedar Ridge Trail (great for day hike; vistas and forests)	4.2	Moderate
238.5	Bluff Mountain Trail (parallels Parkway to milepost 244.7)	7.5	Moderate
241.0	Fodder Stack Trail (great variety of plants)	1.0	Moderate
241.0	Bluff Ridge Trail (primitive trail with steep slopes)	2.8	Moderate
243.7	Grassy Gap Fire Road (wide enough for side-by-side hiking)	6.5	Moderate
243.7	Basin Creek Trail (access from back-country campground)	3.3	Moderate
244.7	Flat Rock Ridge Trail (forest path with vistas)	5.0	Moderate
260.3	Jumpingoff Rocks Trail (forest path to vista)	1.0	Easy
264.4	The Lump Trail (to hilltop view)	0.3	Easy
271.9	Cascades Trail (self-guiding loop to view of falls)	0.5	Moderate
272.5	Tompkins Knob Trail (to Jesse Brown Cabin)	0.6	Easy
294.0	Rich Mountain Carriage, Horse & Hiking Trail	4.3	Moderate
294.0	Flat Top Mountain Carriage, Horse & Hiking Trail	3.0	Moderate
294.0	Watkins Carriage, Horse & Hiking Trail	3.3	Easy/Moderate
294.0	Black Bottom Carriage, Horse & Hiking Trail	0.5	Easy
294.0	Bass Lake Carriage, Horse & Hiking Trail	1.7	Easy
294.0	Deer Park Carriage, Horse & Hiking Trail	0.8	Moderate
294.0	Maze Carriage, Horse & Hiking Trail	2.3	Moderate
294.0	Duncan Carriage, Horse & Hiking Trail	2.5	Moderate
294.0	Rock Creek Bridge Carriage, Horse & Hiking Trail	1.0	Easy
294.1	Figure 8 Trail (short self-guiding loop around nature trail)	0.7	Easy
294.6	Trout Lake Hiking & Horse Trail (loop)	1.0	Easy
295.9	Green Knob Trail (to Green Knob)	2.3	Moderate/Strenuous
296.5	Boone Fork Trail (stream, forest and meadows)	5.5	Moderate/Strenuous
297.0	Price Lake Loop Trail (loop around Price Lake)	2.7	Moderate
304.4	Linn Cove Viaduct Access Trail	0.16	Easy
305.2	Beacon Heights Trail (10 minutes to view)	0.2	Moderate
305.5	Tanawha Trail (diverse features, parallels Parkway to Price Park)	13.5	Moderate/Strenuous
308.2	Flat Rock Trail (self-guiding loop)	0.6	Easy
315.5	Camp Creek Trail (leg stretcher through laurel and rhododendron)	0.1	Easy
316.4	Linville Falls Trail (view of upper falls)	0.8	Moderate
316.4	Linville Gorge Trail (view of lower falls)	0.5	Strenuous
316.4	Duggers Creek Trail (loop to view of Duggers Falls)	0.25	Easy
316.5	Linville River Bridge Trail (leg stretcher to view of unusual bridge)	0.1	Easy
320.8	Chestoa View Trail (30-minute loop to vista)	0.6	Easy

* Mileage indicates length of trail one-way unless otherwise noted

Milepost	Trail	Mileage*	Difficulty
339.5	Crabtree Falls Loop Trail (loop to view of falls)	2.5	Strenuous
344.1	Woods Mountain Trail (USES)	2.0	Moderate
350.4	Lost Cove Ridge Trail (USFS)	0.6	Moderate
351.9	Deep Gap Trail (USFS)	0.2	Easy
355.0	Bald Knob Ridge Trail (USFS)	0.1	Easy
359.8	Big Butt Trail (USFS) (trail continues on USFS lands)	0.2	Strenuous
361.2	Glassmine Falls (view of falls)	0.05	Moderate
364.2	Craggy Pinnacle Trail (to panoramic view)	0.7	Moderate
364.6	Craggy Gardens Trail (first portion is self-guiding nature trail)	0.8	Moderate
374.4	Rattlesnake Lodge Trail (woodland walk)	0.5	Moderate
382.0	Mountain-to-Sea Trail/MTS Trail (Folk Art Center to Mt. Mitchell; spring wildflowers & views, parallels Parkway; many accesses to trail segments)		Moderate/Strenuous
393.7	Shut-in Trail/MTS Trail (Bent Creek-Walnut Cove)	3.1	Strenuous
396.4	Shut-in Trail/MTS Trail (Walnut Cove-Sleepy Gap)	1.7	Moderate
397.3	Grassy Knob Trail (steep trail to USFS area)	0.9	Strenuous
397.3	Shut-in Trail/MTS Trail (Sleepy Gap-Chestnut Cove)	0.7	Moderate
398.3	Shut-in Trail/MTS Trail (Chestnut Cove-Bent Creek Gap)	2.8	Strenuous
400.3	Shut-in Trail/MTS Trail (Bent Creek Gap-Beaver Dam Gap)	1.9	Moderate
401.7	Shut-in Trail/MTS Trail (Beaver Dam Gap-Stoney Bald)	0.9	Moderate
402.6	Shut-in Trail/MTS Trail (Stoney Bald-Big Ridge)	1.2	Strenuous
403.6	Shut-in Trail/MTS Trail (Big Ridge-Mills River Valley)	1.1	Moderate/Strenuous
404.5	Shut-in Trail/MTS Trail (Elk Pasture Gap-Mt. Pisgah)	1.7	Strenuous
407.6	Mt. Pisgah Trail (summit view)	1.3	Moderate/Strenuous
407.6	Buck Springs Trail (Pisgah Lodge to view)	1.06	Easy/Moderate
408.5	Frying-Pan Mountain Trail	1.06	Moderate/Strenuous
417.0	East Fork Trail (USFS, access to Shining Rock Trail System)	0.1	Easy/Moderate
418.8	Graveyard Fields Loop Trail (loop by a stream)	2.3	Moderate
419.4	John Rock Trail (leg stretcher to view)	0.1	Easy
422.4	Devil's Courthouse Trail (panoramic summit view)	0.4	Moderate/Strenuous
427.6	Bear Pen Gap Trail (access to Mountains-to-Sea Trail)	0.2	Easy
431.0	Richland Balsam Trail (self-guiding loop through spruce-fir forest)	1.5	Moderate
433.8	Roy Taylor Overlook Trail (paved trail to overlook)	0.1	Easy
451.2	Waterrock Knob Trail (summit view; .6 mile one way)	1.2	Moderate/Strenuous

* Mileage indicates length of trail one-way unless otherwise noted

Outfitters

There are a number of excellent camping, rafting, and hiking suppliers in the Asheville/Hendersonville area. The three best outfitters, listed below, can not only supply you with the right equipment but also the right advice. They also offer guide services and are very knowledgeable about hiking, rafting, backpacking, and other outdoor activities in our are.

Black Dome Mountain Sports: 140 Tunnel Rd., Asheville, NC 28805; 251-2001; www.blackdome.com/Mtnhome.htm

Diamond Brand Paddle Sports: 172 Charlotte St., Asheville, NC 28804; 251-4668

Nantahala Outdoor Center Outfitter's Store: 52 Westgate Prkwy., Asheville, NC 28806; 232-0110 www.noc.com/store/ashsto1.htm

The local office of the U.S. Forest Service is another valuable resource and can also answer questions you might have regarding hiking trails in the Pisgah National Forest. Contact them at the U.S. Forest Service, P.O. Box 7148, Asheville, NC 28802; 257-4200.

The choice of possible hikes is so vast that no attempt will be made to even begin to cover what trails are available. I strongly suggest that you first visit one of the three outfitters mentioned above and start there. They will be able to help you make some good choices based on your preferences and skill level. These stores also have maps and books for sale about hiking in the mountains.

Hiking Clubs

High Country Hikers: 697-9743

Carolina Mountain Club: 299-8126, 274-0057, www.carolinamtnclub.com

Horseback Riding

Horseback riding and horse shows are very popular activities in the mountains. Many local horse stables provide not only traditional riding instruction and facilities but also can serve as outfitters for trail rides into the hills and mountains. Two excellent horse and tackle stores in the area are Balsam Quarter Tack, located at 521 Long Shoals Rd., Arden NC 28704 (684-8445) and Jackson Trading Company at 641 Patton Ave., Asheville, NC 28806 (254-1812).

Asheville Area

Alpine Stables: 250 acres of trails, stadium jumping, field, pasture and lighted riding ring. Big Cove, Candler; 667-8281.

Berry Patch Stables: Trail rides, lessons, Olympic-size riding ring, pony rides and petting zoo. 300 Baird Cove Rd., Asheville, NC 28804; 645-7271.

Biltmore Estate Equestrian Center: Guided horseback riding on the grounds of America's largest private estate. 100 miles of trails in forest and riding pastures. Horse stalls and paddocks available. Enter the Estate Stables off Racquet Club Rd. from Hendersonville Rd. in South Asheville; 277-4485.

Horseback riding is a popular pastime in WNC.

Cane Creek Farm: Located in the beautiful Cane Creek Valley of Fletcher, this world-class training facility specializes in hunters and jumpers. Training, showing, boarding and sales. If you are interested in showing and competing in the Hunter/Jumper classes, this facility is for you. 912 Cane Creek Rd., Fletcher, NC 28730; 681-5975.

Encore Stables: Full board, daily turnout. Lessons from beginner to advanced. 338 Youngs Dr. Extension, Candler; 665-0790.

Lazy B Stables: 310 Emmas Grove Rd., Fletcher, NC 28732; 628-0681.

Pisgah View Ranch: Guided rates to guests and general public April through October. Four one-hour rides daily. Pisgah View Ranch is a well-known area country inn also, serving a great evening family-style meal. 70 Pisgah View Ranch Rd., Candler; 667-9100.

In addition, the Western North Carolina Agricultural Center (SEE Section Three, Chapter 2) regularly schedules championship horse shows and related events. Another equestrian facility fairly close to Asheville and Hendersonville is the Foothills Equestrian Nature Center (FENCE), located in Tryon, which is about an hour's drive south. They have world-class equestrian facilities, steeplechase and cross-country courses and regularly host horse shows of all types and classes. (SEE Section Five, Chapter 2)

Hendersonville/Flat Rock

Etowah Valley Stables: Brickyard Rd., Etowah, NC 28729; 891-3340

Red Top Farm and Stables: 3535 Hebron Rd., Hendersonville, NC 28739; 692-4068

Hot Air Balloon Rides

A number of local companies offer hot-air balloon rides that take you floating above the green fields and mountains. Costs are just over $100 per person, and reservations are required. Flight times vary but a typical outing is between 2 and 2½ hours in the air. A really unique way to experience the mountains!

Mount Pisgah Balloons: In operation since 1981, this company is located in Candler, just west of Asheville. Flights are $110 per person. Route 1, P.O. Box 232, Candler, NC 28715; 667-9943.

Llama Trekking

An unusual way to experience the mountain trails is by llama trek. A couple of local companies offer guide service, camping gear, food and gentle llamas to carry the equipment. These friendly relatives of the camel are sure-footed and capable of carrying loads of up to 90 pounds. They are also kind to the trails and do much less damage than would horses.

WindDancer's Llama Treks: Gourmet meals on trips. Day trips or overnight trips lasting up to four days. Day treks start at $60 per person. 1966 Martins Creek Rd., Clyde, NC 28721; 627-6986; www.winddancersnc.com.

Miniature Golf

Asheville

Boyd Park (City of Hendersonville Park): Free. Located between N. Main and Church Sts. at 8th St., Hendersonville.

Shadowbrook Golf & Games: Approximately 15 miles east of Asheville in Black Mountain. 701 NC Hwy. 9, 669-5499.

Tropical Gardens Mini Golf: West Asheville. 956 Patton Ave., 252-2207.

Rock & Mountain Climbing

The mountains of Western North Carolina offer a wealth of climbs if you are interested in rock climbing. Rock cliffs, outcroppings, and slopes are to be found in abundance. Every year, professional and amateur climbers alike visit our area to test their skills.

Asheville has two primary centers that offer advice, sell climbing equipment and apparel, and offer guide services and instruction. It is advisable that you check in with one of the centers before attempting any climb in our area. They are more than willing to help you select climbs or get you started if you have never climbed before.

Black Dome Mountain Sports: One of the premier rock climbing and mountaineering resources in our area, Black Dome has the South's most extensive collection of rock and mountain climbing equipment. They also have a great selection of guidebooks and maps and are more than willing to offer advice on local climbs. If you need climbing equipment or information, this is the best place to find it.

Address:	140 Tunnel Rd., Asheville, NC 28805
Telephone:	251-2001
Hours:	Monday-Saturday 10 a.m.-8 p.m.
	Sunday 1:00-5 p.m.
Rates:	Beginner and Intermediate Clinics $75-$90 per person. Call for private instruction and guide service rates.
Website:	www.blackdome.com

Climbmax: A climbing center located in downtown Asheville offering instruction, guide services, apparel sales, and two on-site climbing walls—one 40-foot outdoor wall and an indoor climbing gym with a 20-foot wall geared to all skill levels, with staff on duty at all times to insure safety. Outdoor guided climbs range from local one-day climbs to multi-day Alpine-class climbs. Climbmax guides are members of the American Mountain Guide Association (AMGA).

Address:	43 Wall St., Asheville, NC 28801
Telephone:	252-9996
Hours:	Summer: Tuesday-Friday noon-10 p.m., Saturday 10 a.m.-10 p.m., Sunday 1:00-6 p.m.
	Winter: Tuesday and Thursday 3:30-10 p.m., Wednesday and Friday noon-10 p.m., Saturday 10 a.m.-10 p.m., Sunday 1:00-6 p.m.

Rates: In-center fees range from $6-30 depending on type of climbing. Guided outdoor climb fees depend on the extent of climb, number of persons, etc. Call for specifics.

Website: www.asheville.com/climbmax/

Rock Hounding

The mountains of Western North Carolina are one of the richest areas in the United States for gemstones and minerals. There are close to 40 different minerals that rock hounds look for in the mountains. Corundum, beryl, moonstone, garnet, olivine, quartz, opal, amethyst, jasper, ruby, sapphires, spinel, turquoise, chrysoprase and zircon are among the most sought-after. And gold is still found occasionally in some of the streams.

A very popular attraction are the gemstone mines, open to the public, where you may sift through buckets of dirt to discover any treasure. The buckets are usually enriched, so everyone is guaranteed a find. Lots of fun for the kids especially! Many of these roadside facilities are to be found in the Franklin area, about three hours west of Asheville.

A great place to see gems in Asheville is the **Colburn Gem and Mineral Museum** at Pack Place. (SEE Section Three, Chapter 2)

Also fairly close to Asheville is the **Museum of North Carolina Minerals** at milepost 331 on the Blue Ridge Parkway. (SEE Section Five, Chapter 1) In the Hendersonville area is the newly opened **Mineral & Lapidary Museum.** (SEE Section Four, Chapter 2) This museum is run by the Henderson County Gem & Mineral Society, a valuable source of information for those people interested in rock hounding in the mountains. The **Franklin Gem and Mineral Museum** in Franklin has interesting exhibits also of regional minerals and gemstones. (SEE Section Five, Chapter 2) Franklin itself has a number of gem shops, as well as the gemstone mines mentioned previously. Located to the east of Asheville is the **Emerald Village,** a fascinating attraction that has a museum, mine tours, and rock-hounding expeditions for those interested. (SEE Section Five, Chapter 2)

One of the most famous of the mines in our area is found in Canton, about 30 minutes west of Asheville. This is the **Old Pressley Sapphire Mine,** where the world's largest blue star sapphires were found. Flumes are available for washing ore provided by the mine. 240 Pressley Mines Rd., Canton, NC 28716; 648-6320.

Other Gem Mines and Mineral Centers in the Mountains

Franklin Area:

Cowee Mountain Ruby Mine: US 441, Franklin, 369-5271

Gold City Gem Mine: 9410 Sylva Rd., Franklin, 369-3905

Mason Mountain Mine and Cowee Gift Shop: 5315 Bryson City Rd., Franklin, 524-4570

Mason's Ruby and Sapphire Mine: 6961 Upper Burningtown Rd., Franklin, 369-9742

Rocky Face Gem Mine: 260 Sanderstown Rd., Franklin, 524-3148
Rose Creek Mine, Gift and Rock Shop: Sylva Rd., Franklin, 369-3905
Sheffield Mine: 385 Sheffield Farms Rd., Franklin, 369-8383
The Old Cardinal Gem Mine: 71 Rockhaven Dr., Franklin, 369-7534

Little Switzerland:
Blue Ridge Gemstone Mine: PO Box 327, Little Switzerland, 765-5264
Emerald Village: (SEE Section Five, Chapter 2), PO Box 98, Little Switzerland, 765-6483
Rio Doce Gem Mine: PO Box 296, Little Switzerland, 765-2099, www.riodoce.com
World of Gems: PO Box 249, Little Switzerland, 765-6832

The World's Largest Blue Star Sapphire

Located just a short drive west of Asheville, in Canton, is the Old Pressley Sapphire Mine. In 1986 and 1987, two blue sapphires were found there that were truly spectacular. Craig Peden and Steve Meyers, prospecting in the area of the mine, found one that was 1035 carats and was named the "Southern Star." At the time it was the world's largest. Around the same time, Bruce Camanitti found an even larger one. When it was cut in 1988, it was named the "Star of the Carolinas" and was an astounding 1445 carats! It is listed in the Guiness Book of World Records, and was cut by the master gem cutter, John Robinson.

Spruce Pine:
Gem Mountain Gemstone Mine: PO Box 488, Spruce Pine, 765-6130
Spruce Pine Gem & Gold Mine: 15090 Highway 226, at the Blue Ridge Parkway, Spruce Pine, 765-7981

Running

Since its founding in 1972, the Asheville Track Club has been instrumental in promoting running as a sport and providing a means for interested individuals to participate and improve as runners. Another object of the club has been the holding of races for all levels and types, from fun runs for young children to championship races such as the Shut-in-Ridge Trail Run. For kids aged 6 to 18, Asheville has one of the country's premier Junior Olympics Track and Field teams, the Asheville Lightning. For more information about USATF Junior Olympics and their summer track and field and fall cross-country programs, visit their website at www.ashevillelightning.org.

Asheville also has a great store devoted exclusively to runners. Jus Running, at 523 Merrimon Ave. (252-7867), can answer all of your questions about running in the WNC mountains as well as provide you with shoes, apparel, books, etc.

The Asheville Track Club (www.AshevilleTrackClub.org) has provided the directions for a 5.75-mile run that takes you through some of Asheville's most beautiful and historic areas, and if you are interested in entering a race, a list of established area races is also provided.

The Kimberly Avenue Special!

Begin in downtown Asheville at the YMCA parking lot on Woodfin Street, across from the Renaissance Hotel and beside the Best Western Central hotel.

From the lot, turn left on Woodfin Street to the first traffic light. (.2 miles)

Turn left at the light on College Street to Charlotte Street. (.3 miles)

Turn left on Charlotte Street; cross over I-240; past Fuddrucker's on your left; down the street to the historic Manor (a large turn-of-the-century structure, now apartments) on your right; turn left on tree-shaded Edwin Place just past the park. (1.1 miles)

Edwin Place becomes Kimberly Avenue. You will have the golf course on your right and can see the Grove Park Inn in the distance. Continue up Kimberly Avenue to the stop sign at Griffing Blvd.. (2.5 miles)

Turn right and loop the head of the rose garden in the center of Griffing. (2.9 miles)

Retrace your steps back to the YMCA. Going downhill may make the views of the Grove Park Inn more enjoyable! (5.75 miles)

The total run will entail 5.75 miles, but as it is an out-and-back route, the distance can be reduced to whatever length suits your fancy! Hills on this run are rather gentle, at least in comparison to the surrounding mountains! The route, which takes you up beautiful Kimberly Avenue with its grand homes, is one of the most popular with area walkers and runners.

Area Race Calendar

Month	Race name	Location	Distance
January	Observer 10-K & Marathon	Charlotte	10K/Marathon
February	Frostbite 5-Miler	Fletcher	5 miles
March	Reedy River Run	Greenville, SC	10 km.
April	Cooper River Bridge Run	Charleston, SC	10 km.
May	Biltmore Estate 15K Classic	Asheville	15 km
June	Rhododendron Run	Bakersville	10 km.
July	Bele Chere Road Race	Asheville	5 km.
August	Moonlight Run	Maggie Valley	8 km.
September	Ducky Derby Run	Asheville	5 km.
October	Thomas Wolfe Road Race	Asheville	8 km.
November	Shut-in-Ridge Trail Run	Asheville	17 miles
December	Reindeer Romp	Asheville	5 km.

Shuffleboard

Toms Park: Located on West Allen Street in Hendersonville, it is the site of state and national shuffleboard tournaments. For more information, call the Hendersonville Shuffleboard Club at 697-3016.

Hawksnest Golf & Ski Resort: Skiing and tubing. Highway 105 South between Boone and Banner Elk; (800) 822-4295. www.hawksnest-resort.com

Ski Slopes

The slopes of the Western North Carolina mountains provide a wide variety of trails, from easy beginner to expert. The views are breathtaking and the facilities modern. Many of the resorts feature their own snow making equipment. Most people don't associate the south with skiing, but the Western North Carolina mountains, with their higher elevations and colder winters, do have excellent skiing. Wolf Laurel Ski Resort is the closest to Asheville, a 30-minute drive north on Highway 19/23. Ski Country Sports (254-2771), located at 960 Merrimon Avenue in Asheville, is an excellent resource for skiing and snowboarding equipment.

Appalachian Ski Mountain: Open since 1962. Nine slopes, two quad chairlifts, one double chairlift, outdoor ice skating. Excellent ski school and a large number of family-oriented programs. 940 Ski Mountain Rd., Blowing Rock; 295-7828, (800) 322-2373. www.appskimtn.com

Cataloochee Ski Area: Cataloochee has nine slopes and trails with a 740-foot vertical drop. Full-service rental shop and PSIA ski school. Cataloochee is the oldest ski resort in North Carolina. Route 1, Maggie Valley; 926-0285, (800) 768-0285. www.cataloochee.com

Sapphire Valley Ski Area: Excellent conditions for beginner and intermediate skiing and snowboarding. 4350 Hwy. 64 West, Sapphire; 743-1164.

Scaly Mountain Ski Area: Four slopes, snow tubing only. NC Highway 106, Dillard Road, Scaly Mountain; 526-3737.

Ski Beech: Beech Mountain is the highest ski area in Eastern North America. Peak elevation of 5,506 feet; 4,675-foot base elevation. Lifts: one high-speed quad, six doubles, one J-bar and one rope tow. 1007 Beech Mountain Prkwy., Beech Mountain; 387-2011, (800) 438-2093. www.skibeech.com

Sugar Mountain Resort and Ski Area: A full-service alpine snow ski area. Features a 1,200-foot vertical drop, 18 slopes and trails, eight lifts, and a longest run of 1½ miles. 1009 Sugar Mountain Drive, Banner Elk; 898-4521, (800) SUGARMT. www.skisugar.com

Wolf Laurel Ski Resort: Skiing serviced by quad-chair; 14 runs with 100 percent snowmaking, night skiing, expanded lounge. Ski slopes closest to Asheville and Hendersonville. Route 3, Wolf Laurel Rd., Mars Hill; 689-4111, (800) 817-4111. www.skiwolflaurel.com

Skateboarding

Asheville Food Lion Skateboard Park: A 17,000 sq.ft. facility including bowls, quarter pipes, hips, boxes, ledges, handrails and a pyramid. Open daily until dark. Small fee. Corner of Cherry and Flynn Sts.; 259-5800.

Zero Gravity Skateboard: 12,000 sq.ft. indoor skate park near Brevard. Spine mini-ramp, fun boxes, mini-three quarter bowl, bank ramps and more. 1800 Old Hendersonville Hwy., Brevard; 862-6700. www.zerogravitypark.com

Swimming
Asheville

Buncombe County Parks and Recreation Services offers six outdoor parks located in all areas of Buncombe County. The pools are open in June, July and the early part of August. The water is heated in every pool and admission is $3 per person. Visit the Buncombe County website, www.buncombecounty.org, for more information and maps to the pools.

Cane Creek Pool (Southern Buncombe): 590 Lower Brush Creek Rd., Fletcher
Erwin Community Pool (Western Buncombe): 55 Lees Creek Rd., Asheville
Hominy Valley Park Pool (Western Buncombe): 25 Twin Lakes Rd., Candler
North Buncombe Park Pool (Northern Buncombe): 82 Clarks Chapel Rd., Weaverville
Owen Pool (Eastern Buncombe): 117 Stone Dr., Swannanoa

Hendersonville

The Hendersonville YMCA at 810 West Sixth Ave. (692-5774) offers swimming at $5 per session. The best outdoor pool is the Patton Pool located in Patton Park on Highway 25 in Hendersonville. There is a $3 fee to swim here. If lake swimming is what you want, drive to Lake Lure and try the public beach. This is a gorgeous lake and worth the 45-minute drive. (SEE Section Five, Chapter 1) A couple of unique river swimming spots are Mills River Recreation Area (SEE Section Four, Chapter 7) and Sliding Rock (SEE Section Five, Chapter 1 Pisgah National Forest), both in the Pisgah National Forest.

Tennis

For tennis players, both Asheville and Hendersonville have a number of city parks that have tennis courts available. The Asheville Parks and Recreation Department sponsors an Open Tennis Championship Tournament for Adult and Junior divisions. Sanctioned by USTA, STA and NCTA, this popular tournament is held in July at the Aston Park Tennis Center. Information about the tournament can be obtained by calling the Parks and Recreation Department, 259-5800.

Asheville

Aston Park Tennis Center: 336 Hilliard Ave. at South French Broad Ave., 255-5193. An excellent tennis complex, with twelve lighted clay courts, picnic shelter, playground, club house, racket stringing service, concession and ministore. Ball machines. Private or semiprivate lessons available. Open April 15 to December 15, 9 a.m.-9 p.m. Monday-Thursday, 9 a.m.-7 p.m. Friday-Sunday. Reservations requested.
Weaver Park: Merrimon Avenue: 258-2453. Very easy to find North Asheville park near UNC-Asheville. Park and tennis courts will be on the right. (SEE Section Three, Chapter 9 Asheville Parks) No reservations needed—first come, first served basis.

Hendersonville/Flat Rock

(SEE also Section Four, Chapter 7: Hendersonville Area Parks)

Jackson Park: 4th Ave. East, 697-4888. Four lighted tennis courts in the best Hendersonville park.

Whitewater Rafting, Canoeing & Kayaking

The rivers of Western North Carolina and the Tennessee border offer Class I through Class IV rapids for whitewater rafting. Major rafting rivers are the French Broad, Nolichucky, Nantahala, Ocoee, Chattooga and Green River. These six rivers in the North Carolina mountains are considered the best whitewater in the Southeast.

There are few better ways to experience the excitement of the mountains than a whitewater rafting trip, and Western North Carolina has it all, from peaceful gentle streams to big tumbling rivers that roar through the deepest gorges.

The most popular whitewater stream for professional and amateur alike is the Nantahala River in the Bryson City area. A class II and III stream, the Nantahala begins in the mountains of Macon County and flows northward through the beautiful Nantahala Gorge and on into Graham County where it joins the Little Tennessee River. The eight-mile run on the Nantahala takes about three hours. Be advised, though, on summer weekends the river can get very crowded.

There are a number of outfitters that provide rental equipment and guided raft trips on the area streams. The larger outfitters, like Nantahala Outdoor Center, provide guide services worldwide. Prices for a guided raft trip will vary from outfitter to outfitter and usually are higher on weekends. Plan to spend around $30 per person per float.

Basic gear requirements are a life jacket and protective foot wear such as river-runner sandals or booties. Be sure and wear quick-drying clothes!

Located north of Asheville in Woodfin on the French Broad River, the Ledges Whitewater Park is the closest whitewater section of the river for canoeing and kayaking without guided service. Recommended for experienced canoeists and kayakers only.... The Ledges playspots, of which there are several, begin to warm up at levels over 1,000 cfs, and rise to 3,500 cfs. The park is complete with movable holding "gates" that kayakers can paddle through to practice for slalom competition and to improve their dexterity and water skills. To get there from Asheville, take I-240 to 19-23 North (Exit 4) and continue six miles to the New Stock Road exit. Turn left off the exit ramp and drive 0.7 miles to left on Aiken Road, then first right onto Goldview Road. Follow Goldview Road to the river. Turn right onto NC 251. The Ledges Whitewater Park and Picnic Area will be on your right almost immediately. If you wish, you can continue north on NC 251 2.0 miles to the Alexander Bridge for put-in.

Stream Classifications

Class I: Easy. Moving water with a few riffles, small waves and few obstructions. Requires basic paddling knowledge.

Class II: Moderate. Easy rapids with up to three-foot waves and few obstructions. Requires intermediate skill level.

Class III: Difficult. High rapids and narrow channels. Requires intermediate skill level.

Class IV: Very difficult. Long difficult rapids, constricted channels and turbulent water. Requires experienced skill level.

Class V: Exceedingly difficult. Extremely difficult, long and often violent rapids. Requires high skill level.

Class VI: Utmost difficulty. Very dangerous and for experts only.

Outfitters

Asheville:

Southern Waterways: 521 Amboy Rd., Asheville, NC 28806; 232-1970, (800) 849-1970. Quiet-water canoe trips through Biltmore Estate property. Scenic, relaxing and fun. All ages. www.paddlewithus.com

Zippy Boat Works: Sweeten Creek Rd., 684-5107. Guided canoe trips down French Broad River.

Banner Elk:

Edge of the World Outfitters: (800) 789-3343. www.edgeoworld.com

Blowing Rock:

High Country Expeditions: (800) 262-9036. Nolichucky and Watauga Rivers. www.highcountryexpeditions.com

Boone:

Wahoo's Adventures: (800) 444-7238. Six convenient locations in the mountains, serving more than nine rivers.

Bryson City-Nantahala River:

Endless River Adventures: Whitewater rafting on the Nantahala and Ocoee Rivers. (800) 224-7238. www.endlessrivers.com

Nantahala Outdoor Center: 13077 U.S. Hwy. 19 West, Bryson City, NC 28713. (800) 232-7238. The Southeast's most experienced outfitter since 1972. All classes of whitewater, complete range of guided trips. Located on Nantahala River. www.noc.com

Rolling Thunder River Company: Hwy. 19 South, 74 West, Bryson City, NC 28713; (800) 408-7238. Nantahala and Ocoee guided trips.

Carolina Outfitters: U.S. Hwy. 19W, Bryson City, NC 28713; (800) 468-7238. www.carolinaoutfitters.com

Rafting in the Smokies: Since 1978, whitewater rafting on the Ocoee, Nantahala, and Big Pigeon Rivers. (800) 776-7238. www.rollingthunderriverco.com

USA Raft: Guided trips on French Broad River, Nantahala, Pigeon and Nolichucky rivers. More than 15 years in business. (800) 872-7238. www.usaraft.com/nantahala.htm

Wildwater Rafting: A major outfitter for more than 26 years. Whitewater rafting adventures on the Chattooga, Pigeon, Nantahala and Ocoee rivers for all ages and skill levels. (800) 451-9972. www.wildwaterrafting.com

Hot Springs-French Broad River:

Blue Ridge Rafting: Professional guides in every raft. Class I to Class IV, including trips with beach buffets served riverside, and overnight camping. Creekside Inn & Mountain Cottage rentals available. Just 35 miles north of Asheville. Creekside Inn, Bridge St., Hot Springs, NC 28743; 622-3544, (800) 303-7238. www.blueridgerafting.com

Marshall-French Broad River:

French Broad Rafting Company: 1 Thomas Branch Rd., Marshall, NC 28753; (800) 842-3189. French Broad river trips. Canoes, funyaks and guided rafts. 45 minutes from Asheville. www.frenchbroadrafting.com

USA Raft: (800) 872-7238. www.usaraft.com/frenchbroad.htm

Dillsboro:

Tuckaseegee Outfitters: Whitewater float trips on the Tuckaseegee river. Rafts, funyaks, ducks, and tubes available for self-guided float trips. Fun for the entire family. Hwy. 74 and 441 at Barkers Creek (P.O. Box 1201), Dillsboro, NC 28725; (800) 539-5683. www.tuckfloat.com

Rosman:

Headwaters Outfitters Inc.: Hwy. 64 & 215, Rosman, NC 28772; 877-3106. Canoe rental and sales; kayak and tubing, April-October. www.headwatersoutfitters.com

Chapter Seventeen
Popular Indoor Sports

Roller Skating

Skate-A-Round USA: 310 Weaverville Rd., Weaverville; 645-4715

Tarwheels Skateway: 978 Hwy. 70, Swannanoa. (I-240 East to I-40 East, V.A. Hospital Exit, U.S. 70 East—if you reach Black Mountain, you've gone too far. Rink will be on the left.) Rink also available for parties, skating classes, and hockey leagues.

Bowling Alleys

All of the area bowling alleys recommend that you call ahead to check lane availability.

AMF Star Lanes: 491 Kenilworth Rd. (off Tunnel Rd. near Asheville Mall), 254-6161. Monday noon-11 p.m., Tuesday-Thursday 9 a.m.-11 p.m., Friday-Saturday 9 a.m.-2 a.m., Sunday 9 a.m.-11 p.m.

Sky-Lanes: 1477 Patton Ave. (West Asheville), 252-2269. Monday-Thursday 9 a.m.-11 p.m., Friday-Saturday 9 a.m.-2 a.m., Sunday 1:00-11 p.m.

Tarheel Lanes Bowling Center: 3275 Asheville Highway (North Hendersonville on Hwy. 25), 253-2695. Sunday-Monday 11 a.m.-11 p.m., Tuesday and Thursday 9 a.m.-11 p.m., Wednesday 10 a.m.-11 p.m., Friday 11 a.m.-midnight, Saturday 10 a.m.-midnight.

Section Three
Asheville, All-America City

Chapter One
About Asheville

L ocated at the hub of the Great Smoky and Blue Ridge mountains, 2,216 feet above sea level on the Asheville Plateau, Asheville is the largest city in Western North Carolina and the tenth largest municipality in the state, covering an area of 40.99 square miles. Asheville's population is estimated at approximately 70,000 and the city is located at the confluence of the French Broad and Swannanoa rivers in a river-formed valley that runs 18 miles north and south. Chartered in 1797 and named after Samuel Ashe, a former governor of North Carolina, Asheville attracts millions of visitors and tourists each year who come for the timeless natural beauty, the crisp highland air, the magnificent mountains and cosmopolitan vibrant hospitality the city offers. Recent noteworthy rankings by national magazines and travel organizations include: Money Magazine (1998) 10th best small southern city in which to live, American Style Magazine (2000) 6th among top 25 Arts Destinations, Money Magazine (2000) one of the best places to retire. Places Rated Almanac (2000) 8th Best Small Metro Area, Policom (2000) 71st out of 315 for Overall Economy, Demographics (2000) 26th out of 276 metros for Small Business Vitality and Industry Standard (2001) one of the five Top Places for Wired Companies Who Want To Run a Small Business From Paradise.

Surrounded by thousands of acres of majestic mountains, plateaus, rolling valleys and mystical coves, Asheville is a city not easily forgotten once visited. With its winding hilly streets graced by architectural gems from the past, Asheville has come to be known as the "Paris of the South." Every section of this enchanting city is blessed with unique and irreplaceable buildings that few cities in America can match. From the awesomely majestic Biltmore House to the Art Deco masterpiece S&W Building to the stately rock-hewn beauty of the Grove Park Inn, Asheville is overflowing with architectural treasures. More than 170 historic buildings have been preserved, some of which were designed by world-famous architects Richard S. Smith, Douglas Ellington, Richard M. Hunt and Rafael Guastavino. Couple this with all of the cultural, business and entertainment possibilities and you have an extraordinary city to experience.

A major tourist destination with more than 5,000,000 visitors annually, Asheville is also known for its varied and rich arts and crafts communities. Hundreds of galleries, craft shops, and artisans studios are to be found here. Asheville has become an important center for traditional Appalachian as well as contemporary crafts and the variety and quality of the craft galleries and the many craft exhibits and shows attest to this fact.

Located only minutes from national forests and green valleys, outdoor recreation opportunities abound. White-water rafting, golf, hiking, fishing, horseback riding, llama trekking, rock climbing, camping and ballooning are just a few of the choices.

As you would expect, Asheville is rich in museums, nature centers, historic sites and other attractions for the visitor. During your stay, you may wish to attend a performance of the Civic Ballet, the Asheville Symphony Orchestra or one of the many local theatre companies. A wonderful way to spend a summer evening is to take in a game at historic McCormick Field, where Babe Ruth once played baseball. Throughout the year Asheville celebrates with many festivals, from the renowned fairs of the Southern Highland Handicraft guild to the world famous street festival, Bele Chere.

Asheville is also a major medical center. Modern hospitals and numerous specialized medical facilities, as well as a large resident population of doctors and medical professionals combine to make Asheville the regional center for health care.

The largest city in Western North Carolina, Asheville is the regional center for manufacturing, transportation, banking and professional services and shopping. A superb book sponsored by the Asheville Area Chamber of Commerce is *Asheville, A View From the Top,* which gives an in-depth look at this important corporate dimension. It is available at the Asheville Visitor Center and area bookstores.

Asheville has also in recent years experienced a downtown revitalization that is establishing it as Western North Carolina's entertainment mecca. Nightclubs, cafes, galleries, theatres, coffeehouses, pubs and superb restaurants all add to the mix that now creates one of the most exciting and cosmopolitan downtown districts in the South.

Voted an All-America City in 1997 by the National Civic League, Asheville was one of only ten U.S. cities to receive this prestigious award. The award is given only to those cities that are judged truly superior for collaborative problem-solving among the public, private and nonprofit sectors. Citizen participation, community leadership, government performance, volunteerism and philanthropy, intergroup relations, civic education, community information sharing, capacity for cooperation and consensus building, community vision and pride, and regional cooperation are the criteria by which the candidate cities are judged.

History

Surrounded by towering mountains, Asheville was a small crossroads town when it was founded by pioneer town planner John Burton in 1792. Known as Morristown during the early years, the city was also called Buncombe Courthouse until 1797, when it was incorporated and named Asheville in honor of North Carolina governor Samuel Ashe.

Buncombe attained county status in 1792 and was named for Revolutionary War hero Col. Edward Buncombe. Growth was slow until 1880, when the first railroad system was constructed. This first steam train changed Asheville forever, bringing in the outside world. This small mountain settlement went from a population of 2,616 to 10,328 in just ten years. A trickle of summer visitors that had journeyed to Asheville for half a century turned into a torrent. By 1886, an estimated 30,000 "summer people" visited the city annually. In 1885, the building of the first Battery Park Hotel was noted as the beginning of a great period of expansion for Asheville. Near the turn of the century, George Vanderbilt also began construction of the now world famous Biltmore House.

The greatest boom period in Asheville's history came during the 1920s with the construction of many new buildings throughout downtown, including the Grove Arcade, City Hall, Buncombe County Courthouse, Flat Iron Building and others. Many Art Deco buildings were also constructed in this period, the best example being the S&W Cafeteria building.

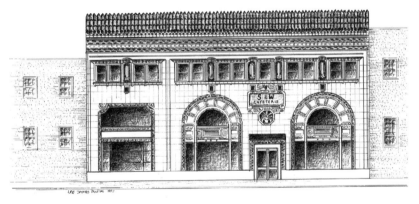

The S&W Cafeteria, 56 Patton Avenue, Asheville

Today, Asheville is experiencing another period of tremendous growth and revitalization. The downtown district, with its wealth of historic buildings, is one of the most vibrant city centers in the South. Major, ecologically sound riverfront development is also occurring along the French Broad River, with parks, greenways and cultural centers emerging. Asheville continues to attract people from around the world as an exciting vacation destination, and as a wonderful and beautiful place to live.

Downtown Neighborhoods

As a visitor to Asheville, it will be helpful to know that the downtown district is divided into a number of diverse neighborhoods, each with its own unique history and ambience. One of the very best ways to experience these neighborhoods is to walk the Asheville Urban Trail. This short self-guided walking tour visits all four of the neighborhoods discussed below, with stations and thematic markers along the way. For more information about this extraordinary way to trace the footsteps of Asheville's historic past, see Section Three, Chapter 5, The Asheville Urban Trail.

For those interested in historic architecture, see Section Three, Chapter 4, Historic Asheville. Each of Asheville's official historic districts are presented and the most important and historic buildings are highlighted. For some districts, self-guided tours are presented.

1. **Battery Hill Neighborhood:** This neighborhood is crowned by the magnificent Basilica of St. Lawrence, D.M., the former Battery Park Hotel and the historic Grove Arcade. This area contains some of Asheville's best shopping and dining. Be sure to take a stroll down quaint Wall Street and visit some of its interesting and unusual stores. Farther down on Haywood Street is the Asheville Civic Center and the main library.

2. **Lexington Park Neighborhood:** This is Asheville's antique shop district. If you are at all interested in antiques, a visit to this district is a must. There you will also find trendy boutiques, the oldest store in town, coffeehouses, galleries and nightclubs.

3. **Pack Square Neighborhood:** The heart of Asheville is Pack Square, a wonderful space surrounded by stunning architecture, from Art Deco to contemporary. This is a district that overflows with nightlife from the many art galleries, pubs, coffeehouse, theatres and restaurants. Asheville's Pack Place and YMI Center for African-American Culture are also found here.

4. **Thomas Wolfe Plaza Neighborhood:** Crowned by the historic home of author Thomas Wolfe, the Thomas Wolfe Plaza area is home to the Asheville Community Theatre, historic churches, craft shops and art galleries.

In addition to the districts already mentioned, there are some others of special interest to visitors. You will want to be sure and visit Biltmore Village, located just outside the entrance to the Biltmore Estate. There you will find unique and enchanting gift shops, art and craft galleries, and specialty stores, including Chelsea's Village Cafe and Tea Room, where lunch begins at 11:30 a.m. and their quintessentially English afternoon tea begins at 3:30 p.m.

Four other districts that have distinctive and historically important architecture in abundance are Montford, Chestnut Hill, Albermarle Park and the Grove Park areas. All of these neighborhoods, including Biltmore Village, are presented in depth in Section Three, Chapter 4 Historic Asheville.

Asheville Trolley Tours

Asheville's only professionally narrated city tour, on restored vintage touring trolleys. Boarding passes allow you to get off at city attractions, shops and points of interest and reboard at a later time on another trolley. Major stops are the Asheville Visitor Center, the Grove Park Inn Resort & Spa, Biltmore Village and Pack Square. (888)-667-3600, www.ashevilletrolleytours.com.

Biltmore Village Shops, Asheville

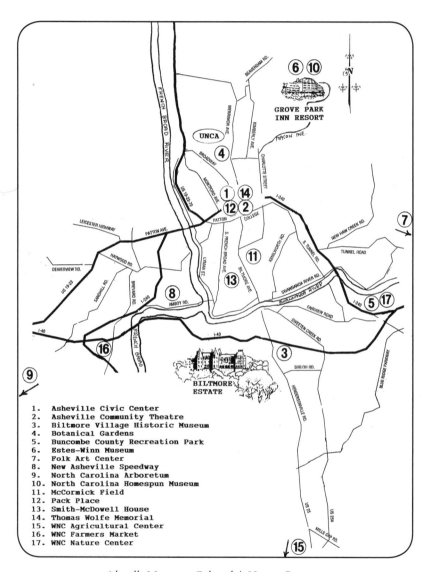

1. Asheville Civic Center
2. Asheville Community Theatre
3. Biltmore Village Historic Museum
4. Botanical Gardens
5. Buncombe County Recreation Park
6. Estes-Winn Museum
7. Folk Art Center
8. New Asheville Speedway
9. North Carolina Arboretum
10. North Carolina Homespun Museum
11. McCormick Field
12. Pack Place
13. Smith-McDowell House
14. Thomas Wolfe Memorial
15. WNC Agricultural Center
16. WNC Farmers Market
17. WNC Nature Center

Asheville Museums, Cultural & Nature Centers

Chapter Two
Museums, Cultural & Nature Centers

This chapter is devoted to the major cultural attractions and centers that Asheville has to offer. Those included here are very important to the life of Asheville as a city and each attracts thousands of visitors each year. The range of attractions is wide, from world-class crafts to baseball games at a park where Babe Ruth once swung a bat. Each is uniquely different and the one criteria that insured placement in this guidebook is a high level of excellence and professionalism.

Asheville Civic Center

Located on Haywood Street near the Asheville Area Visitor Center, the Asheville Civic Center is the major entertainment facility for Western North Carolina. It includes an Exhibition Hall on the bottom level, an Arena Floor immediately above, and a third level complex which includes a glass-enclosed concourse. The Civic Center is home to the Thomas Wolfe Auditorium, the venue for many dramas, music performances, pageants, conventions, and festivals. Equipped with excellent acoustic and lighting systems, it is also the performance space for the Asheville Symphony Orchestra.

The Asheville Civic Center, 87 Haywood St., Asheville

The building itself contains historic elements from the previous Art Deco auditorium. The lobby of the current structure features Art Deco terrazzo floors and gilded plaster molding and anthemia-ornamented columns.

Location: Downtown Asheville
Address: 87 Haywood St., Asheville, NC 28801
Telephone: 259-5736
FAX: 259-5777
Website: www.ci.asheville.nc.us
Hours: Business office open Monday-Friday 8:30 a.m.-5 p.m.; ticket office open Monday-Friday 10 a.m.-5:30 p.m., Saturday 10 a.m.-1 p.m.
Of Note: Listed in the National Register of Historic Places. Ice skating available on the Asheville Smoke rink in season (call for hours).
Nearby: Basilica of St. Lawrence, D.M.
Directions: Walking from Pack Square, take Patton Avenue to Pritchard Park. Turn right onto Haywood Street.

Asheville Community Theatre (ACT)

For more than 50 years, the Asheville Community Theatre has presented productions that have ranged from classics to contemporary comedies. The theater's Heston Auditorium (named after Charlton Heston and his wife, actress Lydia Clark, who served as artistic co-directors in 1947) is designed to provide an intimate theatre setting; the back row is only 55 feet from the stage edge. Air-conditioned and equipped with a Bose sound enhancement system, ACT is also home to youth acting classes, special student matinees and the Autumn Players outreach program, produced by, for and about senior citizens.

Asheville Community Theatre (ACT), 35 Walnut Street, Asheville

Location: Downtown Asheville
Address: 35 Walnut St., Asheville, NC 28801
Telephone: 253-4931 main, 254-1320 tickets, 252-4723 business office
FAX: 252-4723
Website: www.ashevilletheatre.org
Hours: Business hours Monday-Friday 10 a.m.-4 p.m.
Of Note: Call 253-4931 to find out about upcoming shows.
Nearby: Thomas Wolfe Memorial
Directions: From I-240 heading east, take exit 5A Merrimon Avenue. Go straight up the hill through the light onto Market Street. Make first left, in front of Magnolia's Grill and Bar. I-240 heading west, left off exit ramp. Left at light onto Woodfin Street. Right on Market Street. First left on Walnut Street.

Asheville's Fun Depot

One of Asheville's newest attractions, designed with kids in mind. Facilities include state-of-the-art arcade gallery, 18-hole indoor mini-golf, outdoor go-kart track, multi-level laser tag, soft play area, climbing wall, batting cages and the Depot Diner.

Location: Southeast Asheville just off Interstate 1-40 at exit 5
Address: 7 Roberts Road, Asheville, NC 28803
Telephone: 277-2386, (866) 303-4386
Website: www.AshevillesFunDepot.com
Hours: 10:00 a.m.-10:00 p.m. Monday-Friday
            9:00 a.m.-10:00 p.m. Saturday
            Closed Sunday
Fees: Call for prices
Of Note: Restaurant on premises
Directions: Take exit 5 off of Interstate 1-40, turn left at bottom of the ramp onto Sweeten Creek Road. Turn left onto Roberts Road.

Biltmore Village Historic Museum

Founded in 1989, the Biltmore Village Historic Museum houses a large and fascinating collection of photographs and artifacts associated with the early development of Biltmore Village and the Biltmore Estate. The purpose of the museum is to share information about the Village through photographs, maps, antique post cards and artifacts. On display are original maps, copies of original drawings for the Biltmore Village cottages and an extensive collection of Biltmore carvings by students of the estate. Handmade silver of W.W. Doge, architect and silversmith, highlights the museum's collection.

Location: Biltmore Village
Address: 7 Biltmore Plaza, Asheville, NC 28803
Telephone: 274-9707

Website: www.biltmorevillage.com
Hours: Monday-Saturday 1-4:30 p.m., April through December. Limited hours January through March. Call first.
Fees: None
Allow: 1½ hours to see museum
Of Note: Building listed in the National Register of Historic Places
Nearby: Biltmore Estate
Directions: From Pack Square, take Biltmore Avenue south to Biltmore Village. Turn left onto Brook Street and then left onto Biltmore Plaza.

Botanical Gardens at Asheville

The Botanical Gardens at Asheville are located on a ten-acre site next to the campus of the University of North Carolina at Asheville. The Gardens were organized in 1960 by the Asheville Garden Club and were designed by Doan Ogden, a nationally known landscape architect. They were created to preserve and display the native plants and flowers of the Southern Appalachian Mountains and are noted for both their landscaping and great variety of plant life present on the grounds.

The gardens are open year round and are intertwined with peaceful walking trails through varied habitats. There is a Botany Center, library and gift shop.

Location: North Asheville
Address: 151 W.T. Weaver Blvd., Asheville NC 28804
Telephone: 252-5190

Botanical Gardens at Asheville, 151 W.T. Weaver Boulevard, Asheville

Hours:	Open year round, dawn to dusk
Fees:	None
Allow:	About two hours
Of Note:	April is a special time in the gardens when all of the native plants and shrubs are in bloom.
Nearby:	The University of North Carolina at Asheville
Directions:	From I-240 take Exit 5A Merrimon Avenue. Go north to W.T. Weaver Boulevard and turn left.

Estes-Winn Memorial Automobile Museum

Located in the Homespun Shops area next to the Grove Park Inn Resort is the Estes-Winn Memorial Automobile Museum. More than twenty restored cars including a 1926 Cadillac, a 1927 La Salle convertible and a 1922 La France fire engine now fill this building. Greeting you at the door is a 1913 Model T much like the ones Henry Ford and Thomas Edison traveled to Asheville in during their stays at the Grove Park Inn. A visit to the Estes-Winn Museum is to step into the past for a few hours.

Location:	North Asheville, behind Grove Park Inn in Homespun Shops
Address:	111 Grovewood Rd., Asheville, NC 28804
Telephone:	253-7651
Website:	www.grovewood.com
Hours:	February-March: 10 a.m.-5 p.m. Friday and Saturday; April-December: 10 a.m.-5 p.m. Monday-Saturday and 1:00-5 p.m. Sunday

Estes-Winn Memorial Automobile Museum, 111 Grovewood Road, Asheville

Fees: Donations accepted for Cancer Society
Allow: One hour
Of Note: Historic Biltmore Industries Cottage, listed in National Register of Historic Places. Owned by Grovewood Gallery
Nearby: Grove Park Inn Resort, North Carolina Homespun Museum
Directions: From I-240 take Exit 5B. North on Charlotte Street. Right on Macon Avenue to Grove Park Inn. Museum is in Homespun Shops area behind the inn, opposite the Vanderbilt wing garage.

Folk Art Center of the Southern Highland Craft Guild

Opened in 1980 on the 50th anniversary of the Southern Highland Craft Guild (SHCG), the Folk Art Center is home to Allanstand Craft Shop, one of Appalachia's oldest and best-known craft shops. Allanstand sells the work of more than 200 members of the SHCG. Both the finest in traditional mountain crafts of the region as well as the very best in contemporary American crafts are available for the discriminating visitor.

The center's upper level contains the museum space of the SHCG as well as the offices and the center's comprehensive craft library. The changing exhibition schedule showcases the works of SHCG members in addition to specially selected traveling exhibitions reflecting the traditions of the Southern Highlands. If crafts are of interest to you, a visit to the Folk Art Center is a must. Set in a forested glen just off the Blue Ridge Parkway, this special Asheville attraction is for young and old alike.

The Folk Art Center, off the Blue Ridge Parkway at milepost 382

Location:	Milepost 382 just east of Asheville on the Blue Ridge Parkway
Address:	P.O. Box 9545, Asheville, NC 28815
Telephone:	298-7928
FAX:	298-7962
Website:	www.southernhighlandguild.com
Hours:	Open daily 9 a.m.-5 p.m. except Thanksgiving, Christmas, and New Year's Day. Call to confirm hours because the facilities are closed periodically for exhibition changes and inventory.
Fees:	None
Allow:	Two hours
Directions:	Located on the Blue Ridge Parkway just east of Asheville at milepost 382. Access the parkway at Highway 74A (I-240, Exit 9) and head north.

The Grove Arcade Public Market

The Grove Arcade was the dream of E.W. Grove, a self-made millionaire who moved to Asheville in the early 1900s, where he conceived of the Arcade as "the most elegant building in America," and as a new type of retail center. When the Arcade opened in 1929, it quickly became home to a collection of local shops and services. For 13 years, the Arcade was the major commercial and civic center in Western North Carolina. The Federal Government took over the building in 1942, following America's entry into World War II, evicting all retail and office tenants. Following the war's end, the Arcade continued under Federal ownership. In 1992 a group of community leaders and concerned citizens formed the Grove Arcade Public Market Foundation, a non-profit organization. In that same year, the Federal Government announced plans to build a new facility. Three years later it was completed and in 1997 the City of Asheville acquired title to the Grove Arcade under the National Monument Act. The U.S. General Services Administration formally gave the building to the City of Asheville at no cost, and a 198-year lease was promptly signed with the Foundation at $1.00 per year. The revitalized Grove Arcade now features over 50 specialty stores, restaurants, offices and apartments and is open to the public daily. Check out the great stone griffins that guard the north entrance! The Arcade is located just west of Haywood Street and the Civic Center, an easy walk 10-minute from Pack Square. Grove Arcade Public Market Foundation, 252-7799, www.grovearcade.com

McCormick Field

Opened in 1924, McCormick Field is one of the oldest operating minor-league baseball parks in North America. A 1992 remodeling replaced the field's rickety wooden grandstand with one of steel and brick and expanded the concession area. Despite the facelift, the field retained its signature short right field, a scant 300 feet down the line from home plate. As a result of remodeling, though, the wall is now an imposing 35 feet high. The entire outfield wall is surrounded by tall, verdant

trees, and during the summer the smell of honeysuckle is heavy throughout the park. Scenes from
the movie "Bull Durham" were filmed at the park.

McCormick Field is home to the Asheville
Tourists, a Class A farm team of the Colorado
Rockies. Ty Cobb, Jackie Rob-
inson and the immortal Babe
Ruth all played at McCormick
Field. The field has a well-
stocked souvenir shop and
you can also purchase a bottle
of the team's private label
wine, Championship White.
Several food items at the concession stand are noteworthy,
especially the grilled chicken
sandwich and the tangy chili
dogs. Check local listings for

*Historic McCormick
Field, opened in 1924
and remodeled in 1992,
can be seen in the film
"Bull Durham."*

the Asheville Tourists home game schedule. Local sporting goods stores usually
have schedules available during the baseball season.

Location: Downtown Asheville
Address: Asheville Tourists, P.O. Box 1556, Asheville, NC 28802; McCormick
Field, 30 Buchanan Pl., Asheville, NC 28802
Telephone: 258-0428
FAX: 258-0320
Website: www.theashevilletourists.com
Hours: Most games are played at night, starting at 7:05 p.m. (Schedules
available at ticket window and souvenir store). Sunday games begin
at 5:05 p.m.
Fees: Box seats $7 adults, $5 children and seniors
Allow: Three hours for game
Of Note: Babe Ruth, Ty Cobb, and Jackie Robinson played here.
Directions: Take I-240 to Exit 5B Charlotte Street. Go south on Charlotte
Street to McCormick Place.

North Carolina Arboretum

Established in 1986 as an interinstitutional facility of the University of North
Carolina, the Arboretum is located within the 6,300-acre Bent Creek Experi-
mental Forest and is surrounded by the 480,000-acre Pisgah National Forest.
The 426-acre site is nestled in one of the most beautiful natural settings in the
Southeast. The Arboretum has wonderful varied gardens, walking trails and
natural habitats.

North Carolina Arboretum, 100 Frederick Law Olmsted Way, Asheville

The Arboretum focuses on education, economic development, research, conservation, and garden demonstration with respect to landscape architecture and plant sciences. It is becoming the major state-supported attraction in Western North Carolina. A wide variety of classes and workshops are taught by the garden's staff and other plant experts. Educational programs target all ages and range from bonsai demonstrations to nature walks.

Location:	Southwest of Asheville
Address:	100 Frederick Law Olmsted Way, Asheville NC 28806
Telephone:	665-2492
FAX:	665-2371
Website:	www.ncarboretum.org
Hours:	Daily from 7 a.m.-9 p.m. (daylight savings time) and 8 a.m.-9 p.m. (Eastern Standard Time)
Fees:	None
Tips:	Beautiful anytime of year, but spring is especially spectacular
Allow:	Three hours
Directions:	From the Blue Ridge Parkway: N.C. 191 exit (Milepost 393.6). On the exit ramp, the entrance is on the left. From I-40: Exit 40 (Farmers Market). 191 south, follow signs.

North Carolina Homespun Museum

The North Carolina Homespun Museum is located in the Homespun Shops section next to Grove Park Inn Resort. Exhibits and artifacts on display portray the history of Biltmore Industries' hand weaving operation from 1901 to 1980. The museum houses storyboards, weaving examples and a major collection of mountain crafts. Weaving demonstrations are held on a regular basis.

Location:	Behind the Grove Park Inn in the Homespun Shops
Address:	111 Grovewood Road, Asheville NC 28804
Telephone:	253-7651
Hours:	April to December 10 a.m.-5 p.m. Monday-Saturday, 1-5 p.m. Sunday; January to May 10 a.m.-5 p.m. Friday and Saturday only.
Fees:	None
Allow:	One hour
Of Note:	Historic Biltmore Industries Cottage; listed in the National Register of Historic Places
Nearby:	Grove Park Inn Resort, Estes Winn Memorial Automobile Museum.
Directions:	Exit 5B of I-240. Charlotte Street ½ mile north. Right on Macon Avenue. Museum is located behind the Grove Park Inn opposite the Vanderbilt wing parking garage.

Pack Place Education, Arts & Science Center

Located in the heart of downtown Asheville on Pack Square, the Pack Place Education, Arts & Science Center is a marvelous combination of science, arts, culture and entertainment all under one roof. This 92,000 square-foot complex boasts museums, performance spaces, courtyards, exhibition and lobby galleries, as well as a permanent exhibit "Here is the Square ..." which traces the story of Asheville from its earliest days.

Location:	Downtown Asheville
Address:	2 South Pack Square, Asheville, NC 28801
Telephone:	Pack Place: 257-4500
	Asheville Art Museum: 253-3227
	Colburn Gem & Mineral Museum: 254-7162
	Diana Wortham Theatre: 257-4530 (tickets), 257-4512 (office)
	The Health Adventure: 254-6373
	YMI Cultural Center: 252-4614
FAX:	Pack Place: 251-5652
	Asheville Art Museum: 257-4503
	Colburn Gem & Mineral Museum: 251-5652
	Diana Wortham Theatre: 251-5652
	The Health Adventure: 257-4521
	YMI Cultural Center: 257-4539
Websites:	Main: www.main.nc.us/packplace/
	Asheville Art Museum: www.ashevilleart.org
	Colburn Gem & Mineral Museum: www.main.nc.us/colburn
	Diana Wortham Theatre: www.dwtheatre.com

Pack Place at Pack Square is many museums in one complex.

The Health Adventure: www.health-adventure.com

Hours: All Year: 10 a.m.-5 p.m. Tuesday-Saturday
June-October Only: 1:00-5 p.m. Sunday

Fees: $6.50 ticket accesses all museums and facilities; less expensive tickets available for each museum

Allow: Four hours to see all exhibits

Of Note: Building listed in the National Register of Historic Places

Directions: From I-240 take exit 5A Merrimon Avenue and follow signs for Highway 25 south for three blocks. Pack Place is located on Pack Square, directly in front of the Vance Monument.

Within Pack Place are the following facilities:

Asheville Art Museum

Enter a world of 20th Century American art set within the elegance of a restored 1926 structure of Italian Renaissance design. The museum's permanent collection features America's impressionists, regionalist and contemporary abstract artists. In the spacious galleries above, traveling exhibitions spotlight a broad range of artistic talent in a full spectrum of media and highlight nationally renowned collections of sculpture, paintings, traditional and contemporary crafts.

Colburn Gem & Mineral Museum

Explore the beauty of crystals, the magnificence of gemstones and the fantastic shapes and colors of minerals from around the world. The museum highlights the treasures that make North Carolina a geologic paradise, and regularly schedules exhibitions covering the full range of gem and mineral related subjects.

Diana Wortham Theatre

State-of-the-art acoustics and lighting, exquisitely detailed woodwork, plus a full-sized stage and orchestra pit, excellent sight lines, and accessibility for the handicapped make this a gem of a performance space for audiences, performers and technicians alike. The 500-seat theater is a dramatic and sophisticated setting that attracts a diverse range of local, regional and national companies, and touring shows.

The Health Adventure

Founded in 1968, The Health Adventure is one of the first health education centers in the country to let you explore the wonders of the body and mind with dozens of exhibits full of amazing health and science information and fascinating photography. At The Health Adventure, you'll find unique hands-on exhibits that make learning exciting and fun. The Health Adventure, and the Colburn Gem & Mineral Museum are two must-see places for kids!

YMI Cultural Center

The YMI Cultural Center is an enduring asset in the city of Asheville. Housed in a local landmark building that is listed on the National Register of Historic Places, the YMICC runs programs in cultural arts, community education and economic development. Commissioned by George Vanderbilt in 1892, this beautiful pebbledash and brick building of Tudor design was built by and to serve several hundred black craftsmen who helped construct the Biltmore Estate. Today, the newly refurbished center continues its tradition of community service. Its galleries feature exhibits, programs, classes and performance that present African-American art, culture and history at their best. The YMI Cultural Center is located behind Pack Place at Eagle and Market streets.

Vintage Mercury

Smith-McDowell House, 283 Victoria Road, Asheville

Smith-McDowell House

Delve into mountain history and enjoy the Victorian splendor of Asheville's oldest brick residence by visiting the Smith-McDowell House. This elegant structure, circa 1840, is now open to the public as a local history museum.

The Smith-McDowell House was built by James McConnell Smith as a private residence. A later owner, Charles Van Bergen, commissioned the famous Olmsted Brothers Firm to landscape the property. In 1974, Asheville-Buncombe Technical College purchased the structure, and leased it to the Western North Carolina Historical Association. Five years later, after restoration, it was opened as a museum.

One of Asheville's architectural jewels, the Smith-McDowell House presents a wonderful opportunity to experience the past in a truly elegant restoration. Especially delightful at Christmas time when all of the Victorian decorations are up. For an in-depth look at Smith-McDowell House's architecture and history, see Section Three, Chapter 4 Historic Asheville.

Location: South Asheville hospital district
Address: 283 Victoria Rd., Asheville, NC 28801
Telephone: 253-9231
FAX: 253-9231
Website: www.wnchistory.org
Hours: Open year-round. Tuesday-Saturday 10 a.m.-4 p.m.
November 1-April 30: Tuesday-Saturday 10 a.m.-2 p.m.
Fees: $5 adults, $3 children

Of Note: Local Historic Landmark and listed in the National Register of Historic Places. Great attraction anytime, but the Christmas season is special.
Allow: Two hours
Nearby: Biltmore Village, Biltmore Estate
Directions: From Pack Square take Biltmore Avenue south toward hospitals. Just before Memorial Mission Hospital, make a right onto Victoria Road.

Thomas Wolfe Memorial

Thomas Wolfe left an indelible mark on American letters. His mother's boardinghouse in Asheville, now the Thomas Wolfe Memorial, has become one of literature's most famous landmarks. In his epic autobiographical novel, *Look Homeward Angel,* Wolfe immortalized the rambling Victorian structure, originally called "Old Kentucky Home," as "Dixieland." A classic of American literature, *Look Homeward Angel* has never gone out of print since its publication in 1929, keeping interest in Wolfe alive and attracting visitors to the setting of this great novel.

The Memorial is administered by the North Carolina Department of Cultural Resources and is open to the visiting public. For an in-depth look at the architecture and history of the Thomas Wolfe House, see Section Three, Chapter 4 Historic Asheville.

The Visitor Center has an orientation program and exhibits that cover Wolfe's years in New York, Woodfin Street House and his father's monument workshop as well as other details of family history. There is also a gift shop with books, notecards, and prints, including prints and notecards of the illustration shown on the next page.

Location: Downtown Asheville
Address: 52 North Market St., Asheville, NC 28801
Telephone: 253-8304
FAX: 252-8171
Website: www.wolfememorial.com
Hours: April 1-October 31: Monday-Saturday 9 a.m.-5 p.m.; Sunday 1:00-5 p.m.
November 1-March 31: Tuesday-Saturday 10 a.m.-4 p.m.; Sunday 1:00-4 p.m.
Fees: $1.00 Adults, 50¢ Students
Allow: Two hours
Of Note: Local Historic Landmark, North Carolina Historic Site, National Register of Historic Places, National Historic Landmark. The Thomas Wolfe Festival is held every October 3rd with activities and events centered around Wolfe's life.
Nearby: Pack Place, First Baptist Church, Lexington Avenue antique district, Grove Park Inn.

Thomas Wolfe Memorial, 52 North Market Street, Asheville

Directions: I-240 heading east: Take Exit 5A straight up hill through light onto North Market Street.
I-240 heading west: turn left off exit, then left onto Woodfin Street and right onto North Market Street.

Western North Carolina Agricultural Center

One of the country's premier agricultural centers, the WNC Agricultural Center schedules over 50 events yearly, including 35 horse shows. The Center has a 65,000 square-foot fully enclosed show arena, with a 3,000-person seating capacity. There is also a 120' x 240' show ring, outdoor covered rings, and two outside, well lighted warm-up rings.

The Agricultural Center is host yearly to horse and livestock events, trade shows, RV and car shows, festivals, cat and dog shows, and many other events. This world-class multiuse facility is open year round.

Location: Fifteen minutes south of Asheville
Address: 1301 Fanning Bridge Rd., Fletcher, NC 28732
Telephone: 687-1414
FAX: 687-9272
Website: www.agr.state.nc.us/markets/facil/agcenter/western/
Hours: Vary depending upon event
Fees: Vary depending upon event
Of Note: Call business office or check local listings for scheduled events.
Directions: I-26 Exit 9. Follow airport signs off ramp. Continue past airport to make left onto Fanning Bridge Road.

Western North Carolina Farmers Market

The Western North Carolina Farmers Market first opened for business September 1977. This model project involving input from local, state and national leaders, is one of the most modern and best planned markets in the United States. Hundreds of thousands of visitors come to the market each year not only to shop but just to take in the wonderful country atmosphere. Fruits and vegetables can be purchased by the piece, pound, bushel or truckload. Commissioner of Agriculture James A. Graham states it this way; "Think of shopping at a 36-acre roadside stand featuring farm-fresh fruits and vegetables, flowers and ornamental plants, mountain crafts and scores of gift items."

Retail vendors offer a year-round selection of farm fresh produce, canned goods, honey and handcrafted items. Five truck sheds provide space for farmers and dealers to display and sell their produce. Restaurants and a retail garden center are also located on Market grounds. A visit to the WNC Farmers Market is a truly enjoyable experience, as well as a practical place to shop.

Location: West Asheville
Address: 570 Brevard Rd., Asheville, NC 28806
Telephone: 253-1691
FAX: 252-2025
Website: www.wncfarmersmarket.org
Hours: Open year-round, 7 days a week. (April-October) 8 a.m. to 6 p.m. (November-March) 8 a.m. to 5 p.m.
Fees: None

At the Western North Carolina Farmers Market, 570 Brevard Road, Asheville

Allow: One hour
Of Note: Great buys on fresh produce
Directions: I-40 Exit 47. South on Hwy. 191/Brevard Road. Market on left.

Western North Carolina Nature Center

Owned and maintained by Buncombe County, the Western North Carolina Nature Center is open year-round with indoor and outdoor exhibits. This outstanding 42-acre center features indigenous wildlife and plantlife of the Appalachian region.

Voted "the best place to take kids" in Western North Carolina, the center has animals both large and small, from cougars and wolves to the tiniest insects. Special programs, demonstrations and "hands-on" activities are available for anyone who wishes to learn about the rich natural heritage of the Southern Appalachian mountains. And nowhere else will you find such diverse wildlife, gardens, trails, indoor exhibits, habitats and farm animals in one setting.

Cougars can be seen at WNC Nature Center

Location: East Asheville
Address: 75 Gashes Creek Rd., Asheville, NC 28805
Telephone: 298-5600
FAX: 298-2744
Website: www.wildwnc.org
Hours: Open daily year-round 10 a.m.-5 p.m. except Thanksgiving, Christmas, New Year's Day, and Martin Luther King Day.
Fees: $5 Adults, $4 Seniors, $3 Youth (3-14)
Allow: One-two hours
Nearby: Buncombe County Recreation Park
Directions: I-240 Exit 8 (74A West). East off ramp. Right onto Swannanoa River Road. Right onto Gashes Creek Road.

The Red Wolf: A Nature Center Project

The Red Wolf, one of the lesser-known wolf species native to North America, once roamed throughout much of the Southeastern United States but have been eliminated from almost all of their natural range. The Nature Center located in Asheville is part of a breeding program to raise red wolves for eventual release into the wild.

Red Wolves average between 55 and 80 pounds, somewhat smaller than the better known gray wolf, but larger than the coyote which it resembles. Although many red wolves have a reddish cast to their fur, some do not. The usual coloration is a blend of cinnamon-brown, black and grayish-brown.

Western North Carolina Nature Center, 75 Gashes Creek Road, Asheville

Not as much is known about the red wolf as it's more well-known cousin, and it is believed that they do not form large packs like gray wolves. Most of their food consists of smaller animals such as raccoons, rabbits, rodents and birds. Like other wolf species, the red wolf has been persecuted by man because of our hatred, fear and misconception of these large predators. Over the years, the red wolves were shot, trapped and poisoned as their habitat was cleared for use by man. Today, thanks to the efforts of organizations such as the Western North Carolina Nature Center, the red wolf is returning to the wild habitats of its ancestors.

Chapter Three
Biltmore Estate

This chapter is devoted exclusively to Biltmore Estate. A national treasure, Biltmore Estate's importance to Asheville cannot be understated, and as one of the major attractions in Western North Carolina warrants a chapter unto itself. A visit to Biltmore Estate, in the opinion of the author, is a must for anyone coming to Asheville.

Although it is not formally part of the present Biltmore Estate, Biltmore Village is included here since it was originally conceived of by George Vanderbilt. The architecture of the original village buildings, especially the Cathedral of All Souls, clearly reflects the spirit of Vanderbilt's vision.

Biltmore Village

When George W. Vanderbilt began building Biltmore Estate near Asheville in the late 1880s, he planned a picturesque manorial village to be built just outside the entrance to Biltmore Estate.

Constructed in the early 1900s, the Village was primarily the work of Richard Hunt, Frederick Law Olmsted and Richard Smith. Today, Biltmore Village is a charming community of shops, restaurants and galleries offering world class shopping in an historic setting. Be sure and take time to park your car and take a walking tour of the many shops housed in the original historic buildings.

Planning began in 1889 and by 1896 the streets were laid in a fan shape. At the front of the railroad depot, Olmsted (who was instrumental in developing the village plan) placed a plaza, a simple diamond-shaped area framed by larger commercial buildings. At the opposite end of this axis, the Church of All Souls dominated the view as the tallest building in the Village. These primary elements of the central spine of the Village still dominate the scene today.

All other streets were laid out in short lengths, with views terminated into lots at the end. The result is that views are contained within the Village so that the "outside world" does not intrude into the setting. All Souls Church (now Cathedral of All Souls), parish house, estate office and the railway station were then built. Buildings were added to the Village until about 1910, and shortly after Vanderbilt's death, the Village was sold. It was declared a National Historic

District and a Local Historic District in 1989. See Section Three, Chapter 4, Historic Asheville for an in-depth look at the history and architecture of the Biltmore Village Historical District.

Buildings of special historical interest in Biltmore Village are the Cathedral Of All Souls, the Administration Building at 1 Biltmore Plaza, the Depot, The Samuel Harrison Reed House at 119 Dodge Street and the cottages throughout the main section of the village.

Located at 7 Biltmore Plaza is the Biltmore Village Historic Museum, a free, nonprofit museum. Its purpose is to share information about the Village from 1889 to the present through displays of pictures, maps, antique postcards and artifacts. For more information call 274-9707. (SEE Section Three, Chapter 2)

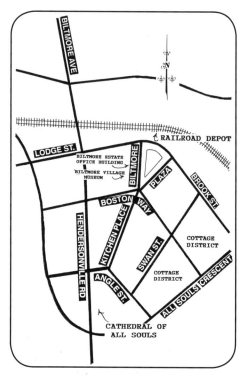

Biltmore Village

Biltmore Village is also noted for its Christmas festival that surrounds the enacting of Charles Dickens' "A Christmas Carol." This enchanting festival includes concerts, lighting displays and arts and crafts exhibits.

Directions: I-40 Exit 50 North on Highway 25/Biltmore Avenue. Right immediately after All Souls Cathedral. From downtown Asheville, take Biltmore Avenue south from Pack Square through the hospital district. Left directly before Pedro's Porch.

Website: www.biltmorevillage.com

Biltmore Estate
Your Visit

A visit to Biltmore is an event, so you'll want to give yourself at least 4-6 hours to explore the house, grounds, and winery.

You'll find eight shops throughout the estate, all with an uncommon selection of special gifts, accessories, and mementos of your visit. Don't forget to allow time to browse them all.

Like the estate itself, Biltmore's restaurants offer a delicious blend of American and European flavors. Dining choices range from the distinctly American fare of the Stable Café to the seasonal buffets of the Deerpark Restaurant. The newest restaurant, The Bistro, located in the winery, offers wonderful Bistro-style fare.

Every trip to Biltmore, no matter the time of year, is a new and exciting experience, whether you come for the breathtaking Festival of Flowers in the spring or the celebrated Candlelight Christmas Evenings.

The beauty of Biltmore Estate is ever-changing, with new wonders and delights appearing every season. In the springtime, the gardens explode with brilliant color, calling for the celebration of the spring Festival of Flowers. Summertime brings lush greenery to the hillsides, deep shade in the cool, wooded groves, and Summer Evenings Concerts performed on the South Terrace. In autumn, the surrounding mountains are ablaze with fiery color, and the estate commemorates its agricultural legacy with Michaelmas: An English Harvest Fair. December brings the splendor of an elaborate 19th century Christmas to every corner of the decorated mansion. Finally, winter is a time when guests can enjoy the special presentations regarding many of the preservation projects taking place in the house.

Many people dream of living in a house as grand as Biltmore House but few people get to realize their dreams the way George Vanderbilt did in 1895, when construction of his new country home was completed.

George Vanderbilt's dream first began to take shape in 1887, when he visited Asheville on holiday. Enchanted by the remote majesty of the Blue Ridge Mountains, he decided to make Asheville the site of his country estate. Commissioning architect Richard Morris Hunt, he set out to create a mansion modeled after the châteaux of France's Loire Valley. They began to collect the finest building materials from all over the United States. It took an army of stonecutters and artisans six years to construct Biltmore House, which is today the largest private home in America, situated on more than eight thousand acres.

George Vanderbilt filled his 250-room mansion with treasures he had collected during his world travels. Works by Albrect Dürer, John Singer Sargent, and Pierre Auguste Renoir cover the walls. Exquisite furniture and oriental rugs fill each room. And Minton china graces elaborate table settings.

Guests of Mr. Vanderbilt had their choice of 32 guest rooms, and could pass the time in the Billiard Room, Winter Garden, Tapestry Gallery, or countless other sitting rooms and be entertained in the Gymnasium, Bowling Alley, or indoor swimming pool.

Ever mindful of his guests' comfort, Mr. Vanderbilt equipped his house with a centralized heating system, mechanical refrigeration, electric lights and appliances, and indoor bathrooms—all unheard of luxuries at the turn of the century.

Today, Biltmore House visitors can see the house virtually as it was in George Vanderbilt's day because its sculptures, paintings, furnishings, and household items have been carefully preserved.

Biltmore Estate Information

Location: South Asheville, adjacent to Biltmore Village

Address: Corporate Offices: Biltmore Estate, One North Pack Sq., Asheville, NC 28801

Telephone: General Information, (800) 543-2961, 274-6333
Corporate Offices, 255-1776
Group Ticket Sales, 274-6230
Employment Hotline, 255-1144
Catering/Social Events, 274-6264
Deerpark Restaurant, 274-6260
Stable Cafe, 274-6370
Bistro, 274-6341
Inn on Biltmore Estate, (800) 858-4130, 225-1600

FAX: 255-1111

Website: www.biltmore.com

Hours: Biltmore Estate is closed Thanksgiving and Christmas but open on New Year's Day. Biltmore Estate also has a number of special events including Summer Evenings Concerts, Michaelmas: An English Harvest Fair, and Candlelight Christmas Evenings (early November

Biltmore Estate

through Christmas, taking place after normal hours.) Reservations are required.

Estate Entrance Hours (Subject to change without notice):
January-March daily 9 a.m.-5 p.m.
April-December daily 8:30 a.m.-5 p.m.

Reception and Ticket Center Hours:
January-March daily 9 a.m.-5 p.m.
April-December daily 8:30 a.m.-5 p.m.

Biltmore House Hours:
January-December daily 9 a.m.-6 p.m.

Winery Hours:
January-March Sunday 12 noon-6 p.m.
Monday-Saturday 11 a.m.-6 p.m.
April-December Sunday 12 noon-7 p.m.
Monday-Saturday 11 a.m.-7 p.m.

Fees: Prices vary seasonally with special events priced separately. Adults over 16: $32; Youth 10-15: $24; Children nine and under: Free when accompanied by paying adult

Allow: Four to six hours minimum.

Tips: Wear walking shoes. Plan to eat in one of the three restaurants.

Of Note: National Register of Places, National Historic Landmark.
While a great attraction year-round, Spring during the Festival of Flowers (April and May), Fall during Michaelmas (Sept. 26-Oct. 26), and Christmas are special times.
The Inn on Biltmore Estate is expected to open in the spring of 2000. This world-class inn will be located near the Biltmore Estate Winery.

Nearby: The Thomas Wolfe Memorial, Grove Park Inn Resort, and Biltmore Village

Directions: From I-40: Exit 50 or 50B. North on Highway 25. Left at fork. Entrance gate on left. From downtown Asheville: Biltmore Avenue south from Pack Square through hospital district. Left on Lodge Street.

The Gardens

George Vanderbilt commissioned Frederick Law Olmsted, designer of New York's Central Park, to create the stunning backdrop for his château. The resulting gardens and grounds are as spectacular as the house itself. A feast for the eyes, the ten acres of gardens also feature a remarkable array of flowers—many blooming through most of the year. From the orderly, manicured grounds framing the house to the lush forestland covering the mountains, the estate was carefully planned and designed by Olmsted's judicious hand.

Today the grounds are still exquisitely maintained, and you are invited to explore them at your leisure.

Estate Blooming Schedule

Early April: Early-flowering shrubs and trees: forsythia, spirea, magnolias, and flowering cherries.

Mid-April: Tulips and other spring bulbs, dogwoods, redbuds.

Late April to Early May: Azaleas (hybrid), various flowering shrubs.

May: Native azaleas (first week is usually the peak), various flowering shrubs.

Late May to October: Roses and perennials.

June to Early July: Native rhododendron, perennials.

July to August: Annual flowers: marigolds, salvia, impatiens, cannas, coleus, globe amaranth, and many others.

September to October: Chrysanthemums, also the grape harvest begins.

October: Fall foliage colors.

The Winery

Your visit to Biltmore Estate is not complete without a visit to the winery, which is located in the Estate's original dairy barns. Here you will find a charming and relaxed atmosphere. While there, you may view the production areas and see the careful attention that goes into producing Biltmore's award-winning wines. After deciding on your favorite wines during the complimentary tasting, a delightful shopping experience awaits you in the Wine Shop, where you can purchase a wide selection of Biltmore wines.

(The preceding estate information was provided courtesy of The Biltmore Company for use in this chapter as an introduction to the Biltmore Estate.)

Biltmore Estate Lodging

Inn on Biltmore Estate: Superb is the one word to describe the Inn on Biltmore Estate. Opened in 2001, it is the newest addition to George Vanderbilt's turn-of-the-century retreat. The 213-room luxury accommodation provides guests with an opportunity to enjoy Vanderbilt-style hospitality firsthand. Located on the east side of the estate above the Winery, it affords spectacular views of Biltmore House. At 165,000 sq. ft., the Inn offers banquet meeting rooms, two executive boardrooms, 213 exquisitely appointed guest rooms and suites, a 150-seat dining room, library, lobby bar, exterior swimming pool and fitness center. Amenities offered to guests include walking and hiking trails, carriage rides, horseback riding, mountain hiking and river float trips. The design of this world-class facility is in keeping with gracious resorts of the turn-of-the-century, and elements and accents from the magnificent Biltmore House are everywhere.

Many design materials and elements reflect other estate structures incorporating fieldstone stucco and a slate roof similar to that found on the house. The large lobby fireplace, the inn library and Indiana fieldstone reception desk all further reinforce the perception that one is truly in a creation inspired by the vision of George Vanderbilt. Landscaping reflects the style of landscape architect Frederick Law Olmstead and his overall plan for Biltmore Estate.

Fine dining is provided in The Dining Room at the Inn on Biltmore Estate with breakfast, lunch and dinner available to inn guests. The restaurant features estate-raised products and a regional cuisine paired with Biltmore Estate wines. Room service is available 24 hours a day.

One Antler Ridge Rd., Asheville, NC 28801, (800) 858-4130, 225-1600.

Biltmore Estate Dining

Stable Cafe: Formerly the Biltmore Estate carriage house and stables, the Stable Café is open from 11 a.m. to 5 p.m. The menu includes rotisserie chicken, Biltmore beef, fresh salads, burgers, desserts, and a full selection of drinks including wine and beer. Open year-round. 274-6370

Bistro: Open daily for lunch and dinner. The menu includes soups, salads, wood-fired pizza, homemade pasta, desserts, a children's menu, and entrées featuring estate-raised beef, lamb, and veal. Located at the Winery, the Bistro opens year-round at 11 a.m. 274-6341

Deerpark Restaurant: Originally part of the estate's farm operation, Deerpark is open late March-December 11 a.m.-3 p.m. Deerpark offers delicious southern specialties served buffet-style in an outdoor atmosphere. To make arrangements for group dining, call 274-6260.

Ice Cream Parlor: Located in the stable courtyard next to the house, the Ice Cream Parlor serves specialty ice cream, yogurt treats, beverages, and picnics for two. Open year-round 9 a.m.-6 p.m.

Bake Shop: Serves espresso, gourmet coffees, herbal teas, and freshly baked goods daily 9 a.m.-6 p.m.

Food & Beverage Carts: Carts offering snacks and drinks are located near the house and gardens on a seasonal basis.

Biltmore Estate Shops

The Carriage House: Carries gifts, decorative accessories, and Biltmore Estate wines.

A Christmas Past: Offers an assortment of Christmas ornaments and music.

The Toymaker Shop: Features old-fashioned toys and games.

The Bookbinder's Shop: Filled with books relating to the Vanderbilt family and the Gilded Age.

The Confectionery: Offers a delectable array of sweets.

The Gate House Gift Shop: Located near the main entrance. Features Biltmore Estate reproductions, decorative accessories, and a full selection of fine estate wines. The only estate shop accessible without ticket purchase.

The Wine Shop: Offers fine wines, gourmet foods, kitchen accessories, and other gifts.

A Gardener's Place: Features estate-grown plants, gardening accessories, books and gifts.

Lodge Gate

The entrance to Biltmore Estate is through the Lodge Gate opposite Biltmore Village. Both its bricks and roof tiles were made on the Estate. Beyond the Lodge Gate, the approach road winds for three miles through a deliberately controlled landscape. The road runs along the ravines instead of the ridges, creating a deep natural forest with pools, springs and streams. Around the last turn, the visitor passes through

The Lodge Gate at Biltmore Estate

the iron gates and pillars that are topped by early 19th century stone sphinxes, and then into the expansive court of Biltmore House.

Statue of Diana

Statue of Diana

Located inside a small temple at the top of the hill beyond the Rampe Douce at Biltmore Estate is a statue which represents Diana. Diana was the daughter of Zeus and Leto, twin sister of Apollo and one of the twelve Olympians. As protector of wild animals, deer were especially sacred to her, which is particularly appropriate for Biltmore, with its large native deer population. Diana is usually portrayed with a bow and arrow and quiver, as she is here. The dog next to her in the statue could represent fidelity or chastity. The sculpture is a replacement of the original and was carved out of Carrara marble in the 1970s by the Italian sculptor H. Whinery Oppice.

The Entrance Lions

Guarding the main entrance at Biltmore House are two massive carved stone lions that survey visitors with magnificently serene countenances. Carved of Rosso di Verona marble that is from near San Ambrogio Valpolicello in Italy, these lions are believed to date to the late nineteenth century and were not put in place until late 1899 or early 1900.

Biltmore House

George Vanderbilt commissioned two of America's most renowned designers to help plan his estate. His friend Richard Morris Hunt, the first American to receive an architectural degree from the Ecole des Beaux Arts in Paris, was the architect of Biltmore House, and Frederick Law Olmsted was chosen to lay out the gardens and parks surrounding the house.

One of the Entrance Lions

For his house, Mr. Vanderbilt chose the period of the great 16th century châteaux, known as the Francis I style. In 1895, when the house was formally opened, it was named Biltmore from Bildt, the name of the Dutch town from which the family's ancestors came (van der Bildt), and "more," an old English word for rolling, upland country.

Biltmore House became a favorite home for Mr. Vanderbilt and his wife, Edith Stuyvesant Dresser and their only child, Cornelia. Upon Cornelia's marriage to John Francis Amherst Cecil, it became the Cecils' residence.

Biltmore House

To build Biltmore House, beginning in the summer of 1890, a thousand workers were steadily engaged for six years. A three-mile railway spur from the present Biltmore Station had to be built to carry materials to the site. Hundreds of workmen from the local area and artisans from all over the country and Europe came to carve and fit limestone that came from Indiana. So massive are some of these limestone blocks that one in the retaining wall weighs over three tons. So great was the project that a brick manufacturing facility was established on the estate grounds to satisfy the need for building materials. One of the greatest private houses in America, Biltmore House, once seen, will never be forgotten.

The Building of a Legend

The following section was provided courtesy of The Biltmore Company for use in this chapter:

"Biltmore House took six years and 1,000 men to build it; it opened its doors on Christmas Eve in 1895. With its 390-foot facade, the House has more than 11 million bricks, 250 rooms, 65 fireplaces, 43 bathrooms, 34 bedrooms, and three kitchens, all of which are contained in more than four acres of floor space. The massive stone spiral staircase rises four floors and has 102 steps. Through its center hangs an iron chandelier suspended from a single point containing 72 electric light bulbs.

At its completion, Biltmore House was one of the most innovative and technologically advanced homes in the world. Imagine having hot and cold running water, elevators, indoor heating, a fire alarm system, refrigeration, electric light bulbs and 10 Bell telephones—all of which were unheard of luxuries at the turn of the century.

Imagine what it must have been like to call this your home. Dozens of servants to meet your every need. A vast collection of art and furniture comprising more than 70,000 items, including approximately 23,000 books, furniture from 13 countries, over 1,600 art prints, and many paintings.

If you were lucky enough to be one of Vanderbilt's guests, your choice of inside activities included bowling, billiards, an exercise room, swimming, and games of all sorts. Outdoors, guests could ride horseback, swim, play croquet, hunt, camp, fish, and hike, The Vanderbilts could entertain as many as 64 guests at their dinner table in the massive Banquet Hall. The room spans 72 feet by 42 feet and is 70 feet high. Meals served in the Banquet Hall were usually seven courses and required as many as 15 utensils per person. Enough fresh fish to feed 50 people was often shipped daily from New York, and the same amount of lobster was often shipped twice a week to feed the ever-changing guest list.

You'll experience a different kind of awe when you walk the Estate's grounds. Originally more than 125,000 acres of land, the Estate includes wooded parks, six pleasure gardens, a conservatory, and 30 miles of paved roadway. You will be overwhelmed every spring with the sight of tens of thousands of tulips in the Walled Garden. Or stroll among the carpets of mums that decorate the grounds each fall. The rest of the year the grounds will amaze you with their colors, shapes, aromas, and natural beauty."

The Tea House

The Tea House in the southwest corner of the South Terrace was an addition landscape-architect Frederick Law Olmsted advocated throughout the construction of Biltmore House. He viewed it as a much-needed focal point and an ideal spot from which to contemplate the mountains.

The Tea House

Italian Garden at Biltmore House

The Italian Garden

Designed by Olmsted, the Italian Garden is located to the east of the lower terrace adjacent to Biltmore House. Its three formal pools are part of a design concept that dates back to the 16th century. These gardens have an architectural purity in which the plantings are secondary to the design. Nature is completely controlled and the gardens serve as an extension of the house. The outline of the three pools, grass areas and the paths are all part of a symmetrical design. The nearest pool contains the sacred lotus of Egypt. In the second are aquatic plants and in the third, water lilies.

The Conservatory at Biltmore House

The Conservatory

The Conservatory was used to provide citrus fruit, flowers, and plants for Biltmore House during Vanderbilt's time. It is located at the far end of the four-acre Walled Garden, the lower half of which contains the Rose Garden featuring 159 of 161 All-American Rose selections as well as more than 2,300 other roses of the finest varieties. The Conservatory, restored in 1999, serves the same function today as it did in Vanderbilt's time: providing cut flowers and ornamental plants for the house and growing bedding plants for the estate's gardens.

The Winery Clock Tower

One of the highlights at Biltmore Estate's Winery is Richard Morris Hunt's European winery clock tower. Since the winery was previously a dairy, the central clock tower with its "candle-snuffer" roof originally had only three working faces; the side toward the pasture featured a painted-on clock, as the grazing cows did not need to know the time.

The Clock Tower at the Winery

The Winery

The Winery, opened in 1985, followed George Vanderbilt's original concept of a self-supporting European estate. The 96,500 square-foot facility is located in buildings designed by Richard Morris Hunt as part of the dairy operation on Biltmore Estate. The winery complex with its half-timbered woodwork, pebbledash plaster and decorative

The Winery on Biltmore Estate

brickwork is reminiscent of a rural landscape of the 19th century. Today the buildings house state-of-the-art wine making equipment, cellars for wine storage, an elaborately stenciled tasting room, and the spacious Wine Shop. The winery is also home to the Bistro, which offers excellent continental Bistro-style fare.

Deerpark Restaurant

Deerpark Restaurant is part of a series of handsome outbuildings designed by architect Richard Morris Hunt in the 1890s for George Vanderbilt's farm operations at Biltmore Estate. Originally a dairy barn, Deerpark has been renovated into a unique open-air restaurant in a beautiful pastoral setting. The historic architectural detailing includes pebbledash plaster, half-timbered woodwork, and decorative brickwork. The name Deerpark is taken from a nearby area of the estate which George Vanderbilt set aside as a deer preserve.

Deerpark Restaurant on Biltmore Estate

Vignette:
George Washington Vanderbilt, III

William Henry Vanderbilt's youngest son, George, was born in the Vanderbilt farmhouse in New Dorp, Staten Island, New York on November 18, 1862, the youngest of eight children. Little interested in his father's business affairs, Vanderbilt was influenced instead by the collection of art and antiques in his father's home.

A quite shy person, he began collecting books and art objects at a young age. After his mother died, George inherited the family home at 640 Fifth Avenue in New York City and all the art objects within it, including the large collection of paintings his father had assembled. He showed no interest in the social world of the Vanderbilt family, instead preferring the adventure of travel and the world of books.

After visiting Asheville in the 1880s, which was then a fashionable resort, he decided to create a home for himself away from the noise and pace of New York City. During the five years of the construction of Biltmore House, he was a bachelor. However, on a trip to Europe in 1896 he met Edith Stuyvesant Dresser and on June 1, 1898, they were married in a civil ceremony in Paris, followed the next day by a religious ceremony at the American Church. Their only child, Cornelia, was born on August 22, 1900.

While George Vanderbilt is well known for his creation of Biltmore Estate, he also accomplished a number of important good works in his lifetime. He established the first school of scientific forestry management practices in the United States and he also brought modern farming techniques to the relatively rural area surrounding his estate. Together, the Vanderbilts started Biltmore Estate Industries in 1901. In this apprenticeship program, young people were instructed in skills to produce furniture, baskets, needlework and woven fabric for resale.

George Vanderbilt died in 1914 and was buried in the family vault on Staten Island. In the memorial service held at All Souls Church in Biltmore Village, the following remarks were made:

"Courteous in manner, dignified in deportment, kind in heart and pure in morals, he was beloved by his friends, honored by his acquaintances and respected by everyone..."

Chapter Four
Historic Asheville

One encounters Asheville today as a modern city that is rapidly growing and expanding out into the surrounding Buncombe County. Asheville today does not look at all like the Asheville from before the turn of the century. Regrettably, much of the best of that time has vanished, including the elegant Queen Anne style Battery Park Hotel and the very hilltop on which it stood and dominated the city landscape. Only scattered buildings remain from that period.

Much of the city landscape remains, however, from the early days of the century through to the present day, especially downtown Asheville, which retains a strong presence from the early third of this century. Asheville's slow recovery from the Great Depression did not allow it to wholesale demolish these early buildings as did so many American cities, and because of that, they have been preserved intact to this day. Within the central downtown district for example, one can find excellent examples of Neo-Gothic, Neo-Georgian, Commercial Classical, Art Deco, Romanesque Revival and other style structures that make up the most extensive collection of early twentieth century architecture in the state. They remain an open-air museum, reminders of the optimism and unbounded investment that characterized Asheville in its boom period. Asheville is the only city of its magnitude in which such a urban landscape survives almost intact.

Asheville, through the efforts of local preservation and historic resources organizations, as well as the North Carolina Department of Cultural Resources, has been divided into a number of historic districts. These districts form the basis for this chapter and also the framework for a series of mini-tours, should you wish to experience some of the wonderful and diverse architectural heritage of Asheville during your visit.

Before we present this material however, it is necessary to acquaint you with some organizations and with terms that will enrich your understanding of what you see.

Historic Designations
Historic District

    Historic District refers to a district of Asheville that has been so designated by the United States Department of the Interior. These districts serve as frameworks for further discussion of the historic buildings and sites of Asheville and in some cases as self-guided mini-tours. Some of these Historic Districts include whole neighborhoods while others are only a small cluster of buildings.

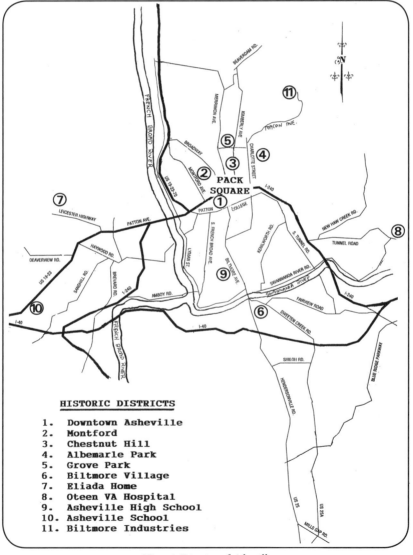

HISTORIC DISTRICTS

1. Downtown Asheville
2. Montford
3. Chestnut Hill
4. Albemarle Park
5. Grove Park
6. Biltmore Village
7. Eliada Home
8. Oteen VA Hospital
9. Asheville High School
10. Asheville School
11. Biltmore Industries

Historic Districts of Asheville

Local Historic Landmarks (LHL)

These are designated by the Asheville City Council or the Buncombe County Board of Commissioners. The list in the Asheville area is maintained by the Historic Resources Commission of Asheville and Buncombe County and at present contains over 35 listings. Buildings and sites that are Local Historic Landmarks will be indicated so as they are discussed later in this chapter. The designation LHL indicates the building or site is a Local Historic Landmark.

National Historic Landmarks (NHL)

National Historic Landmark are structures, buildings or sites which are of significance to all Americans. This designation is by the Secretary of the Interior and the listings are registered with the United States Department of the Interior National Park Service. In the Asheville and Hendersonville/Flat Rock area there are three National Historic Landmarks: Biltmore Estate and the Thomas Wolfe Memorial in Asheville, and the Carl Sandburg Home in Flat Rock. The designation NHL indicates the building or site is a National Historic Landmark. www. cr.nps.gov/nhl/

National Register of Historic Places (NRHP)

The National Register is the official list of the nation's cultural resources worthy of preservation. Authorized under the National Historic Preservation Act of 1966, the National Register is part of a national program to coordinate and support public and private efforts to identify, evaluate, and protect our historic and archeological resources. The National Register is administered by the National Park Service under the Secretary of the Interior. Properties listed in the National Register include districts, sites, buildings, properties and objects that are significant in American history, architecture, archaeology, engineering, and culture. The designation NRHP will be used throughout this book to indicate properties listed in the National Register.

The National Register includes all historic areas in the National Park System, National Historic Landmarks, and properties significant to the nation, state or community which have been nominated by the states, federal agencies and others and have been approved by the National Park Service. Asheville has many listings in the National Register. To present them all in this book is beyond our space and scope. Only the most important and interesting have been presented, through the recommendation of various authorities and experts, including John Horton, Maggie O'Connor, Jennifer Martin and Harry Weiss, among others. You can obtain a full listing of all of the National Register properties by contacting The Division of Archives and History, North Carolina Department of Cultural Resources. Their office in Asheville is at 1 Village Lane, Suite 3, Biltmore Village, NC 28803 (274-6789, www.hpo.dcr.state.nc.us). They can supply the interested visitor with not only more information about local National Register listings but also information about the National Register itself. This Western

Office of the N.C. Department of Cultural Resources offers professional expertise in historic resource management. They are not a repository for historical
records and do not have facilities for genealogical research. However, one of
their major functions is to assist private citizens, institutions, local governments
and agencies of state and federal government in the identification, evaluation,
protections and enhancement of properties significant in North Carolina history and archaeology.

It is interesting to note that buildings can be listed in the National Register for
two reasons. They can be "individually listed," significant unto themselves and as
such warranting inclusion. Good examples are the Grove Park Inn and Biltmore
Estate. Others buildings listed in the National Register can be so because they are
"contributing structures" and are located in a designated National Historic District. A good example of this would be a bed & breakfast that is in such a historic
district. In itself, the building has not been individually listed but because of its
location and contribution to the whole, it is. I shall not attempt to differentiate
between these two type of listings but simply indicate that the building or site
being discussed is in the Register, and therefore definitely noteworthy from an
historical perspective.

Local History Resources
The Historic Resources Commission of Asheville and Buncombe County
An Asheville organization very much concerned with the city's historical
districts and buildings, The Historic Resources Commission is located in the
Asheville City Building, P.O. Box 7148, Asheville, NC 28807 (259-5836).

This organization was created in 1979 to evaluate historically significant
neighborhoods, areas and individual sites and to recommend their designation
as a Local Historic District or Local Historic Landmark. It administers design
review of new construction or rehabilitation within those areas. The Commission also serves as an educational resource promoting the merits of historical
preservation and providing technical assistance to property owners and residents
in the entire region.

The Old Buncombe County Genealogical Society
Another valuable community resource, especially if you are interested in
family history, the Old Buncombe County Genealogical Society is located on
Tunnel Road in the Innsbruck Mall. This society has been in existence for over 20
years and has an extensive library of books and documents relating to genealogy
and local history. The organization produces an excellent quarterly, "A Lot of
Bunkum," and has a first-class webpage that is both entertaining and informative
(www.main.nc.us/OBCGS/). The staff handle inquires from the public on a fee
basis and have published two encyclopedia-sized books, "The Heritage of Old
Buncombe County" volumes I and II, which compile over 500 sketches each of
former and current area residents' ancestral backgrounds. Membership is open

to the public and the society offers many opportunities for office volunteers to learn about genealogical research and local history. The office is located at 85 Tunnel Rd., Suite 22, Innsbruck Mall, Asheville, NC 28805, but mail should be sent to P.O. Box 2122, Asheville, NC 28802-2122. Call 253-1894 for more information.

The Preservation Society of Asheville and Buncombe County

The Preservation Society is primarily concerned with the preservation, maintenance and enhancement of historic properties. It is a private organization that promotes the preservation of Asheville and Buncombe County heritage by providing educational and technical services to the community and through direct advocacy activities. They help to educate the public through lectures, workshops, tours, research and publications. They also provide historical information and technical preservation assistance to property owners undertaking preservation and restoration projects. The Preservation Society also provides financial assistance to targeted preservation needs in the community and they also acquire endangered historic properties for resale to sympathetic buyers. Their office is located at 13 Biltmore Avenue, Asheville, NC 28801, just down from Pack Square (254-2343).

Downtown Asheville Historic District

Downtown Asheville itself has four distinct neighborhoods, each with their own distinctive qualities and ambience: **Battery Park,** the area that includes Haywood Street, Wall Street, and Battery Park Avenue; **Lexington Park,** spanning Lexington Avenue and Broadway; **Pack Square,** encompassing Pack Square, South Pack Square, Biltmore Avenue, and Patton Avenue; and **Thomas Wolfe Plaza,** centered on Market Street and Spruce Street.

One of the very best ways to experience these neighborhoods and most of the downtown Asheville historic buildings presented below is to walk the Asheville Urban Trail. This self-guided walking tour visits all four of the neighborhoods discussed here, with stations and thematic markers along the way. For more information about this extraordinary way to trace the footsteps of Asheville's historic past, see Section Three, Chapter 5, The Asheville Urban Trail.

Pack Square (NRHP)

Pack Square, and the nearby South Pack Square, Biltmore Avenue, and Patton Avenue, is the heart of Asheville. Located at the intersection of Biltmore Avenue, Broadway, and College Street, it was once known as Public Square and was renamed in 1901 for city benefactor George Willis Pack when he moved the courthouse off the square and, in agreement with county commissioners, the square was designated a public park. This spacious square is surrounded by wonderful examples of Classical, Gothic, Art Deco, and Contemporary architecture.

Pack Square, the heart of downtown Asheville

Today, Pack Square and its surrounding streets are a vibrant and historic city center that not only boasts elegant architecture but superb museums, shops, music halls, art galleries and world class restaurants. A visit to Pack Square will show you immediately why Asheville has been called "Paris of the South."

Vance Monument (NRHP)   Pack Square
Located in the square's center is a 75-foot tall granite obelisk, the Vance Monument, erected in 1896 and named in honor of Zebulon B. Vance, an Asheville attorney who was twice governor of North Carolina and was also a U.S. Senator.

Two-thirds of the $3,000 cost was paid by philanthropist George W. Pack, and the architect R.S. Smith donated his services. The granite obelisk was cut from the Pacolet quarries in Henderson County.

Pack Memorial Library Building (NRHP, LHL)   2 South Pack Square
Located on the southern side of Pack Square is the Pack Memorial Library Building. Today this noble Second Renaissance Revival structure is home to the Asheville Art Museum, part of the Pack Place Education, Arts & Science Center. Built in 1925-26 and designed by New York Library architect Edward L. Tilton, the four-story building presents symmetrically arranged elevations faced with white Georgia marble and ornamented with a low-relief classical cornice.

Jackson Building (NRHP)   22 South Pack Square
To the left of the Library Building is the wonderfully elegant Jackson Building. Built in 1923-24 by real estate developer L.B. Jackson and it was the first skyscraper in Western North Carolina. The architect was Ronald Greene and the building he designed rises 13 stories on a small 27 x 60 foot lot. Neo-Gothic in style, the building originally had a searchlight on top that illuminated the surrounding mountains.

Asheville City Hall (NRHP, LHL)   70 Court Plaza

To the east of Pack Square
is the Art Deco masterpiece
designed by Douglas D.
Ellington, and built in
1926-28. One of the crown
jewels of Asheville it is set
on a marble base and topped
with a pink and green tiled
octagonal ziggurat roof. A
wonderful unity of appearance is achieved through the
luxurious use of color and
form. The main entrance
is through a loggia of pink
marble with multicolored
groin vaults. One of the most
striking and beautiful buildings in all of North Carolina,
City Hall is a show stopper in
a city graced by many unusual
and beautiful buildings:

Asheville City Hall

Buncombe County Courthouse (NRHP)   60 Court Plaza

To the left of the City Hall is
the Buncombe County Courthouse. Designed by Milburn
and Heister of Washington,
DC, and built in 1927-28, this
steel frame seventeen-story
courthouse has a brick and limestone classical surface. It has an
opulent lobby ornamented with
polychrome classical plaster
work and marble balustrades.
Polished granite columns at the
entrance are echoed by similar
columns above at the jail section.
The large superior court room
has a coffered plaster ceiling and
elegant woodwork.

Buncombe County Courthouse

Young Men's Institute Building (NRHP, LHL)   Market and Eagle St.

Located behind the Pack Place Education, Arts, & Science Center on the corner of South Market and Eagle streets is the Young Men's Institute (YMI) Building, built by George Vanderbilt in 1892 to serve as a recreational and cultural center for black men and boys. It was sold to the Young Men's Institute in 1906 and became a center for social activity in the black community and contained professional offices and a black public library. Designed by R.S. Smith in a simplified English Cottage style with a pebbledash and brick surface, today it houses the YMI Cultural Center, part of Pack Place Education, Arts & Science Center.

Eagle and Market Streets (NRHP)

This district was the heart of the black community in Asheville in the early days and today contains many fine buildings of historic importance, including the YMI Building mentioned earlier. Of interest are the Campbell Building at 38 South Market Street, originally an office building, and the former Black Masonic Temple Building at 44 South Market Street.

Mount Zion Missionary Baptist Church (NRHP)   47 Eagle St.

Also in this historic area is the large and handsome Mount Zion Missionary Baptist Church. A three-tower red brick Late Victorian Gothic structure built in 1919, it has a tin-shingled roof that has ornamental sheet-metal finials. The large number of Art Glass windows that grace the church are another unusual feature. It was home to one of Asheville's largest black congregations, organized in 1880 by the noted Reverend Rumley.

Kress Building (NRHP, LHL)   21 Patton Ave.

Just down from Pack Square on Patton Avenue, you will encounter one of Asheville's finest commercial buildings, the Kress building. Housing today an antique and crafts emporium, this four-story building was built in 1926-27. Distinctive features are the cream colored glazed terra-cotta with orange and blue rosette borders that face the front three bays of the building. In addition the side elevations above the first level are tan brick with terra-cotta inserts. This classical design preceded the many Art Deco Kress stores built around the country in the late 1930s and is unique in that sense.

Drhumor Building (NRHP)   48 Patton Ave.

Farther west is the splendid Romanesque Revival Drhumor Building. Built in 1895, this structure is an imposing four stories of brick trimmed with rock-faced limestone and graced by a marvelous first floor frieze by sculptor Fred Miles. One of the bearded visages is supposedly of local merchant E.C. Deake, who watched Miles sculpt. Miles was also the sculptor who did the figures atop the Basilica of St. Lawrence. A complementary limestone frontispiece was added to the north side of the building in the 1920s and the original corner entrance was filled in.

Detail from Drhumor Building

The building was designed by A.L. Melton for Will J. Cocke and his relatives, Mrs. Marie Johnson and Miss Mattie. The name Drhumor comes from the Johnson family's ancestral home in Ireland.

S&W Cafeteria Building (NRHP, LHL)   56 Patton Ave.

A little farther down Patton Avenue is another of the crown jewels of Asheville, and one of the finest examples of Art Deco architecture in North Carolina, the S&W Cafeteria Building. It was built in 1929 for the cafeteria chain which occupied the building until 1973. The building was designed by Douglas D. Ellington, and is two stories with a polychrome cream, green, blue, black and gilt glazed terra cotta facade that employs geometrically-stylized Indian and classical motifs. The interior is divided into dining rooms and lobbies with Art Deco decorations of superb quality. The building today is used for catering of meetings, receptions and banquets. (SEE illustration Section Three, Chapter 1)

Public Service Building (NRHP, LHL)   89-93 Patton Ave.

Farther west is the Public Service Building built in 1929. This imposing eight-story Neo-Spanish Romanesque steel frame office building is one of North Carolina's most attractive 1920s skyscrapers. Built of red brick and glazed terra cotta, its first two and upper floors are lavishly ornamented with polychrome terra cotta including such whimsical details as Leda-and-the-Swan spring blocks on the second-floor windows.

Flatiron Building (NRHP, LHL)

10-20 Battery Park Ave.

The Flatiron Building is an eight-story tan brick building that has classical detailing and a "flatiron" plan. Built in 1925-26, and designed by Albert C. Wirth, this elegant and unique building is faced with limestone ashlar and is perched at the entrance to the historic Wall Street district. A large metal sculpture of a household iron sits outside on the Wall Street side of the building.

The Flatiron Building

Wall Street (NRHP)

This charming one-block street of small shops was named Wall Street after the retaining wall built behind the structures that face Pritchard Park. In 1926 Tench Coxe and Ed Ray remodeled and repainted the rear entrances to these building to create a boutique district, which they called "Greenwich Village." That name never caught on, and the district was simply called Wall Street. Today it is a one of Asheville's most interesting shopping districts, with many top-quality gift and specialty shops. When there, notice the unusual gingko trees planted along the street.

Grove Arcade (NRHP, LHL)   10-20 Battery Park Ave.

Located just north of Wall Street, the grand Grove Arcade building occupies a full city block. This imposing building was begun in 1926 by E.W. Grove to be a commercial mall topped with an office skyscraper. Completed after Grove's death minus the skyscraper, the building is surfaced with cream glazed terra-cotta in a Neo-Tudor Gothic style. It is one of several major buildings for which the millionaire was responsible, with the most noteworthy among them being the Grove Park Inn. The arcade was designed by Charles N. Parker. Among the most interesting details are a pair of winged Griffin statues guarding the Battle Square entrance of the building. After years of service as offices for the federal government, the Grove Arcade is now home to commercial shops and venues.

Griffin from Grove Arcade

Battery Park Hotel (NRHP, LHL)

1 Battle Square

The hotel is a huge 14-story T-plan Neo-Georgian hotel erected by E.W. Grove in 1923-24. This extraordinary building was designed by hotel architect W.L. Stoddart of New York and replaced a previous Queen Anne style hotel of the same name. It is surfaced in brick with limestone and terra-cotta trim. The hotel building today houses apartments and is located just north of the Grove Arcade.

United States Post Office and Courthouse (NRHP)   100 Otis St.

Located just west of the Grove Arcade is the former post office and courthouse building, one of the state's finest Depression-era Federal buildings. This Art-Deco influenced building was designed by the Federal Architect's Office under James A. Wetmore. The building has a majestically massed central entrance in which the Art Deco influence can be seen.

First Church of Christ Scientist (NRHP)

First Church of Christ Scientist

64 North French Broad Ave.

The First Church of Christ Scientist is of a refined Jeffersonian, Neo-Classical Revival style, constructed of orange brick. Built between 1909 and 1912, it was designed by S.S. Beaman of Chicago.

Basilica of Saint Lawrence, D.M. (NRHP)   97 Haywood St.

To the north of the Grove Arcade area is the Basilica of Saint Lawrence, Deacon and Martyr, built in 1909. A Spanish Baroque Revival Roman Catholic Church built of red brick with polychrome glazed terra-cotta inserts and limestone trim, it was designed by world-famous architect/engineer Raphael Guastavino. The church employs his "cohesive construction" techniques in its large oval tile dome and Catalan-style vaulting in its two towers. The massive stone foundations and the solid brick superstructure give silent testimony to the architect's desire to build an edifice that would endure for generations. There are no beams of wood or steel in the entire structure; all walls, floors, ceilings and pillars are of tile or other masonry materials. The dome is entirely self supporting, has a clear span of 58 x 82 feet and is reputed to be the largest unsupported dome in North America. The Crucifixion tableaux of the Basilica altar features a rare example of seventeenth century Spanish woodcarving. The windows are of German origin, and the Basilica

Basilica of Saint Lawrence, D.M.

has two chapels. Attached by an arcade is the 1929 Neo-Tuscan Renaissance brick rectory designed by Father Michael of Belmont Abbey. Self-guided tour brochures are available at the church, and guided tours are given after Sunday masses.

Loughran Building (NRHP, LHL)   43 Haywood St.

The Loughran Building was in 1923 and is a six-story steel-frame commercial building that has a restrained white glazed terra cotta classical facade. It was designed by Smith and Carrier for Frank Loughran and its first occupant was Denton's Department Store.

Central United Methodist Church (NRHP)   27 Church St.

Located on Church Street, south of Patton Avenue, this Gothic limestone-faced church was designed by R.H. Hunt of Chattanooga, Tennessee. The church is noted for its fine stained and Art Glass windows and was built between 1902 and 1905.

First Presbyterian Church (NRHP)   40 Church St.

This Gothic Revival church is home to one of Asheville's oldest congregations and is one of the oldest church buildings in the city. Located on the corner of Church and Aston streets, the brick nave and steeple were constructed in 1884-85 and have deep, corbelled cornices, hoodmolded windows and blind arcading at the eaves. The north chapel and the south building were added in 1968.

Trinity Episcopal Church (NRHP)   Church and Aston St.

Located on the opposite corner of Church and Aston Streets, the Trinity Episcopal Church is the third of the three churches in this Church Street neighborhood. Built in 1921, it is a Tudor Gothic Revival style brick with granite trim building and was designed by Bertram Goodhue of Cram, Goodhue and Ferguson, well-known church architects. This lovely building has a simple gable roofed sanctuary with transepts and a short gable-roofed blunt tower.

Ravenscroft School Building (NRHP, LHL)   29 Ravenscroft Dr.

Built in the 1840s, this two-and-a-half story brick Greek Revival house is probably the oldest structure in the downtown area and one of the oldest in Asheville. It housed the Ravenscroft Episcopal Boys' Classical and Theological School after 1856 until the Civil War. Thereafter it was

Ravenscroft School Building

used as a training school for the ministry. In 1886 it was used again as a boys' school. After the turn of the century, it was a rooming house, and today it is used for professional offices. Details of the house in Academic Greek Revival are of a type not common to Western North Carolina.

Mears House (NRHP) · 137 Biltmore Ave.

Located on Biltmore Avenue, the Mears House is a wonderful example of Queen Anne style architecture. Built around 1885, this brick residence has a slate-shingled mansard roof, gables and dormers. This is the most distinguished of the remaining late nineteenth century residences near downtown.

Scottish Rite Cathedral and Masonic Temple (NRHP) · 80 Broadway

Built in 1913, this imposing four-story building is constructed of pressed brick and trimmed in limestone and grey brick. A two-story limestone portico with a pair of Ionic columns graces the Broadway entrance. The building was designed by Smith and Carrier.

Lexington Avenue (NRHP)

This once thriving market district was where farmers and others once came to water their horses and buy and sell local produce. Because natural springs kept it wet, Lexington Avenue was first called Water Street. Double doorways accommodating farmers' wagons are still evident on renovated buildings. Lexington Avenue is Asheville's premier antique district and also home to Asheville's oldest store, T.S. Morrison (circa 1891). Many antique shops, specialty stores, galleries and nightclubs are found today in this interesting neighborhood.

Lexington Avenue is home to T.S. Morrison, Asheville's oldest store.

First Baptist Church of Asheville (NRHP)   5 Oak St.

Built in 1927, the First Baptist Church of Asheville was designed by noted architect Douglas Ellington from his sketches of a cathedral in Florence, Italy. Three major additions have been made to the building. The Children's Wing was added in 1968, and the Sherman Family Center in 1980. This wonderfully elegant building is an unusual combination of an Early Italian Renaissance form and color scheme arranged in a beaux arts plan with Art Deco detailing. Of particular interest is the Art Deco copper lantern atop the dome and the subtle gradation of color in the roofing tiles. The walls are an effective combination of orange bricks, terra-cotta moldings and pink marble. This striking building is at the corner of Oak and Woodfin Streets.

First Baptist Church of Asheville

First Christian Church (NRHP)   20 Oak St.

Right across the street is the First Christian Church, built between 1925 and 1926 in a traditional Late Gothic Style, and constructed of rock-faced grey granite masonry with smooth granite trim. Designed by the home office, it has an unusual feature in that the placement of the tower is at the intersection of the nave and transept.

Montford Historic District

The Montford Historic District is Asheville's oldest and largest with over 600 buildings reflecting a variety of late 19th and early 20th century styles. Montford is a culturally diverse and thriving community, and was the creation of Asheville's boomtimes, having its origins as an upper middle class suburb in 1889. Asheville's most famous son, writer Thomas Wolfe, describes Montford Avenue in *Look Homeward Angel* as "the most fashionable street in town."

Montford's Riverside Cemetery is well worth a visit for scenic beauty alone; but is also notable as the final resting place for two of America's most important writers: O. Henry (William Sidney Porter) and Thomas Wolfe.

Located just across I-240 from downtown Asheville, a drive through Montford reveals a collection of architecture from the Queen Anne to Georgian Revival styles, with many variations in between. Quite a few of these majestic old homes have been converted to bed & breakfasts, making Montford one of Asheville's premier destinations for those seeking a pleasant stay in a historic setting. The best way to see Montford is by car and the historic sites in this section will be presented as a self guided tour. Plan at least an hour, perhaps more if you wish to get out and visit Riverside Cemetery on foot, for the tour.

From I-240, take Exit 4C Haywood Street/Montford Avenue. Begin at the top of Montford Avenue just on the north side of I-240. Montford Avenue turns off of Haywood Street just west of the Asheville Visitor Center. Continue down Montford to 276, The Lion and The Rose Bed & Breakfast on your left.

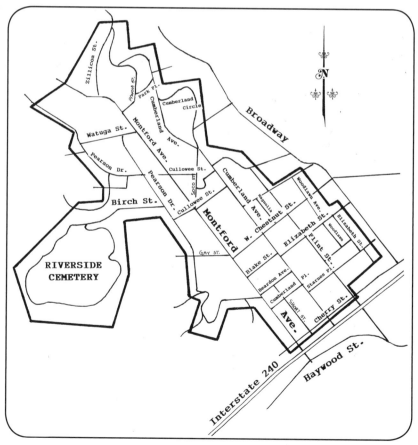

Montford Historic District

The Lion & The Rose Bed & Breakfast (NRHP)   276 Montford Ave.

This beautifully landscaped bed & breakfast is housed in a charming three-story Queen Anne/Georgian Revival style pebbledash building and is officially known as the Craig-Toms House. Interesting features are the double Doric posts on stone pedestals and the elaborate center gable. Built in 1898, this house has been faithfully restored to its original elegance, with all its rooms furnished with antiques, oriental rugs and period appointments. High embossed ceilings, golden oak, classic leaded and stained glass windows create a feeling of the Victorian era.

Right next door is The Black Walnut Bed & Breakfast Inn.

The Black Walnut Bed & Breakfast Inn (NRHP)   288 Montford Ave.

This large handsome residence, designed by Richard Sharp Smith was constructed around 1900. Known historically as the Otis Green House, after Otis Green who owned the residence for many years, it embodies the eclecticism characteristic of Smith's work, combining flourishes of the Shingle style, Queen Anne and Colonial Revival styles of architecture. Beautifully landscaped also, this striking building is faithfully restored and decorated throughout with antiques and fine traditional furniture.

The third of three bed & breakfasts located on this side of the street is The Inn on Montford, next door to The Black Walnut.

The Inn on Montford (NRHP)   296 Montford Ave.

Originally known as the Dr. Charles S. Jordan House, this "Old English" style house at 296 Montford Avenue was designed by Richard Sharp Smith. The house is typical of architect Smith's interpretation of the "Old English" style. Two major gables with splayed eaves are presented to the street at attic level, and a combination of shingles and pebbledash are employed. Construction of the house dates back to around 1900. This lovely bed & breakfast has period landscaping with rows of neatly trimmed boxwoods and other plantings. Queen-sized poster beds, English and American antiques and fine paintings all add to the atmosphere of an "English Cottage." After viewing these three inns, turn left on Watauga Street and proceed to Pearson Drive. Turn left on Pearson. On your left will be the romantic Wright Inn.

The Wright Inn and Carriage House (NRHP)   235 Pearson Dr.

The Wright Inn is one of the finest examples of Queen Anne architecture in the Montford District and in all of Western North Carolina. With stylized Doric porch posts on paneled pedestals, multiple gables and slate roof, this wonderfully restored building is a delight to behold. Elegantly appointed inside with antiques and family heirlooms, the 1899-1900 Victorian masterpiece was designed by George Barber.

Right across the street is the Colby House, another bed & breakfast.

The Colby House (NRHP) 230 Pearson Dr.

This bed & breakfast was built in 1924, and is a Dutch Colonial Revival-style dwelling with Gambrel roof. Interesting features include the elliptical leaded fanlight at the entrance door and the exterior of North Carolina blue granite with beaded mortar joints. Originally called the Dr. Charles Hartwell Cocke House, the Colby House today welcomes guests to a relaxing refined environment.

Continue down Pearson Drive and turn right onto Birch Street to the historic Riverside Cemetery.

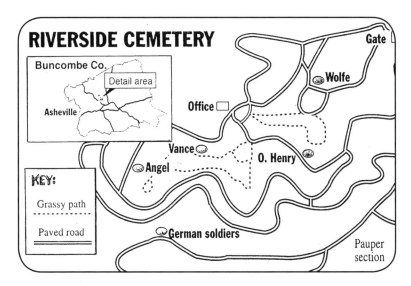

Riverside Cemetery (NRHP) 53 Birch St.

Historic Riverside Cemetery at the end of Birch Street and is operated under the direction of the City of Asheville Parks, Recreation and Public Facilities Department. It is the burial site of Thomas Wolfe, O. Henry (William Sidney Porter), Zebulon Vance (N.C. Governor and U.S. Senator), three Civil War Confederate Generals, Thomas L. Clingman and Robert R. Reynolds (U.S. Senators), and many of Asheville's founding families. Group tours are welcomed at this 87-acre cemetery. A walk through Riverside Cemetery is a walk through a rich source of area history. More than 13,000 people lie in marked graves, many with grave sites marked with angels and lambs crafted of Italian Carrera marble. The cemetery is open around the clock, but office hours are Monday-Friday, 8 a.m.-4:30 p.m. The office phone number is 258-8480. Website: www.ci.asheville.nc.us/parksrec/riversid.htm

Leaving the cemetery, return by way of Birch Street back to Pearson Drive and turn right. Continue down Pearson to West Chestnut Street and turn left. On West Chestnut you will cross Montford Avenue and continue on to Cumberland Avenue. Turn left at Cumberland and look for another lovely Victorian bed & breakfast, A Bed of Roses, immediately on your right.

Thomas Wolfe's gravestone at Riverside Cemetery in historic Montford

A Bed of Roses (NRHP)   135 Cumberland Ave.

This splendidly restored house dates back to around 1897 and is a playful vari-
ant of the Queen Anne style, with the dominant feature being the large second
store polygonal corner projection with a broad ogee roof. The front porch also
has stylized Doric type posts on stone pedestals. It was built by O.D. Revell and
is officially named after the first long-term occupant Marvin B. Wilkinson who
purchased it in 1904. Today, the house welcomes guests to its rooms furnished
with antiques, handmade quilts and fresh flowers. (SEE illustration Section Two,
Chapter 1)

Continuing on down Cumberland Avenue you will see the Maria T. Brown
House on your right at 177, restored as the Carolina Bed & Breakfast.

The Carolina Bed & Breakfast (NRHP)   177 Cumberland Ave.

This 2½-story stucco dwelling was designed by Richard Sharp Smith and built
before 1901. The porch has unusual brackets, shed dormers and a high hipped
roof. The pebbledash stucco is typical of that period of architecture. The Carolina
Bed & Breakfast has been graciously restored and features warm heart-pine floors,
spacious rooms and seven working fireplaces.

Farther down Cumberland on your left is The Arbor Rose Inn at 254 Cumberland Avenue.

Cumberland Falls Bed & Breakfast (NRHP)   254 Cumberland Ave.

This early 20th century house is a 2½-story vernacular shingle dwelling which
features shingles over weatherboards, bay windows and porch. Charming rooms

with antique furnishings, ornamental fireplaces and ceiling fans await the visitors to this graciously restored dwelling.

At this point you will want to take the right fork onto Cumberland Circle. Ahead on the left will be the Wythe Peyton House at 46 Cumberland Circle, known today as Abbington Green Bed & Breakfast Inn.

Abbington Green Bed & Breakfast Inn (NRHP)   46 & 48 Cumberland Cir.

This stunning Colonial Revival home was built in 1908 for businessman David Latourette Jackson and was officially named the Wythe Peyton House for another prominent resident who lived here during the 1950s. It was designed by Richard Sharp Smith and has been lovingly restored to all of its former glory. It features shingles over weatherboards, Doric porch posts, molded trim and a central gable. Inside, each of the eight stylishly appointed guest rooms is named after parks and gardens in London.

Continuing on Cumberland Circle you will see the red Applewood Manor Inn on your left.

Applewood Manor Inn (NRHP)   62 Cumberland Cir.

Built before 1917, this shingle-sided Colonial Revival building features a pedimented entrance supported on Doric columns and flanking porches. Located on an acre and a half this finely restored bed & breakfast is a touch of country in the city!

Continue on Cumberland Circle until it rejoins Cumberland Avenue and turn right. Take Cumberland Avenue until you reach Panola Street. Turn left and go to Montford Avenue. Turn right on Montford and then right again on Zillicoa Street. Directly ahead on your left is the Homewood School Building and just beyond it is the magnificent Rumbough House.

Applewood Manor Inn

Homewood (NRHP)　　　　　　　　　　49 Zillicoa St.
Constructed in 1934 and designed by Dr. Robert S. Carroll, founder of High-land Hospital, Homewood was for many years the home to Dr. Carroll and his second wife Grace Potter Carroll. The castle-like Homewood was constructed of uncoursed stone masonry, with an asymmetrical facade and entrance deeply recessed beneath a basket arch. A crenellated polygonal tower at the building's southeast corner and additional crenellation atop a projecting bay at the north end give the former residence the romantic image of a fortified castle.

Rumbough House (NRHP)　　　　　　　49 Zillicoa St.
Built in 1892 by James H. Rumbough, this elegant building, featuring a com-bination of Queen Anne, Colonial Revival and Neoclassical elements, is generally considered to be the most impressive residence in the Montford area. It features weatherboarding, wide porches and pairs of tapered and molded porch posts on stone pedestals. It is also known for its elaborately finished rooms. The house was owned by James Edwin Rumbough (1861-1941) who became the first and only mayor of the autonomous village of Montford when it was incorporated in 1893. Among his various other distinctions he is credited with being the first person to drive an automobile across the Appalachian Mountains, a feat that he accomplished in 1911. The house was purchased in 1952 by Duke University to become the administration building for the former Highland Hospital. It now houses the Carolina Center for Metabolic Medicine.

Turn around here and return on Zillicoa Street to Montford Avenue and turn left. Continue down Montford for 3 blocks to Blake Street and turn left on Blake to the stop sign. Turn right onto Cumberland Avenue and you'll find The Red-wood House immediately on your right.

Redwood House (NRHP)　　　　　　　90 Cumberland Ave.
This early 20th century house is officially known as Redwood House and is a fine example of Colonial Revival architecture. It features shingles over stucco, Doric porch posts and a high pitched roof.

Turn left in front of Redwood House onto Elizabeth Street and continue to Flint Street. Turn right on Flint. Just ahead on your right you'll see the Flint Street Inns.

Flint Street Inns (NRHP)　　　　　　100 & 116 Flint St.
The Flint Street Inns are two, side by side, distinguished old family homes that date back to the turn of the century. The structure at 100 Flint Street is a half-timbered stucco gable end dwelling. 116 Flint Street is thought to be one of Richard Sharp Smith's designs and features shingle over weatherboard, bracketed eaves, Montford brackets and a large dormer. Rooms in the Inns are furnished in turn-of-the-century style.

Your tour of Historic Montford is now over. Continue straight ahead up Flint Street to Haywood Street and downtown Asheville.

Vignette:
Richard Sharp Smith

Few persons have left their mark upon the face of a city as British-born Richard Sharp Smith has upon Asheville. Employed in his younger years by the prestigious architectural firm of Hunt and Hunt, he was sent to Asheville to supervise the construction of Biltmore House, which had been designed by Richard Morris Hunt. Smith stayed in Asheville, married here and raised two sons and two daughters. He became an American citizen and opened a private practice. During his life, he designed scores of private homes and dozens of commercial buildings in downtown Asheville. His distinctive architectural style has a British accent and Smith is remembered today as one of the most prominent of the many architects who helped shape Asheville.

Chestnut Hill Historic District

The Chestnut Hill Historic District is centered around Chestnut Hill, the apex of a knoll running west from Patton Mountain just 500 yards north of the center of Asheville. The neighborhood surrounding the hill was once an extension of the nineteenth-century residential streets that began a block off the city's Public Square. This district is a relatively compact late-nineteenth and early-twentieth-century residential neighborhood whose architectural styles and landscaping form a well-defined place. Tree-lined streets, brick-paved sidewalks and granite curbing are all unique features.

Practically all of the more than 200 buildings in the district were originally dwellings. Architecturally they range from the local in-town vernacular of the period to sophisticated versions of the nationally popular Queen Anne, Colonial Revival and Shingle styles.

The district dates from Asheville's post-railroad (post-1880) boom period and its finer homes reflect the relative sophistication of the city's more substantial citizens of that time. Besides a continuous growth in permanent residents, Asheville experienced an annual influx of thousands of summer and winter tourists and a number of Chestnut Hill "cottages" were built as high quality rental properties.

In this section, some of the more important houses will be presented as a self-guided driving tour. This is a very convenient way to see the Chestnut Hill district. Allow about an hour for the tour, and slightly more if you wish to park occasionally to get out and examine some of the buildings closer. As a note, Chestnut Hill District and the following two districts, Albermarle Park and Grove Park are very close together. It is possible to see all three of these important neighborhoods in a few hours.

Begin your tour by taking Merrimon Avenue north to Hillside Street. Turn right onto Hillside and go to second right North Liberty Street. Turn right onto North Liberty. A short distance on the left you'll see a classic Victorian House.

North Liberty Victorian House   76 North Liberty St.

A wonderful example of Victorian architecture, the elegant house is intricate in its detail and styling. It is a multi-gabled structure with flaring eaves and standing-seam tin roof, and has a square tower with a mansard-like shingled cap dominating the house adjacent to two projecting bays. The house's elaborate porch features turned posts, a scroll-bracketed cornice above a ladder frieze and a Chinese-Chippendale-like balustrade. Currently the building is undergoing restoration.

Continuing on North Liberty you will come upon the historic Beaufort House Bed & Breakfast on your left.

Beaufort House   61 North Liberty St.

This Victorian bed & breakfast is a grand 2½-story pink Queen Anne style house built in 1895 by former State Attorney general and prominent Asheville resident Theodore Davidson. This elegant building features a roof line that sweeps down upon an ample veranda accented at its southern end by a fanciful pergola. Elaborate interior woodwork includes paneled wainscoting and a closed-stringer stairway with intricately carved newel post and balusters. The building has been wonderfully restored as Beaufort House Bed & Breakfast and is furnished with antiques and period furniture.

From this unique house continue down North Liberty and turn left on East Chestnut Street. Located just one block down are two wonderfully restored bed & breakfasts. Chestnut Street is noted for its many fine examples of Colonial Revival, Queen Anne-influenced and bracketed Victorian homes.

White Gate Inn & Cottage   173 East Chestnut St.

Known officially as the Kent House, it was built circa 1889 and is a tall 2½-story Shingle style house. The building features tall exterior chimneys centered on minor gables. Mr. Kent who owned the house reportedly ran the Asheville Ice Company. Today it houses the White Gate Inn that is beautifully furnished with period antiques, fine furniture and collectibles.

Directly across the street is the newly restored Chestnut Street Inn.

Chestnut Street Inn   176 East Chestnut St.

Officially known as the William R. Whitson house, this Grand Colonial Revival House was built circa 1905. The house is constructed out of pressed brick and is two and a half stories with hip-on-hip roof with central Palladian dormer. The house, constructed for Whitson by J. M. Westall, has some of the finest wood-work in Asheville, including a graceful closed stringer stairway, beautiful arts & crafts wainscoting, and elaborate mirrored mantles. Today, Chestnut Street Inn

Chestnut Street Inn

welcomes visitors to its gracious and exquisite interior impeccably furnished with antiques and period decorations.

Just down the street on the right is the Annie West House.

Annie West House
189 East Chestnut St.

Built around 1900, this picturesque half-timbered cottage was designed by Richard Sharp Smith. Standing 1½ stories, it features a "veranda" across facade beneath a large central gable and smaller flanking dormers. This detail links it stylistically to early Biltmore Village architecture. Continue down East Chestnut to the Jeter Pritchard House.

Jeter Pritchard House
223 East Chestnut St.

This imposing two-story frame house was built by architect and builder James A. Tennent, who sold it to Senator Jeter Conly Pritchard in 1904. Construction dates back to around 1895. The building is a boxy weatherboard form under a multi-gabled roof. The interior of the house features exceptional woodworking.

Continue down East Chestnut to Charlotte Street and turn left. Take a right onto Baird Street and take your second left onto Albemarle Place to find The Carl Von Ruck House on your left.

Carl Von Ruck House (NRHP, LHL)
52 Albemarle Pl.

This rambling three-story house was built in three distinct stages by Dr. Carl Von Ruck, famed tuberculosis specialist who founded the Winyah Sanitorium on Sunset Mountain. In 1904 he bought twenty acres, including two houses that were on the property. One of the houses is incorporated into the north end of the present structure. In 1912 he built a separate house for his resident MDs just to the south and in 1915 he built between these two buildings, connecting them with a grand two-story music room with twin elliptic conservatories to either side. The music room features Viennese-crafted mahogany woodwork and houses Dr. Ruck's sixty-seven rank Aeolian Organ, with 4800 handmade wooden pipes rising two stories behind a curved mahogany screen.

At this point, turn around and return down Albemarle Place to Baird Street. At Baird turn left and look on the left for the Edward I. Holmes House.

Edward I. Holmes House   60 Baird St.

Built around 1883, this wonderfully restored house is an elaborated frame two-story double-pile plan design. There is a hip roof with internal brick chimneys and gabled projecting bays on each elevation. Other unique features are chamfered posts on opaque shoulder brackets and an elaborate scrollwork balustrade. No other 20th-century building in Asheville, especially of the finer structures, is as little altered as this house.

Edward I. Holmes House

Turn right onto Furman Avenue across from the Holmes House and continue down to East Chestnut Street. Turn right onto East Chestnut and just before you reach Charlotte Street you will see the white Thomas Patton House on your left. The main entrance is off Charlotte Street but virtually impossible to see from that direction because of the trees and landscaping. Turn left onto Charlotte Street and continue south to downtown Asheville.

Thomas Patton House   95 Charlotte St.

Built in 1869, the Thomas Patton House is a two-story frame house formally organized around central and traverse hallways. It has very interesting external features in chevron-latticed bargeboards. Tradition maintains that the house was built by black carpenters working from the plans of Thomas Patton. Patton was the grandson of James Patton, mayor of Asheville and active public servant.

Albemarle Park Historic District

Albemarle Park, located off Charlotte Street, is a planned residential community that is composed of 45 residences reflecting diverse and very attractive architectural styles that were built on a 32.42-acre tract of land acquired by William Green Raoul in 1886. Raoul, who served as president of both Georgian and Mexican railroads, was the visionary who conceived of Albemarle Park and who purchased the land from a local farmer named Deaver. It was his third son, Thomas Wadley Raoul, however who was to be the foreman of the project and the one who made the vision a reality. For almost twenty-five years he devoted his energies to overseeing the construction and management of The Manor and cottages.

The main building, The Manor, was built in 1898 by Thomas. He conceived the idea of a twenty-five room English style country inn to be used as a boarding house. He later modified his plan to include several individually designed cottages to complement the main house. From these beginnings the Albemarle Park neighborhood began to take shape, with Raoul insisting upon only the finest materials and workmanship to be used in the construction.

This neighborhood has very narrow curving streets that preserve much of the wooded landscape of the area. It is situated on the western slope of Sunset Mountain and is crowned by The Manor that graces a knoll that slopes down to Charlotte Street. This district is evocative of Asheville's dramatic turn-of-the-century resort town boom era, and its rich craftsmanship and informal picturesqueness is related to Biltmore Village.

The original site plan was designed by Samuel Parsons Jr., the landscape architect of New York's Central Park. The design catered to wealthy lowlanders from

The Manor

Georgia and North and South Carolina who saw the mountains as a summer refuge. The crown jewel of this marvelous complex is The Manor, one of the last intact grand hotels from the late 19th century resort era. It was used for the filming of one of the scenes for the recent movie "The Last of the Mohicans." This historic building also hosted the film crews for the movie, "The Swan," and Grace Kelly, who starred in the film was a guest at the inn. Her former rooms are now known as the Princess Suite. Alec Guiness, Agnes Morehead and Louis Jordan also stayed at The Manor during that time.

The Manor was converted to a retirement hotel in 1961 by Charles Lavin. By 1976 The Manor had changed owners again and at this time it became a residential hotel, and in 1984, after severe winter damage, it was closed. The Preservation Society bought The Manor in 1989 when it was threatened with demolition, and in 1991, it was sold and restored in an historically sensitive way as an apartment complex. Without the efforts of this important local organization, this historical treasure would have been lost forever.

Each building in the neighborhood was intended to have a distinctive architectural style. A walk through the neighborhood reveals cottages that show Italian, French and Swiss influences as well as Georgian Revival, Appalachian and Adirondack styles of architecture. The primary architect of Albemarle Park was Bradford Lee Gilbert, who also designed the Virginia Beach Hotel (1888) in Virginia Beach, Virginia, and the Berkeley Arms Hotel (1883) in Berkeley, New Jersey.

If you would like to learn more about this fascinating Historic District, you may purchase a copy of The Manor Cottages, a book published by the Albemarle Park-Manor Grounds Association, Inc. (P.O. Box 2231, Asheville, NC 28802), 258-1283. This excellent publication gives an in-depth look at the history and architecture.

To reach Albemarle Park take Charlotte Street north till you come to the original Gatehouse on your right at 265. Turn right onto Cherokee Road. The Manor will be on your left. Park your car if you wish in the small parking lot on Cherokee Road.

The Manor (NRHP, LHL)　　　265 Charlotte St.

Constructed in 1889, The Manor is a rambling group of interconnecting wings which combine elements of Shingle, Tudoresque and Dutch Colonial Revival architecture. The main portion of The Manor was built soon after the property, originally part of the Deaver Farm, was purchased in 1886 by the elder Raoul. This main portion of the inn is a twenty-five room five-part structure of rough field rock above which is a stucco and timber level.

A second wing, built in 1903, angles out from the main body of the inn towards the road. The main level of this wing is Tudoresque and has cross timbering beneath the windows that is painted a deep red color.

A third wing projects in the opposite direction and is composed of rough stone below green shingles. This wing was added in 1913-1914.

The interior of The Manor is wonderfully executed craftsmanship that is believed to have been done by Italian workmen from Biltmore Estate. An immense brick fireplace, a long, curved glass-enclosed sun corridor and Tiffany-type stained glass windows are among the notable features.

Just below The Manor are the Gatehouse and the Clubhouse.

The Gatehouse (NRHP)

Also referred to as the Lodge, this building was the first structure built in Albemarle Park, erected by James A. Tennent in 1898. It was designed by Gilbert in the Tudoresque Shingle style with pebbledash stucco at the first floor and granite foundation. The Lodge arched over the entrance drive leading from Charlotte Street into The Park. During the early years of the development, the offices of the Albemarle Park Company were on the ground floor of the two-story shingle and stone turret. Today the Gatehouse is used for commercial office space.

The Club House (NRHP)

Built around 1903, it originally contained the tennis courts, bowling alleys, pool and billiard rooms and a reading lounge. It is an L-shaped building of stone and timber that has a long gallery on the second floor. Three small hexagonal offices now dot the area between the old tennis court and the Gatehouse, and though modern, are in character with the round and polygonal forms found on several of the earlier buildings. The Club House today is used for commercial office space.

After viewing these main buildings, you may wish to venture on foot to see some of the lovely cottages throughout Albemarle Park. Dogwood Cottage, Foxhall and Rose Bank are all within walking distance.

Dogwood Cottage Inn (NRHP) 40 Canterbury Rd.

This large 1½-story rustic shingle cottage is now operated as a bed & breakfast, the Dogwood Cottage Inn. Main features are a continuous shed dormer across the main facade, casement windows and a bracketed hood over the entrance. It was built as a home for William Green and Mary Raoul in 1910 and sits on a commanding mountainside site offering views of the mountains to the west. The rustic style of the Dogwood Cottage relates to the traditional architecture of the Appalachians.

Dogwood Cottage Inn

Foxhall and Fox Den (NRHP)   60 Terrace Rd.

Foxhall is the larger of the two and was built in 1914 by E.A. Fordtran, who was the owner of the New Orleans Times/Picayune newspaper. It is a 2½-story building, originally stucco and shingle, which has been refaced with brick veneer and siding. The building has graceful roof lines and fenestration and is beautifully landscaped. Fox Den is a two-story gambrel roofed garage apartment of stucco and timber that adjoins Foxhall.

Rose Bank (NRHP)   106 Orchard Rd.

Rose Bank is a two-story shingle cottage with a projecting Dutch gambrel wing and double porches, designed in the Dutch Colonial Revival Style. Built around 1905, Rose Bank has distinctive windows that have diamond-paned upper sashes playfully arranged. Windows of various sizes and shapes are tied together with simple trim.

Grove Park Historic District

The Grove Park Historic District is located in an area that adjoins the Grove Park Country Club golf course and extends on either side of Charlotte Street. This district also includes part of Kimberly Avenue that runs along side the golf course in a northerly direction.

The Grove Park neighborhood was designed and developed by St. Louis entrepreneur Edwin Wiley Grove with the help of Chauncey Beadle, landscape designer and later superintendent of Biltmore Estate and is a superb example of early twentieth century planned residential development. Grove wanted his development, like every other real estate venture he engaged in, to be exciting and innovative. Some of his ventures, such as the Grove Arcade and the Battery Park Hotel, were on the cutting edge of design and planning and his Grove Park Inn stands today as a monument to Grove's vision and genius.

The early phases of Grove Park were laid out by Chauncey Beadle and have curvilinear streets, large tree canopies, stone retaining walls and a grand entry park. There are many architectural styles represented and these include Shingle, Neo-Classical, American Foursquare, Colonial Revival, Tudor Revival, Georgian Revival, Bungalow, Italian Renaissance, Queen Anne and Chateauesque. Many nationally known and historically important architects worked within the Grove Park neighborhood. These included Richard Sharp Smith, Ronald Greene, Henry I. Gaines and James Gamble Rogers. Local Asheville developers E.A. Jackson and W.H. Westall also contributed to Grove Park's growth, buying and developing many lots in the 1920s.

Especially notable in this lovely neighborhood are the large number of deciduous and evergreen trees. Stonework in retaining walls and stairs are found throughout and many of the houses are on terraced grounds.

Like the Montford and Chestnut Hill historic districts, Grove Park is easily seen by car, and a self-guided tour is presented below.

To reach Grove Park take Charlotte Street north to 324 Charlotte Street where you will see Mr. Grove's Real Estate Office on the left.

E.W. Grove's Office (NRHP)   324 Charlotte St.

This building is a small one-story rubble rock structure with rough-faced ashlar covering. It features a tile-on-gable roof. It was constructed around 1909 and is said to have been used by Grove when he was building the Grove Park Inn and developing the Grove Park neighborhood. The building was designed by Richard Sharp Smith and is the only structure of its type in the area. Grove left the building and the adjacent park to the City of Asheville. Note also the handsome stone gates to the right, entrances into the park.

Continue on Charlotte Street to 337 where you will see the beautiful St. Mary's Parish Church just ahead on your right.

St. Mary's Parish, Grove Park (NRHP)   337 Charlotte St.

Described in the year of her founding in 1914 as a "Wayside Shrine in the Mountains of Western North Carolina," beautiful little St. Mary's Church has attracted countless visitors over the years. Designed by Richard Sharp Smith and built in 1914, the church is English Gothic in style and cruciform in plan. Constructed out of red brick with steeply pitched gable roofs, the building is like those dotting the hilly landscape of County Durham, Northumberland and Cumbria in northern England. The English cottage-style Rectory, also designed by Smith, was built and set in beautiful landscaped grounds. The landscape architect was the famous Frederick Law Olmsted, architect for Biltmore Estate and designer

St. Mary's Parish at Grove Park

of New York's Central Park. International attention was brought to St. Mary's by the writer Gail Godwin when she immortalized the church in her novel Father Melancholy's Daughter.

From St. Mary's Parish, return down Charlotte Street and turn left onto Sunset Parkway. Continue on Sunset to the end where you will turn left onto Glendale Road. Look for 50 on your right, the Edgar Fordtran House. It is up on a hill at the intersection of Ridgewood Street, behind ivy covered stone walls.

Edgar Fordtran House (NRHP)   50 Glendale Rd.

This Tudor Revival style house was built in 1936 for Edgar Fordtran for $30,000. It is constructed of cut ashlar stone with stucco infill as part of the half-timbering in the front gable. This lovely building features outstanding chimneys and a decorative wrought iron front door. The landscaping is especially noteworthy and includes a winding drive, stone retaining wall and large wrought iron gates. This residence was the ASID Designer House for 1994.

Continue on Glendale Road to the stop sign and turn left onto Macon Avenue. Look for the Ralph Worthington House on your left.

Edgar Fordtran House

Ralph Worthington House (NRHP)   41 Macon Ave.

This handsome house was built in 1920 by Ralph Worthington and is a wonderful example of the quality of the houses that abound in the Grove Park District. The ASID Designer House for 1992, it is an excellent blend of Colonial Revival and Spanish Revival styles of architecture. It was operated as a boarding house from 1942 to 1959 but is now a private residence.

Continue on Macon to Charlotte Street and at the stop sign take a right onto Charlotte Street. Turn left onto Evelyn Place just beyond the park. Immediately on your left, just past the intersection of Gertrude Place, is the J.R. Oates House.

Ralph Worthington House

J.R. Oates House (NRHP)
90 Gertrude Pl.

Built in 1913 for J.R. Oates, a local banker, the house was designed by the architectural firm of Smith and Carrier. It is an excellent example of the Prairie style of architecture. A striking two-story house with smooth stucco and a cross gable roof with wide overhanging eaves. According to the portfolio of Richard Sharp Smith, the building was designated as "fireproof." It is noteworthy also for the superb craftsmanship of the interior as well as the exterior spaces, including the beautifully landscaped grounds.

Directly across the street on Evelyn Place is the Reuben Robertson House.

Reuben Robertson House (NRHP)   1 Evelyn Pl.

This elegant house was built for Reuben Robertson in 1922 and was designed by New York architect James Gamble Rogers. This is an excellent example of the Colonial Revival style of architecture.

Continue on Evelyn Place to 107, The William Bryan Jennings House, which will be on your right.

Reuben Robertson House

Residence on Kimberly Avenue

William Jennings Bryan House (NRHP)   107 Evelyn Pl.

William Jennings Bryan, famous orator, statesman, politician and presidential candidate spent many summers in this house. Built in 1917, it was designed also by Richard Sharp Smith, and is a refined example of a Colonial Revival style house. Exceptional details include paired columns and pilasters on front stoop and dentil molding beneath the roof lines.

After viewing the Jennings House, turn right onto Kimberly Avenue and continue on up Kimberly.

Kimberly Avenue

Kimberly Avenue is one of the finer residential streets in all of Asheville, bordered on one side by the Grove Park Inn golf course and one the other by grand houses from the 1920s. The Avenue is a favorite for local walkers and joggers and the views of the Grove Park Inn and nearby mountains from the tree-lined street are outstanding.

This concludes your tour of the historic Grove Park District. To return to downtown Asheville, retrace your path down Kimberly Avenue and Edwin Place to Charlotte Street. While you are in the vicinity, you may wish to visit the Grove Park Inn and The Biltmore Industries Buildings which are close by. Both of these are presented later in this chapter.

Biltmore Village Historic District

Biltmore Village was built by George W. Vanderbilt on the south bank of the Swannanoa River at the edge of his vast estate. Much has changed over the years by the flood tide of urban sprawl, Biltmore Village nonetheless has some remaining buildings from that early period. Many of these form a small neighborhood which evokes the village's original ambience. The landscaping, the quaintness of the cottages, the presence of other remaining buildings and the street pattern all form an important historic district.

The symmetrical, fan-shaped street plan is the least changed element of the original design. At the north end, Brook and Lodge streets join at an obtuse angle at the railway station and plaza. All Souls Crescent swings south from these streets to form the boundaries of the village, and within the village itself a network of streets forms the fan pattern.

Vanderbilt planned Biltmore Village as a picturesque manorial village, to complement his estate and grounds and as a practical solution to solving the housing problem of estate workers and servants. This model village, English in flavor with

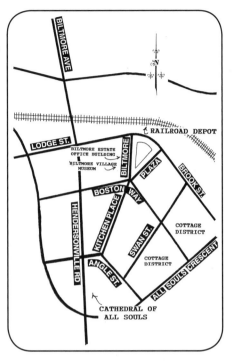

Biltmore Village

its Tudor buildings, was primarily the work of three men: Richard Morris Hunt (1827-1895), the nationally prominent architect who designed Biltmore House itself, the village church of All Souls, the railway station and the estate office; Frederick Law Olmsted (1822-1903), the renowned landscape architect who designed the grounds of the estate and the village plan; and Richard Sharp Smith (1852-1924), an architect employed by Hunt who designed the cottages, school, post office, infirmary and other village buildings.

The site along the Swannanoa River, a small crossroads known as Asheville Junction or Best (for William J. Best, an owner of the Western North Carolina Railroad) was chosen for Biltmore Village, planning for which began in 1889. Vanderbilt bought the village, relocated the residents and constructed an entirely new town. Construction was largely complete by 1910. Shortly after Vanderbilt's death, the village was sold and over the years, many changes were made, not all compatible with the original concept and design of Vanderbilt and his architects. Recently however, through the efforts of the Historic Resources Commission of Asheville and Buncombe County, the Preservation Society and the Biltmore Village Merchants Association, much restoration has been accomplished and an enlightened program of adaptive use instituted. At the heart of Biltmore Village's recent revival has been the conversion of former cottages into commercial spaces that include gift shops, restaurants, art and craft galleries and clothing stores.

The Village is a Local as well as a National Historic District which will insure its preservation and continued restoration.

Biltmore Village is an ideal setting for a walking self-guided tour and the historic buildings highlighted in this section will be presented in that fashion. I suggest also that you visit the Biltmore Village Historic Museum at 7 Biltmore Plaza, one building to the left of the Biltmore Estate Office Building on the plaza. (SEE Section Three, Chapter 2)

Begin your walking tour by parking near the plaza, across from the old railroad depot, which will be your first stop.

Biltmore Village Railway Depot (NRHP)   1 Biltmore Plaza

This Southern Railway passenger depot was designed by Richard Morris Hunt and is a symmetrical one-story structure with half-timbered pebbledash walls. It is significant as one of the four structures that were designed by Hunt for the Village and it serves as one of the major functional and architectural landmarks of the community. It was built in 1896.

Walk across the Plaza and you will see the Biltmore Estate Office on your right.

Biltmore Estate Office (NRHP)   10 Biltmore Plaza

Another of the four structures designed by Hunt it is a combination of the design motifs and materials utilized in other structures in the village. It is a 1½-story building that features pebbledash walls, half-timbering, brick trim, chamfered and bracketed porch posts and stylized classical ornament. This building served as the office for the operations of Biltmore Estate and was constructed also in 1896. It is still in use today by the Biltmore Company for offices.

After viewing the Biltmore Estate Office Building, you will see the Biltmore Village Historic Museum, also on the plaza. If they are open, stop in for a visit. After leaving the museum, continue on your way from the plaza area and walk south on Kitchen Place towards The Cathedral of All Souls directly ahead.

The Cathedral of All Souls (NRHP)   9 Swan St.

Originally known as All Souls Church, it was designated an Episcopal Cathedral in January 1995. The largest structure in Biltmore Village, it is an exquisite, lovely building of fine Romanesque style. Designed by Richard Morris Hunt, this complex building combines pebbledash wall surfaces, brick and wood trim, and expansive tiles roofs. In spite of the complexity however, the church is a simple cruciform with a tall tower rising in the center which contains most of the interior space. The Parish House features the same materials but is considerably different in design.

The interior is relatively simple but no less elegant and features wonderful stained glass windows created for the Vanderbilts by Maitland Armstrong and his daughter Helen. They illuminate a variety of scenes from the Old and New Testaments.

The Cathedral of All Souls

George Vanderbilt was one of the organizers of the congregation in 1896, financed the construction of the church and parish house and selected the furnishings. The church was consecrated on November 8, 1896.

From this lovely building, you may now begin to explore the Cottage District which is found on Swan Street, All Souls Crescent, and Boston Way. There are fourteen cottages in this district, which will be on your left and behind you as you face the front of the church and the Parish House.

Biltmore Village Cottage District (NRHP)

The English Tudor cottages on the east side of Biltmore Village were designed by architect Richard Sharp Smith. All are one-and-one-half to two-story pebble-dash cottages with recessed porches, multiple gables and steeply pitched roofs. No two cottages are alike although they are closely similar and in some cases mirror images. They are located at 1 and 3 Swan Street, 2, 4, 6, 7, 10 and 11 All Souls Crescent and 5 and 6 Boston Way. Besides being architecturally interesting, these cottages now house specialty shops and restaurants.

This concludes the walking tour of Biltmore Village. Another structure of historical importance, The Reed House, is in the district and can be visited by car. From the plaza area take Lodge Street to Hendersonville Road (Highway 25) and turn left. Go south on Hendersonville Road to Irwin Street and turn left. Turn left at the end onto Dodge Street and look for 119, The Samuel Harrison Reed House.

Biltmore Cottage District

Samuel Harrison Reed House (NRHP)   119 Dodge St.

Built in 1892, this house is one of the most important Queen Anne style residences in Asheville. The frame structure features a prominent corner turret with an ogee dome and a wraparound porch. It is historically significant for its associations with Mr. Reed, who sold to George Vanderbilt and his land agents the property on which Biltmore Village was constructed.

Eliada Home Historic District

The Eliada Home is a youth home complex located in the Leicester neighborhood of Asheville. This historic district includes the early administrative, residential and agricultural buildings of the home as well as associated sites that include a residence, a tabernacle site, a log guest cabin and cemetery. Eliada Home is in a parklike setting with concrete walks and shade trees, and is situated on a hilltop.

Eliada Home was founded by Lucius B. Compton as a refuge for unwed mothers in 1903. The first facility was "Faith Cottage" on Atkinson Street in Asheville. The children's home was established in 1906, with buildings on the property dating back to 1907, and is still in operation today.

To reach Eliada Home, take Patton Avenue west from Asheville and turn right onto Leicester Highway. Turn right again onto Compton Drive. Eliada Home is at the end of Compton Drive. www.eliada.org

Main Building (NRHP)   2 Compton Dr.

The main building is a two-and-a half story, five-course American-bond brick structure that originally served as a dormitory and was used also for administration, food processing (canning) and as an outlet store for excess clothing and as a chapel. The exterior style is Colonial Revival and Foursquare-inspired, and was designed by architect Thomas E. Davis.

Located behind the Main Building and accessible down a short gravel drive is the most impressive of the structures at Eliada Home, the Dairy Barn.

Dairy Barn (NRHP)

This magnificent barn was built between 1930 and 1931 and is a two-level, six course American-bond brick building with room for forty dairy cows on the fire-proof first level and machinery and tools on the second level. The barn was used for milk production and the motto "Eliada Dairy, Pure Bred Guernseys" was originally painted on the west side of the roof. This has been replaced with the motto "Eliada Home Outlet Barn," indicating its use as a retail outlet since the late 1970s.

Oteen Veterans Administration Hospital Historic District

Located in the Oteen district of Asheville on US Highway 70 just beyond the intersection of Highway 70 and Riceville Road, the Oteen Veterans Administration Hospital District is a striking collection of massive yellow stucco Georgian Revival and white frame Colonial Revival buildings. As Riceville Road leaves Highway 70 at the foot of the hospital's lawn it runs north through the district and divides employees' dormitories and other residential structures to its west from the facility's main campus.

The structures included in the Historic District were built between 1924 and 1940 to replace a large collection of frame buildings which had served as U.S. Army General Hospital No. 19 in the late teens and early twenties. The work accomplished at the Oteen location turned out to be one of the nation's best and most beautiful permanent military hospitals. The focus of care at the hospital was tubercular and respiratory treatment. Today the hospital still functions as a major care center, although some of the outlying buildings have been converted to apartment use. For more information about the current medical programs at the VA Hospital, see Section Three, Chapter 8 Asheville VA Medical Center.

Asheville High School Historic District (NRHP)

To reach the Asheville High School Historic District, take Patton Avenue west from Pritchard Park. Turn left onto Asheland Avenue until you reach McDowell Street. Continue on McDowell until you reach the high school at 419.

Asheville High School is an Italian Renaissance and Art Deco pink granite building that was a state-of-the-art facility when it opened February 5, 1929. It cost $1,362,601 when it was built by general contractor Palmer-Spivey Construction Co. of Charlotte, using the plans of architect Douglas D. Ellington. The main school building is visible from McDowell Street and is a large Art Deco/Italian Renaissance style structure that features a tile roof. The landscaping in front is extraordinary and the formal stairs, drives and walkways of Ellington's plan serve as a graceful setting for the magnificent building. The whole school complex is

Asheville High School

contained within this district. Originally named Asheville High School, it was renamed Lee H. Edwards High School but was changed back to Asheville High School in 1969 when the city schools were integrated.

Asheville School Historic District (NRHP)

To reach the Asheville School Historic District, take Patton Avenue west from Pritchard Park. Continue on Patton Avenue (19-23 South); 3.4 miles after you cross over the French Broad River, look for Asheville School Road on your left just beyond Goodwill Industries.

The Asheville School and its attendant buildings compose the Asheville School Historic District. This lovely parklike campus is approximately 276 acres, with a winding entrance road lined with native evergreens. These were planted by Chauncey Beadle, landscape gardener for Biltmore Estate, who donated his design services to the school. Asheville School is still in operation today, many years after its founding in 1900, and still provides excellent secondary education as a private boarding school. It was founded by Newton Anderson and Charles Mitchell. Over the years, they commissioned many prominent architects to design the campus buildings, including John Milton Dyer, Thomas Hibben, and Anthony Lord. The result was a collection of wonderful and architecturally impressive buildings. www.asheville-school.org

Following the entrance road you will pass in front of the three main administration buildings and then around to the larger structures, Anderson Hall, Mitchell Hall and Lawrence Hall, all on your right.

Anderson Hall (NRHP)   Asheville School Rd.

This building was built as the main academic building in 1900 and is the oldest one on the campus. It was designed by John Milton Dyer of Cleveland and is Tudor Revival in style. Constructed primarily of brick with limestone lintels and sills on the first and second floor windows, it is three stories tall.

Mitchell Hall, Asheville School Historic District

Mitchell Hall (NRHP) Asheville School Rd.

Built in 1903, this building was also designed by Dyer and is a long, linear plan with porches on the front and rear of the building. Walls on the lower floors are brick, with half-timbering on the uppermost floors. The exterior and interior design of this superb building is Art Deco with Tudor Revival detailing.

Lawrence Hall (NRHP) Asheville School Rd.

Lawrence Hall is the third of the main campus buildings and was constructed in 1907. It is likely that Dyer also designed this building. The building was originally used as a dormitory, which it remains today along with administrative use. Three stories high, it is Tudor Revival in style.

Biltmore Industries Historic District (NRHP)

Directions: Take Charlotte Street to Macon Avenue. Turn right on Macon and go to Grove Park Inn Resort, 290 Macon Avenue. Turn left into the inn's parking area and bear right to go down the hill and left at the stop sign to Grovewood Road and Grovewood Shops area.

The Biltmore Industries complex of buildings is situated on an eleven and one-half acre tract adjacent to the Grove Park Inn Resort. The seven buildings of the grouping, which vary in size and form, lie in a row along the top of a ridge. These cottages were constructed in 1917 under the supervision of Fred Seely, designer and owner of the Grove Park Inn. The purpose was to provide workshops for the production of high-quality crafts and fine hand-woven cloth that would be pleasing to the workers, and to provide a special to visitors at the Grove Park by offering the opportunity to observe the manufacturing process and to purchase completed items.

*Biltmore Industries buildings include Estes-Winn Automobile Museum.
The buildings are adjacent to the Grove Park Inn Resort & Spa.*

Today the Biltmore Industries Buildings house the Grovewood Gallery, the Estes-Winn Automobile Museum, the North Carolina Homespun Museum and the Grovewood Cafe.

Other Historic Asheville Sites & Buildings

This section of Historic Asheville is devoted to those sites and buildings of architectural or historic importance that have not been covered in the previous section.

Albemarle Inn Bed & Breakfast (NRHP, LHL)   86 Edgemont Rd.

Officially known as the Dr. Carl V. Reynolds House, this large frame Neo-Classical Greek Revival building is today the Albemarle Inn Bed & Breakfast. It is distinguished by a gable roof and a two-story portico with twin pairs of Corinthian columns and half-round pilasters. The interior features oak paneling and an exquisite carved oak stairway with a unique circular landing and balcony. Dr. Carl Reynolds built this house in 1909 and occupied it until 1920. Thereafter it was leased to the Grove Park School and then to the Plonk sisters, who operated an arts school there until it became the Albemarle Inn in 1941. Hungarian composer Bela Bartok stayed at the Inn during 1943 and while there completed his Third Piano Concerto, also known as the Asheville Concerto or Concerto of Birds. (SEE also Section Two, Chapter 1)

Directions: From Pack Square, take College Street east to Charlotte Street. Turn left and go 0.9 miles. Turn right onto Edgemont Road.

Albemarle Inn Bed & Breakfast

Beaucatcher Tunnel (NRHP) College St.

This two-lane tunnel was originally built in 1930 to replace a winding road that went over Beaucatcher Mountain. The tunnel was blasted out of solid granite and has served Asheville for these many years. In 1997 it was refurbished and modernized and new granite stonework installed over the entrances.

Directions: From Pack Square take College Street east to the nearby tunnel entrance.

Biltmore Estate (NRHP, NHL) Entrance opposite Biltmore Village

This magnificent estate built by George Vanderbilt is a national treasure. Biltmore House, the largest privately owned house in America, is visited by hundreds of thousands of visitors each year. For architectural and historical information see Section Three, Chapter 3 Biltmore Estate.

Biltmore Forest

Biltmore Forest is an area of fine residential homes that adjoins part of Biltmore Estate. Driving through this lovely parklike neighborhood you will see many architecturally interesting and historic buildings. Notice also the street lamps, antique ornamental fixtures still in use throughout that combine lighting and signage functions. The high quality copper and bronze swan-neck lamp posts are thought to have been manufactured in California and bought by a Judge Adams before 1928. Of special interest are the Biltmore Forest Municipal Buildings (circa 1927) at Vanderbilt Place, the Silver Shop Building (circa 1930) at 365 Vanderbilt Road and the Biltmore Forest Country Club (circa 1922) at Country Club Road.

Residence in Biltmore Forest

Although Biltmore Forest is not a Historic District, many of the buildings are individually listed in the National Register of Historic Places.

Directions: Biltmore Forest can be entered at many places along Hendersonville Road going south from Biltmore Village. An easy-to-find entrance is Vanderbilt Road that enters the Forest just to the right of the Quality Inn Biltmore.

Cedar Crest (NRHP, LHL)   674 Biltmore Ave.

Officially known as the William E. Breese, Sr. House, this is one of the largest and most opulent residences surviving from Asheville's 1890s boom period. A wonderful Queen Anne-style dwelling, it was constructed by contractor Charles B. Leonard in 1891. It features a prominent turret, expansive side and rear porches and interior woodwork of extraordinary beauty. It was opened as a tourist home with the present name "Cedar Crest" in the 1930s. Today, it is a Victorian bed & breakfast. (SEE also Section Two, Chapter 1)

Directions: From Pack Square take Biltmore Avenue south.

Church of the Redeemer (NRHP)   1201 Riverside Dr.

This small, coursed-ashlar church was reportedly built in 1886 by a Dr. Willis, an immigrant from England. It features a cruciform plan, patterned slate roof and round arched windows with beautiful stained glass. An Episcopal Church, it still is in operation and visitors are welcome.

Directions: From Pack Square take Broadway north to Riverside Drive. Turn right onto Riverside Drive.

Grove Park Inn Resort & Spa (NRHP, NHL) 290 Macon St.

The Grove Park Inn Resort & Spa is one of the largest resort and conference centers in the Carolinas. Built in 1913 by Edwin Wiley Grove of native granite boulders, the main block of the inn is four double bays wide and four stories deep with a deep hip roof pierced by two rows of eyelid dormers, thus making six floors in all. The granite for the inn was quarried locally from nearby Sunset Mountain.

A magnificent building, it has many noteworthy architectural features including more than 600 handmade solid copper lighting fixtures still in use, the main lobby with the huge fireplaces at each end and the striking red clay tile roof. Recently wings were added to each side of the hotel, thus providing over 500 rooms. (SEE Section Three, Chapter 6 for more about the history of the Grove Park Inn Resort & Spa)

Directions: Take exit 5B onto Charlotte Street off I-240. Go one-half mile north on Charlotte Street to Macon Avenue. Turn right. The Inn is one-half mile up Macon Avenue.

Grove Park Inn Country Club (NRHP) Country Club Rd.

Formerly the Asheville Country Club, this rambling stucco-on-masonry structure was designed in a chateauesque style by English architect H.T. Linderberg in 1925. Distinctive features include a diminutive round tower with tall conical cap and weathervane adjacent to the archway drive and a grand Flemish bond chimney on the west side of the north-south section of the building. The Country Club building is owned today by the Grove Park Inn Resort and houses the Golf Pro Shop, swimming pool facilities and is also used to host meetings and weddings.

Directions: Take exit 5B onto Charlotte Street off I-240. Go one-half mile north on Charlotte Street to Macon Avenue. Turn right. Inn is one-half mile up Macon. Enter into main driveway and in front of the hotel bear right. Go down hill to stop sign and turn left and then left again at stop sign onto access road. Country Club building in on your left.

The Hop Ice Cream Shop (NRHP) 507 Merrimon Ave.

The Hop is a Late Art Deco 1950s gasoline station that has been converted to an ice cream parlor with a drive-through window in one of its two service bays. Still serving delicious ice cream, the Hop is a window into the past. Neon lighting, stainless steel and appropriate painting schemes all accentuate the image and feeling of a 1950s drive-through.

Directions: From Pack Square take Broadway north to Merrimon Avenue. Follow Merrimon past Weaver Park, and The Hop will be on your right.

Longchamps Apartments (NRHP)   185 Macon Ave.

This imposing six-story structure was designed by Ronald Greene and built around 1925. Chateauesque and Tudor elements are combined in the unusual facade. The body of the building is a combination of half-timbers, rectilinear and half-round towers and brick and slate. A controversial building because of the unusual combination of elements, the building is nevertheless pleasing and has a majestic presence.

Directions: From I-240 take the Charlotte Street exit 5B. Take Charlotte Street north and turn right onto Macon Avenue.

The Old Reynolds Mansion (NRHP)   100 Reynolds Hghts.

Officially known as the Reynolds-Reynolds House, this two-story American bond brick structure is supposed to have been built around 1846. During the 1920s the house was completely remodeled at which time a third floor within a mansard roof with dormers as well as other rooms were added giving the house a Second-Empire look. Today the house is known as The Old Reynolds Mansion and is operated as a bed breakfast.

Directions: From Pack Square, take Broadway to the juncture of Merrimon Avenue. Follow Merrimon Avenue north past Beaver Lake and turn right just past next stop light onto Beaver Drive. Turn left up gravel lane.

Richmond Hill Inn (NRHP, LHL)   45 Richmond Hill Rd.

The grand Victorian mansion known as Richmond Hill was built in 1889-1890 as the private residence of Ambassador and Congressman Richard Pearson. Designed by James G. Hill, it was one of the most elegant residential structures of its time. It had ten master fireplaces, a communications system, running water, and a pulley-operated elevator for transporting baggage from one floor to the next. The mansion combines the materials, irregular form and complex plan of the Queen Anne style but has restrained Neoclassical ornamentation.

The elegant mansion was the center of social and political activity for many years. Today, it is a lovely country inn surrounded by rolling grounds with gardens overlooking the French Broad River. Restored to its original splendor, the estate was opened as an inn in 1989. The 12 guest rooms in the mansion are decorated in a style reflecting the spirit of the 1890s. Of particular note are the wonderfully restored interior surfaces—rich oak, cherry and other fine woods.

Richmond Hill Inn was saved from demolition through the relentless efforts of Asheville's Preservation Society. Thanks to their work, Richmond Hill shines today as one of the jewels in Asheville's crown of architectural treasures. The Richmond Hill today is owned by Jake and Marge Michael and is considered one of the premier country inns in Western North Carolina.

Directions: From I-240 take Highway 19/23 (Weaverville exit). Once on 19/23 take exit 251 (UNC-Asheville) and turn left at the bottom of the ramp. At the first stoplight, turn left onto Riverside Drive. Off Riverside Drive turn right onto Pearson Bridge Road and at the sharp curve, turn right onto Richmond Hill Drive.

Richmond Hill Inn, 45 Richmond Hill Road

Sherrill's Inn (NRHP)   Hwy. 74A, Fairview

This large weatherboarded house was operated as an inn that served travelers passing through Hickory Nut Gap during the 19th century. Bedford Sherrill began operating the inn in 1834. It is a two-story saddlebag-plan structure that probably dates back to around 1801. Also located on the property is a very old smokehouse and tradition maintains that this building served as a frontier "fort" in the 1790s. More than likely this small rectangular building is the area's oldest structure. The inn, which is a private residence today, is visible on the right as you drive up the winding Hickory Nut Gap Road from Fairview going towards the Lake Lure area. As a note, if you happen to be in Asheville or Hendersonville in the fall during apple harvest the owners of the house sell excellent homemade cider and fresh apples grown in the property's orchards.

Directions: From Asheville take I-240 east to exit 9 (Bat Cave, Lake Lure and Highway 74A east). Take Highway 74A east through Fairview to the very end of the valley. As you climb up the winding road to Hickory Nut Gap, look for the State Historic Sign and Sherrill's Inn on your right up on a hill.

St. Luke's Episcopal Church (NRHP)   219 Chunns Cove Rd.

St. Luke's is a tiny historic country frame church located in the Chunns Cove section of Asheville. The building was consecrated on July 9th, 1898 and features triangular arched windows with simple geometric stained glass. The building is noteworthy for its simple, honest beauty.

Directions: From I-240 take Exit 6 Chunns Cove Road. Look for the church on your right.

St. Matthias Church

St. Matthias Church (NRHP)   One Dundee St.

Saint Matthias began as Trinity Chapel in 1867 on land donated by Captain Thomas Patton. It has the distinction of being Asheville's first black congregation. In addition, a strong Sunday School and Day School flourished on the site and offered the only formal education at that time for the children of the black community. However, they soon outgrew the smaller structure and the present building was begun in 1894. It was completed two years later under the supervision of James Vester Miller, whose crew then went to begin work on Biltmore House. At this time it was renamed Saint Matthias to honor the 13th apostle and the first missionary to Africa. A handsome Gothic-brick structure, the building features elaborate interior woodwork.

Directions: Located in downtown Asheville. Take exit 5B off I-240 onto Charlotte Street heading south. Take a left on Carver Street, then a quick right on Grail Street, and then turn right onto Dundee Street.

Smith-McDowell House (NRHP, LHL)   283 Victoria Rd.

The Smith-McDowell House is one of Asheville's major historic structures. Built around 1848, the house is an impressive two-story double-pile plan Flemish-bond brick house with a graceful two-tier porch. It is one of the oldest buildings surviving in Asheville and definitely the oldest brick structure in Buncombe County. The house was constructed for James M. Smith, one of the wealthiest and most influential men in antebellum Asheville. It is open today as a museum. See Section Three, Chapter 2, Smith-McDowell House for more information about the museum and the programs offered.

The Smith-McDowell House as it appeared in 1848

Directions: From Pack Square take Biltmore Avenue south. Just past St. Joseph Hospital and just before Memorial Mission Hospital turn right onto Victoria Road.

Thomas Wolfe House (NHL, NRHP, LHL) 48 Spruce St.

This historic two-story Queen Anne style house was the childhood home of North Carolina's most famous writer, Thomas Wolfe. The building was built around 1883 and features a decoratively-shingled slate roof, colored glass windows and bracketed cornice. In 1906 it was purchased by Wolfe's mother, Julia, who operated it as a boarding house that she called Dixieland. Wolfe immortalized it in his novel *Look Homeward Angel*. Almost destroyed by fire in 1998, the house was authentically restored in 2004. It is operated today as the Thomas Wolfe Memorial and is open to the public. For more information about this important house, see Section Three, Chapter 2, Thomas Wolfe Memorial.

Directions: From Pack Square take Broadway north and turn right onto Woodfin Street. Take first right onto Market Street. Memorial parking lot is ahead on the left (Spruce Street, the official address for the house no longer exists as a operational city street.)

Thomas Wolfe House, "Dixieland"

Chapter Five
The Asheville Urban Trail

One of the most creative projects that has accompanied the revitalization of downtown Asheville has been the development of the Asheville Urban Trail, a walking route through downtown that is centered around Pack Square, the birthplace of Asheville. The trail is highlighted with interpretive displays which commemorate people, places and events of historic, cultural and architectural significance.

In this chapter, we will explore this special Asheville attraction, through the gracious cooperation of the Urban Trail Committee and especially writer Mickie Booth, who contributed the following article about the Trail for this book.

In walking the trail, your starting point will be the Pack Place Education, Arts & Science Center located on Pack Square across from the Vance Monument. Here you can pick up a free map for the self-guided tour. The 1.7 mile-long trail should take an hour or so, depending on your walking pace. And of course, along the way there are plenty of opportunities for refreshment in Asheville's many cafes and coffeehouses. Maps are available at the Asheville Visitors Center.

Should you wish to get involved in helping to fund or develop the Trail, which is dependent on private donations and is a work-in-progress contact Asheville's Public Art Administrator at 259-5855, FAX 259-5606, or write to: Public Art Administrator, Asheville Parks and Recreation Department, PO Box 7148, Asheville, NC 28802. Plaques and artwork may be given in memory of family and friends, or to honor someone who contributed significantly to the lives of others. The donor's name or honoree can then be reflected on a plaque at a chosen station.

Location:	Downtown Asheville
Address:	Pick up maps and rent cassettes at main desk of Pack Place, located on Pack Square
Telephone:	258-0710 (Asheville Area Arts Council)
FAX:	259-5606
Website:	www.ashevillearts.com
Hours:	None, visit anytime

Fees: Self-guided tours, using audiocassettes ($5 per cassette rental).
Guided tours are available beginning at 3 p.m. every Saturday. $5
donation per adult, children under 12 free.

Tips: The trail may be started at any point.

"The Asheville Urban Trail" by Mickie Booth

Beginning and ending at Pack Square, the Urban Trail is a self-guided celebration of Asheville's history and architectural treasures. Indeed, the Urban Trail has
often been likened to "a museum without walls." Located in Asheville's historic
district, the trail—by means of informative plaques and creative artifacts—seeks to
inform and delight those treading its path. Sometimes serious, sometimes whimsical, the trail is immensely appealing, presenting its visitors with an opportunity to
pause and experience the very heart of Asheville.

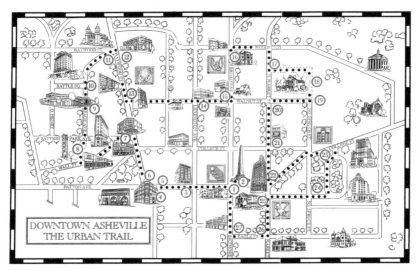

The Asheville Urban Trail

The trail presently consists of thirty stations located at strategic spots throughout the downtown area. Each station has been carefully planned to reflect the
people and events which over the years have made Asheville unique. Beginning
as a crossroads and layover for drovers and settlers, the city mushroomed with
the coming of the railroad in 1880. Asheville's climate and natural beauty soon
attracted men of vision and wealth, and the city more than tripled its population.
These stories and many more await the visitor along the Urban Trail.

At present, the Urban Trail is 1.6 miles in length, but one is free to walk as
much or as little as desired. The pace is a matter of personal choice. At several
stations, benches are an integral part of the art work, and provide a charming spot
for rest or contemplation.

Each station is unique. Carefully designed and executed, stops commemorate Asheville's most significant cultural, educational, social and historic trends, and highlight the myriad of architectural treasures contained within the downtown historic district. To create a station, designers employed informative plaques and a widely diverse selection of art works in stone, bronze, tile, brick and wrought iron, as well as sixteen-inch square thematic markers. Plans call for thematic markers to be placed every fifty feet to guide walkers and allow them to follow the trail unaided. The markers, etched with a logo, represent the five distinct themes of the trail: Asheville's Earliest Years (a horseshoe), the Gilded Age (a stylized feather), Thomas Wolfe's Era (an angel), Civic Pride (Asheville's court house of 1876), and the Age of Diversity (an eagle).

In addition to the thematic markers, each station has an interpretative plaque cast in bronze. Carefully researched information about the site is inscribed on the plaques, as well as the name of the station's donor or honoree.

Throughout the trail are beautifully wrought and uniquely designed works of art which catch the eye and further develop the theme of the station. Seeking to engage all the senses, trail designers not only make use of bas-relief, embedded objects and free-standing works, but also employ sound and stereoptic devices to reflect the mood of the station and delight the visitor.

Station 14 is an excellent example of art reflecting mood. A sunbonnet and basket of apples—worked in bronze—are set upon a bench in an area where farmers and their wives once came to sell baskets of produce. Perhaps on this very spot, a young wife—wearied by her travels—paused to lay aside her bonnet and rest before returning to her outlying farm. Careful observation in this area will reveal the outline of market doorways with extraordinary height and breath. These oversized entryways were needed to accommodate farmer's massive delivery wagons piled high with goods.

"Childhood" in Pack Square

Some stations make use of skillfully executed freestanding bronzes. Perhaps the best known of these is a work by sculptor, James Barnhill, appropriately called "Childhood."

This lovely bronze portrays a slender young girl gracefully bending to drink from a horse-head fountain. Located at station 22 in Pack Square, "Childhood" charms all who visit her. Interestingly enough, there are still those in Asheville who can recall playing in the square as a child, and drinking from just such a fountain. Elaine McPherson, who donated the plaque at this station, remembers Pack Square as "her playground."

A quilt, fiddle, and full-size bronze dancers at the entrance to the Civic Center serve as reminders of the city's mountain heritage. Indeed, the Civic Center has long celebrated Asheville's "heritage of the hills," hosting many performances by local dancers, storytellers, crafters and musicians.

At the corner of College and Market streets, walkers pass a handsome, full-sized bronze bell, reminiscent of the bronze bell which once hung in the old city hall and was rung to warn of fire. The present bell, cast at about the same time as the old fire bell, has a lovely tone and is rung to mark special occasions.

Another interpretation in bronze, interactive and especially appealing to the young-at-heart, is the station commemorating the life and works of Thomas Wolfe. The author possessed rather large feet, and his size thirteen shoes, cast in bronze, invite the visitor to try them on for size.

Innovative and exciting, a large bronze frieze at station 29 depicts the Afro-American contribution to the commercial and spiritual development of Asheville. Innovative as well are the sound boxes and stereoptic viewers planned for several of the other stations. The stereoptic viewer will picture the city as it was in bygone days before the modern street lights and traffic signals were installed and auditory boxes will echo such sounds as hooves striking cobblestone and the clanging of an arriving trolley.

Much progress has been made since the Urban Trail's inception in 1990. What was once simply the dream of a group of dedicated and gifted residents has become after years of hard work an exciting reality. As news of the trail has spread, tourists, city workers, children, retirees, and residents of the city and surrounding counties have expressed their interest, and many realizing the value of such an endeavor, have answered the call to become involved. Some have generously funded the markers, plaques and large works of art which are the heart of the trail. Others, city and office worker, gardener, student, homemaker and historian, give to the trail the valuable gifts of time and talents. Together they have watched with pride the dynamic evolution of Asheville's "path through history"—Asheville's own Urban Trail.

Chapter Six
The Grove Park Inn Resort & Spa

The Grove Park Inn was the dream of Edwin Wiley Grove and his son-in-law, Fred Loring Seely, who envisioned the building of a resort hotel in the beautiful and restful mountains of the Southern Appalachians. Mr. Grove, who was the owner of a pharmaceutical company in St. Louis, Missouri, had come to Asheville for health reasons and liked the area so much he bought land here, including acreage on the western slope of Sunset Mountain. It was on this land that he eventually built a unique resort, the Grove Park Inn, patterned after the Old Faithful Inn in Yellowstone National Park, but built of native stone instead of logs.

Over the years, this grand hotel has had many distinguished guests. President Franklin D. Roosevelt and his wife, Eleanor, President Woodrow Wilson, F. Scott Fitzgerald, William Jennings Bryan and Will Rogers all journeyed to E.W. Grove's luxurious mountainside inn. The attraction of the inn was compelling and guests came in great numbers from all over the world. Other noteworthy visitors were John D. Rockefeller, General Pershing, Chief Justice Taft and Thomas Edison.

The hotel was designed by Mr. Seely and was constructed of granite boulders which were brought from nearby Sunset Mountain or from land owned by Mr. Grove. Hundreds of North Carolina laborers helped in the construction was well as Italian stone masons. Each rock was used only if it fit perfectly where it was needed, and the great fireplaces, which are thirty-six feet wide required one hundred and twenty tons of boulders to build. The hotel was completed in just over a year and was opened on July 1, 1913.

Originally a guard house protected the main entrance to the hotel grounds. The roads leading up the hill along Macon Avenue were also originally paved in smooth brick and converged on a circular parking area in front of the east porch, now the main entrance. Seven hundred pieces of furniture and over six hundred lighting fixtures were handmade by Roycrofters of East Aurora, New York, and the bedroom furniture was made by the White Furniture Company of Mebane, North Carolina. The rugs were woven in Aubusson, France, and lasted until 1955, when Charles and Elaine Sammons of Dallas came to the resort and refurnished the entire property. In the early years, entertainment at the hotel included bowling, swimming and billiards, and in the Great Hall there were concerts, organ recitals and movies,

Grove Park Inn Resort & Spa on Sunset Mountain

after which each guest received an apple wrapped in gray paper for depositing the core. Another hotel practice which amazed visitors was the presenting of change at the cashier's window in washed and polished silver and crisp new paper money.

The rocking chairs on the porches and terraces were very popular as guests would sit for hours enjoying the mountain views and refreshing air. Walking paths on the grounds were also provided for the guests.

During the years of the Second World War, the U.S. State Department leased the property for an internment center for Axis diplomats. Later, the Navy Department took over the hotel as a rest and rehabilitation center for soldiers returning from the war, and the Philippine Government in exile functioned from the Presidential Cottage on the hotel grounds. For a decade after the war, the hotel was operated as such by the owner, Ike Hall.

The complete restoration and modernization, begun in 1955, included private baths in every room, electric and water lines replaced, American fabrics and rugs installed and furniture cleaned, restored and reupholstered. A beautiful swimming pool was added, tennis courts were resurfaced and a putting green constructed. In later years, wings were added to the original stone hotel body to provide needed guest accommodations.

In 1917, the Biltmore Industries, a cottage craft industry started by Mrs. George Vanderbilt, was sold to Mr. Seely who installed it in the Old English type shops at the edge of the Grove Park Inn grounds. Visitors to the Grove Park Inn could watch the spinning and carding of wool and the looming of cloth. These cottages still operate in much the same spirit and are home to the Grovewood Gallery, the Estes-Winn Memorial Automobile Museum and the North Carolina Homespun Museum.

In the early 1980s the famous resort hotel was converted from a seasonal enterprise into a year-round resort and convention center. Refurbishing of all the guest rooms, public areas, dining rooms and meeting rooms was undertaken, and the electric and plumbing system fully modernized. New wings included complete meeting and conference facilities.

Today, the Grove Park Inn Resort & Spa is the epitome of a world-class resort. This grand lady has it all—superb facilities, a rich history, overwhelmingly beautiful mountain setting, a Four Diamond Restaurant, and championship golf course. The hotel has over 40 meeting rooms offering 50,000 square feet of space, complete in-house support services, 510 guest rooms, including 12 suites.

Deluxe accommodations are also provided on the Club Floor, a concierge-attended floor which features oversized guest rooms with jacuzzis, newspaper delivery and a private Club Lounge. There are six outdoor tennis courts and three indoor plexipave courts, as well as racquetball, squash, Nautilus and aerobics facilities.

Recent renovations and additions to the resort include an updated Sports Center with indoor pool, the restoration of the historic main Inn's roof, new outdoor tennis courts and an extraordinary 40,000 sq. ft. spa complex that is one of the finest in the world (SEE review of the spa). These improvements tally over $24 million and further secure the Grove Park Inn Resort and Spa's position as one of the world's great hotels.

Vignette: Stone Poems

One of the many surprises that await guests of the Grove Park Inn are the two magnificent fireplaces that grace both ends of the great entrance hall. Made out of massive boulders and large enough for a bunch of kids to camp out in, these transcendently massive stone structures also have a delicate literary side, and if you look closely, you will find written here and there on some of the stones poems and quotations. The one below is from the north fireplace:

"This old world we're living in
is mighty hard to beat
We get a thorn with every rose
but ain't the roses sweet?

Location: Sunset Mountain, Asheville, NC
Address: 290 Macon Ave., Asheville, NC 28804
Telephone: (800) 438-5800, 252-2711
FAX: 253-7053
Website: www.groveparkinn.com
Fees: $109-$500. These rates are based on double occupancy during the April-December season only and are subject to change. Rates go up $10 on weekends. Rates during remainder of year are lower.

Tips:	The Inn has a number of great festivals and special event weekends that include "All That Jazz Weekend" in January, "Big Band Dance Weekend" in February, and "A Grove Park Inn Christmas" ongoing during late November and December.
Of Note:	Listed in the National Register of Historic Places. AAA "Four Diamond," Mobil "Four Star," Family Circle "Fun Resort," Mid-Atlantic Country's "50 Finest Hotels & Resorts," Successful Meetings "Pinacle Award," Medical Meetings "Merit & Distinction." USAir magazine voted the hotel golf course one of the top 10 American golf courses, and Tennis Magazine voted the hotel among the top 50 USA Tennis Resorts. Southern Living magazine awarded the inn the Readers Choice Award—Favorite Country Inn and Favorite Resort.
Nearby:	Thomas Wolfe Memorial, Biltmore Estate.
Directions:	From I-40 or I-26, take I-240 into Asheville. Take exit 5B, Charlotte Street. Proceed north on Charlotte Street for ½ miles, then turn right on Macon Avenue. After ½ mile, take Grove Park Inn entrance on left.

Grove Park Inn Restaurants   Reservations: 252-2711

Horizons: Award-winning wine selection. Innovative, classic cuisine. AAA Four Diamond.
Blue Ridge Dining Room: Lavish buffets, panoramic views.
Sunset Terrace: Spectacular outdoor dining veranda.

The Spa at
The Grove Park Inn Resort

Completed in 2001, the 40,000 square foot spa is one of the finest in the world and features stone and timber construction, cascading waterfalls, waterscaped gardens and harmonious landscaping. Built into the face of Sunset Mountain and largely underground, the spa reflects the strong mountain arts and crafts traditions with a palette of soft greens, rust and ochre. Arts and crafts decorations abound, including torchieres that illuminate the main spa pool. The pool area, with its ocean themes, is absolutely spectacular. In addition to a relaxation pool and a lap pool, the area also boasts plunge pools and whirlpools. Saunas, steam rooms, inhalation rooms, treatment rooms and outdoor sun decks are only steps away. There are a wide range of services and treatments offered and these can be reviewed at the spa's website (www.groveparkinn.com). The following personal account of her own experience by writer Liza Schillo will give you an insider's view of just how wonderful the Spa at the Grove Park Inn Resort really is:

"In order to get to The Spa at the Grove Park Inn, you must walk through the resort's grand lobby, which is breathtaking enough—all stone, vast ceiling and a fireplace at each end large enough to fit a handful of people. But stepping out onto the Sunset Terrace overlooking Asheville, and descending the stone steps winding through the garden and around a lit waterfall, pennies scattered over every rock the water touches, a feeling quite overwhelming wells inside me. The anticipation and excitement of spending an entire day of pampering, inside one of the world's best spas! The feeling augments the closer I get to the entrance, where I can catch the fragrant scent of herbs, and that warm, spicy smell that saunas give when they are warm.

"Upon stepping inside I was amazed at the interior design. The theme I was told is "Rock, Water, Fire, and Light," and this is apparent as the lighting resembles torches in increments along the walls, which are all of rock. The ambience is one of an ancient library, or a revered museum. I am immediately greeted with the fine manners of one of their receptionists, who takes my name and hands me a black notebook in which is an itinerary and a question sheet. He courteously explains to me what I will be doing, and I take a seat. Not a minute later another spa employee comes out to give me and the other waiting ladies a tour before our treatments! We are lead through the back and I learn that only paying customers over the age of 18 are allowed here, to ensure maximum comfort and quiet to The Spa's clients. I also learned that no matter what treatment you are undergoing, you are permitted to remain at the spa, using the full facilities, for the entirety of the day, coming and going as you please! The spa divides into men and women's halves, and we are all taken to a very classy locker room where we change into robes and flip flops. The robes I was pleased to learn may be found in the spa store, as well as most of the products used during massages. A hall leading to the ladies' fireside lounge stems from it a shower room (with large showers, all of tile in a teal color, the "water" portion of their decorating theme I'd assume), bathroom and vanity room. Let me speak some on the vanity room: it was built for *two* Marilyn Monroes. The Hollywood lights that run above the wrap-around mirror highlight every amenity you could possibly need during your stay at The Spa. Mouthwash, hair gel, razors, deodorant, you name it and it is there at your fingertips! Tiny windows throughout the interior allow peeks at things to come, some looking over the huge pool room that I will come to momentarily. In the lounge fancy snacks and cucumber water are provided, as well as a spot by the fireplace, but if you'd rather, the ladies' sundeck, complete with a hammock, is right outside. I was soon led to my massage, but I do not want to ruin this surprise for you! Let me just say that after I came out, my skin was literally glowing and my head was huge from so much attention given just to me for a solid 80 minutes! I can't remember the last time my body felt so good, so cool and relaxed, yet strengthened. It is a feeling that can only be created when you allow yourself enough time to drop everything you are currently worrying with and simply focus on the now, on how your body feels and what can ease that stress that so many of us today are under too often. You can be assured that every masseuse at the Grove Park Inn Spa is an absolute expert. I myself have applied for various positions at the resort with an above-average resume, and I know from experience that there is quite an extensive and selective application process. They know exactly what they are looking for, and at the Grove Park, they get it. My masseuse was one of the younger ones; he told me that a lot of the staff is around 50 years of age. He also described to me some of the other massage rooms, and all are different; mine was The Dome Room: waterproof, containing a bathtub and a water massager, as well as other special treats.

"After my treatment, I am taken to another lounge and provided with a neck warmer until I am guided through another tour. This one leads me to the pool that I've seen so many pictures of. However there is much more to it than just the simple lap pool. There are of course more king-size showers, and an unlimited stock of towels. Then the women rejoin the men in this cavernous space containing several pools and whirlpools. There is a sauna, what I caught a waft of outside. To get to the sauna however you enter a room I'd never heard of, an Inhalation Room. This room remains at room temperature but inside is burning essential oils to breathe in! There is a double whirlpool next to it titled the Contrast Pools. One pool of 103 degrees and an adjoining one of 65. After minutes in the hot one, you are to plunge into the icy one! This is good for circulation and detoxification of the bloodstream, especially good after massages or strenuous workouts. Needless to say I did not spend much time here but my body certainly tingled with a refreshing cleanliness afterwards. I decide to try the large pools next. There is one in the back of the "cave," where the lights are dimmer. This pool is unique because in the ceiling there are tiny, twinkling fiber optic cable stars, just beautiful. A waterfall cuts through between this pool and the front one, which is a mineral salts pool. This was my favorite, at 86 degrees (several degrees above the latter), I could open my eyes without the burning of strong chlorine! Both pools are no deeper than 4 feet, and have speakers underwater so that their soft, soothing music may still be heard while you are swimming. Massage waterfall whirlpools bank this pool on either side, and I test them out. These are like hot tubs but with two streams of water that are just strong enough to sit beneath for a good, hard massage on the shoulders. For the remainder of the day I rotate between these varying pools of water, and spend a good deal of time on their large patio with comfy lounge chairs and another large fireplace. Here I order lunch, and it is brought to me on a silver platter! The spa café is not just hot dogs; I enjoyed the vegetarian BLT—their menu is clearly health conscious, though if you're not counting calories I recommend their fruit creams, made with real fruit! Though menu items may seem a little pricey, believe me you get more than what you pay for. That is probably the most remarkable thing I found during my visit. I noticed two outdoor gazebos while on the patio, and learned that these are available if you wish to upgrade a massage to the outdoors, with a view of our Blue Ridge Mountains. I shared the patio with a good number of people, though I was astounded at how vacant and spacious it seemed for such a renowned spa. Upon questioning I found that there is usually a constant 30 to 40 people at The Spa during busy summer months, yet even in the winter they stay pretty full. This is because they have found that now spouses and other acquaintances of people arriving at the Grove Park for business have discovered The Spa! These otherwise stay-at-homes now tag along for treatment while their significant other is in meetings (a good idea, I think).

Though 30 to 40 people may sound like a lot, spread throughout The Spa it is a tiny number for the size of the building, which I greatly appreciated. For most of the day I had the pools to myself! It is good to make reservations several weeks in advance, especially on weekends and summer days.

"After inspection of the spa's store in the front (in which I was very happy to find that my robe is carried there!), I exit the building sometime around dusk, sorry to be returning to what I'd left behind that morning. But as I stare into the wishing well of the waterfall as I climb the steps, I feel no need to toss a penny in, because tonight, I can't wish for anything else."

Chapter Seven
Universities, Colleges & Schools

No guidebook would be complete without a listing of area universities and colleges. Not only are these institutions culturally important but they are many times architecturally interesting. In this chapter a listing is also included of the public and private schools—elementary through high school.

Post-Secondary Institutions
Asheville-Buncombe Technical Community College

Established in 1959, Asheville-Buncombe Technical Community College has grown from a trade school to a fully accredited comprehensive community college that offers 39 career programs plus college transfer. Four academic divisions—Allied Health and Public Service, Business and Hospitality Education, Engineering and Applied Technology, and Arts and Sciences—prepare students for employment and further education. A fifth division, Continuing Education, provides noncredit academic, avocational, practical skills, and occupational classes. A-B Tech has 21 buildings on over 144 acres of land, and in 1990, the college established a campus in Madison County.

Asheville-Buncombe Technical Community College

Address: 340 Victoria Rd., Asheville, NC 28801
Telephone: 254-1921
FAX: 251-6355
Website: www.abtech.com
Directions: From Pack Square take Biltmore Avenue south to the hospital district. Take right onto Victoria Road.

South College

Founded in 1905 by Robert Talmadge Cecil, South College is a secular, coeducation institution of higher education and offers Associate of Applied Science degrees and certificates in Junior College programs. Located on an eight acre campus off Patton Avenue in West Asheville, Cecils is the only private junior college in Asheville. Its mission centers on career placement in high demand and high growth fields, and it is ACICS accredited.

Address: 1567 Patton Ave., Asheville, NC 28806
Telephone: 252-2486
FAX: 252-8558
Website: www.southcollegenc.com
Directions: From downtown Asheville, take Patton Avenue west.

Mars Hill College

Located to the north of Asheville in Mars Hill, Mars Hill College is the oldest college on an original site in Western North Carolina. The 180-acre campus is set against the majestic backdrop of the Blue Ridge Mountains in a rural traditional area. Opened in the fall of 1856, Mars Hill is accredited to award bachelor's degrees. This lovely campus boasts many unique buildings dating back to the 1800s.

Address: P.O. Box 370, Mars Hill, NC 28754
Telephone: 689-1201, (800) 543-1514
FAX: 689-1473
Website: www.mhc.edu
Directions: From I-240, take 19/23 (Weaverville/UNC-A) exit north to Mars Hill exit.

Montreat College

Located 15 miles east of Asheville in Montreat, N.C. Montreat is a four-year coeducational, Christian liberal arts college with an established heritage of over 75 years with the Presbyterian Church (U.S.A.).

Address: 310 Gaither Cir. (P.O. Box 1267), Montreat, NC 28757
Telephone: 669-8012
FAX: 669-9554
Website: www.montreat.edu
Directions: Take I-40 east to Black Mountain exit 64. Go north on Route 9 through Black Mountain two miles through Montreat Gate. Continue on to college.

Shaw University

Shaw University was founded in 1865 by Rev. Henry Martin Tupper. It is a four-year college, which offers a Bachelor of Arts or Bachelor of Science degree. The university's Center for Alternative Programs of Education allows working students to arrange their classes around their job hours. Programs are offered in the following subjects: Business Management, Public Administration, Religion and Philosophy, Criminal Justice, Liberal Studies and Behavioral Science. Shaw also offers evening classes.

Address: 31 College St., Asheville, NC 28801
Telephone: 252-7635
FAX: 252-4050
Website: www.shawuniversity.edu
Directions: Take College Street from Pack Square in downtown Asheville.

University of North Carolina at Asheville

University of North Carolina at Asheville

UNC-A was founded in 1927 as Buncombe County Junior College. In 1961 it was relocated to its present site in north Asheville, and in 1966 it joined the University of North Carolina system. The 265-acre campus comprises 30 buildings for classrooms, administration, residence and recreation. In its years as UNC-A, the university has maintained a distinctive position within the 16-member UNC system in its primary mission: to offer an undergraduate liberal arts education of superior quality for serious and able students.

Ramsey Library at UNC-A

Address: One University Hghts., Asheville, NC 28804
Telephone: 251-6600
FAX: 251-6495
Website: www.unca.edu
Directions: From I-240, take exit 5A Merrimon Avenue (US 25) north. Left onto W.T. Weaver Blvd. opposite Boston Pizza. Then right on University Heights.

Holden Art Center at Warren Wilson College

Warren Wilson College

Founded in 1894, Warren Wilson College has educated students with a unique triad of a strong liberal arts program, work for the college, and service to those in need, which makes Warren Wilson unlike any other college. The Bachelor of Arts degree is offered, with the goal of the degree program the completion of three well-designated areas of study. The 1,000-acre campus includes a 300-acre working farm, 600 acres of forest, 25 miles of hiking trails, and a white-water kayaking course. The campus and the area are havens for outdoor activities, such as white-water sports, hiking, camping, mountain biking, and rock climbing.

Address: 701 Warren Wilson Rd., Swannanoa, NC 28778
           P.O. Box 9000, Asheville, NC 28815
Telephone: (800) 934-3536, 298-3325
FAX: 298-1440
Website: www.warren-wilson.edu
Directions: From Asheville take I-40 west. Use exit 55 and turn left to access Hwy. 70. Follow Hwy 70 east and take left onto Warren Wilson Road.

Western Carolina University At Asheville

Western Carolina University is one of the 16 senior institutions of the University of North Carolina. The University has four undergraduate schools: Applied Sciences, Arts and Sciences, Business, and Education and Psychology, as well as a Graduate School. The main campus of Western Carolina University is in Cullowhee, North Carolina. At the Asheville campus, WCU offers primary study areas in education, business administration, human resource development, nursing and health sciences, public affairs, engineering and industrial technology, and criminal justice.

Address: One University Heights/UNCA, Asheville, NC 28804
Telephone: 251-6642
FAX: 232-2274
Website: www.wcu.edu
Directions: From I-240, take exit 5A Merrimon Avenue (US 25) north. Left onto W.T. Weaver Blvd. opposite Boston Pizza. Then right on University Heights.

Secondary Schools

Buncombe County Public Schools

Buncombe County has the largest concentration of students in Western North Carolina—over 25,000. There are six high schools, seven middle schools and over 20 elementary schools. 255-5921 (www.buncombe.k12.nc.us)

Asheville City Schools

With a student population of over 5,000, Asheville has eight schools, including Asheville High School, one middle school and six elementary schools. 255-5304 (www.asheville.k12.nc.us)

Private Schools

Asheville Catholic School: 252-7896
Asheville Christian Academy: 298-1600
Asheville School: 254-6345
Carolina Day School: 274-0757
Christ School: 684-6232
Merrimon Baptist School: 252-9305
Mount Pisgah Academy: 667-2535
Nazarene Christian School: 252-9713
Rhema Christian School: 254-5727
Swannanoa Christian Academy: 686-3977

Chapter Eight
Hospitals

A sheville is the major medical center for Western North Carolina and has a large number of medical facilities, physicians, medical personnel and a number of hospitals. Since these are so important to the life of Asheville, the primary institutions, the hospital are included here. Some are new and some are old, yet all impose their presence on Asheville in a quiet and purposeful way. Institutions this important to a community require significant recognition in any guidebook.

Asheville VA Medical Center

A major hospital and surgical facility, it serves as a primary referral center within the VA system for heart surgery, primary and secondary care and tertiary care in all areas except neurosurgery, plastic surgery and hemodialysis. The Asheville Center has a strong affiliation with Duke University Medical Center.

Address: 1100 Tunnel Rd., Asheville, NC 28805
Telephone: 298-7911
Directions: Take exit 7 off I-240 onto Tunnel Road east. Follow Tunnel Road to Riceville Road. Hospital is just beyond Riceville Road on the left.

New Vistas Behavioral Services

A public agency that provides mental health, developmental disability, and substance abuse services to Buncombe, Madison, Mitchell, and Yancey county residents. The center helps with problems such as marital unhappiness, depression, anxiety, job stress, alcoholism, drug abuse, difficulties with children, developmental disabilities, stress-related health problems, long-term mental illnesses, learning problems, and difficulties related to aging. A comprehensive array of services are also available to individuals and families who are affected by addiction, through the Center's Substance Abuse Services.

Address: 356 Biltmore Ave., Asheville, NC 28801
Telephone: 258-3500
Directions: From Pack Square in downtown Asheville, take Biltmore Avenue south to the hospital district. Blue Ridge Center will be on your left.

Mission+St. Joseph's Health System

Newcomers to Western North Carolina are often surprised by the sophistication of the region's medical community. At its center is the Mission+St. Joseph's Health System, a partnership between the area's two largest private, not for profit, acute care hospitals: Memorial Mission Hospital and St. Joseph's Hospital.

The Mission+St. Joseph's Health System was formed by the two hospitals to strengthen them for rapid changes in the nation's health care delivery system. The partnership has three goals: To maintain and enhance excellence in care, to better control costs, and to improve health care for people in the Western North Carolina region. The Mission+St. Joseph's Health System offers almost every medical specialty and subspecialty, from neonatology to gerontology. These are organized within clinical services lines, which focus the expertise and commitment of physicians and hospital staff on providing excellent, up-to-date procedures, technology and care. www.msj.org

St. Joseph's Hospital

St. Joseph's Hospital was founded in 1900 by the Sisters of Mercy, and is a not-for-profit hospital and a medical referral center for the region. It has over 300 beds and is staffed with over 1,500 employees and 385 physicians. St. Joseph's specializes in laser surgery, oncology, orthopedics, urology and general surgery.

Address:	428 Biltmore Ave., Asheville, NC 28801
Telephone:	213-1111
Directions:	From Pack Square in downtown Asheville, take Biltmore Avenue south to the hospital district. St. Joseph's will be on your left.

St. Joseph's Hospital, 428 Biltmore Avenue

Mission Memorial Hospital, 509 Biltmore Avenue

Memorial Mission Hospital

Mission is a private, not-for-profit, community owned hospital founded in 1885. It also serves as a regional referral center for Western North Carolina. It has over 470 beds and is staffed with over 2,500 employees and 380 physicians. Memorial Mission specializes in trauma, neurology and neurosurgery, radiation and medical oncology, pediatrics, maternity, gynecology, neonatal intensive care, diagnostic radiology and endoscopy.

Address: 509 Biltmore Ave., Asheville, NC 28801
Telephone: 213-1111
Directions: From Pack Square in downtown Asheville take Biltmore Avenue south to the hospital district. Memorial Mission will be on your right.

Thoms Rehabilitation Hospital

This 80-plus bed hospital offers inpatient and outpatient rehabilitation services to individuals with physical, cognitive and developmental impairments, including brain injury, chronic pain, problems of aging, orthopedic disabilities, and treatment of children with difficulties in development and learning.

Address: 68 Sweeten Creek Rd., Asheville, NC 28803
Telephone: 274-2400
Directions: From Pack Square in downtown Asheville take Biltmore Avenue south to Biltmore Village. Just beyond the railroad tracks, take left onto Brook Street which turns into Sweeten Creek Road.

Chapter Nine
Natural Attractions

S urrounded on all sides by majestic mountains, with a major river, the French Broad, flowing through its center, Asheville is blessed with nearby outdoor recreation opportunities and natural attractions for visitors. Excellent golf courses, parks, lakes and the river itself are within a few minutes drive from downtown.

Some of the area's natural attractions—Blue Ridge Parkway, Chimney Rock Park, Lake Lure, Mount Mitchell, Pisgah National Forest, and nearby waterfalls—are covered in depth in Section Five, Chapter 1 and are therefore not repeated here.

Asheville Parks

Woven throughout the Asheville community are 11 neighborhood recreation centers, two pools, over 35 parks and play areas, 20 tennis courts, and a stadium complex supervised and maintained by the Asheville Parks and Recreation Department (www.ci.asheville.nc.us/parksrec/parks.htm). The Asheville Parks and Recreation Department also sponsors or supports many cultural festivals and special events that enrich the Asheville area. Some of these include Montford Park Players' Shakespeare Theatre, Sunday in the Park, Fourth of July Celebration, Goombay Festival, Martin Luther King Jr. Prayer Breakfast, Light Up Your Holidays Festival, Shindig On The Green, Teen Street Dances, Greek Festival, Tell It In The Mountains, Bele Chere, Very Special Arts Festival, and USATF Junior Olympics Track and Field and Cross Country Meets.

Asheville parks are full of activity in the summer.

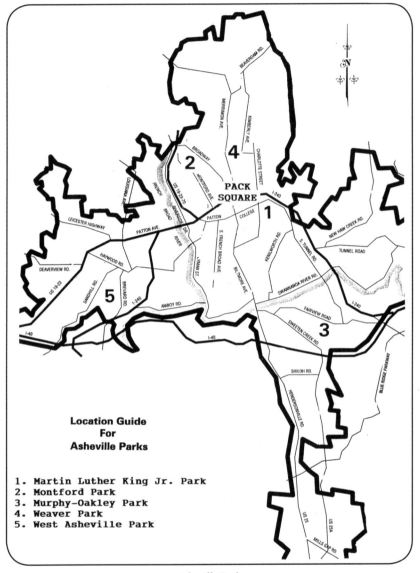

Asheville Parks

Recommended Parks

The following listing of Asheville Parks were recommended to the author by the Asheville Parks and Recreation Department for first-time Asheville visitors. They are easy to find, and offer outstanding facilities. For a more complete listing of all other recreational facilities in the Asheville Park system, or for directions to the listed parks, call 259-5800.

French Broad River Park: The most popular park in Asheville, it is located on Amboy Road along the French Broad River. One of Asheville's most beautiful parks, this 14-acre park meanders alongside the tranquil French Broad River. The property features a vast area of open green space with gracious old trees, a wildflower garden, a paved half-mile walking path, a large gazebo, picnic tables and grills, a fishing/observation deck, and a small playground. The natural beauty of this park makes it a popular spot for warm weather weddings and romantic picnics in the meadow. The newest addition of the property is the Dog Park, which features a large fenced-in area made just for exercising and socializing your pooch! Off-street parking and restrooms are also available.

Martin Luther King Jr. Park: (Martin Luther King Jr. Dr., 259-5800) Ball field, concession stand, fitness course, soccer field, picnic tables, playground, restrooms, open shelters.

Montford Park: (Montford Ave., 253-3714) Outdoor basketball court, playground, restrooms, open shelters, tennis.

Murphy-Oakley Park: (Fairview Rd., 274-7088) Ball field, outdoor basketball court, concession stand, picnic tables and grills, playground, restrooms.

Weaver Park: (Murdock/Merrimon Ave., 258-2453) Ball field, outdoor basketball court, concession stand, soccer field, picnic tables and grills, playground, restrooms, open shelters, summer playground.

West Asheville Park: (Vermont Ave., 258-2235) Ball field, concession stand, picnic tables, restrooms, open shelters, summer playground, tennis.

Lake Julian District Park

Lake Julian is an ideal family recreational facility and an excellent spot for the fishing enthusiast. Located near Skyland, N.C., the park offers opportunities for picnicking, canoeing, sailing and outdoor games. The park is open

Lake Julian, off Long Shoals Road in South Asheville

year-round for all county residents and visitors to enjoy. Many local residents are amazed to find some of this area's best fishing in their own backyard. Lake Julian has an abundance of bass, brim and crappie, as well as an imported fish, the tilapia. Because Lake Julian is a "thermal" lake (it is used as a cooling agent for CP&L), some of the best fishing occurs from October through March. Fishermen may fish from the shore or from jonboats that are available on a rental basis. Patrons must provide their own electric boat motor, gasoline motors are not allowed. N.C. fishing laws are enforced and a local lake permit is required. Lake Julian was named in honor of Julian Byrd Stepp.

Location: South Asheville

Address: Entrance is off Long Shoals Rd. (Hwy 146)

Telephone: 684-0376

Hours: Open year-round except Thanksgiving, Christmas, and New Year's Day. October-March: 8 a.m.-6 p.m.; April: 8 a.m.-8 p.m.; May-September: 8 a.m.-9 p.m.

Fees: Fishing boat rental: $3-$15 (depending on length of rental); Canoe rental: $1.50-$2.00; Paddle boat rental per hour: $4.50-$5.00; Picnic Shelters: $20-$45

Directions: Take Hendersonville Highway south from Biltmore Village. Turn left onto Long Shoals Road in south Asheville. The entrance to the park is a few miles on the left opposite Overlook Road.

The French Broad River

The French Broad River flows north through 117 miles of Western North Carolina from its headwaters in Rosman to Paint Rock. In Tennessee it joins the Holston to form the Tennessee River and eventually reaches the Mississippi. Named by early explorers because it flowed toward French Territory to the west, it is a great recreational resource offering splendid scenery, perfect picnic spots, Class I through IV whitewater, and good fishing. It flows right though Asheville on its journey north.

One of the Cherokee names was Tah-kee-os-tee, "racing waters." Others, frequently used for only a part of the river, were Poe-li-co, Ariqua, and Zillicoah. By 1776 the present name French Broad River was in use.

On its way through Asheville, the river is accessible at a number of places. Riverlink, a local organization dedicated to the economic and environmental revitalization of the French Broad, has begun to turn a dream into reality. This organization, an association of recreation experts, garden clubs, city planners, businesses, economic professionals and private citizens has developed a vision for the future of the river as it flows through the Asheville area.

The French Broad River Park is the newest access point on the river developed by Riverlink. Located on the river at Amboy Road, this park features fishing sites, playground, restrooms, bicycling and walking trails, interpretive displays and a picnic shelter that echoes the 1905 architecture of the original Riverside Park.

The French Broad River runs through 117 miles of Western North Carolina.

Greenways and other river parks are currently also under development as part of Riverlink's vision.

The Buncombe County Department of Recreation Services also maintains a number of river parks on the French Broad River in the Asheville area. One of these, the Jean Webb Park is located just north of the French Broad River Park along Riverside Drive which parallels the river. This small park is convenient to downtown and a good spot for picnic lunch. For more information about the other river parks maintained by Buncombe County, contact the Department of Recreation Services at 250-4260.

Location: West of downtown Asheville

Telephone: Riverlink: 252-8474 (P.O. Box 15488, Asheville, NC 28813; www. riverlink.org);
Buncombe County Department of Recreation Services: 250-4260

Directions: The French Broad River is accessible from many points in Asheville. To reach the Riverlink French Broad River Park, take Meadow Road west from Biltmore Village. This road eventually begins to parallel the river. Turn left at Amboy Road to access the park.

Buncombe County River Access Sites

Glenn Bridge River Park (Mile 54)
Sandy Bottom River Park (Mile 59.5)
Bent Creek River Park (Mile 60)
Hominy Creek River Park (Mile 66)

Southern Waterways Access (Mile 68)
French Broad River Park (Mile 69)
Jean Webb Park (Mile 70)
French Broad River Campground (Mile 79.5)
The Ledges Whitewater Park (Mile 80)
Walnut Island River Park (Mile 86)

Jewel of the Appalachians

Visitors to the mountains are often surprised by how often during the summer months they encounter the ruby-throated hummingbird. This tiny creature belongs to a family that numbers more than 300 tropical species, but the ruby-throated is the only one found in the mountains. It is a great migratory flier and strong enough to make the 500-mile flight across the Gulf of Mexico each spring and fall. During the summers it can be found in the mountains sipping nectar from flowers garden variety and wildflower alike. They are very good flyers and posses incredible stamina and endurance. In fact, they can hover in mid-air and even go backwards when necessary.

Section Four
Hendersonville & Flat Rock

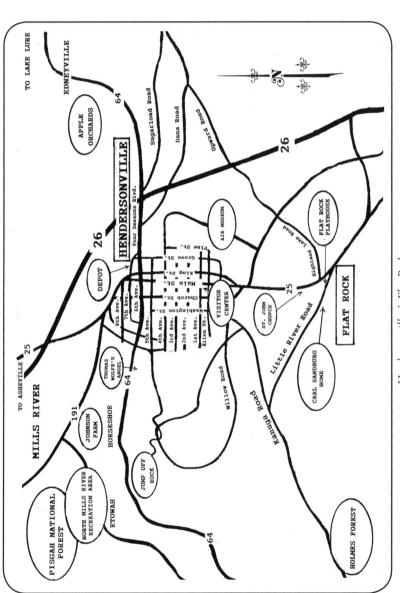

Hendersonville & Flat Rock

Chapter One
Hendersonville & Flat Rock

Hendersonville

Located amidst the majestic mountains of the Southern Appalachians, Hendersonville (population approximately 10,000) has come to be known as the "City of Four Seasons" and as an ideal retirement community. Since before the turn of the century, Hendersonville has attracted visitors and families seeking a gentle climate, lovely mountain scenery, and great recreational resources. It is located in Henderson County, which has a population of over 90,000.

Situated 2,200 feet above sea level, on a mountain plateau between the Blue Ridge and the Great Smoky Mountains, Hendersonville is blessed with a moderate and mild climate, yet the area still experiences the four seasons. With a mean summer temperature of around 70 degrees and 40 degrees in the winter, the climate is conducive to year-round outdoor recreation.

Tourism is a major industry in Hendersonville, with agriculture and industry also strong economic forces. Noted for its scenic beauty and tranquility, Hendersonville has industrial development restrictions that encourage small industries that will not disturb the peaceful quality of Henderson County life. Retirement development is also a major economic force in Hendersonville as retirees continue to flock to the area.

Blessed with an abundance of cultural opportunities, Hendersonville offers something for all ages. Symphony orchestra, theatres, libraries, and festivals throughout the year enrich the life of Hendersonville residents. Henderson County is also rich in parks, picnic areas, hiking trails and other outdoor attractions.

Over the years, Hendersonville has preserved its traditional downtown Main Street area from the decline which has happened in so many other cities. And Main Street has been transformed into a beautiful tree-lined avenue complete with flower-filled brick planters. A stroll down Main Street will surround you with sounds of classical music, sights of exquisite seasonal plantings in a hometown setting of boutiques, numerous antique and clothing shops and an old fashioned pharmacy, plus benches on which to sit and people-watch. Few hometowns have remained as beautiful, vital, and alive as historic downtown

Downtown Hendersonville

Hendersonville. The streets bring history to life and bring the best of yesteryear into the excitement of today.

Hendersonville was an uninhabited Cherokee hunting ground before Revolutionary War solder William Mills discovered it in the late 1780s. He received one of the first land grants west of the Blue Ridge and established the first community. By right of discovery, Mills christened some of Henderson County's picturesque regions: Mills River and Mills Gap are names that are still in use today.

The county was named for Chief Justice of the State Supreme Court Judge Leonard Henderson and has four incorporated areas: the city of Hendersonville, the village of Flat Rock, the town of Fletcher, and the town of Laurel Park. Agriculture was the sole industry for early Hendersonville citizens. Tourism came later as visitors from the lowlands in South Carolina and Georgia discovered the scenic beauty and cooler climate. Industrial development became important after World War II, with the founding of the Chamber of Commerce program. Henderson County has long been known for its superior apples, and apple production still continues to be a major industry. Hendersonville celebrates this fact every summer with its famous "Apple Festival."

Flat Rock

Flat Rock began about a century and a half ago with large summer estates being built in the English manner by the affluent Charlestonians, Europeans and prominent plantation owners of the South's low country. The first great estate was built in 1827 by Charles Baring of Baring Brothers Banking firm of London, consisting of 3,000 acres, which he named Mountain Lodge. Baring also built a private chapel on his estate which is now St. John in the Wilderness Episcopal Church.

The second large estate was built by Judge Mitchell King of Charleston, South Carolina, and was named Argyle. He later donated the land on which Hendersonville was built and directed the laying out of Main Street.

Many other coastal families soon followed, until the settlement grew to about fifty estates. They came to Flat Rock to escape the sweltering heat, yellow fever and malaria, which were running rampant. Summers in Flat Rock became a round of southern gaiety in antebellum days. South Carolina's low country gentry called Flat Rock "The Little Charleston of the Mountains."

Most of these old estate homes still stand, surrounded by wide lawns, gardens, towering trees and graced by white pillar porches. A few of these gracious homes remain in the possession of the families of the original owners. Many of these grand estates are now lovely planned communities.

Flat Rock is built around a tremendous outcropping of granite which is said to have been the site of Cherokee gatherings. A great deal of rock has been blasted away and used for highway material. The main "rock" can be found on the grounds of the Flat Rock Playhouse.

Chapter Two
Museums, Cultural Attractions & Nature Centers

This chapter is devoted to the major cultural attractions and centers that the Hendersonville/Flat Rock area has to offer. The ones included here are very important and each year attract thousands of visitors. The range of attractions is wide, from an writer's home to a museum of vintage aircraft. Each is uniquely different and the one criterion that insured placement in this guidebook is a high level of excellence and professionalism.

Carl Sandburg Home

A very popular attraction, Pulitzer Prize winning writer Carl Sandburg's farm, "Connemara," is open to the public for visitation. The farm includes 264 acres of rolling hills, forests, lakes, pastures, goat barn, and buildings.

Carl Sandburg Home

Located in Flat Rock, three miles south of Hendersonville, the grounds are open for self-guided tours. Guided tours of the home are also scheduled daily. The goat barn and the many delightful goats are a hit with the kids!

Location:	Flat Rock
Address:	1928 Little River Rd., Flat Rock, NC 28731
Telephone:	693-4178
FAX:	693-4179
Website:	www.nps.gov/carl/
Hours:	Open-year round, 9 a.m. to 5 p.m. Closed Christmas Day.
Fees:	Guided house tour $3 adults, children free

Allow:	Two hours
Of Note:	National Historic Landmark, listed in the National Register of Historic Places.
	The Carl Sandburg Festival is held at the home every Memorial Day.
Nearby:	Flat Rock Playhouse, Woodfield Inn, St. John in the Wilderness Church
Directions:	Connemara is located 3 miles south of Hendersonville in Flat Rock. Take Highway 25 south from Hendersonville and turn right just beyond the Flat Rock Playhouse onto Little River Road.

Flat Rock Playhouse, home of the Vagabond Players

Flat Rock Playhouse

The State Theatre of North Carolina, Flat Rock Playhouse, is one of the top ten summer theatres in the nation. Broadway-mountain style is the best way to describe this professional equity theatre to be found in a lovely forested setting in Flat Rock. Actors at the Playhouse come from across the nation and have acting credits including Broadway, feature films, national tours, television, off-Broadway and regional theatres. Sets are designed by the resident scenic designer and in the scenic studio adjacent to the theatre by playhouse carpenters.

Flat Rock Playhouse (The Vagabond School of the Drama, Inc.) was established in 1952. In 1961, the playhouse was given special status with the honorary title of The State Theatre of North Carolina by the N.C. State Legislation in recognition of its high production standards. As the State Theatre, the Playhouse strives to offer a variety of fare each year with an emphasis on diversity.

Location:	Flat Rock
Address:	P.O. Box 310, 2661 Greenville Hwy., Flat Rock, NC 28731

Telephone: 693-0731
FAX: 693-6795
Website: www.flatrockplayhouse.org
Hours: Ticket and Business Office: 9 a.m.-6 p.m. Monday-Tuesday, 9 a.m.-8:30 p.m. Wed-Sat, and 11 a.m.-4 p.m. Sunday during summer season. Summer Season: late May to Mid-October
Curtain Times: 2:15 and 8:15 p.m.
Fees: Ticket prices vary with performance and seating.
Allow: Performances last from two to three hours.
Of Note: The Lowndes Place, near to theatre, is listed in the National Register of Historic Places. The Flat Rock Playhouse is the State Theatre of North Carolina.
Nearby: Carl Sandburg Home, Woodfield Inn, St. John in the Wilderness Church
Directions: From downtown Hendersonville take Highway 25 south to Flat Rock. The Playhouse is on the right at the intersection of Highway 25 and Little River Road.

Henderson County Curb Market

The Henderson County Curb Market, in continuous operation since 1924, offers home-grown fresh vegetables and fruits, baked goods, home-made jams and jellies and gifts and handicrafts of all kinds.

The Curb Market was started on Main Street in 1924 with eight sellers using umbrellas. It has grown to the present number of 137 selling spaces, with many sellers being third and fourth generation. The sellers are required to be residents of Henderson County and to make or grow all items sold.

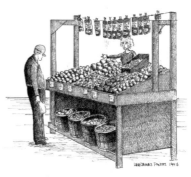

Henderson County Curb Market

Location: Downtown Hendersonville
Address: 221 N. Church St., Hendersonville, NC 28739
Telephone: 692-8012
Hours: January-April: Tuesday & Saturday, 8 a.m.-1 p.m.
May-December: Tuesday, Thursday, & Saturday, 8 a.m.-1 p.m.
Fees: None
Nearby: Historic Main Street, Old Henderson County Courthouse
Directions: Heading south on Main Street, take any right turn to take you to Church Street. It parallels Main Street. The market is behind the historic old Courthouse.

Henderson County Historical Center

Located on Main Street in downtown Hendersonville, the Henderson County Historical Center consists of four separate entities under one roof: 1) Henderson County Historical Museum; 2) Henderson County Archives; 3) Henderson County Genealogical and Historical Society; and 4) Mineral and Lapidary Museum of Henderson County. The Henderson County Historical Center has grown over the years under the direction of Dr. Jack Jones, noted local historian, into one of the area's most prestigious attractions.

Location:	Downtown Hendersonville
Address:	400 North Main St. (P.O. Box 2616), Hendersonville, NC 28793
Telephone:	Genealogical & Historical Society: 693-1531
	Mineral and Lapidary Museum: 698-1977
	County Archives: 693-1531
	County Historical Museum: 693-1531
FAX:	Mineral and Lapidary Museum: 891-6060
Hours:	Geneaological and Historical Society Center, County Archives and County Historical Museum: 9 a.m.-4 p.m. Monday through Friday; 9 a.m.-2 p.m. Saturdays;
	All other times by appointment only.
	Mineral and Lapidary Museum: Open Monday-Friday 10:00 a.m.-4 p.m.; Saturday 10 a.m.-1 p.m.
Fees:	None. Dues to join Society $20/year
Tips:	If your interests include history, minerals and architecture, and you would like to know more about the Henderson County area, this is the place to start.
Directions:	Located on east side of North Main Street.

Henderson County Historical Museum

The Henderson County Historical Museum has exhibits of documents, photographs, artifacts, and records pertaining to the history and development of Henderson County including Hendersonville.

Henderson County Archives

The repository of all the historic Henderson County documents, including old hand-written records.

Henderson County Genealogical and Historical Society

The purpose of the Society, which was organized in 1983, is to promote research into the heritage of Henderson County by collecting, preserving, and publishing the history of Henderson County, and of her people. A non-profit educational and cultural organization, the society welcomes visitors to its center on Main Street.

At the center, various displays and exhibits illustrate aspects of local history, publications are available for further exploration and research, and volunteer staff members stand ready to answer any questions about Henderson County's history. The Historical Center also maintains an extensive library.

Mineral and Lapidary Museum of Henderson County

The purpose of the museum is to support the education of the children of Henderson and neighboring counties in the Earth Science areas of Mineralogy, Geology, Paleontology and the associated Lapidary Arts. The museum has ongoing exhibits of regional minerals and gemstones of interest to the general public and a workshop where gem-cutting and polishing demonstrations are held.

Historic Johnson Farm, just northwest of Hendersonville

Historic Johnson Farm

The Johnson Farm originally was the home of a wealthy tobacco farmer, Oliver Moss. Construction began in 1876 and was completed by 1880, handmade entirely of bricks fired on site from French Broad River mud. Over the years various outbuildings were added, including a toolshed/blacksmith shop, barn, boarding house and cottage. In 1913 Sallie Leverett Johnson inherited the farm, a new era began and the farm was operated as farm and summer boarding home for tourists. It is owned and administered by the Henderson County Board of Education and operates today as a community museum and heritage center, with guided tours available for visitors. Especially suitable for children.

Location: Just northwest of Hendersonville
Address: 3346 Haywood Road, (Route 191), Hendersonville, NC 28791
Telephone: 891-6585
Website: www.johnsonfarm.org

Hours: Year-round: Tuesday-Saturday 9 a.m. to 2:30 p.m.
Fees: $3 adults, $2 students, preschoolers free.
Allow: Two hours
Of Note: Listed in the National Register of Historic Places
Directions: From Hendersonville take Haywood Road (Rt. 191) north four miles.

Holmes Educational State Forest

North Carolina has six Educational State Forests that have been developed as living environmental education centers. These forests are designed to promote a better understanding of the value of forests in our lives.

Holmes Forest, located in the Great Smoky Mountains, offers a rich mixture of mountain hardwoods, rhododendron, flame azaleas and a variety of wildflowers. These features are accessible to the visiting public by a series of well-marked trails accented by exhibits and displays depicting the ecology of the managed forest. Picnic sites with tables and grills are provided, and ranger-conducted programs are available to groups visiting the 235-acre Forest.

Holmes Educational State Forest

Location: Just west of Hendersonville
Address: Crab Creek Rd., Route 4 (Box 308) Hendersonville, NC 28739
Telephone: 692-0100
FAX: 698-0086
Website: www.dfr.state.nc.us/esf/holmes_esf.htm
Hours: Mid-March to the day Friday before Thanksgiving. Closed Mondays. 9 a.m.-5 p.m. Tuesday through Friday, 11 a.m.-8 p.m. DST/11 a.m.-5 p.m. ST Saturday and Sunday.
Fees: None
Allow: Two hours
Directions: From Hendersonville take Kanuga Road west 8 miles. Forest is on the left.

Western North Carolina Air Museum

The Western North Carolina Air Museum is a private organization dedicated to preserving and promoting the flying heritage of the Western North Carolina region. The museum has on display a large number of vintage aircraft, including

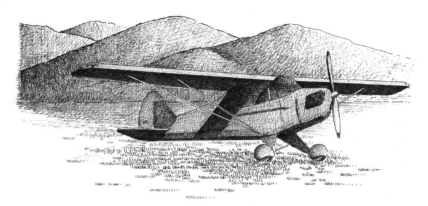

Impromptu rides sometimes happen at the N.C. Air Museum

a bi-winged 1942 Stearman, and the North American SNJ-5 Texan, the classic two-seat advanced trainer, which turned young fliers into combat pilots.

Location: Hendersonville Airport
Address: 1340 Gilbert St., Hendersonville, NC 28792
Telephone: 698-2482
Website: www.wncairmuseum.com
Hours: Wednesday, Saturday, and Sunday noon-6 p.m., weather permitting
Fees: None
Allow: One-two hours
Tips: A very informal museum. Rides sometimes are possible if you happen to be there when a flight is about to happen.
Directions: From I-26 south take exit 22 Upward Road. Take right onto Spartanburg Highway (US 176) and then another right onto Shepherd Street. Museum is on Gilbert Street.

Chapter Three
Historic Hendersonville

Hendersonville, while in existence as early as 1841, did not reach its peak of development until the late 19th and early 20th centuries. The boom started in 1879 when the railroad arrived and commercial development expanded greatly, both in the downtown Main Street area and in the district around the railroad depot. The influx of tourists at that time greatly increased and this in turn spurred the building of resort hotels and boarding houses, as well as fine residential homes for those tourists who decided to stay in Hendersonville. This building and development continued into the early 20th century but stopped abruptly in 1929 with the advent of the Great Depression.

During the early years of development, two individuals, W.F. Edwards and Erle G. Stilwell had major influence on the shape and character of Hendersonville. Edwards was a builder, and was responsible for the construction of many important commercial and residential buildings, including the early Town Hall and Opera House which stood on Main from 1893 to the 1920s, the Neo-Classical People's Bank at 225-231 North Main Street and the historic Henderson County Courthouse. Stilwell was an architect who had considerable influence on the shape of municipal, religious and commercial architecture in Hendersonville by bringing a new level of sophistication and competence to the local architecture. Among his important works were the Hendersonville High School, City Hall and the Citizens National Bank.

The face of domestic architecture was changed significantly with the arrival of the railroad. The industrial growth that the railroads brought also resulted in fine homes being built in the Queen Anne, Eastlake, Colonial Revival and Neo-Classical styles to house the wealthy industrialists. Today, in modern Hendersonville, many of these remaining significant residential properties in downtown have survived and continue to grace the city with their historic presence.

In this chapter, a selection of important historic buildings and structures will be presented, both as part of the two major downtown historic districts; Main Street and the 7th Avenue Depot area, and as separate structures not part of any designated historic district.

As in the chapter on Historic Asheville, certain abbreviations will be used to signify buildings of historical importance. NRHP indicates the structure is listed in the National Register of Historic Places, NHL indicates a National Historic Landmark property and LHL means the building is a Local Historic Landmark. Discussion of these designations is given in depth in the Historic Asheville chapter. (SEE Section Three, Chapter 4)

The Hendersonville Preservation Society is instrumental in the preservation and restoration of historic properties. They are a valuable resource for anyone interested in historic Hendersonville. The Preservation Society may be reached by calling the Henderson County Genealogical & Historical Society offices at 693-1531, also an excellent historical resource. They are located at 400 North Main Street, Hendersonville, NC 28792.

Historic Districts of Hendersonville
Main Street Historic District

This district will be presented in the form of a self-guided walking tour. The best place to start is to park at the Hendersonville and Flat Rock Area Visitors Information Center located at 201 South Main Street. From there your tour will take you up and back on Main Street. Allow about an hour for the stroll.

Leaving the Visitors Center proceed north up Main Street. One block up on your left will be the Historic Henderson County Courthouse.

Historic Henderson County Courthouse (NRHP)   113 North Main St.

Built in 1905, the historic Henderson County Courthouse overlooks Main Street. Graced with a gold dome and a statue of Lady Justice, this imposing building was constructed by W.F. Edwards, father of A.V. Edwards, who served

The Historic Henderson County Courthouse

as Hendersonville's mayor for 36 years. Neo-Classical Revival in style, this building replaced an earlier two-story stuccoed brick structure. The architect was Richard Sharp Smith and is Smith's only structure in Hendersonville. The most notable feature of the courthouse is the gold domed three-stage cupola, which consists of a columned drum and domical roof, crowned by a statue of Lady Justice. This Lady Justice is thought to be the only one in the United States that does not wear a blindfold.

Although its main function was as a courthouse, the graceful building served other purposes over the years. The main courtroom was used in the early 1900s for various purposes, including speeches by governors, and as a gathering place for church congregations. Although it no longer is Henderson County's courthouse, it remains a dignified and majestic reminder of the past. The sophistication and grandeur reflect the past aspirations of a small county seat at a time when the economy was booming and whose population was beginning to soar.

Farther up Main Street in the next block you will see the People's National Bank Building on your left.

People's National Bank Building (NRHP)   227-231 North Main St.

This building, dating back to around 1910, is a two story Neo-Classical structure of cream colored brick and was built by W.F. Edwards. It has a recessed central entrance beneath entablature supported by Ionic columns, and storefronts to either side. The bank building was the earliest use of Neo-Classical style and reinforced concrete construction for a commercial building in Hendersonville.

Continuing on up North Main Street to the end, look for the Maxwell Store Building on your left, which is now home to Mast General Store.

People's National Bank Building

Maxwell Store Building (NRHP)   529 North Main St.
This building once housed a fancy grocery business run by Maxwell Brown, a longtime proprietor. It was built around 1910 and is a two-story pressed brick structure. Highlights are round and segmentally arched windows with fanlights.

Turn around at this point and continue south on North Main. Turn left at 5th Avenue and look for the Hendersonville City Hall on your left.

Hendersonville City Hall (NRHP)   145 5th Ave. East
Built between 1926 and 1928, this Neo-Classical Revival building was designed by Erle Stilwell. A flight of stairs leads up to the main entrance which is under a tetrastyle portico, on which is inscribed "'Erected by the People, Dedicated to the Perpetuation of Civic Progress, Liberty and the Security of Public Honor." This building reflects the prosperity of Hendersonville during the 1920s and the architectural refinement that Stilwell brought to the city.

After viewing the City Hall, return to Main Street, and turn left. Proceed south on Main. The Ripley-Shepherd Building will be three blocks down on your left.

Ripley-Shepherd Building (NRHP)   218 North Main St.
This building is believed to be the second-oldest building on Main Street, one of several buildings built by Colonel Valentine Ripley and once known as the "Ripley Brick Store House." It is said to have served as a district commissary under a Major Noe during the Civil War. Later it was also a post office for Hendersonville. Later still it was the home of Shepherd and Hart's furniture store and undertaking business. Notable features are the high hip roof and bracketed eaves.

7th Avenue Depot Historic District
This district is located two blocks northeast of Main Street and separated from Main Street by new commercial development. The district still shows a cohesive grouping of commercial, residential and transportation-related structures typical of the early development of Hendersonville, especially the period after the arrival of the railroad.

Seventh Avenue East developed as a commercial district during the late 19th and early 20th centuries and was centered around the first depot built in 1879. The majority of buildings are one and two story brick commercial and warehouse structures located along 7th Avenue. Only minor alterations to the commercial buildings have occurred and these are mainly at the storefront level. Very little construction took place after the Great Depression. This district, with its frame depot, approximately 28 brick commercial buildings and the Station Hotel is one of the best surviving examples of a railroad district in western North Carolina. The buildings in the district are primarily commercial in function and provided services that were associated with a shipping point for locally grown cash crops.

Directions: Take North Main Street north to 6th Avenue. Turn right and go 2 blocks. Turn left onto North Grove Street. Proceed on North Grove across Four Seasons Boulevard. Take a right onto East 7th Avenue. The Depot is just ahead on your right.

Hendersonville Depot, built between 1902 and 1904

Hendersonville Depot (NRHP)
SE Corner of 7th Avenue and Maple St.

This depot was the second station to be built by Southern Railway in the city and was built between 1902 and 1904. A frame structure with characteristics of the Craftsman style of architecture, it originally was 87 feet long and consisted of two waiting rooms, an agent's office and had indoor plumbing. In 1906, 15 more feet were added to each end of the station to provide a ladies waiting room and more baggage space. A few years later, an open pavilion area was added to the north end, and in 1916 another 50 feet were added to the roofed over, open pavilion area.

The railroad line was opened from Spartanburg, S.C. to Hendersonville in 1879, a year before Asheville was to receive a line from the east. The railroad brought large numbers of visitors to Hendersonville and allowed the county's produce to reach a wider market in other cities. The last passenger service ended in 1968. Since then the depot has been restored to its original color, and a Southern Railway caboose located at the south end. Restoration is ongoing, and the depot currently houses an operating model railroad in the baggage room. Visitors are invited to visit this historic station. The Depot is open for visitors year-round, Saturday 10 a.m.-2 p.m. Free. Call 890-0436 for more information.

Just north of the Depot, on the same side of the railroad tracks is the Station Hotel Building.

Station Hotel (NRHP)
729 Maple St.

Built between 1912-1922, the Station Hotel is a two story brick building that features a low tripped roof and a two tiered, full facade frame porch. This relatively plain hotel was built near the tracks to serve the visitors who came to Hendersonville by the railroad. The building is still operated today as a hotel, although without its former polish and poise.

Other Historic Sites & Buildings

This section of Historic Hendersonville is devoted to those sites and buildings of architectural or historic importance that have not been covered in the previous section.

Aloah Hotel (NRHP)   201 3rd Ave. West

The Aloah Hotel, called the Hendersonville Inn since the 1930s, is a large three-story brick building built in the early years of the 20th century. The building has a modest Classical Revival porch and entrance and is remarkably unaltered on its exterior and very well preserved on the interior. One of the few hotels in Hendersonville still operated as such, it was also known as the Carson House and then the Hendersonville Inn. Its plain sturdy brick design and great wraparound porch reflect comfort and integrity, and is a good example of the type of hotel built to handle the influx of visitors and tourists to Hendersonville in the early years. This sector of town was originally filled with other hotels catering to the tourist boom.

Directions: From Main Street take 3rd Avenue heading west. The Aloah Hotel, known today as the Hendersonville Inn, is on your right just beyond Church Street.

The Cedars (NRHP)   227 7th Ave.

The Cedars is a large 3½-story brick veneer hotel built in a Neo-Classical Revival style. It derives its name from the large ancient cedars on the lot in which it stands. The building is highlighted by a monumental Ionic portico that has a deck with railing. The Cedars is the largest and one of the most important of the historic tourist accommodations in Hendersonville. It was built in 1914 for Jennie Bailey, wife of a local Southern Railroad executive. Mrs. Bailey and, later, her daughter operated the hotel until 1976. Today it is privately owned and used for weddings, receptions, parties and club meetings.

The Cedars

Directions: Take 7th Avenue west off of Main Street.

Chewning House (NRHP) 755 North Main St.
Located on the same shady street as the Waverly Inn, Chewning House is also one of Hendersonville's treasures. Built sometime between 1888 and 1906 by W.A. Smith, the inn's original name was "The Smith-Green House." The house underwent a complete transformation between 1912 and 1922 when it was enlarged from a two-story building to the present three-story structure. It is a prime example of the simpler domestic architectural styles of the 1920s. Chewning House, like the Waverly next door, still serves its original purpose and today is known as the Claddagh Inn.

Directions: Located on Main Street in downtown Hendersonville.

Clarke-Hobbs-Davidson House (NRHP) 229 5th Ave. West
Built about 1907, the Clarke-Hobbs-Davidson House is one of the most imposing historic residences remaining near downtown Hendersonville. Purchased by the Masons in 1958, it is a 2½-story brick Queen Anne-Colonial Revival style house that has had a rear brick wing added, nearly doubling the size of the building. The house was probably built by Charles S. Clarke and his wife Louise, and in 1907 it was sold to Alfred J. Hobbs, and thereafter to Charles A. Hobbs and his wife Harriet. In 1911 it was again sold to a Mrs. Davidson who left the property to her brother Edgar Sutton and his wife Eleanor. Since that time it has had a number of other owners, including the Masons, who now operate it as a Masonic Lodge. It is a rare example of a large brick house in Hendersonville at the time of the tourism boom during the early part of the 20th century.

Directions: From Main Street, take 5th Avenue heading west. The Clarke-Hobbs-Davidson House will be on your right.

Henderson County Courthouse 200 North Grove St.
Dedicated on April 29, 1995, the Henderson County Courthouse occupies approximately 99,100 square feet on a 13-acre site. Designed by Grier-Fripp Architects of Charlotte, NC, and built by M.B. Kahn Construction Company

The Henderson County Courthouse, dedicated in 1995

of Greenville, SC, this imposing structure replaced the historic old courthouse on Main Street.

The ceilings in the lobby and court waiting areas are painted to resemble the sky with clouds. The clock over the main steps is over five feet in diameter, and the grounds are planted with Japanese Yoshino cherry trees, Japanese Zelkova, and Sugar Maples.

Directions: Located in downtown Hendersonville on North Grove Street. North Grove Street parallels North Main Street and is two blocks to the east.

King-Waldrop House (NRHP)   103 South Washington St.

The King-Waldrop House was built around 1881 and shows features of both the Queen Anne and the Italianate building styles. Its main feature is a square three-stage cupola with a concave pyramidal roof. The general condition of the house is excellent and both the inside, with its dark woodwork and Victorian detailing, and the outside are little altered. The house is an excellent example of the large spacious residences built for the wealthy in Hendersonville in the 1880s. It is one of the few surviving 19th century dwellings in downtown Hendersonville. It was built for Laura V. King, the daughter of Colonel Valentine Ripley, one of Hendersonville's earliest businessmen and entrepreneurs. In 1897, Laura King and Dr. J.G. Waldrop traded houses, and the residence was then titled "Maple Grove" by Dr. Waldrop, who occupied the home with his wife, Nancy, and their eight children.

Directions: Take First Avenue west from Main Street and turn left onto Washington Street. The King-Waldrop House is on your right at 103.

Mary Mills Coxe House (NRHP)   1210 Greenville Hwy.

The Mary Mills Coxe House is located south of Hendersonville on the Greenville Highway, formerly known as Flat Rock Road. Built around 1911 as a single family residence, it is notable as one of only a handful of pebbledash houses remaining in Henderson County. A Colonial-Revival style dwelling, it is two-and-a-half stories and has as distinctive features a large porch formed by fifteen columns and a roof of pressed metal shingles. The house was built by Mary Mills Coxe, widow of Colonel Franklin Coxe, one of the more influential and wealthy men in Henderson and Buncombe counties. The building is significant historically since it is a very well-preserved pebbledash house that is a rare, unchanged structure that has not been modernized stylistically. The pebbledash stucco walls reflect the influence of noted Asheville architect Richard Sharp Smith.

Directions: Take Main Street heading south. This street turns into Greenville Highway. The Mary Mills Coxe House is on your left heading toward Flat Rock.

Reese House (NRHP)   202 South Washington St.

The Reese House, built in 1885 by Harriet Louise and William Reese is one of the best preserved Queen Anne style houses in Hendersonville. Wonderfully restored, the house boasts rich, red heart of pine floors, seven fireplaces and hand-carved gingerbread mouldings. On the front lawn is a buckeye tree that was one of the original plantings.

Directions: Just down the street to the south of the King-Waldrop House on South Washington Street.

St. James Episcopal Church   766 North Main St.

St. James Episcopal Church, located on Main Street in downtown Hendersonville, is one of the area's most picturesque churches. Consecrated in 1861, the first rector was Rev. N. Collin Hughes. From 1970 to 1980, Henderson County experienced an unprecedented population growth. New economic developments, discovery of Hendersonville as an outstanding retirement area, and growth in tourism marked this period. Consequently, St. James Church flourished and became the largest parish in the Episcopal Diocese of Western North Carolina during that time.

Directions: Located on North Main Street.

LEE JAMES PANTAS 1993

St. James Episcopal Church

Thomas Wolfe's Angel   Oakdale Cemetery, Hwy. 64 West

The marble angel statue immortalized by Thomas Wolfe in his novel *Look Homeward Angel* now stands at Oakdale Cemetery in Hendersonville. The statue was imported from Carrara, Italy by Wolfe's father, and was bought by members of the Johnson family after the death of Mrs. Johnson in 1905. The gravesite belongs to Reverend and Mrs. H.F. Johnson and their son. In 1975, when the statue was

accidentally knocked from its stand, the Henderson County Commissioners had the graves
enclosed with a six-foot tall iron picket fence set
on a stone wall. This still allows visitors to view
the statue and reduces the possibility of damage
to the monument.

Directions: From downtown Hendersonville,
take Highway 64 west. Look for Oakdale Cemetery on your left. The Angel Statue is visible
from the road, and the location is indicated by
a State Highway Marker.

The Waverly Inn (NRHP)

783 North Main St.

Built just after 1898, the Waverly Inn is a three-

Thomas Wolf's Angel
in Oakdale Cemetery

story Queen Anne style inn. The third story was
added in 1910 after a fire did extensive roof damage. With the exception of minor
changes, the Waverly has undergone relatively little change and is in remarkably
pristine condition. The interior boasts a magnificent Eastlake style stair and
twenty-one guest rooms, with seventeen bathrooms. Today the Waverly is still
operated as an inn.

Directions: Located on North Main Street in downtown Hendersonville.

The Waverly Inn

Chapter Four
Historic Flat Rock

Flat Rock, located a few miles south of Hendersonville, grew up along the road up the mountain from South Carolina. The road is winding and narrow and lined with large old trees and most of the houses are set back from the road. For many, the only visible sign of their presence are the stone gates at the entrances to the driveways. Flat Rock is characterized by peaceful, uncluttered roads, large open spaces interrupted only by tree-lined drives and the absence of any major commercial intrusions among the stone fences and gates that lead to the many concealed estates and great houses.

Tourism was a major factor in shaping Flat Rock since the area was settled largely by wealthy South Carolinians in search of a cooler climate in which to escape the hot lowland summers. The country estates represent a unique segment of Southern social history and preserve as a living record the scale and quality of life led by these affluent South Carolinians.

One of the most important landowners in Flat Rock was Charles Baring, a prominent rice planter in South Carolina and a member of a well-known banking family of England. He settled in Flat Rock with his wife, Susan, in 1827 where he purchased substantial acreage and began construction of a home, Mountain Lodge, the first Flat Rock house built by Charlestonians. After the Barings settled at Flat Rock, others followed and also began to live in the mountain area. Baring is credited with being among the first of many to find the climate and terrain of Flat Rock to their liking. He and his wife also constructed the beautiful church St. John in the Wilderness as a private chapel which they later donated to the Episcopal Diocese of North Carolina.

In this chapter, some of the historic homes and structures will be presented. The ones included are those that are visible from the road. They will be presented in the form of a self-guided auto tour that begins at the Flat Rock Playhouse and ends with a tour of Connemara, the Carl Sandburg Home. Flat Rock is rich with many historic residences and buildings but many of these will not be presented since they are inaccessible and not visible from public domain. All of Flat Rock has been declared an Historic District and is listed in the National Register of Historic Places.

An organization which is instrumental in preservation work in Flat Rock is
Historic Flat Rock, Inc. Chartered in
1968, Historic Flat Rock, Inc. is actively
involved in education, preservation and
restoration projects. Recently they were
responsible for the restoration of the
Lowndes House. The organization may
be reached by writing to P.O. Box 295,
Flat Rock, NC 28731.

The following self-guided auto tour
of this area will start at the Flat Rock
Playhouse located on Highway 25
south at the junction of Little River
Road. Right next to the Playhouse is The
Lowndes Place.

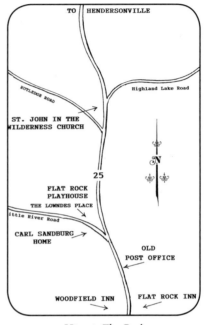

Historic Flat Rock

The Lowndes Place (NRHP)

Juncture of Hwy. 25 South and Little River Rd.

Built in 1885 by Richard I. Lowndes, it
was named "The Rock" because it is near
the rock outcropping from which Flat Rock takes its name. The Vagabond School of
the Drama acquired the building in 1956 and used it as an administrative office building and dormitory in its operation of the Flat Rock Playhouse and Drama School.
The two-story, five-bay house has some distinctive features in the use of splayed eaves
without brackets and a one-bay gable porch at the central bay of the second floor.

While at this site, you will of course want to take a look at the Flat Rock Playhouse itself. (See Section Four, Chapter 2) From the Lowndes Place take Highway
25 north to St. John in the Wilderness Church on your left.

St. John in the Wilderness Church (NRHP)   1895 Greenville Hwy.

A unique spot of southern history in a setting of idyllic beauty, St. John in the
Wilderness Episcopal Church in Flat Rock is a gable roof brick church that has at
its southeast corner a three-story square tower with pyramidal roof.

In 1833, Charles and Susan Baring built the church as a private chapel, and at
the formation of the Episcopal Diocese of Western North Carolina in 1836, the
Baring family gave up their rights to the church as a private chapel, turning the
deed to the bishop of the newly-formed diocese.

Among the family plots in the graveyard are the graves of Christopher Memminger, first secretary of the Confederate treasury; Rev. John Grimke Drayton,
developer of the world famous Magnolia Gardens; members of families of three
signers of the Declaration of Independence; and Edward P. King, the World War
II general who led the infamous Bataan death march.

St. John in the Wilderness

The church and graveyard are open daily 9 a.m.-4 p.m. for visitation.

Continue your tour by returning down Highway 25 heading south. After you pass the Flat Rock Playhouse, look for the Old Post Office Building on your left.

Old Post Office (NRHP)   Greenville Hwy. at Little River Rd.

This small frame building was built around 1846 by Peter Stradley, a blacksmith who was appointed postmaster in 1845. It is two stories high and its three-bay gable end sits almost flush with the highway. The building was used as a post office until 1877, and then intermittently the following years until 1965. Currently it is home to a bookstore, The Book Exchange.

Continue past the Old Post Office a half a mile and look for the Flat Rock Inn on your left at 2810 Greenville Highway. Turn into the inn's driveway. Park if you wish and get out and take a close look at this wonderful old building. The inn's owners welcome visitors.

Flat Rock Inn (NRHP)   2810 Greenville Hwy.

The Flat Rock Inn was built in 1888 as a summer retreat by R. Withers Memminger, a minister from Charleston, South Carolina and a son of C.G. Memminger, the first Secretary of the Treasury for the Confederate States. Officially known as Five Oaks, the Inn served as a summer home until 1911 when it was purchased by Thomas Grimshawe, who resided there with his wife, Elizabeth, until 1930. The home was given to their daughter Greta Grimshawe King and her husband, Campbell. Sold in 1940, the house was used as a summer residence by a number of owners for the next 45 years. Beginning in 1985, the inn was renovated by Barthela Galloway and ultimately purchased in 1992 by Dennis and Sandi Page, who own and manage the property as The Flat Rock Inn.

After leaving the Flat Rock Inn, you will see directly across the street the entrance to the Woodfield Inn.

Woodfield Inn (NRHP)
Greenville Hwy.

Built in 1852, the Woodfield Inn has been a favorite destination for travelers and vacationers for over 135 years, and is one of the most visible landmarks of Flat Rock. It is a three-story, hip-roof, frame structure with a two-story porch running the length of the building.

The Inn was conceived in 1847 when several prominent landowners in Flat Rock purchased four hundred acres in the center of the community "with the design of promoting the establishment of a good, commodious tavern at or near the Saluda Road." Construction was completed under the direction of Henry Tudor Farmer, who purchased the property in 1853 and operated it as an inn under the name "Farmer's Hotel" until his death in 1883. Mrs. Annie T. Martin, a later owner, changed the name to the Woodfield Inn.

The Woodfield Inn has played host to many famous people throughout its century-old history, and during the Civil War, a company of Confererate soldiers was bivouacked at the inn to protect the Flat Rock community from renegades. The Woodfield Inn today is owned by Mike and Rhonda Horton and is considered one of the premier country inns in Western North Carolina.

After leaving the Woodfield Inn, turn left and continue north on Greenville Highway. Turn left onto Little River Road and look for the parking lot of the Carl Sandburg Home on your left. In order to see the house and grounds properly you will have to park here and proceed on foot. Allow one to two hours for your visit.

Woodfield Inn, built in 1852

(See Section Four, Chapter 2 Carl Sandburg Home for fees, hours, and other information) Connemara, as it is known, will be the last stop on your tour of historic Flat Rock.

Connemara (NRHP, NHL) Little River Rd.
Designated a National Historic site because of its association with Carl Sandburg, who lived there from 1945 until his death in 1967. It was built in 1838-1839 by Christopher Gustavus Memminger, later secretary of the treasury of the Confederacy, on land purchased from Charles Baring. Memminger named the house Rock Hill and after his death, the new owner Captain Ellison Adder Smyth, a textile executive, changed the name to Connemara. The farm today includes 264 acres of rolling hills, forests, lakes, goat barn and buildings. The grounds and farm are open for self-guided tours, and guided tours (admission charged) of the home are scheduled daily. (SEE Section Four, Chapter 2 Carl Sandburg Home)

Chapter Five
Colleges & Schools

In addition to the local listings below, those relocating to the area should also consider the proximity of Hendersonville to the metropolitan area of Greenville/Spartanburg, SC, which offers a plethora of continuing education. Within the state, also remember the nearby Brevard College.

Colleges

Blue Ridge Community College

Blue Ridge Community College was established in May, 1969 as one of the 58 similar institutions throughout the state. It is fully accredited by the Commission on Colleges of the Southern Association of Colleges and Schools.

Address: 180 West Campus Drive, Flat Rock, NC 28731
Telephone: 684-1700
FAX: 694-1690
Website: www.blueridge.edu
Directions: I-26 Exit 22 (Upward Road). Right on Upward Road, then right on South Allen Road, and then left onto College Drive.

Brevard College

Located in nearby Brevard, this four-year liberal arts institution is known for small classes and a gifted and caring faculty. Spiritual and ethical development are elements of the educational process at Brevard College in keeping with its affiliation with the United Methodist Church.

Address: 400 North Broad St. Brevard, NC 28712
Telephone: 883-8292, (800) 527-9090
Website: www.brevard.edu
Directions: From Asheville, take I-26 east to Airport Road (NC 280) and head south to Brevard. From Hendersonville, take Highway 64 west to Brevard.

Secondary Schools

Henderson County Public Schools

Henderson County school system has more than 10,000 students and 19 schools.

Address: 414 4th Ave. West, Hendersonville, NC 28739
Telephone: 697-4733
Website: www.henderson.k12.nc.us

Henderson County Private Schools

Captain Gilmore School: (Seventh Day Adventist) 684-8221
Faith Christian Day School: 692-0556
Fletcher Academy: 684-4751
Fruitland Baptist Bible Institute: 685-8886
Heritage Hall School: 693-6845
Immaculata Catholic School: 693-3277
Pathway Christian Academy: 693-5099

Chapter Six
Hospitals

While Asheville has a larger medical community including a huge hospital complex, the Hendersonville area is blessed by competition between hospitals, which some feel increases the quality of service.

Margaret R. Pardee Memorial Hospital

This full-service hospital is licensed for 222 beds plus a 40-bed nursing facility. Pardee provides medical, surgical, orthopedic, maternal, pediatric, intensive and coronary care, radiation therapy, and mental health services. A 52,000 square foot surgical facility has been opened housing six large operating rooms, 22 day-surgery rooms, a 13 bay-recovery room, and Central Sterile Supply and Materials Management departments.

Pardee's Home Care includes OB and pediatric nursing, psychiatric nursing and personal care services. Pardee also recently opened Hendersonville Family Health Center to furnish comprehensive medical care to all ages. Free access to medical assistance is offered by Pardee's Ask-A-Nurse, and since 1989 the Pardee Health Education Center at the Blue Ridge Mall has been serving the community in health promotion and wellness.

Address: 800 N. Justice St., Hendersonville, NC 28791
Telephone: 696-1000
Website: www.pardeehospital.org
Directions: Located in downtown Hendersonville on Fleming Street off Highway 64 west.

Park Ridge Hospital

This 103-bed hospital provides general inpatient services, mental health services, and Lifeline Emergency Services. The oldest medical facility in Henderson County, Park Ridge was established in 1910 as Mountain Sanitarium and known for many years as Fletcher Hospital.

Park Ridge Hospital, a not-for-profit facility is operated by the Seventh-Day Adventists, who, for more than 120 years, have been promoting wellness and healthy lifestyle philosophies. Park Ridge has a tradition of providing quality personalized patient care.

Address: Naples Rd. (P.O. Box 1569), Fletcher, NC 28732
Telephone: 684-8501
Website: www.parkridgehospital.org
Directions: I-26 Exit 13 onto Highway 25 South. Take left onto Naples Road, then right onto Hospital Drive.

Chapter Seven
Natural Attractions

Natural beauty abounds in the Hendersonville and Flat Rock areas, from enchanting apple orchards to lush green valleys and rugged mountains. Visitors to the area are only minutes away from a wide variety of natural attractions and opportunities for outdoor recreation. Chimney Rock Park, Lake Lure, and area waterfalls are covered separately in Section Five, Chapter 1.

Apple Orchards in Henderson County

Henderson County, North Carolina, is the seventh largest apple producing county in the United States. Its main city, Hendersonville, is home to the famous North Carolina Apple Festival, held every summer. Apple orchards in the county range in size from small family backyard plantings to some over 600 acres. The most popular varieties are Rome, Red Delicious, Golden Delicious, Gala, Fugi, and Jonagold. An average of one million mature apple trees are growing on nine thousand acres producing approxi- mately 5 million bushels of apples per year. A drive in the country out Route 64 heading east through Edneyville towards Chimney Rock will take you past some very scenic apple orchards, as well as past roadside stands that sell fresh apples and cider. There are also a number of orchards where you may pick you own apples. Contact the Visitors Center for current listings during the apple harvesting season

Apple orchards in Hendersonville area

in late summer and early fall. Additionally, the N.C. Apple Growers Association provides a comprehensive directory of roadside markets in WNC where you may buy apples or pick your own. Check the association's website (www.ncapple growers.com) or write them at P.O. Box 58, Edneyville, NC 28727.

Nearby Apple Sources

While visiting the area during apple season, you might want to visit the WNC Farmer's Market at 570 Brevard Road in South Asheville. (SEE WNC Farmer's Market, Section Three, Chapter 2) This is by far the biggest and best "roadside stand" in the region. In the market square and tailgate section you will find a great variety of apples for sale in any quantity you wish. They are open 8 a.m.-6 p.m. daily. Another favorite source for apples in season is Hickory Nut Gap Farm. In addition to their own homegrown apples, they also sell honey, ham, and great cider. To get there take 74A east through Fairview to Hickory Nut Gap and follow the small signs. The stand is located next to historic Sherril's Inn. (SEE Section Three, Chapter 4) Hours of operation are 8 a.m.-6 p.m. daily during apple season.

Bottomless Pools

The Bottomless Pools, located at the east end of Hickory Nut Gorge in Lake Lure, is a series of three separate pools each with their own beautiful waterfall. This popular attraction has been open since 1916 and was formed where Pool Creek on its rush to Lake Lure found weaknesses in the hard, resistant rock of the stream bed. The pools were created by the swirling current as it carried stones and pebbles, carving steep circular walls. Thousands of years old, the Bottomless Pools are an interesting geological phenomena and a refreshing place to visit.

Location: Lake Lure
Address: 200 Pool Creek Rd., Lake Lure, NC 28748
Telephone: 625-8324
Hours: Daily 9 a.m.-6:30 p.m., April through October.
Fees: $3 adults, $1 children 7 to 12, under 7 free.
Allow: 30 minutes
Tips: Picnic tables available as well as walking trails.
Nearby: Lake Lure, Lake Lure Boat Tours, Chimney Rock
Directions: Hwy. 64 East. Right on Hwy. 74A to Lake Lure and turn right at the beach onto Pool Creek Rd. to Bottomless Pools.

City of Hendersonville Parks

Hendersonville maintains seven city parks, listed below, that are easily accessible. The most popular is the 20-acre Patton Park.

Address: Hendersonville City Parks, Public Works Department, 415 8th Avenue East, Hendersonville, NC 28792
Telephone: 697-3084

Patton Park: Hwy. 25 north to Patton Avenue
Boyd Park: 840 Church Street
Edwards Park: North Main Street and Locust Street
Green Meadows Park: Ash Street and Park View Drive
King Memorial Park: 7th Avenue and Robinson Terrace

Toms Park: Allen Street and Lily Pond Road, shuffleboard
Lennox Park: Park Drive off Whitted Street

Hendersonville Area Parks
Henderson County Parks
Maintained by the Henderson County Parks and Recreation Department, these parks total over 259 acres of playing fields, recreation facilities, woodland and playgrounds. The Parks and Recreation Department also sponsors special events that include The March for Parks Bicycle Tour, Easter Egg Hunt, Four Seasons Senior Games, USATF Junior Olympics Track Meet, Fourth of July Festivities, Farm-City Day and Halloween Fest.

Address: Henderson County Parks & Recreation Department, 801 Glover St., Hendersonville, NC 28792
Telephone: 697-4884
FAX: 697-4886

Jackson Park   4th Avenue East, Hendersonville
The southeastern city limits of Hendersonville touch the edges of this busy 212-acre park. The largest municipal-owned park in Western North Carolina, Jackson Park offers activities and facilities for all ages. The park is open 7:30 a.m. to 11 p.m. daily. It features 4 lighted tennis courts, 8 lighted softball/baseball fields, 3 soccer fields, 2 lighted basketball courts, 3 large playgrounds, 4 covered picnic shelters, 20 woodland picnic tables, restrooms and a 1.5-mile Nature Trail. Jackson Park is noted for its great birdwatching also. 697-4888, www.jacksonbmx.com

Edneyville Park   Hwy. 64, Edneyville
Located behind Edneyville Volunteer Fire Department about ten miles from downtown Hendersonville, this four-acre park has 2 tennis courts, 1 basketball court, a well-equipped children's playground, a picnic area, and restrooms.

Dana Park   Upward Rd., Dana
Approximately eight miles from downtown Hendersonville, this six-acre park has a Community Building, covered picnic shelter, softball field, and children's playground.

Stoney Mountain Activity Center   Stoney Mountain Rd., Hendersonville
This Activity Center has classes and special activities in art, calligraphy, fitness and aerobics, and other types of instruction. Follow US 25 north from Hendersonville about one mile to Stoney Mountain Road. The center is one mile down on the right.

Westfeldt River Park   Fanning Bridge Rd.
River access, canoe landing ramp, and an open recreation area are found at this park. Follow US Hwy. 280 to Fanning Bridge Road.

Jump Off Rock

Legend has it that more than 300 years ago a young Indian maiden leapt from this rock to her death when she learned that her lover, a Cherokee chief, had been killed in battle. Indian lore to this day maintains that on some moon-lit nights the ghost of the heartbroken maiden can be seen on the rock. Views from the rock during daylight hours are breathtaking of the valleys below. The rock itself is surrounded by landscaped grounds.

Jump Off Rock

Location: Laurel Park section of Hendersonville.
Address: End of Laurel Park Hwy.
Fees: None
Tips: Great views anytime but spectacular at sunset.
Good spot for a picnic.
Directions: Located a few miles west of Hendersonville, via 5th Ave. West, at the very end of Laurel Park Highway.

North Mills River Recreation Area

The North Mills River Recreation Area and Campground is part of the Pisgah District of the Pisgah National Forest and is a great place to take kids on a picnic. Bring inner tubes and rubber rafts. A gentle yet bold stream provides the perfect place for summer fun. The section of the stream where the kids tube even has a natural beach area.

There are over 39 picnic units with grills along the river for cookouts, and large ball playing fields and walking trails along the river. For campers there are 32 excellent campsites which can accommodate tents or RVs up to 22 feet in length. The sparkling river offers excellent trout fishing as well as the popular tubing. (SEE also Section Five, Chapter 1 Pisgah National Forest)

Location: 20 minutes west of Hendersonville
Address: North Mills River Rd.
Telephone: (Pisgah District Ranger Station) 877-3350
FAX: 884-7527
Hours: Always open
Fees: Campsites $6 per night.
Tips: Hot summer days in July and August are great for tubing. Other times, trout fishing and hiking are good.

Kids love this place in the summer.

Nearby: Historic Johnson Farm, Lake Powhatan

Directions: From downtown Hendersonville take Highway 191 north towards the community of Mills River. Go approximately 13 miles. Turn left onto North Mills Road to the recreation area.

Black Bears:
Spirit of the Mountains

If any one animal personifies the spirit of the Western North Carolina mountains, it is the black bear. They inhabited these mountains long before the Cherokees arrived and it is estimated that the entire population numbers around 4,000 for the Southern Appalachians, with the heart of bear country located in the Great Smoky Mountains National Park. With over 500,000 acres, it is the largest protected bear habitat east of the Mississippi. Over 1,000 bears are estimated to live in the park, one of the highest densities anywhere.

Although only one human death has ever been recorded in the Great Smokies, bears are to be respected. Each year there are an average of seven bear incidents reported that involve human injury, and over 150 incidents each year of property damage—coolers destroyed, backpacks ripped open, cars scratched and tents torn down. Most of these incidents involved violation of a primary rule—don't feed the bears!

The black bear has long been held as a symbol of power by the Cherokee Indians, both on the land and in the psyche. And to visitors, the bear is the one animal that is hoped to be seen, perhaps for similar reasons. More than any other animal, it is an embodiment of the wilderness and represents the mystery and power of the mountains.

Section Five
Western North Carolina

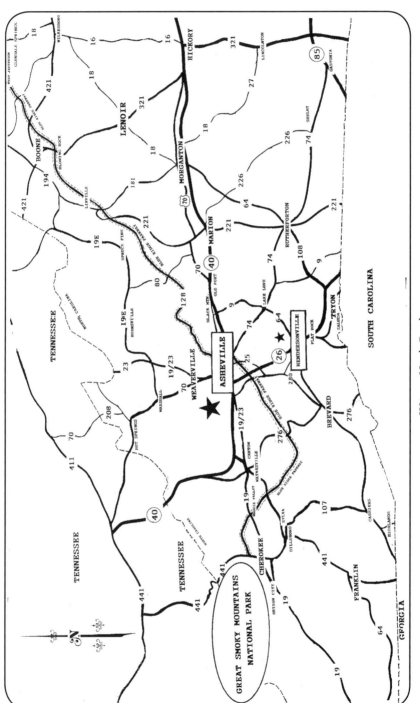

Western North Carolina

Chapter One
Natural Attractions

Western North Carolina is blessed with towering verdant mountains, lovely gentle valleys, flower-filled coves, virgin stands of untouched forest and crystal clear lakes and streams. A vacationer's paradise, Western North Carolina is home to major national forests and other natural attractions. Hundreds of thousands of visitors flock to this region of the state each year to camp, hike, fish and participate in many other outdoor recreations. In this chapter, the major natural attractions will be presented according to location; either north, south, east, or west of Asheville.

North of Asheville
Appalachian National Scenic Trail
The Appalachian Trail is a 2,167-mile footpath from Maine to Georgia which follows the ridgetops of the fourteen states through which it passes. Each day, as many as two hundred backpackers are in the process of hiking the full length of the trail. On average, it takes about four to five months to hike the entire length.

The Trail, which passes though North Carolina, was conceived by Benton MacKaye in the 1920s. With the support of local hiking clubs and interested individuals, MacKaye's dream eventually became a reality. By 1937 the trail was completed by opening a two-mile stretch in a densely wooded area between Spaulding and Sugarloaf Mountains in Maine.

The Appalachian Trail Conference (ATC), an organization consisting of local hiking clubs and volunteers, oversees maintenance and improvement of the trail. Every year, more than 6,000 volunteers improve and maintain the trail from Maine to Georgia. It may be entered at many points as it passes through North Carolina for over 300 miles. For reliable advice about the trail in our area, I strongly suggest you contact the Southern Regional Office of

Swallowtail butterfly

The Appalachian Trail Conference at 254-3708 or visit Black Dome Mountain Sports in Asheville. They are one of the two best hiking and camping outfitters in our area, offer excellent guide service and can help you plan any hike. They are located at 140 Tunnel Rd. in Asheville, telephone 251-2001 or (800) 678-2367.

Location: The trail passes to the north of Asheville
Address: Appalachian Trail Conference Southern Regional Offices: 160-A Zillicoa St., Asheville, NC 28801
Distance: From Asheville, approximately 30 miles—a 45-minute drive
Telephone: (Appalachian Trail Conference) 254-3708
FAX: (Appalachian Trail Conference) 254-3754
Website: www.atconf.org or www.nps.gov/aptr
Directions: Closest access is at Sams Gap, on the North Carolina/Tennessee line. Take US 19/23 north to the state line. Look for the parking on the west side. Just before the parking lot at the crest of the ridge is a trail sign. The parking lot is just before 19/23 becomes a four-lane road. After parking, walk back along 19/23 about 100 meters to access the trail.

Max Patch

Max Patch is one of Western North Carolina's best kept secrets, and it is located about 40 miles north of Asheville in the Hot Springs area. It is 300 acres of a grassy bald that is 4,629 feet at its highest point, and from which, on clear days, one can see Mount Mitchell to the east and the Great Smokies far off in the west! Some balds are naturally occurring areas in the mountains where trees do not grow and only flowers and grasses have taken hold. In Max's case, evidently it was cleared by sheep and cattle in the 1800s and has remained as such, with a little mowing help from the U.S. Forest Service. Max Patch is a premier example of a southern mountain bald, and if you have a half-day free, it is well worth the trip. Absolute panoramic views and a thousand places to picnic or camp await those making the trip.

Directions: From Asheville take Leicester Hwy. North 30 miles to NC 209. Follow 209 about 7 miles to Meadow Fork Rd. (State Rd. 1175). Follow this road south 5.3 miles to State Rd. 1181. Follow 1181 for 2 miles (will turn into gravel). At the top of the mountain, the road intersects with State Rd. 1182. Turn right and drive about 3 miles to the Max Patch parking area, which will be on your right. From the parking area, it is a short 1.4 miles to the top.

South of Asheville

Chimney Rock Park

Chimney Rock Park is a privately owned, natural scenic attraction nestled in the foothills of the Blue Ridge Mountains just above Lake Lure. Southeast of Asheville and only a short drive from Hendersonville, this 1000-acre park provides breathtaking views from its many trails and from the top of the 315-foot monolithic "Chimney Rock." The park features three hiking trails that lead to the 404-foot Hickory Nut Falls, one of the highest waterfalls in the eastern United States. At 2,280 feet above sea level, Chimney Rock is a 535-million-year-old remnant of igneous rock. You can climb a trail to its top, or take the 26-story elevator carved out of solid rock if you wish.

The movie "Last of the Mohicans" was filmed at Chimney Rock, and you may recognize part of the Cliff Trail from scenes in the film. Picnic tables and grills are located along the roadway to the Chimney Rock, and a less strenu-

Chimney Rock Park

ous trail leads to the base of Hickory Nut Falls. There is also a nature center on the access road where you may learn about the flora, fauna and geology of the park.

Location:	Southeast of Asheville
Address:	Box 39, Chimney Rock, NC 28740
Distance:	From Asheville, approximately 25 miles—a 45-minute drive
Telephone:	625-9611, (800) 277-9611
FAX:	625-9610
Website:	www.chimneyrockpark.com
Hours:	Open year-round except Thanksgiving, Christmas and New Year's Day; 8:30 a.m.-4:30 p.m. EST (5:30 DST). Park closes 1½ hour after ticket office closes.
Fees:	$12 Adults, $5.50 Children 6-15, Children under 6 free
Allow:	2-3 hours
Tips:	Best long-distance views on clear days Take good hiking shoes
Nearby:	Lake Lure, Bottomless Pools
Directions:	From Hendersonville, take Hwy. 64 East. Turn right on Hwy. 74 to Chimney Rock. From Asheville, take I-240 East to Exit 9 (Bat Cave, Blue Ridge Parkway) and continue on Hwy. 74A through Fairview and Hickory Nut Gap to Chimney Rock.

Lake Lure

Located southeast of Hendersonville just below Chimney Rock is sparkling Lake Lure, selected by National Geographic as one of the ten most spectacular and beautiful man-made lakes in the world. Over 1,500 acres of crystal clear water and 27 miles of inviting shoreline await the visitor to this majestic body of water. Marina and sandy beaches are open to the public. The lake has excellent fishing, and boat tours of the lake, offered by Lake Lure Tours, are a popular attraction. The boat tour dock is located at Lake Lure Marina, off of highway 64/74A.

Location: Southeast of Asheville
Distance: From Asheville, approximately 30 miles— a 45-minute drive
Address: Lake Lure Boat Tours, P.O. Box 541, Lake Lure, NC 28746 (located at Lake Lure Marina)
Telephone: Lake Lure Tours: 386-4255 or (877) 386-4255
Website: www.lakelure.com
Hours: Lake Lure Tours: March-November. Daily cruises on the hour from 10 a.m.-5 p.m. Dinner Cruise 7 p.m. (Reservation required for Dinner Cruise).
Fees: Lake Lure Tours: $8 adults, $4 children 6-15, 5 and under free; Dinner Cruise: $12 adults, $8 children 6-15, 5 and under free. Swimming at beach, no fee.
Allow: Cruises take one hour
Tips: Lake Lure has an excellent beach at the northern end of the lake near the Marina. Opens in May.
Nearby: Chimney Rock Park, Bottomless Pools
Directions: From Hendersonville, take Hwy. 64 West. Turn right on Hwy. 74. Go through Chimney Rock to Lake Lure.
From Asheville, take I-240 East to Exit 9 (Bat Cave, Blue Ridge Parkway) and continue on Hwy. 74A through Hickory Nut Gap and Chimney Rock. Lake Lure is one mile past Chimney Rock.

East of Asheville
The Blowing Rock

The Blowing Rock, located near Boone, is an immense cliff rising about 1,000 feet above the Johns River Gorge below. The rock is named Blowing Rock because the cliff walls of the gorge form a flume through which the northwest wind sweeps with such force that it returns light objects cast over the cliff. This phenomena prompted the Ripley's "Believe It or Not" cartoon about "the only place in the world where snow falls upside down."

The Blowing Rock

Location: Blowing Rock, NC
Distance: 2 hours from Asheville
Address: Hwy. 321 South, Blowing Rock, NC 28605
Telephone: 295-7111
Hours: March, April, May and November: 9 a.m.-6 p.m.; June-October: 8
           a.m. to 8 p.m.; Closed December-February
Fees: $6 adults, $5 seniors, $1 ages 6-11, under 5 free
Allow: ½-1 hour
Nearby: Mast General Store, Tweetsie Railroad, Linville Caverns, Linville
           Gorge, Grandfather Mountain, Ben Long Frescoes
Directions: From Blue Ridge Parkway take Boone exit to 321 South to Blowing
           Rock. A faster route from Asheville is to take I-40 East to Marion
           and take Hwy. 221 North to Blowing Rock.

Blue Ridge Parkway

The Blue Ridge Parkway is ranked "America's most scenic drive" by leading travel writers. Following mountain crests from Shenandoah National Park in Virginia to the Great Smoky Mountains National Park in North Carolina and Tennessee, the Parkway is the gateway to a wondrous Appalachian empire. The Parkway's 469 toll-free miles of awesome natural beauty combined with the pioneer history of gristmills, weathered cabins and split-rail fences create one of the most popular areas in the national park system. This extraordinary region encompasses a world of mountain forest, wildlife and wildflowers thousands of feet above a patchwork of villages, fields and farms.

Passing right through Asheville, the Parkway is easily accessible to visitors. Located at Milepost 384 just southeast of Asheville is the newly constructed Blue Ridge Parkway Headquarters. A unique feature about the Parkway is that there are no tolls. Speed limits are set at a leisurely 45 miles per hour, and stops are frequent with more than 250 overlooks on the parkway that offer magnificent uninterrupted views. More that 600 million visitors have traveled the Parkway over the years since it opened in the 1930s.

A free Parkway trip planning information packet is available by writing to the Blue Ridge Parkway Association, P.O. Box 453, Asheville, NC 28802. This packet contains maps, the official Park Service Trip map, guides, and other useful information. Much of this information is also available at the parkway website (www.blueridgeparkway.org). A complete list of hiking trails that can be accessed from the Blue Ridge Parkway is presented in Section Two, Chapter 16.

A nonprofit organization, Friends of the Blue Ridge Parkway, continues to work towards the preservation of the environmental heritage of the Parkway. This grass-roots organization welcomes memberships in its work to preserve and protect the Parkway. Information about Friends of the Blue Ridge Parkway can be obtained by calling 687-8722, (800) 228-7275 or by writing them at 3536 Brambleton Avenue S.W., Building B. Roanoke, VA 24108. Another organization dedicated to preserving the Blue Ridge Parkway is the Blue Ridge Parkway

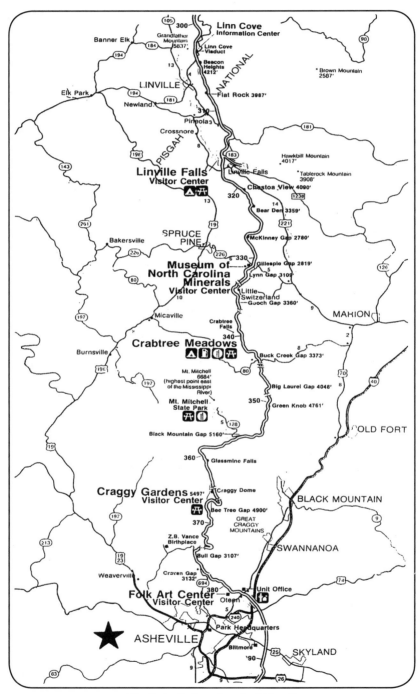

Blue Ridge Parkway North of Asheville

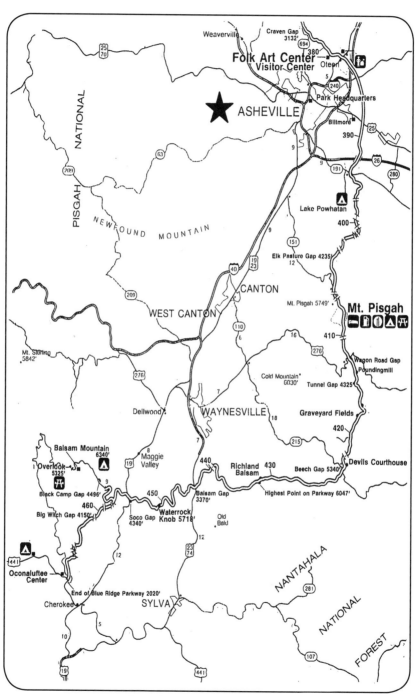

Blue Ridge Parkway South of Asheville

Foundation. They fund specific programs and projects that further the parkway's preservations, protection, and enhancement. For further information, call (910) 721-0260 or write P.O. Box 10427 Salem Station, Winston-Salem, NC 27108.

Camping is allowed along the parkway May-October at designated sites, many requiring a small fee that covers the use of a fireplace and table. Winter camping is allowed, weather permitting. Facilities are limited and you will need to check in advance. Copies of campground regulations are available at Parkway Visitor Centers, and are posted at all campgrounds. Campgrounds near Asheville are at Linville Falls (Milepost 316.3; 50 tent, 20 RV sites), Crabtree Meadows (Milepost 339.5; 71 tent, 22 RV sites) and Mount Pisgah (Milepost 408.6; 70 tent, 70 RV sites).

Location: The Parkway begins at Fort Royal, Virginia, and ends in Cherokee, North Carolina. It goes right through the east side of Asheville, running north to south overall.

Address: Superintendent, Blue Ridge Parkway, 400 BB&T Building, Asheville, NC 28801.

Telephone: Parkway Information: 298-0398, 259-0701, 271-4779
Emergency Parkway Telephone: (800) 727-5928
Parkway Headquarters: 271-4779
Visitor Information: 271-4779, xtn. 245
Human Resources: 271-4779, xtn. 249
Public Affairs: 271-4779, xtn. 203
Maintenance: 271-4779, xtn. 214
Rangers: 271-4779, xtn. 241

FAX: 271-4313

Websites: www.nps.gov/blri/
www.blueridgeparkway.org
www.virtualblueridge.com

Fees: None

Tips: The Parkway is closed intermittently during the winter due to ice and snow. Peak traffic is during the summer months and especially the autumn leaf season. With a 45-mph speed limit on a winding two-lane road, be prepared for a leisurely trip.

Directions: From Asheville, take I-240 East and get off at Exit 9 (Bat Cave, Blue Ridge Parkway). Take Hwy. 74A East to parkway entrance roads. It is also accessible off of Tunnel Rd. (US 70) near the V.A. Hospital in East Asheville and Brevard Rd. (Hwy. 191) in South Asheville past the Biltmore Square Mall.

The entries that follow are some of the major attractions found on the Parkway within a short drive of Asheville.

Parkway North of Asheville:

Milepost 382, Folk Art Center: Located just east of Asheville, the Folk Art Center offers a look at traditional and contemporary crafts of the Appalachian

Craggy Gardens

region through interpretive programs, a museum and library. (SEE Section Three, Chapter 2)

Milepost 364, Craggy Gardens: Craggy Gardens is an area of exposed rocks and high peaks that provides breathtaking views. Large expanses of native rhododendron cover its slopes and summits. In mid-June, pink and purple blooms of these Catawba rhododendrons are at their peak. This popular stop has restrooms, nature exhibits, and is open May-October. Well-marked trails lead through the rhododendron thickets to Craggy Dome's awe-inspiring views.

Milepost 355, Mount Mitchell: Mount Mitchell State Park offers tent camping, trails, nature study, picnic area, natural history museum and restaurant. At 6,684 feet above sea level, it is the highest peak in the eastern United States. 675-4611. (SEE other listing on Mount Mitchell in this chapter for complete information)

Milepost 331, Museum of North Carolina Minerals: Displays of over 300 varieties of minerals found in North Carolina. Open 9-5 daily. 765-2761 or 298-0398. (SEE Section Five, Chapter 2)

Milepost 317, Linville Caverns: North Carolina's only caverns open year-round. Smooth paths takes visitors deep into the innermost recesses of this beautiful underground fairyland. Located on route 221, between Linville and Marion, NC. (800) 419-0540. (SEE main Linville Caverns listing later in this chapter for complete information)

Milepost 316, Linville Gorge: Located off NC 105 in the Pisgah National Forest. Excellent hiking trails that lead to superb views of Linville Falls. Linville Gorge is one of the most spectacular sites in North Carolina. (SEE main Linville Gorge listing later in this chapter for complete information)

Milepost 305, Grandfather Mountain: One of North Carolina's top scenic attractions. Extraordinary views, wildlife habitats, famous Mile High Swinging

Linn Cove Viaduct

Bridge, trails, picnic areas, nature museum, restaurant and theatre. (SEE main Grandfather Mountain listing in this chapter for complete information)

Milepost 304, Linn Cove Viaduct: Linn Cove Viaduct is a spectacular bridge that offers outstanding views and is noteworthy for its elegant and unique construction. Opened in 1987, this engineering marvel represents the final link in the construction of the Blue Ridge Parkway. The Viaduct is the most complicated concrete bridge ever built, snaking around boulder-strewn Linn Cove in a sweeping "S" curve.

Milepost 294, Moses H. Cone Memorial Park: This great mountain park has hiking and horseback riding trails, and Flat Top Manor houses the Parkway Craft Center. No fees, and the Craft Center is open from Mid-March to November, 9:00 a.m. to 5:00 p.m. Ranger-guided activities are also available throughout the summer.

Parkway South of Asheville:

Milepost 408, Pisgah Inn at Mount Pisgah: Mount Pisgah was part of the original 145,000-acre estate bought in the 1800s by George Vanderbilt. The area is now the Pisgah National Forest. Located on the parkway is the famous Pisgah Inn, a great place to stop for a meal. The inn is open April through Autumn. Their phone number is 235-8228. A moderately strenuous hiking trail leads from the Inn to the Mount Pisgah Overlook.

The old Pisgah Inn

Milepost 412, Cradle of Forestry: Four miles south of the parkway on US 276 is the Cradle of Forestry, a National Historic Site located in the Pisgah National Forest. The Cradle of Forestry was the birthplace of American forestry. Visitors will find forestry exhibits, guided tours, restored historic buildings, craft exhibits and more. 1002 Pisgah Hwy. 884-5713. (SEE Section Five, Chapter 2)

Milepost 419, Graveyard Fields: An unusual flat area that takes its name from the mounds dotting the site, which are remains of fallen trees, victims of a 1925 Thanksgiving Eve fire.

Milepost 469, Mountain Farm Museum: Located at the southern end of the Parkway on US Hwy. 441, the Mountain Farm Museum is a National Park Service reconstruction of early pioneer farm buildings that show a past lifestyle. 497-1900. Located nearby also is Oconoluftee Visitors Center, which has restrooms, exhibits and park information.

Brown Mountain Lights

To the east of Asheville, near Morganton in Burke County, lies Brown Mountain. Rising to an elevation of only 2,600 feet, this foothills mountain has been at the center of a mystery since the earliest days of recorded history. For hundreds of years, lights have been seen on the mountain to the astonishment of all that have seen them. Cherokee Indians were familiar with the lights as far back as the year 1200, and their legends claim the lights are the spirits of Indian maidens searching for their fallen husbands and sweethearts. Early scientists, including German engineer Gerard Will de Brahm, Dr. W.J. Humphries of the Weather Bureau, and members of the U.S. Geological Survey, studied the lights and offered various explanations, none of which has stood the test of time. In fact, there has been no satisfactory explanation to date, making the lights one of North Carolina's most enduring mysteries as well as one of its most famous legends. Possible explanations that have been rejected by the scientific community include nitrous vapor emissions, locomotive or automobile reflections, "Andes Light" manifestations, marsh gas spontaneous combustion, moonshine still reflections, electrical phenomenon such as St. Elmo's Fire, mirages, UFOs, radioactive uranium ore emissions, and atmospheric reflections from nearby Hickory, Lenoir, or other area towns.

The lights are visible from several locations, the most popular being Brown Mountain Overlook, located 20 miles north of Morganton on NC Hwy. 181 one mile south of the Barkhouse Picnic area; Wiseman's View Overlook, located five miles south of the village of Linville Falls on Kistler Memorial Hwy. (Old NC 105/SR 1238); and Lost Cove Cliffs Overlook, located on the Blue Ridge Parkway at Milepost 310 two miles north of the NC 181 junction.

Brown Mountain's lights have been seen as far away as Blowing Rock and the old Yonahlossee Trail over Grandfather Mountain over twelve miles away. The lights are an irregular and somewhat rare occurrence and are not always visible. Your best chance of seeing them is on a night with clear weather conditions, good visibility, and little to no moonlight. Witnesses have reported seeing them at all hours of the night between sundown and sunrise. The lights vary widely in appearance, at times seeming large like balls of fire from a Roman candle, sometimes rising to various heights and fading, others expanding as they rise to finally burst without a sound.

It is best to keep your expectations low since there is absolutely no certainty that the lights will be visible. In this case, the journey is just as important as the destination. The adventure of looking, not finding, should be your focus. In any event, you will be participating in a North Carolina mystery that has baffled plenty of smart people over the years!

Location: Near Morganton, North Carolina (see viewing locations above)
Distance: 1½-2 hours from Asheville
Telephone: 433-6793, Morganton Visitor Information Center
Directions: From Asheville, take I-40 East to Morganton and NC 181 North. The Blue Ridge Parkway is a more scenic though slower alternative (allow three hours). Follow the parkway north from the Tunnel Rd. (US 70) entrance to Milepost 310.

Grandfather Mountain

Grandfather Mountain is one of the most environmentally significant mountains in the world. It is set apart by the United Nations as an International Biosphere Reserve. Grandfather Mountain is famous for its swinging bridge, the highest in America. Crossing this bridge suspends visitors more than a mile above sea level. Hiking and picnicking are favorite activities at Grandfather, and the mountain boasts wildlife habitats with bears, deer, panthers, otters and eagles. There is also a Nature Museum and gift shop.

Location:	Linville, N.C.
Distance:	2 hours from Asheville
Address:	US 221 & Blue Ridge Parkway, Linville, NC 28846
Telephone:	(800) 468-7325, 733-4337
FAX:	733-2608
Website:	www.grandfather.com
Hours:	8 a.m. to dusk year-round except Thanksgiving and Christmas.
Fees:	$12 adults, $6 children 4-12, under 4 free
Allow:	2½ hours
Of Note:	An International Biosphere Reserve
Tips:	Take good walking shoes
Nearby:	Linville Caverns, Linville Gorge, Ben Long Frescoes, The Blowing Rock, Horn in the West, Mast General Store, Tweetsie Railroad
Directions:	Take Linville exit, Milepost 305 off of Blue Ridge Parkway onto US 221 or take I-40 from Asheville. Get off in Marion and take Hwy. 221 North 35 miles to Linville. Look for Grandfather Mountain signs.

Lake James State Park

Tucked away in rolling hills at the base of Linville Gorge is Lake James, a 6,510-acre lake with more than 150 miles of shoreline. This impressive waterway is the centerpiece of Lake James State Park. The park offers a variety of activities, including swimming, boating and fishing.

Location:	Nebo, NC. Lake James State Park is located in Burke and McDowell counties, five miles northeast of Marion on NC 126.
Distance:	About an hour's drive
Address:	PO Box 340, Nebo, NC 28761
Telephone:	652-5047
Website:	www.ils.unc.edu/parkproiect/visit/laja/home
Hours:	November-February: 8 a.m.-6 p.m.
	March and October: 8 a.m.-7 p.m.
	April, May, September: 8 a.m.-8 p.m.
	June-August: 8 a.m.-9 p.m.
	Closed Christmas Day
Directions:	Traveling east on I-40: From I-40, take the Nebo/Lake James exit (Exit 90) and head north. After a half-mile, turn right onto Harmony Grove Rd., and follow it for 2 miles to a stoplight. Proceed straight across the intersection and past Nebo Elementary School to a stop sign. Turn right onto NC 126, and follow the signs to the park entrance 2.3 miles on the left.

Linville Caverns

At the head of beautiful Linville Valley, Linville Caverns lie deep under Humpback Mountain. The caverns entrance is in a beautiful glade and they are open year-round. In the winter many of the skiers from various popular ski slopes in the Banner Elk, Boone and Blowing Rock areas add a visit to Linville Caverns, "Inside the Mountain" as a delightful contrast to their skiing on the slopes above. The wondrous splendors deep inside Humpback Mountain were unknown to the white man until they were explored by H.E. Colton, an eastern Carolinian, and his local guide, Dave Franklin, more than one hundred years ago. The mysterious appearance of fish swimming out of the mountains led the explorers to probe deep into the mountain, following the underground stream through passageways and rooms whose ceilings when lit by torches "looked like the arch of some grand cathedral." Linville Caverns have lighted smooth paths that take visitors deep into the innermost recesses. Courteous and experienced guides accompany each party through the caverns, point out the most interesting features and answer all questions.

Location:	Linville, NC
Distance:	1 hour from Asheville
Address:	Hwy. 221 North (P.O. Box 567), Marion NC 28752
Telephone:	(800) 419-0540, 756-4171
Website:	www.linvillecaverns.com
Hours:	Open year-round, closed Thanksgiving and Christmas. June 1-Labor Day: 9 a.m.-6 p.m.; April, May, September, October: 9 a.m.-5 p.m.; November-March: weekends only 9 a.m.-4:30 p.m.
Fees:	$5 adults, $3 children 5-12, under 5 free, seniors (62+) $4
Allow:	One hour
Nearby:	Linville Gorge, Grandfather Mountain, Horn in the West, Tweetsie Railroad, The Blowing Rock, Mast General Store, Ben Long Frescoes
Directions:	Take Linville Falls exit on Blue Ridge Parkway and turn left on US 221. Caverns are 4 miles south of Linville on US 221 north of Marion. A faster route is I-40 from Asheville. Exit in Marion and take Hwy. 221 North.

Linville Gorge

Linville Gorge is a rugged wilderness area in Pisgah National Forest. Excellent hiking trails lead to superb views of Linville Falls. Linville Gorge, carved by the Linville River forming Jonas Ridge on the east and Wiseman's View on the western rim, is one of the most spectacular sites in North Carolina. The Linville Gorge area was originally donated to the Parkway by John D. Rockefeller. Linville Falls is perhaps the best-known waterfall in the entire Appalachian Mountains, and certainly is one of the most scenic. The waterfall marks the beginning of the gorge, one of the deepest canyons in the east, with walls rising to almost 2,000 feet in places. Peregrine falcons and numerous other rare animals and plants are found in the gorge. One species of plant, the mountain golden heather (Hudsonia montana) is found nowhere else in the world.

Location: Linville, NC
Distance: Two hours from Asheville
Address: Linville Falls Visitor Center, spur road off of Blue Ridge Parkway at Milepost 316.4.
Telephone: Grandfather District Ranger Station: 652-2144
Linville Falls Visitor Center: 765-1045
U.S. Forest Service: 768-6062
Hours: The Linville Falls Visitor Center is open 9 a.m.-5:30 p.m.
Fees: None, but permit must be obtained at Information Cabin along top of Gorge in order to enter Gorge area. This cabin is open 8 a.m.-4:30 p.m.
Allow: Minimum of six hours to see Gorge
Tips: Dress appropriately and prepare for day hike. Wear good hiking shoes. Check in first at Visitor Center for maps and information, then obtain permit to enter Gorge area.
Nearby: Linville Falls, Grandfather Mountain, Tweetsie Railroad, Horn in the West, Mast General Store, Ben Long Frescoes
Directions: Turn off of the Blue Ridge Parkway at Milepost 316.3, and follow the paved road 1.4 miles to Linville Falls Visitor Center. Faster route is I-40 East from Asheville. Get off in Marion and take Hwy. 221 North for 26 miles to Linville Falls Community. At intersection of Hwy. 183, take right and go east ¼ mile to entrance.

Mount Jefferson State Natural Area

Mount Jefferson is a National Natural Landmark. Two short trails give hikers spectacular views of the New River and the surrounding mountains. One of the more interesting features of the area is Luther's Rock Overlook. No bicycles or camping are allowed. There are picnic areas and canoeing can be done at the nearby New River State Park. Mount Jefferson has a self-guided nature trail for hikers who wish to take their time and learn about the natural history of the area. By special request, park naturalists lead guided walks explaining the area's natural history and legends. The Park Service also offers a program history that advertises upcoming hikes and events.

Location: Jefferson, NC
Distance: 2-2½ hours from Asheville
Address: P.O. Box 48, Jefferson, NC 28604
Telephone: (336) 246-9653, Park Office
FAX: (336) 246-3386
Website: www/ils.unc.edu/parkproject/moje.html
Hours: November-February 9 a.m.-5 p.m.; March & October 9 a.m.-6 p.m.; April, May, & September 9 a.m.-7 p.m.; June-August 9 a.m.-8 p.m.; closed Christmas. Office hours: 8 a.m.-noon Monday-Friday.
Fees: None

Allow: 3 or more hours
Of Note: Wheelchair accessible parking space, water fountain, and picnic area provided.
Tips: Wear comfortable shoes and bring binoculars.
Nearby: New River State Park, Ben Long Frescoes
Directions: From Asheville, take I-40 East to Hickory. Use 321 North through Blowing Rock and West Jefferson to US 221 North. Mount Jefferson State Natural Area is located a half-mile south of Jefferson. From NC 163, take SR 1149 to the park entrance on SR 1152.

Mount Mitchell State Park

Mount Mitchell State Park is in the Black Mountain range, which reaches higher than the Blue Ridge or Smoky Mountains. At 6,684 feet, its dominant mountain Mount Mitchell is the highest peak in the eastern United States. A cool climate, unique flora and fauna and easy access from the Blue Ridge Parkway make this a very popular vacation spot. Mount Mitchell State Park offers tent camping, six trails of varying difficulty, nature study, picnic areas, Natural History Museum and restaurant. The Park is 1,727 acres in size, and the summit of Mount Mitchell is famous for its spectacular views. On a clear day it is possible to see for more than 70 miles. The Natural History Museum located on the way to the Stone Observation Tower at the summit has dioramas, exhibits and recordings that present some of the unusual higher elevation plants and wildlife.

These high elevations give Mount Mitchell a cooler climate than the surrounding lowlands, a climate more typical of the boreal forests that dominate Canada and Alaska. Flora and fauna associated with the mountain's ecosystem are atypical of the southern Appalachians. Rare and uncommon plant and animal species live in the spruce-fir forest that covers the summit. This spruce-fir forest is among the rarest of forest environments in North Carolina, and one of the most endangered.

The Park was created in 1916 by individuals concerned with the destruction of virgin forests by logging, and the mountain was named for Dr. Elisha Mitchell, the first person to take measurements of the Black Mountains, which include Mt. Mitchell. Dr. Mitchell is buried on the summit of Mount Mitchell at the base of the 42-foot tall observation tower.

Location: Northeast of Asheville.
Distance: 1½ hours from Asheville
Address: Rt. 5 Box 700, Burnsville, NC 28714 (Milepost 355 on the Blue Ridge Parkway)
Telephone: 675-4611, Park Office
FAX: 675-9655
Website: www.ils.unc.edu/parkproject/momi.html
Hours: November-February: 8 a.m.-6 p.m.; March & October: 8 a.m.-7 p.m. ; April, May and September: 8 a.m.-8 p.m.; June-August: 8 a.m.-9 p.m.; tent camping from May 1 through October 31; park closed Christmas day.

Fees: None; campsites $8 per night
Allow: Minimum of two hours to hike to summit and see exhibits
Of Note: Parking and restrooms are wheelchair-accessible but pathways and picnic shelters are not.
Mount Mitchell is the highest peak in the Eastern United States.
Tips: Restrooms available at campground but no showers or hot water. A restaurant is located near the entrance Ranger Station. Maps of the park's trails and further information can be obtained at the station. Mt. Mitchell is visible from Asheville from the River Ridge Shopping Center and from I-240 and I-40 in that part of town.
Directions: Take the Blue Ridge Parkway north from Asheville. The entrance to the park is at Milepost 355.

New River State Park

One of the oldest rivers in the world, the New River is designated as a National Wild and Scenic River and an American Heritage River. At the New River State Park, it is possible to canoe the more than 26 miles of the river's South Fork, embarking for your journey from any of three access points. A trip down the gentle New River promises excellent fishing and picnicking as well as inspiring mountain scenery. The park itself encompasses 1,580 acres and is located in Ashe and Alleghany counties.

The park has a number of hiking trails, picnic areas including a 12-table covered picnic shelter with fireplace and grill, and a community building which includes a large meeting room, kitchen facilities, and restrooms. The community building is available for rent at $125 per day and is often used for family reunions and other groups' meetings.

Canoe camping is very popular on the New River and the three access areas provide over 30 canoe-in or walk-in primitive campgrounds with tables and grills. Pit toilets and drinking water are located nearby. Campers must first register with the park staff or at registration boxes. Campsites require a small fee.

The south and north forks of the New River are known for their excellent smallmouth and redeye bass fishing, while the smaller, faster tributaries are designated trout waters and are stocked regularly with rainbow and brown trout. Muskelunge have also been stocked in the lower portion of the river.

Easy paddling and beautiful scenery make canoeing the New River a spectacular and rewarding trip. Gentle waters with some rapids make it fun for both beginning and advanced paddlers. Canoes may be launched at the three access sites as well as from several bridges and roadways that cross the river.

Location: Jefferson, NC
Distance: 2-2½ hours from Asheville
Address: 1477 Wagoner Access Rd., Jefferson, NC 28640-0048
Telephone: Park Office: (336) 982-2587
FAX: (336) 982-3943

Website: www.ils.unc.edu/parkproject/neri.html
Hours: November-February 8 a.m.-6 p.m.; March & October 8 a.m.-7 p.m.;
April, May, & September 8 a.m.-8 p.m.; June-August 8 a.m.-9 p.m.;
Closed Christmas. Gates remain locked after hours.
Fees: Small fees for camping only
Allow: Depending on activities, can range from a few hours to days
Of Note: Wheelchair-accessible picnic shelter and restrooms available at Wagoner Rd. Access Area.
Tips: Drive-up access areas are at Wagoner Rd. and US 221. There is an access area at river mile one, Alleghany Access Area, that can only be reached by canoe.
Nearby: Mount Jefferson State Natural Area, Ben Long Frescoes
Directions: From Asheville, take I-40 East to Hickory. From there, take US 321 North through Blowing Rock and West Jefferson to US 221 to Jefferson. Wagoner Access Rd. off NC 88 can reach the Wagoner Rd. Access Area, which is eight miles southeast of Jefferson, 1.2 miles east of the intersection of NC 16 and NC 88. The US 221 Access Area, at river mile 15, is located eight miles northeast of Jefferson.

Stone Mountain State Park

Stone Mountain is not immediately visible upon entering the park that bears its name, but this magnificent 600-foot granite dome is well worth the wait. The 132,747-acre park offers 17 miles of designated trout waters and more than 16 miles of hiking trails. Designated as a National Natural Landmark in 1975, Stone Mountain is bounded on the north by the Blue Ridge Parkway and on the west by the Thurmond Chatham Game Lands.

Location: Roaring Gap, NC
Distance: 3 hours
Address: 3042 Frank Parkway, Roaring Gap, NC 28668
Telephone: (336)957-8185
Website: www.ils.unc.edu/parkproject/visit/stmo/home
Hours: November-February: 8 a.m.-6 p.m.
March and October: 8 a.m.-7 p.m.
April, May, September: 8 a.m.-8 p.m.
June-August: 8 a.m.-9 p.m.
Closed Christmas Day
Directions: Stone Mountain State Park is located in Wilkes and Alleghany counties, seven miles southwest of Roaring Gap. From I-77, turn west onto US 21. Veer left onto Traphill Rd. (SR 1002), and follow it to the John P. Frank Parkway. Turn right and follow the parkway to the park. From the west, take NC 18 North and turn right onto Traphill Rd. (SR 1002). Follow the road to the John P. Frank Parkway and turn left, following the parkway to the park.

West of Asheville

Bent Creek Experimental Forest

Bent Creek Experimental Forest (SRS-4101), located just outside Asheville, is one of the oldest research areas maintained by the USDA Forest Service. Since 1925, scientists at Bent Creek have been developing and practicing sound forestry practices. The fruits of their research on fire, insects, wildlife, water, diseases, and recreational uses are being applied today in forests all around the world and in particular the Southern Appalachians. Open to visitors, Bent Creek is popular with area hikers and runners.

Location: Just west of Asheville
Distance: 30 minutes west of Asheville
Address: 1577 Brevard Rd., Asheville, NC 28806
Telephone: 667-5261
FAX: 667-9097
Website: www.srs.fs.fed.us/bentcreek/
Hours: 8 a.m.-4:30 p.m. Monday-Friday
Fees: None
Allow: 2 hours minimum
Of Note: One of the oldest research areas maintained by the USDA Forest Service.
Directions: I-26 Exit 2 (Biltmore Square Mall exit). Follow Hwy. 191 South 1½-2 miles. Turn right onto Bent Creek Ranch Rd. and follow signs to Lake Powatan and the Experimental Forest.

Dupont State Forest

The Dupont State Forest is located between Hendersonville and Brevard and its 10,400 acres of forest feature four major waterfalls on the Little River and several on the Grassy Creek. Originally 7,600 acres and established in 1996 through a donation from the Dupont Corporation, the forest was expanded in 2000 by two property additions, including the spectacular 2,200-acre tract in the center of the forest. It lies in the upland plateau of the Little River valley with elevation between 2,300 and 3,600 feet above sea level. Key waterfalls, all of which are easily accessed by short trails, include Triple Falls (a series of three waterfalls), High Falls, Hooker Falls (an 11-foot drop into Cascade Lake), Bridal Veil Falls (the most unique falls in the State Forest, with a long, shallow veil-like whitewater incline along the lower section), Wintergreen Falls (20-foot cascade on Grassy Creek) and Grassy Creek Falls. Cedar Rock Mountain in the forest has hundreds of acres of exposed granite making it a very popular destination for cyclists and hikers, and Stone Mountain is the forest's high point at 3,600 feet. It offers a 180-degree view during the summer and a full 360 degrees during the winter months.

Location: Between Hendersonville and Brevard
Distance: Approximately 45 minutes to 1 hour from Asheville

Telephone: (828) 251-6509
Address: Division of Forest Resources, 14 Gaston Mountain Rd., Asheville,
NC 28806
E-mail: Friends of Dupont Forest friends@dupontforest.com
DuPont State Forest Supervisor supervisor@dupontforest.com
Website: www.dupontforest.com
Hours: None
Fees: None
Allow: At least half a day
Nearby: Pisgah National Forest, Brevard Area Waterfalls
Directions: From Asheville, take I-26 West to Exit 9, and then take Hwy. 280
to Pisgah Forest. Turn left on US 64 in Pisgah Forest and travel 3.7
miles to the Texaco station in Penrose. Turn right on Crab Creek
Rd. and continue 4.3 miles and turn right onto Dupont Rd. As the
road climbs the hill, turn left at Sky Valley Rd. and continue about
a mile past the farmhouse to the parking lot on the right.

Gorges State Park

Located near Sapphire, Gorges State Park contains spectacular waterfalls, sheer
rock walls, rugged river gorges, and one of the greatest concentrations of rare and
unusual plat species in the Eastern United States. An elevation that rises over
2,000 feet in only three to five miles and an annual rainfall in excess of 80 inches
creates a unique temperate rain forest. Gorges' 7,484 acres were designated a state
park in April of 1999 to protect these nationally significant natural resources, and
it is the newest state park in North Carolina.

Park highlights are Horsepasture River (a National Wild and Scenic River),
Toxaway River, Bearwallow Creek, Thompson River, Bearcamp Creek, Windy
Falls, Lower Bearwallow Falls, Toxaway Creek Falls, Chestnut Mountain, Grind-
stone Mountain, Misery Mountain, many major trout streams, and numerous
wildflowers including rare species.

Location: Sapphire, North Carolina
Distance: Approximately 2 hours from Asheville
Address: P.O. Box 100, Sapphire, NC 28774
Telephone: 966-9099, Park Office
E-mail: gorg@citcom.net
Website: www.ils.unc.edu/parkproject/gorg.html
Hours: November-February 8 a.m.-6 p.m.; March & October 8 a.m.-7 p.m.;
April, May, & September 8 a.m.-8 p.m.; June-August 8 a.m.-9 p.m.;
closed Christmas Day. Gates are locked, except in emergency situa-
tions, after hours.
Office hours: 8 a.m.-5 p.m. Monday-Friday.
Fees: None
Allow: 2 hours minimum

Of Note: Wheelchair-accessible facilities and public restrooms are planned
Tips: Be sure to stay on designated trails. Many of the park's rare plants live on thin soils or wet rocks and are very vulnerable to damage from climbing, scrambling, or scraping. Do not attempt to climb on rocks near or above the waterfalls. Every year people are killed in WNC attempting to climb the rocks near waterfalls.
Nearby: Waterfalls, Pisgah National Forest, Cherokee Indian Reservation, Nantahala National Forest, Great Smoky Mountains National Park
Directions: From Asheville, take the I-26 Airport Rd. Exit (US 280 South) past the airport to Brevard where it will turn into US 64. Continue on Hwy. 64 to Sapphire. Gorges State Park is located in Transylvania County and overlaps the North Carolina/South Carolina state lines. It is approximately 45 miles west of Asheville. The interim park office is located in the same building as the Sapphire Post Office at the intersection of US 64 and NC 281 South. Depending on when you buy this book, the interim office may have been moved. So, call ahead for directions.

Great Smoky Mountains National Park

The Great Smoky Mountains, which lie along the common border of Tennessee and North Carolina, form a majestic climax to the Appalachian Highlands. With outlines softened by a forest mantle, the mountains stretch away to remote horizons in sweeping troughs that recede to evenness in the distance. And shrouding the peaks is a smokelike mist that rises from the dense plant growth. The mountains get their name from this deep blue mist.

The park's boundary wraps around 800 square miles of mountain wilderness, most of it virtually unspoiled. Many peaks rise above 6,000 feet. A great variety of trees, shrubs, herbs and other plants are nourished by the fertile land and heavy rainfall and rushing streams. The Great Smoky Park contains more than 700 miles of rivers and streams, over 200,00 acres of virgin forests, and over 850 miles of trails. It is the most visited national park with over 9,000,000 visitors a year.

From Asheville it will take you a number of hours to get to the border of the park where you will want to check in at the Oconaluftee Visitor Center in Cherokee. Although there are many opportunities to drive through the park, the most rewarding experiences are found along the trails. More than 650 miles of horse and foot trails wind along the crystal clear streams and waterfalls, past forest giants that have been living for hundreds of years, through the wild beauty of flower-filled coves and into high mountain meadows.

The park offers guided nature walks as well as self-guided tours. Copies of maps and schedules are available at Visitors Centers and at all ranger stations.

Not to be missed during your visit is the Mountain Farm Museum, located at the Oconaluftee Visitor Center. It is part of an effort to preserve some of the cultural heritage of the Smokies and is a collection of buildings that were moved from their original locations to form an open-air museum. Highly recommended auto tours include the Roaring Fork Auto Tour, the Newfound Gap Road Auto Tour, the Cades Cove Auto Tour and the Cataloochee Auto Tour. Self-guided tour books are available and will enrich your stops at the many historical sites and natural wonders along the way.

The famed Appalachian Trail (SEE Section Five, Chapter 1), which stretches from Maine to Georgia, enters the park near the eastern boundary. Straddling the boundary line of two states, it zigzags a course for 71 miles along the crest of some of the highest peaks and ultimately leaves the park again at Fontana Dam. If you wish to hike the full distance in the park, you can cover the 71 miles in 6 to 8 days. Trailside shelters and campsites are spaced about a day's journey apart.

Many other horse and foot trails are scattered throughout the park. There are short, self-guiding trails that are perfect for beginners. Just pick up a leaflet at the start of each trail. A backcountry-use permit, required for all overnight hiking parties, can be obtained free at ranger stations or visitors centers (except Cades Cove Visitors Center).

There are ten developed campgrounds in the park; fees are charged at each. Reservations are recommended at Cades Cove, Elkmont and Smokemont from May 15 to October 31; they can be made by calling 1 (800) 365-CAMP. Sites may be reserved up to three months in advance. All other campgrounds are first-come, first-serve. Cosby and Look Rock campgrounds rarely fill up. Campgrounds have tent sites, limited trailer space, water, fireplaces, tables and restrooms. There are no showers or hookups for trailers.

No more than six people may occupy a campsite. Two tents or one RV and one tent are allowed per site. The camping limit is seven days between May 15 and October 31, and 14 days between November 1 and May 14. Some campgrounds close in winter. Sewage disposal stations are located at Smokemont, Cades Cove, Deep Creek and Cosby campgrounds, and across from the Sugarlands Visitor Center. They are not available for use in the winter.

LeConte Lodge (accessible by trail only) provides the only lodging in the park. Call (423) 429-5704 for more information on this secluded retreat.

Saddle horses are available from April 1 to October 31 at Cades Cove, Smokemont, Deep Creek (near Greenbrier on U.S. 321), and near park headquarters. Bicycles are permitted on park roads but prohibited on all trails except Gatlinburg, Oconaluftee River, and lower Deep Creek. Bicycles may be rented from the Cades Cove Store, near the Cades Cove Campground.

Fishing is permitted year-round in the park, but a Tennessee or North Carolina license is required. Either license is valid throughout the entire park and no trout stamp is required.

One of the most biologically diverse regions in all of North America, the Park has been designated an International Biosphere Reserve under the UNESCO "Man in the Biosphere" program. Within its boundaries there are over 1500 species of flowering plants; 100 different types of trees; 600 mosses, lichens and liverworts; 50 species of mammals including black bears, whitetail deer, raccoons, foxes, bobcats, opossum, coyotes, and possibly cougars; more than 80 types of snakes and amphibians; and 70 kinds of fish from small colorful darters to brook, brown and rainbow trout. And over 200 kinds of birds have been observed within the park borders. Bring along your bird book and binoculars; the Great Smokies are a bird-watcher's paradise.

Great Smoky Mountains National Park was formally dedicated on February 6, 1930 by both Tennessee and North Carolina governors. Its mission continues today, to preserve and protect the wild beauty and natural charm of the Great Smoky Mountains for all time.

Location: West of Asheville

Distance: 2-3 hours from Asheville

Address: Headquarters: Great Smoky Mountains National Park, 107 Park Headquarters Rd., Gatlinburg, TN 37738. There are three visitor centers that help orient visitors and provide maps and information: Sugarlands (Tennessee side), Cades Cove (Near the western entrance of the park), and Oconaluftee (in North Carolina). Oconaluftee is the nearest entrance to Asheville. Oconaluftee Visitor Center: 150 Hwy. 441 N., Cherokee, NC 28719.

Telephone: General Information (423) 436-1200
Communications Center: (423) 436-1230
Back Country Information (423) 436-1297
Oconaluftee Visitor Center: 497-1900, 497-1904
Park Headquarters: (423) 436-1294
Campground Reservations: (800) 365-CAMP
Park Literature: (423) 436-0120

FAX: (423) 436-1220, Park Headquarters

Website: www.nps.gov/grsm/

Hours: Visitor Centers open daily except Christmas. Winter: 9 a.m.-5 p.m., Summer: 8 a.m.-7 p.m. Hours vary depending on time of year.

Fees: None to enter park. Fees are charged at developed campgrounds and for certain special programs.

Camping: There are ten developed campgrounds in the park including Cades Cove in Tennessee and Smokemont in North Carolina, which are open year-round. The other developed campgrounds are generally open from late March or April to early November. Fees range from $10-$15 per night. Backcountry camping, on the other hand, is free but requires a permit. Most campsites use self-registration at visitor centers or ranger stations, but shelters and rationed sites require reservations. Reservations can be made 30 days in advance by calling (423) 436-1231 or (800) 365-2267 between 8 a.m. and 6 p.m. any day of the week.

Lodging: LeConte Lodge, which is accessible only by foot or horseback, sits atop 6,593-foot tall Mt. LeConte. This is the Park's third highest peak. Reservations are required and can be made by calling (423)

429-5704. The lodge is open mid-March to mid-November. A variety of lodging facilities are available in the outlying communities.

Of Note: The most visited National Park in America. Hosts the International Biosphere Reserve and the World Heritage Site. Elevations in the park range from 800-6643 feet and topography affects local weather. Temperatures are 10-20 degrees cooler on the mountaintops. Annual precipitation averages 65 inches in lowlands to 88 inches in high country. Spring often brings unpredictable weather, particularly in higher elevations. Summer is hot and humid, but more pleasant in higher elevations. Fall has warm days and cool nights and is the driest period. Frosts occur starting in late September and continue into April. Winter is generally moderate, but extreme conditions become more likely as elevation increases.

Tips: In summer time the park is heavily visited. Expect long lines during this season. Late spring is a great time to visit because of the wildflowers, pleasant weather, and absence of crowds. The Great Smoky Mountains are vast. Plan your trip carefully. Write or call ahead for information to help in planning. During the summer and fall, the park provides regularly scheduled ranger-led interpretive walks and talks, slide presentations, and campfire programs at campgrounds and visitor centers.

Nearby: Cherokee Indian Reservation, Nantahala National Forest.

Directions: From Asheville, take I-40 West to Exit 27. Follow Hwy. 19 South to Cherokee. In Cherokee, take 441 North and follow signs to the park entrance.

Nantahala National Forest

This 526,798-acre National Forest located to the west of Asheville offers family camping, boating, fishing, horse trails and miles of hiking trails. Nantahala is home to the Joyce Kilmer Memorial Forest, one of the nation's most impressive preserves of old-growth forest. Here you may view magnificent examples of over 100 species of trees, some over 20 feet in circumference and 100 feet high. Explored in 1540 by Spanish Conquistador Hernando DeSoto and established in 1920 under the 1911 Weeks

"Trees" by Joyce Kilmer
(1886-1918)

I think I shall never see
A poem lovely as a tree.
A tree whose hungry mouth is pressed
Against the earth's sweet flowing breast;
A tree that looks at God all day
And lifts her leafy arms to pray;
A tree that may in summer wear
A nest of robins in her hair;
Upon whose bosom snow has lain;
Who intimately lives with rain.
Poems are made by fools like me,
But only God can make a tree.

Act, this 3,800-acre forest was set aside in 1936 as a memorial to Joyce Kilmer, the soldier/poet who wrote the famous poem "Trees." Scenic drives, excellent fishing and rafting the whitewaters of the Nantahala River are among the forest's biggest attractions. Nantahala is also renowned for waterfalls and its beautiful chain of pristine lakes. Black bears, bobcats, white-tailed deer and other animals indigenous to the Appalachians abound in the Forest.

Location: West of Asheville
Distance: 2-3 hours from Asheville
Address: Cheoah District Ranger Office, Massey Branch Rd., Rt. 1 (PO Box 16A), Robbinsville, NC 28771
Highlands Ranger District: 2010 Flat Mountain Rd., Highlands, NC 28741 (526-3765)
Telephone: Nantahala National Forest Cheoah District Ranger 479-6431
FAX: 479-6784
Websites: www.franklin-chamber.com/nantahala.html
www.gorp.com/gorp/resource/US_National_Forest/NC_Nanta.htm
Hours: Ranger Office: April-November Daily 8 a.m.-4:30 p.m.; December-March 8 a.m.-4:30 p.m. Monday-Friday
Fees: None to enter park
Camping: Tsali campground, $15/night; Cheoah, Horse Cove, and Cable Cove campgrounds, $5/night
Tips: Joyce Kilmer Memorial Forest is a virgin, never-logged forest. Not to be missed if you visit Nantahala.
Directions: From Asheville take I-40 West. Take Exit 27 to 74 West. Follow 74 West to NC 19. Follow NC 19 to Nantahala.

Pisgah National Forest

Pisgah National Forest is a land of mile-high peaks, cascading waterfalls and heavily forested slopes. It is an ideal place, as are all of the national forests, for outdoor recreation. The forest gets its name from Mount Pisgah, a prominent peak in the area. In the 1700s a Scotch-Irish minister saw the peak and named it for the Biblical mountain from which Moses saw the promised land after 40 years of wandering in the wilderness. Located on two sides of Asheville, the forest is more than 490,000 acres and spreads over 12 western North Carolina counties. The forest is more or less divided in half by the Blue Ridge Parkway, and the Appalachian Trail runs along its border with Tennessee. The Mountains-to-the-Sea Trail crosses through the forest. Pisgah National Forest contains three wilderness areas, Middle Prong, Linville Gorge and the Shining Rock section, and is divided into four districts: Pisgah District, French Broad District, Grandfather District and Tocane District.

A short drive from downtown Asheville, the Pisgah District of the National Forest has a number of outstanding features and points of interest. This district is the most popular of all four, and receives over five million visitors a year. Over 156,000 acres in size, it encompasses parts of Buncombe, Haywood, Henderson,

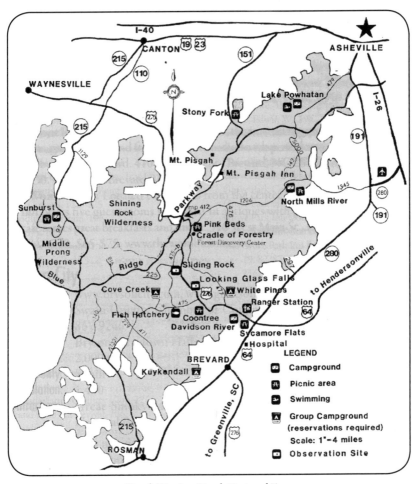

Pisgah District, Pisgah National Forest

and Transylvania counties. There are over 275 miles of trails for hiking, horseback riding, and mountain biking. Two of the three wilderness areas, Shining Rock and Middle Prong, are in this district. There is a Ranger Station and Visitor Center located on US 276 a few miles into the forest from Hwy. 280 in Brevard. I recommend you visit the center before continuing on into the forest.

Location: The Pisgah District of the Pisgah National Forest is located to the west of Asheville

Distance: 45 minutes-1 hour from Asheville

Address: Pisgah District Office, 1001 Pisgah Hwy., Pisgah Forest, NC 28768

Telephone: Pisgah District Office: 877-3350, 257-4203

FAX: 884-7527

The Pisgah View Ranch in Candler, showing Mount Pisgah in the distance

Website: www/ncnatural.com/NCUSFS/Pisgah/

Hours: Pisgah District Ranger Station Visitor Center: Monday-Friday 8 a.m.-5 p.m.; holidays and Saturday 9 a.m.-5 p.m.; Sundays noon-5 p.m.

Fees: None to enter park

Camping: Davidson River, $13/night; Lake Powhatan, $12/night; North Mills River, $6/night; Sunburst, $5/night

Tips: Obtain maps and information at Visitor Center. You may order maps through the mail by calling 884-4734. The forest also has excellent mountain biking trails.

Of Note: The Cradle of Forestry located in the forest was the birthplace of modern forestry in America. It is a National Historic Site.

Nearby: Brevard Area Waterfalls, Blue Ridge Parkway

Directions: From Asheville: Take Airport Rd. (Hwy. 280) off of Hendersonville Hwy. in Arden. Continue on 280 past Asheville airport to Wal-Mart Shopping Plaza just before Brevard. Turn right onto US 276 into Pisgah Forest. The R anger Visitor Center will be located on the right a few miles in.

From Hendersonville: Take US 64 West from downtown to the intersection of Hwy. 280 and Hwy. 276 at the Wal-Mart Shopping Plaza. Continue straight through light to US 276 and into the Forest. Look for the Ranger Visitor Center on your right.

Some major points of interest within the Pisgah District follow.

Andy Cove Nature Trail: A self-guided trail located behind Pisgah Ranger Station (0.7 miles), that goes through several forest habitats. The trail takes about 30 minutes to walk.

Forest Heritage National Scenic Byway: A 79-mile highway loop (US 276, US 64 NC 215 & FS 475) provides numerous opportunities to view the outstanding scenery of the forest, in an area rich in forest history.

The Forest Discovery Center at The Cradle of Forestry in America: This National Historic Site commemorates the birthplace of American forestry and forest education. The Forest Discovery Center features two interpretive exhibits and a gift shop, guided tours on two trails featuring eight historic buildings, restored stationary logging locomotive and living history interpretation by local crafters. www.cradleofforestry.com. Open 9 a.m.-5 p.m. April-October 877-3130. (SEE Section Five, Chapter 2 "Cradle of Forestry")

Lake Powhatan: A family recreation area in Asheville's backyard, Lake Powhatan is located off NC 191 at the end of Bent Creek Rd. The park provides picnic tables with grills and water sources, fishing, swimming beach and hiking trails.

Looking Glass Falls: A beautiful 30-foot wide waterfall that drops more than 60 feet down to a rock cliff. A trail with steps leads to an overlook and to the bottom of the falls. Located along Hwy. 276. Parking is provided.

North Mills River Recreation Area: This popular area offers picnic tables with grills along the beautiful North Mills River. A popular activity here is tubing on the river, as well as trout fishing. 13 miles north of Hendersonville. (SEE Section Four, Chapter 7)

Pisgah Forest State Fish Hatchery and Pisgah Center for Wildlife Education: Different species and size of trout can be observed in the raceways and fish food is available to feed the fish. For group programs and information call 877-4423. www.ncwildlife.org. Located off Hwy. 276 on Davidson River Rd. (FS Rd. 475).

Sliding Rock Recreation Area: This very popular observation and water play area is a natural waterslide located on Hwy. 276. Visitors can slide down a 60-foot rock into a 7-foot deep pool; restrooms, changing areas, large parking lot, observation deck, site attendant on duty Memorial Day through mid-August. Small fee.

Waterfalls

Within an hour's drive of Asheville and Hendersonville are a number of truly spectacular waterfalls in the Brevard area. A great day trip can be planned to visit these easily accessible falls. Be sure and take a picnic lunch. Besides the close-by Brevard area waterfalls, there are a few others worth mentioning.

Chimney Rock Park (SEE Section Five, Chapter 1) has the 404-foot high Hickory Nut Falls, one of the tallest in the eastern United States. The park has an short hiking trail, which leads to the base of this magnificent falls. In the Boone area, about a two hour drive from Asheville is Linville Falls (SEE Section Five, Chapter 1), the best-known waterfall in the Appalachian Mountains, and one of the most scenic. Located in nearby Flat Rock is the little man-made waterfall at the Highland Lake Dam. This delightful spot is worth driving by if you are in the area. It is located on Highland Lake Rd., off Hwy. 25 between Flat Rock and Hendersonville.

The Brevard waterfalls (Transylvania County) are a real treasure and worth a visit at any time of the year. There are hundreds to choose from but due to space restrictions, only some of the major ones will be listed below. It is suggested that if you wish to visit the waterfalls, you first check into the Brevard Chamber of Commerce Visitor Center in Brevard and pick up a copy of their "Land of the Waterfalls" guide and map.

Highland Lake Dam

Brevard Waterfalls

Location: Brevard area waterfalls are to the west of Asheville

Distance: 1 hour from Asheville

Address: Brevard Chamber of Commerce Visitor Center, 35 West Main Street, Brevard, NC 28712

Telephone: Brevard Visitor Center: (800) 648-4523

FAX: 883-8550

Website: www.visitwaterfalls.com

Of Note: While all of the falls are beautiful they can be treacherous. Death or injury may be only seconds away if one misjudges the force of moving water or height of the cascades. Rocks are slippery when wet. Do not attempt to climb the rocks beside the falls or venture near the top. Viewing the falls is safe, family fun only if you stay on the designated trails and viewing areas.

Nearby: Pisgah National Forest, Blue Ridge Parkway

Directions: To reach Brevard from Hendersonville take Hwy. 64 West. From Asheville, take NC 280 South. NC 280 begins as Airport Rd. after you leave Hendersonville Hwy. (US 25).

Bird Rock Falls

Take US 64 West from Brevard 8.5 miles and turn right on NC 215. Continue approximately 9 miles. Falls are on the left just below the confluence of Shoal Creek and the North Fork of the French Broad River in the Balsam Grove Community.

Looking Glass Falls

The most popular waterfall in North Carolina. Located on Hwy. 276, it is a picturesque and unbroken rush of water 30 feet wide and 60 feet high. Take US 64 East 3.5 miles from downtown Brevard to US 276 West in Pisgah Forest. Follow US 276 six miles to falls.

Rainbow Falls

Follow US 64 West from Brevard 18 miles to Whitewater Rd. (NC 281) and turn left 2.5 miles. A trail begins at a turn in the road and continues downstream past Drift Falls a half-mile to the 200 foot high Rainbow Falls.

Toxaway Falls

Take US 64 West from Brevard 15.5 miles. The highway crosses the top of the falls 123 feet just below Toxaway Dam. The area was named Toxaway (Red Bird) by the Cherokee Indians.

Whitewater Falls

A spectacular plunge of 411 feet makes this the tallest waterfall east of the Mississippi. A park with parking and restrooms provides easy access. Take US 64 West from Brevard, go 18 miles to Whitewater Rd. (NC 281), turn left 8 miles to park entrance on left. Falls can be viewed from the end of a paved road 100 yards from the parking area.

Chapter Two
Cultural Attractions

The Western North Carolina mountains Are home to a great number of diverse and very popular cultural attractions. Because of the scope of this book, only the most significant and popular attractions are presented. Most of these are within a few hours drive from Asheville and Hendersonville.

North of Asheville
Dry Ridge Historical Museum

This little-known museum, housed in the Weaverville Public Library, documents the life of the area's first settlers dating back to 1787, especially residents of the Reems Creek and Flat Creek Townships. The museum displays a collection of artifacts that include furniture, tools, clothing, letters, ledgers, books, photographs, and portraits.

Location: Weaverville, NC
Distance: 30 minutes from downtown Asheville
Address: Weaverville Public Library, Lower Level, 41 N. Main St. Weaverville, NC 28787
Telephone: 645-3592
Hours: March-November: Saturdays only from 10 a.m.-4 p.m.
Fees: None
Allow: 1 hour minimum
Nearby: Zebulon B. Vance Birthplace, Gourmet Gardens Herb Farm
Directions: From I-240, take the Weaverville Exit 4A onto 19/23 North. Go seven miles and take the New Stock Rd. Exit. Turn right off the ramp and left onto US 25/70 North. Make a left onto Main Street.

Gourmet Gardens Herb Farm

Located in Weaverville just north of Asheville, Gourmet Gardens has over 500 different herbs in their greenhouse. Display gardens and a gift shop with books on herb growing, herb products and herbs for sale. These gardens have been featured in many magazines and in TimeLife Books, and include a Planned Herb Garden, Culinary Garden and Butterfly Garden.

Location: Weaverville, NC
Distance: 30 minutes from Asheville
Address: 14 Bankstown Rd., Weaverville, NC 28787
Telephone: 658-0766
FAX: 645-2949
Website: www.gourmetgardensherbfarm.com
Hours: March 15-December 1: Tuesday through Saturday 9:30 a.m.-5:30
p.m.; Sunday 10 a.m.-4 p.m.
December 1-March 15 by appointment only
Fees: No admission charge
Tips: Spring and early fall are premium buying seasons.
Allow: 45 minutes to 1 hour
Nearby: Zebulon B. Vance Birthplace, Dry Ridge Historical Museum
Directions: From Asheville take the I-240 Weaverville Exit 4A off of I-240 (US
19/23N) and go seven miles to New Stock Rd. exit. Turn right off
ramp and left at the second light towards Hardee's. Go north on
Merrimon Ave. one mile to bridge. Turn right on Bankstown Rd.
and go 100 meters.

Rural Life Museum

This small museum is housed in an ivy-covered, stone building and is dedicated to preserving mountain farm and craft culture. It focuses on Pre-Industrial Appalachia as well as the Industrial period that followed, with depictions of hearth and home, exhibits of farm and craft implements, and historic photographic murals. An exhibit honoring the Hooked-Rug Industry, which existed in Madison County and other parts of Western North Carolina, is one of the museum's most fascinating displays.

Location: Mars Hill College Campus
Distance: 30 minutes from Asheville
Address: NC 213, Mars Hill College, Mars Hill, NC 28754
Telephone: 689-1424
Hours: Monday-Friday 2-4 p.m. and by appointment
Fees: None
Allow: 1 hour
Nearby: Zebulon B. Vance Birthplace
Directions: From I-240, take Weaverville Exit 4A (19/23N) to the Mars Hill
Exit. Follow Hwy. 213 to the first light. Just ahead will be the college campus. The museum is housed in the native stone building just
inside the gate on the right.

Rush Wray Museum of Yancey County History

Located within the historic McElroy House, this museum focuses on Yancey County's local history and Appalachian mountain heritage. One of their permanent exhibits is "Our people, our heritage, our pride," which features the settlement of Yancey County and Burnsville, NC. The Revolving Exhibit Room hosts changing exhibits including "The Pisgah Village," "Cane River Archeological Site," "The Civil War and the Home Guard," and "The McElroy House."

Location: Burnsville, NC
Distance: 45 minutes to 1 hour from Asheville
Address: 106 West Main St., Burnsville, NC 28714
Telephone: 682-3671
FAX: 682-3671
Hours: April 10-October 10, Saturdays 1-7 p.m. Call for weekday hours.
Fees: None
Allow: 1 hour
Of Note: The McElroy House, circa 1840, is listed in the National Register of Historic Places and was used by Brigadier General J.W. McElroy as the NC Home Guard Headquarters for Western North Carolina during the Civil War. The home is fully restored to its original state under the supervision of the NC Department of Archives and History.
Tips: The Rush Wray is a new museum and they are still adding exhibits. Hours may be added also. So, call ahead.
Nearby: Zebulon B. Vance Birthplace
Directions: From Asheville, take 19/23 North to Mars Hill/Burnsville Exit. Follow 19E to Burnsville. The museum is located behind the visitor center.

Zebulon B. Vance Birthplace

The birthplace of the dynamic "War Governor of the South," Zebulon B. Vance, is located in Weaverville, just a few miles north of Asheville. Administered by the N.C. Department of Cultural Resources, the Vance birthplace is one of North Carolina's Historic Sites and is open to the public year-round. The homestead, a large two-story structure of hewn yellow pine logs, has been reconstructed around the original chimney with its two enormous fireplaces. The furnishings and household items on display today are representative of the period from 1790 to 1840 and include a few pieces original to the home. Clustered about the grounds of the house are six log outbuildings, loom house, slave house, and tool house. Nearby the Visitor Center/Museum houses exhibits portraying the life of Governor Vance.

Each spring and again in the fall, visitors to the Vance home have the opportunity to experience Pioneer Living Days; the grounds come alive with history as costumed staff members and volunteers demonstrate the skills and cherished occupations of settlers in the early days.

Location: Weaverville, NC
Distance: 30 minutes from Asheville
Address: 911 Reems Creek Rd., Weaverville, NC 28787

Telephone: 645-6706
FAX: 645-6706
Website: www.ah.dcr.state.nc.us/sections/hs/vance/vance.htm
Hours: April 1-October 31: Monday-Saturday, 9 a.m. to 5 p.m. Sunday, 1-5 p.m. November 1-March 31: Tuesday-Saturday, 10a.m.-4 p.m. Sunday, 1-4 p.m. Closed Monday.
Fees: None; donations accepted.
Allow: 1-2 hours
Of Note: North Carolina Historic Site, Listed in the National Register of Historic Places.
Nearby: Gourmet Gardens Herb Farm, Dry Ridge Historical Museum
Directions: From Asheville take the I-240 Weaverville Exit 4A off of I-240 (US 19/23N) to New Stock Rd. Turn right off the ramp, left onto US 25/70 North, and follow to Reems Creek Rd. where you will turn right.

Zebulon B. Vance Birthplace

South of Asheville

Foothills Equestrian Nature Center (FENCE)

The Foothills Equestrian Nature Center, also known as FENCE, provides the South Carolina Upstate and Western North Carolina with a nature preserve of over 300 acres, open to the public year-round. FENCE has an award-winning equestrian facility that hosts local, regional and national events, offers birding activities and programs and is a learning center for children. FENCE also hosts youth cross-country meets.

The are over five miles of trails for walking, riding and carriage use, a wildlife pond, quiet meadows and sweeping panoramas. FENCE also hosts steeplechases, horse trails, dressage shows, pleasure driving and cross-country races. Stabling available for over 180 horses, lighted show rings and cross-country and steeplechase courses.

Location: Tryon, NC
Distance: 1 hour from Asheville
Address: 500 Hunting Country Rd. Tryon, NC 28782
Telephone: Foothills Equestrian Trails Association 859-9021; Equestrian Director: 859-9021
FAX: 859-9315
Website: www.fence.org
Hours: Dawn to dusk daily; Office Hours: 9 a.m.-4 p.m.
Fees: None for hiking and nature trails. Equestrian fees charged for Bed and Barn Program (Bring your own horse, rental stalls and apartment are available. Call the Equestrian Director)
Riding Trails: Extensive riding trail system. $5/Day; Guest Tag required from Foothills Equestrian Trails Association.
20-30 equestrian shows per year. No fee to watch. Call office for schedule.
Blockhouse Steeplechase: Sanctioned by National Steeplechase Association. Admissions charged. Held every April.
Of Note: The Blockhouse Steeplechase is one of the major equestrian events in North Carolina.
Directions: Take I-26 East from Asheville or Hendersonville. Take S.C. Exit 1. Turn right towards Landrum. Go 1½ miles and take a right onto Bomar Rd. (Li'l Cricket is on the corner). Go one short block and turn right onto Prince Rd. After 1.7 miles, turn left onto Hunting Country Rd., just before the I-26 overpass. Go slightly over ½ mile to FENCE's entrance on the right.

Maimy Etta Black Fine Arts Museum & Historical Society

The Maimy Etta Black Fine Arts Museum and Historical Society has as its mission to collect, document, preserve, and interpret the art and artifacts of Afro-American and Global Black Art. The museum presents cultural and historic exhibits as well as materials related to the Afro-American experience and to local Black families, including the Thompson Family of Forest City. Key exhibits focus on historical time lines from the 16th century to the present: African art and artifacts, Brazilian art, Caribbean art, Contemporary Black art, descriptions of life in the Thirteen Colonies, and examination of race and politics in the United States.

Location: Forest City, NC
Distance: 1½-2 hours from Asheville
Address: 404 Hardin Rd. (PO Box 1690), Forest City, NC 28043

Telephone: 248-1525
Hours: Tuesday-Friday 11 a.m.-5 p.m.; Saturday 11 a.m.-2 p.m.; Sunday 2-5 p.m.
Fees: Adults (over 12) $2; Children and Seniors $1.50
Tips: Children under 12 must be accompanied by parents
Nearby: Lake Lure, Chimney Rock Park, Bottomless Pools
Directions: From Asheville, take I-240 Exit 9 onto Hwy. 74A. Follow 74A through Fairview, Hickory Nut Gap, Chimney Rock, and Lake Lure to reach Forest City. At the Tri-city Shopping Mall, turn left onto Oak Street and then right onto Hardin Rd.

Polk County Historical Museum

Located in a historic railroad depot, the Polk County Historical Museum contains a large collection that includes artifacts from the Cherokee Indians, early settlers, the Revolutionary War, the Civil War, and World War II. Museum items include tools and clothing of the settlers, various railroad treasures, photos and paintings of historic sites in Polk County, and memorabilia from local residents. They also have a large collection of early maps, records, and pictures including important items in American history.

Location: In the old Tryon Depot in Tryon, NC
Distance: 45 minutes from Asheville
Address: 1 Depot St., Tryon, NC 28782
Telephone: (800) 440-7848, 859-2211
FAX: 859-2300
Website: www.polkcounty.org/county/featured/depot/depot.htm
Hours: Tuesday-Thursday 10 a.m.-noon and by appointment
Fees: None
Allow: 1 hour
Of Note: The old Tryon Depot is listed in the National Register of Historic Places.
Nearby: FENCE (Foothills Equestrian and Nature Center)
Directions: From Asheville, take I-26 East to Exit 36 for Columbia/Tryon. Go right, towards Tryon, and proceed through town on Trade Street to the 4th light. Turn right and then another right onto Depot Street.

East of Asheville

Alleghany County Courthouse

Built in 1933-34 following the destruction by fire of the first courthouse, this two-story brick County Courthouse with white columns is an interesting architectural study of the period.

Location: Sparta, NC
Distance: 3 hours from Asheville

Address: 100 North Main Street, Sparta, NC 28675
Telephone: (336) 372-4179
Admission: Free
Directions: From Asheville, take I-40 East to Marion and take Hwy. 221 North to through Boone to Sparta.

Appalachian Cultural Museum

Located on the campus of Appalachian State University, the Appalachian Cultural Museum is one of the premier museums in the mountains dealing with Appalachian history and culture. Exhibits cover a full range of topics including moonshine, the Civil War, weaving, handicrafts, farming, Native Americans, Blacks in Appalachia, Daniel Boone, mountain furniture, and much more. Professionally exhibited and a wealth of educational information is presented.

Location: Boone, NC
Distance: 1½-2 hours from Asheville
Address: University Hall Dr., Appalachian State University, Boon, NC 28607
Telephone: 262-3117
FAX: 262-2920
Website: www.museum.appstate.edu
Hours: Tuesday-Saturday 10 a.m.-5 p.m.; Sunday 1-5 p.m.
Fees: Adults $4, Seniors $3.50, Youth 10-18 $2, Under 10 Free
Allow: 2 hours
Tips: Visiting groups should call for price and guide arrangements. This museum is a great educational experience for kids.
Nearby: The Blowing Rock, Mystery Hill, Appalachian Heritage Museum, Mast General Store, Grandfather Mountain, Tweetsie Railroad, Linville Caverns
Directions: From Asheville, take I-40 East to Marion and take Hwy. 221 North to Blowing Rock. Then take US 321 North to Boone. In Boone, on turn between Greene's Motel and the Texaco Gas Station onto University Hall Dr. and go to the top of the wooded hill. The museum is located in University Hall.

Appalachian Heritage Museum

The Appalachian Heritage Museum is a living history museum in the same complex as Mystery Hill in Blowing Rock NC. It is housed in the historic Dougherty House, which was the home of the Dougherty Brothers, D.D. and B.B., founders of Appalachian State University. The purpose of the museum is to show visitors how middle class mountain families lived at the turn of the century

Location: Mystery Hill complex between Boone and Blowing Rock, NC
Distance: 2 hours, longer if using the Blue Ridge Parkway
Address: 175 Mystery Hill Ln., Blowing Rock, NC 28605

Telephone: 264-2792
Hours: June-August 8 a.m.-8 p.m.; September-May 9 a.m.-5 p.m.
Fees: Rates vary. Call for current rate schedule. Senior, military, group, and AAA discounts are available.
Allow: 1 hour
Of Note: Original home of the founders of Appalachian State University. Moved twice over the years to its present location.
Nearby: Mystery Hill, The Blowing Rock, Grandfather Mountain, Tweetsie Railroad, Linville Caverns, Horn in the West, Mast General Store, Appalachian Cultural Center.
Directions: From Asheville, take I-40 East to Marion. Take Hwy. 221 North to Blowing Rock. Then, take 321 North four miles to the Mystery Hill complex. Alternately, take the Blue Ridge Parkway north to exit at mile marker 291 and take Hwy. 321 North for 1½ miles.

Avery County Museum

This circa 1912 Avery County Jail is a museum housing displays of early Avery County life. One of the last intact old jails in North Carolina.

Location: Newland, NC
Distance: 2 hours from Asheville
Address: 1829 Schultz Circle, Newland, NC 28657
Telephone: 733-7311
Admission: Free
Directions: From Asheville, take I-40 East to Morganton and take Hwy. 181 North to Pineola, just past the Blue Ridge Parkway. Turn left on Hwy. 221 and then right onto 194 North to Newland.

Ben Long Frescoes

Located in Glendale Springs, Holy Trinity Church features the famous frescoes of Ben Long (Fresco of the Lord's Supper) and Jeffrey Mims (Fresco of Christ's Departure) and other assorted artworks. St. Mary's Church in nearby West Jefferson also features Long's Frescoes of the Mystery of Faith, Mary Great With Child, and John the Baptist.

Fresco painting is an art form based on the immediate application of pigment to wet plaster. It is an ancient art form, with many outstanding examples still existing in European churches. The work in Glendale Springs and West Jefferson was completed 1970-80 by Ben Long and his students. The marvelous luminous beauty of the frescoes attracts approximately 80,000 visitors annually from around the world to St. Mary's and Holy Trinity.

Location: Glendale Springs and West Jefferson, NC
Distance: 2 hours from Asheville
Address: Holy Trinity Church, 195 J.W. Luke Rd., Glendale Springs, NC 28629

Telephone: (336) 982-3076
Address: St. Mary's Church, 400 Beaver Creek School Rd., West Jefferson, NC 28694
Telephone: (336) 246-3552
Hours: 24 hours a day, seven days a week, year-round.
Fees: None
Allow: ½ to 1 hour each church
Directions: From Asheville, take I-40 East to Hickory. Take Exit 131 to NC 16 North to Wilkesboro. Take 421 North towards Watauga. Turn left onto NC 16 North again to Glendale Springs and Holy Trinity Church. From Glendale Springs take NC 16 North to NC 221. Turn left onto NC 221 to West Jefferson and St. Mary's Church.

Caldwell County Historical Society Heritage Museum

Over 35,000 square feet of vertical, horizontal, and floor space have been utilized in the Caldwell County Heritage Museum to show Caldwell Country's history and culture from pre-colonial, pioneer, revolutionary, and Civil War eras to the present day. Specialized collections and exhibits also include antique furniture and farm implements; native American artifacts; World War I and II memorabilia; the Caldwell County Music Preservation collection; antique phonograph, radio, and TV exhibit; and Plains and Western Indian exhibits.

Location: Lenoir, NC
Distance: 1 hour from Asheville
Address: 112 Vaiden St. SE (PO Box 2165), Lenoir, NC 28645
Telephone: 758-4004
Hours: Monday & Wednesday 9:30 a.m.-noon, 1-3:30 p.m.; Saturday 9 a.m.-noon; tours by appointment only.
Fees: None, donations accepted
Allow: 1-2 hours
Of Note: Museum building is listed in the National Register of Historic Places
Nearby: Fort Defiance
Directions: From Asheville, take I-40 East to Rte. 321 in Hickory. Follow 321 North to Lenoir. In Lenoir, you will come to a major intersection (Burger King and Eckerd's Drugstore). Take a left and after 100 yards, bear again to your left. The road turns into Harper Avenue. Stay on Harper and bear to the right in front of the Fire Department and Post Office. Turn right after the Police Department and then left onto Willow. Left again at the stop sign will take you onto Harper. Make a right at the first light and then left at the stop light at the top of the hill. The first street on your right will be Vaiden Street. The museum is on Vaiden at the top of the hill.

Emerald Village

Emerald Village features the North Carolina Mining Museum, a historic tour, gem-cutting shops with resident goldsmith, gem mining with stone identification, and gem cutters at work. In this famous historic mining area, over 45 different rocks, minerals and gems have been found including aquamarine, beryl, emerald, garnet and smoky quartz. The North Carolina Mining Museum is located underground in a real mine. Authentic mining equipment and displays bring to life the early days of North Carolina mining.

Location: Little Switzerland
Distance: 2 hours from Asheville
Address: McKinney Mine Rd., Little Switzerland, NC 28749.
Telephone: 765-6463
FAX: 765-4367
Website: www.glwshows.com/emerald.htm
Hours: 9 a.m.-5 p.m., seven days a week, May through October. Museum is open April-November
Fees: Museum and Displays free.
Underground Mine Tour: $4 adults, $3 seniors and students grades 1-12, preschoolers free.
Rock Hound Mine Tours: 3 hour round hounding excursion with guide, $20 adult, $15 students grades 1-12. Reservations suggested.
Allow: 2 hours
Nearby: Linville Caverns, Linville Gorge
Directions: From Asheville, take I-40 East to Marion. Take NC 221 North to NC 226. Left on NC 226 and go 9 miles to the Blue Ridge Parkway. Go south on parkway and get off at next exit, Little Switzerland, Milepost 334. Take right under parkway onto Chestnut Grove Rd. Turn left onto McKinney Mine Rd.

Fort Defiance

Home of Revolutionary War hero, General William Lenoir, is open to the public. Original clothing and furnishings of 1792 house on display. General Lenoir was a member of the Council of State, served in both houses of the Legislature and was President of the NC Senate. The history of this house is the history of the opening of the Western North Carolina frontier. Furnishings include more than 250 original pieces, from teacups to bedsteads.

Location: Lenoir, NC
Distance: 1½-2 hours from Asheville
Address: Hwy. 268, Lenoir, NC 28645
Telephone: 758-1671
Hours: June-August: 10 a.m.-5 p.m. Friday and Saturday, 1:30-5 p.m. Sunday; April, May, September and October: 1-5 p.m. first and third Sundays only

Fees: $3.50 adults, $1 children 12 and under.
Allow: 1 hour
Of Note: Guided tours with costumed docents have contributed to this being
            rated one of the best restorations in North Carolina.
            Listed in the National Register of Historic Places and designated a
            Cultural Treasure by the State of North Carolina.
Directions: Take I-40 East from Asheville to Rte. 321 in Hickory. North on Rte.
            321 to Patterson. Take 268 East 5½ miles.

From This Day Forward

Held in an amphitheater, this seasonal outdoor drama portrays the compelling story of the Waldensian struggle for religious freedom in the 17th century and their eventual migration to Valdese in 1893.

Location: Valdese, NC
Distance: 1 hour from Asheville
Address: 410 Church St. (PO Box 112), Valdese, NC 28690
Telephone: 874-0176
FAX: 874-0176
Website: www.valdese.com/drama.htm
Hours: July-August 16 evening performances, held on Friday, Saturday, &
            Sunday at 8:15 p.m.
Fees: $10 Adults, seniors and students $8 (SEE "Trail of Faith" later in
            this chapter for Drama/Trail combo ticket information)
Allow: 2½ hours
Tips: WNC can be chilly in the evening, even in summer. Bring a light
            jacket or sweater. Also, bring an umbrella in case it rains.
Nearby: Waldensian Museum, Trail of Faith
Directions: From Asheville, take I-40 East to Exit 111. Take Carolina Street and
            turn left onto Main Street. Turn right on Church Street. You will see
            signs at every intersection.

Hickory Ridge Homestead

Hickory Ridge Homestead is an eighteenth century living history museum that highlights the daily lives of the early settlers of the Appalachian Mountains. Early furniture, period clothing, utensils, farm implements, and many other early artifacts, as well as displays and exhibits, contribute to the experience of Hickory Ridge. This is a great place to take the kids.

Location: Located at Horn in the West, Boone, NC
Distance: 2 hours from Asheville, Blue Ridge Parkway takes longer
Address: 591 Horn in the West Rd., Boone, NC 28607
Telephone: 264-2120
Hours: May-June Saturday 9 a.m.-8 p.m., Sunday noon-8 p.m.; July-October
            9 a.m.-8 p.m. daily; November-April by appointment

Fees: Donations accepted
Allow: 1 hour minimum
Nearby: Horn in the West, Appalachian Cultural Museum, Appalachian Heritage Museum, Mystery Hill, The Blowing Rock, Grandfather Mountain, Linville Caverns, Tweetsie Railroad
Directions: From Asheville, take I-40 East to Marion. In Marion, take NC 221 North to Boone. Located just past the intersection of NC 321.

Wildflowers on the Roadsides

As you drive along some of the major roads and interstates in North Carolina in the spring, summer and fall, you can't help but notice the spectacular plantings of wildflowers. In 1985, the North Carolina Department of Transportation (NCDOT) began planting wildflower beds as an integral part of the highway beautification. The program has been a great success and visitors and residents alike are treated to wonderful colorful displays as they travel throughout the state. If you are planning a trip to North Carolina, I suggest you write to the North Carolina Department of Transportation offices for a copy of their wildflower identification booklet. This guide will allow you to identify and learn about each type of wildflower planting you encounter on your travels. The cost is $6. Checks should be made payable to the NC Wildflower Program. Their address is Roadside Environmental Unit, PO Box 25201, Raleigh, NC 27611.

Hiddenite Center

Housed in the historic Lucas Mansion, the Hiddenite Center, is a step back in time. This folk and cultural arts center features an exhibition of native gems and minerals, one of which is the 294-pound Carolina crystal, as well as a superb doll collection dating from the 1800s. The changing exhibitions of the gallery and the period-house furnishings all contribute to the unique experience of the Hiddenite Center and allow the visitors to this lovely turn-of-the-century Victorian mansion not only to learn about the past but to experience it. Educational activities and arts programming are held on a regular basis.

Location: Hiddenite, NC
Distance: 1 hour from Asheville
Address: 316 Church St. (PO Box 311), Hiddenite, NC 28636
Telephone: 632-6966
FAX: 632-3783
Hours: Monday-Friday 9 a.m.-4:30 p.m., Saturday-Sunday 2-4:30 p.m.
Fees: Members are free. Museum Tours (first floor): Adults $2.50, Seniors and Students $1.50; All other gallery areas are free.
Allow: 1-2 hours

Of Note: The Lucas Mansion is listed in the National Register of Historic Places and is an extraordinarily beautiful building.

Directions: From Asheville, take I-40 East to Exit 149 in Statesville. Go north on NC 90 to Hiddenite. The center is located three blocks north of NC 90.

Historic Carson House

Built in 1793 by Colonel John Carson, the Carson House today is a privately owned history museum that is open to the public. This historic plantation home is filled with furnishings typical of the upper-class of that period. Exhibits and artifacts describe not only the influential Carson family but the culture and history of the region and state.

Location: Between Old Fort and Marion, NC
Distance: 45 minutes from Asheville
Address: Rte. 1 (PO Box 179), Old Fort, NC 28762
Telephone: 724-4640, 724-4948
Hours: May 1-November 1, Tuesday-Saturday 10 a.m.-5 p.m., Sunday 2-5 p.m.
Fees: Adults $3, 16 and under $1.50
Allow: 1 hour
Of Note: Listed in the National Register of Historic Places. Colonel John Carson was a representative to the Fayetteville convention where the North Carolina delegates ratified the United States Constitution in 1789. His son, Samuel Price Carson, was a member of the NC State Senate three times and the US House of Representatives for eight years.
Nearby: Mountain Gateway Museum
Directions: From Asheville, take I-40 East to Old Fort. Take NC 70 North through Pleasant Gardens to the House. It is located on the right just beyond the intersection of NC 80.

Horn in the West

One of North Carolina's best know outdoor drama, "Horn in the West," is a recreation of North Carolina's early pioneers, including Daniel Boone and their struggle for independence from Britain. The production takes place in pre-Revolutionary days and lasts two hours.

Location: Boone, NC
Distance: 2-3 hours from Asheville
Address: 591 Horn in the West Rd., Boone, NC 28607
Telephone: 264-2120
Website: www.boonenc.org/saha/hitw/
Hours: Season is mid-June to mid-August. Performances begin at 8:30 p.m. No show on Mondays.
Fees: $12 adults, $6 children 12 and under, $11 seniors

Allow: Performances last about two hour
Nearby: Tweetsie Railroad, The Blowing Rock, Grandfather Mountain, Mast General Store
Directions: From Asheville, take I-40 East to Marion. In Marion take NC 221 to Boone. Just past intersection of NC 321 look for "Horn in the West" sign.

Mast General Store

The century-old Mast General Store is one of the best remaining examples of old country stores in America. It has featured traditional clothing and quality goods since 1883. There are four other Mast General Stores: Asheville, Boone, Hendersonville, and Waynesville. However, the store in Valle Crucis is the original and as such, is a landmark.

Location: Downtown Valle Crucis
Distance: 2 hours from Asheville
Address: Hwy. 194, Valle Crucis, NC 28691
Telephone: 963-6511
FAX: 963-8405
Website: www.mastgeneralstore.com
Hours: 6:30 a.m.-6:30 p.m. Monday through Saturday; 1-6 p.m. Sunday; Winter: 7 a.m.-6:30 p.m.
Of Note: Listed in the National Register of Historic Places.
Nearby: Horn in the West, Grandfather Mountain, Tweetsie Railroad
Directions: From Asheville take I-40 East to Marion. Take Hwy. 221 North to Hwy. 105. Take 105 North and turn left on Hwy. 194 into Valle Crucis.

Mountain Gateway Museum

The Mountain Gateway Museum offers visitors an opportunity to learn about North Carolina's mountain region. Exhibits, programs, and living history demonstrations depict area history from the earliest original inhabitants through the settlement period and into the twentieth century. The museum site includes a picnic area, amphitheater, two pioneer-era log cabins and the museum itself, all located on the banks of historic Mill Creek, a Catawba River tributary.

Location: Old Fort, NC
Distance: 45 minutes from Asheville
Address: 102 Water St., Old Fort, NC 28762
Telephone: 668-9259
FAX: 668-0041
Hours: 9 a.m.-5 p.m. Monday through Saturday; 2-5 p.m. Sundays. Open year-round, except all main holidays.
Fees: None
Allow: 1 hour

Directions: From Asheville take I-40 East to Old Fort and get off at Exit 73 onto Catawba Avenue. Go left 2 blocks to Water Street.

Museum of North Carolina Minerals

This small museum is located on the Blue Ridge Parkway and has displays of more than 300 varieties of minerals found in North Carolina. Interpretative exhibits, gift shop.

Location: Milepost 331 Blue Ridge Parkway, East of Asheville
Distance: 1-1½ hours
Address: Blue Ridge Parkway, Milepost 331
Telephone: 765-2761
Hours: 9 a.m.-5 p.m. Monday-Sunday, early May through October
Fees: None
Allow: 1-2 hours
Nearby: Craggy Gardens, Mount Mitchell State Park
Directions: Take Blue Ridge Parkway north out of Asheville to Milepost 331

Mystery Hill

Mystery Hill is a hands-on entertainment center for kids and grown-ups alike that has been around for over 50 years. The self-guided tour includes the famous Mystery House where you stand at a 45-degree angle and experience unusual gravitational effects, The Hall of Mystery with over 40 puzzles and science-based experiments, Bubble-Rama with bubble experiments including human-sized bubbles the kids can enter, The Native American Artifacts Museum with over 50,000 relics on display, and the Appalachian Heritage Museum (SEE listing earlier in this chapter).

Location: Between Boone and Blowing Rock, NC
Distance: 2 hours from Asheville
Address: 129 Mystery Hill Ln., Blowing Rock, NC 28605
Telephone: 264-2792
FAX: 262-3292
Website: www.mysteryhill-nc.com
Hours: June-August 8 a.m.-8 p.m.; September-May 9 a.m.-5 p.m.
Fees: Rates vary. Call for current prices. Senior, military, group, and AAA discounts are available
Allow: 1-2 hours
Nearby: The Blowing Rock, Grandfather Mountain, Tweetsie Railroad, Linville Caverns, Horn In The West, Mast General Store, Appalachian Cultural Museum
Directions: From Asheville, take I-40 East to Marion, take Hwy. 221 North to Blowing Rock, and then take 321 North four miles to Mystery Hill. From the Blue Ridge Parkway north out of Asheville, get off at mile marker 291. Take Hwy. 321 North 1½ miles.

Old Burke County Courthouse & Heritage Museum

Built in 1837, the old Burke County Courthouse is a restored 19th century courthouse with displays and exhibits about the building, the early court system, and local history. It features a restored turn-of-the-century lawyer's office, and the museum has changing exhibits on selected aspects of early Burke County life and culture. There is also a 20-minute slide presentation on Burke County heritage.

Location: Morganton, NC
Distance: 1½ hours from Asheville
Address: 102 East Union St. Morganton, NC 28655
          PO Box 915, Morganton, NC 28680
Telephone: 437-4104
Hours: Tuesday-Thursday 10-4 all year
Fees: None
Allow: ½-1 hour
Of Note: Listed in the National Register of Historic Places
Tips: If you love old courthouses, you will really enjoy this restoration. While they do not have a gift shop, they do sell books of regional interest.
Nearby: Quaker Meadows Plantation
Directions: From Asheville, take I-40 East to Exit 105. Turn left off the exit and continue straight into Morganton to Courthouse Square.

Old Fort Railroad Museum

Museum presents the impact of the railroads in the mountains of North Carolina. Train exhibits, original tools and signal lights, furniture and signs are housed in the historic 1890s vintage Old Fort Depot.

Location: Old Fort, NC
Distance: 3/4 hour
Address: 25 West Main Street, Old Fort, NC 28762
Telephone: 668-7223
Admission: None
Directions: Take I-40 East to Old Fort exit.

Old Wilkes Jail Museum

Built in 1859, Old Wilkes Jail was in continuous use as a jail until 1915. The first jail had four cells and included a residence for the jailer and his family. It is now restored as a history museum. One famous inmate, Tom Dula (of the famous ballad "Hang Down Your Head Tom Dooley") was incarcerated here until a change of venue was obtained by his defense attorney, former Governor Zebulon Vance.

Location: Wilkesboro, NC
Distance: 2 hours from Asheville

Address: 203 North Bridge Street, Wilkesboro, NC 28697
Telephone: (336) 667-3712
Hours: 9 a.m.-4 p.m., Monday-Friday; weekends by appointment
Fees: None
Allow: 45 minutes
Of Note: One of the best preserved examples of penal architecture in North Carolina
Directions: From Asheville take I-40 East to Hickory. Exit at Hickory and take Hwy. 16 North to downtown Wilkesboro. Turn right at the light and go through town past the courthouse. Take first left onto to Broad Street to behind the courthouse. Turn left onto North Street and then right onto North Bridge Street.

The Orchard at Altapass

The orchard at Altapass is a unique Blue Ridge experience! This is a great place to take the kids and enjoy an afternoon of Appalachian culture, music, and fun. In addition to the splendid apple orchards, activities include hayrides, storytelling, clogging, performances by local mountain musicians, cider and apple butter making, picnic lunches, craft exhibits, and much more. This is the real thing and a wonderful opportunity to not only have fun but also to learn.

Located on land right next to the Blue Ridge Parkway, the Orchard has always been an important economic base for the local folks. In the 1930s, the Orchard was split in two by the building of the parkway. Because of that proximity, it is the only private business with direct access to the parkway. Nearby railroad lines bring up to thirty trains a day to the area and train whistles are part of the Orchard experience. The trees grown at Altapass are of heritage varieties including the much-prized Virginia Beauty, King Luscious, and Stayman Winesap apples.

Location: Milepost 328.3 at Orchard Rd. near Spruce Pine, NC
Distance: 2 hours by way of the Blue Ridge Parkway
Address: PO Box 245, Little Switzerland, NC 28749
Telephone: (888) 765-9531, 765-9531
FAX: 766-9455
Website: www.altapassorchard.com
Hours: 10 a.m.-6 p.m. daily May-October;
Fees: Orchard: Free; Live music Saturday-Sunday 1:30-4 p.m.: Free; Other music performances: $5/person; Hayride, tour, and storytelling: $3/person, $2/child in school group; Homemade Hot Buffet and Picnic Lunches: $5-$8/person; Guided Tour of Art and Craft Studios: $40/hour; Guided Tour of Mitchell County: $40/hour; Naturalist Talks: $3/person.
Allow: 3 hours minimum
Of Note: The Orchard at Altapass dates back to 1908 when the Clinchfield Railroad worked its way through the mountains on its path to East

Tennessee. It was the railroad that bought the land and established the orchard. Earlier, in 1780, the Overmountain Men traveled along the nearby Orchard Road on the way to the Battle of Kings Mountain during the Revolutionary War. The Orchard is also known as the site which measured a national rainfall record during the Great Flood of 1916.

Nearby: The Blowing Rock, Grandfather Mountain, Linville Caverns
Directions: Take the Blue Ridge Parkway! Hard to find, even with directions by any other route. Get off 3 miles north of the Spruce Pine exit at Milepost 328.3 onto Orchard Rd. Look for little brown signs.

Presbyterian Historical Society

The Presbyterian Historical Society maintains this small religious museum that contains collections of items related to the history of the Presbyterian Church, US, and its missions.

Location: Montreat north of Black Mountain, NC
Distance: 20 minutes from Asheville
Address: 318 Georgia Terrace (PO Box 849), Montreat, NC 28757
Telephone: 669-7061
FAX: 669-5369
Hours: Monday-Friday 8:30 a.m.-4:30 p.m. Closed all major holidays.
Fees: $5 fee for any research done by the Society. Otherwise free.
Allow: ½-1 hour
Of Note: Presbyterian Church (USA) Department of History affiliated
Tips: Montreat is a world-famous retreat center and also the home of Montreat College. Be sure and take a walk around lovely Lake Susan near the Society building.
Directions: From Asheville, take I-40 East to Exit 64. Take Rte. 9 North through Black Mountain and the Montreat Gate. Continue on Assembly Dr. one mile and turn left onto Georgia Terrace.

Quaker Meadows Plantation

Quaker Meadows Plantation is the restored 1812 Catawba Valley Plantation House of Captain Charles McDowell, Jr. It was the site of the 1780 gathering of Overmountain Men, patriots that marched to Kings Mountain and helped defeat the British in the Revolutionary War. This authentically furnished house museum interprets antebellum culture in Burke Country from that era.

Location: Morganton, NC
Distance: 1 hour from Asheville
Address: 119 St. Mary Church Rd., Morganton, NC 28655
Telephone: 437-4104
Hours: Sunday 2-5 p.m. or by appointment
Fees: Adults $3, Under 12 are free

Allow: 1 hour
Of Note: Listed in the National Register of Historic Places
Nearby: Old Burke County Courthouse and Heritage Museum
Directions: From Asheville, take I-40 East to Exit 100. Turn left onto Hwy. 181 and go two blocks to St. Mary's Church Rd. Turn right and the plantation will be on the left.

Rutherford County Farm Museum

This great little museum located in Forest City has exhibits of antique farm equipment and items dating back to the earliest days of the nineteenth century. Two large murals, depicting the cycle of growing cotton and the early textile mills of the county, are outstanding features of the museum.

Location: Forest City
Distance: 45 minutes from Asheville
Address: 240 Depot Street, Forest City, NC 28043
Telephone: (828) 248-1248
Hours: Wed-Sat: 10-4
Fees: $2 adults, children free
Allow: 1 hour
Nearby: Rutherford County Museum
Directions: From Asheville take I-26 South to Exit 35. Take Hwy. 74 East to Alt 221 off of 74 to Forest City.

Rutherford County Museum

The Rutherford County Museum offers exhibits of arts and science, and also has a genealogical library, music studios, offices for cultural groups and a coffeehouse.

Location: Forest City
Distance: 45 minutes from Asheville
Address: 102 W. Main Street, Forest City 28043
Telephone: (828) 245-4000
Allow: 1 hour
Nearby: Rutherford County Farm Museum
Directions: From Asheville take I-26 South to Exit 35. Take Hwy. 74 East to Alt 221 off of 74 to Forest City.

Senator Sam J. Ervin Jr. Library

Located at the library of Western Piedmont Community College is a replica of the late Senator Ervin's home library, as it existed at 515 Lenoir Street in Morganton. A 7,500-item collection of Ervin's books and professional and family memorabilia is housed in the library. Senator Ervin is best known for serving as the Chairman of the Senate Watergate Committee in the 1970s.

Location: Morganton, NC
Distance: 1 hour from Asheville
Address: Western Piedmont Community College, 1001 Burkemont Ave.,
             Morganton, NC 28655
Telephone: 438-6195
Hours: Monday-Friday 8 a.m.-5 p.m.
Fees: None
Allow: 1 hour
Directions: From Asheville, take I-40 East to Morganton. Get off at Exit 103.
             Turn left at the light and go across the bridge on Burkemont Avenue.
             College ½ mile down on the right. The college's library building has
             a black roof.

Swannanoa Valley Museum

The museum resides in what was formerly the Black Mountain Fire Department and was founded in 1989 by the Swannanoa Valley Historical and Preservation Association. Exhibits focus on the Swannanoa Valley history and culture and
include Native American exhibits, artifacts and early tools, plants indigenous to
the region and photographic displays.

Location: Black Mountain, NC
Distance: 20 minutes from Asheville
Address: Corner State and Daugherty St., Black Mountain, NC 28711
Telephone: 669-9566
Hours: April-October: Tuesday-Saturday 10 a.m.-5 p.m.; Sunday 2-5 p.m.
Fees: None
Allow: ½-1 hour
Directions: From Asheville, take I-40 East to Black Mountain. Get off at Exit
             64 and turn left onto Hwy. 9. Proceed to State Street and turn left.
             The museum is two blocks on the left.

Trail of Faith

The Trail of Faith is a walk-through outdoor trail showing the terrible religious
persecution of the Waldensians in Northern Italy and their eventual settling in
Valdese. Over nine life-sized exhibits are on the trail with more being added yearly.
Summer evening dramas reenact the historic struggles of Waldensians (SEE "From
This Day Forward," earlier in this section). Combination trail/drama tickets are
available.

Location: Valdese, NC
Distance: 1 hour from Asheville
Address: 401 Church Street, Valdese, NC 28690
Telephone: (800) 635-4778, 874-1893
FAX: 879-2089

Website: www.valdese.com/trail.htm
Hours: Trail: Saturday-Sunday 2-5 p.m., Weekdays by appointment.
Drama: July-August, times and dates vary, please call ahead
Fees: Trail: Adults $5, Students $3; Tour group rates available
Drama: $10 Adults, $8 Seniors & Students
Trail/Drama Combo: $12 Adults & Seniors, $10 Students
Allow: 1-2 hours for the trail, 2½ for the drama
Tips: Located at the same complex as From This Day Forward mentioned earlier in this chapter. Gift shop and concessions are inside at the Visitor Center on the site.
Nearby: Waldensian Museum, From This Day Forward
Directions: From Asheville, take I-40 East to Exit 111. Take Carolina Street and turn left onto Main Street. Turn right on Church Street and follow the From This Day Forward signs.

Turchin Center for Visual Arts

The Turchin Center has exhibits that focus on a blend of new and historically important artworks, and features the work of regional, national and international artists.

Location: Boone, NC
Distance: 2 hours from Asheville
Address: 423 West King Street, Boone, NC 28608
Telephone: 262-3017
Admission: Free
Website: www.turchincenter.org
Directions: From Asheville, take I-40 East to Marion and take Hwy. 221 North to Blowing Rock. Then take US 321 North to Boone.

Tweetsie Railroad

Tweetsie Railroad is an exciting Western theme park. An authentic early American, full-size coal fired steam locomotive takes you on a 3-mile trip over a scenic route with an enacted Indian raid. There is a complete old-time western town that features live entertainment at the Palace Variety Show. A petting zoo, gift shops, and rides for the kids make for great family entertainment.

Location: Between Boone and Blowing Rock, NC
Distance: 2 hours from Asheville
Address: Hwy. 321 (PO Box 388), Blowing Rock, NC 28605
Telephone: (800) 526-5740
FAX: 264-2234
Website: www.tweetsie-railroad.com
Hours: 9 a.m.-6 p.m. mid-May-late August daily and late August-October Friday-Sunday only.

Halloween Ghost Train: Every weekend on Friday and Saturday, and daily the last week in October. Gates open at 7:30 p.m.; $15 includes train ride and Haunted House activities.

Fees: $23 adults; $16 children (3-12); $19 seniors; 2 & under free
Allow: 5-6 hours to see park and do all rides and activities.
Of Note: Oldest operating family theme park in North Carolina.
Tips: An excellent little railroad museum, The Frank T. Williams Railroad Museum, is also located at Tweetsie Railroad.
Directions: Exit at Milepost 291, Boone Exit, off Blue Ridge Parkway. Tweetsie Railroad is located on US 321 between Boone and Blowing Rock. Faster route: Take I-40 from Asheville and take Hwy. 221 North at Marion. Proceed to Linville and take Hwy. 105 North into Boone. In Boone take 321 South 5 miles.

Waldensian Museum

This museum covers the history of the Waldensians from their life in Italy to their settlement in WNC at Valdese over one hundred years ago.

Location: Downtown Valdese, NC
Distance: 1 hour from Asheville
Address: 109 East Main St., Valdese, NC 28690
Telephone: 874-2531, 879-9010
Website: www.valdese.com/museum.htm
Hours: During "From This Day Forward" 5-8 p.m. Thursday-Sunday; otherwise Sundays only 3-5 p.m. or by appointment.
Fees: None
Allow: 1 hour
Nearby: From This Day Forward, Trail of Faith
Directions: From Asheville, take I-40 East to Valdese, Exit 111.

Wilkes Art Gallery

The Wilkes Art Gallery is a small, nonprofit art gallery that has changing monthly exhibitions of local, regional, student, and nationally known artists. A broad range of contemporary art—oils, watercolors, pottery, sculpture, etc.—are shown in the two primary gallery spaces: The Winkler Gallery and the Vickery Gallery.

Location: North Wilkesboro, NC
Distance: 2 hours from Asheville
Address: 800 Elizabeth St. North Wilkesboro, NC 28659
Telephone: (336) 667-2841
Hours: Tuesday-Friday 10 a.m.-5 p.m.; Saturday noon-4 p.m.
Fees: None
Allow: ½-1 hour
Tips: The Gallery also has a gift shop with hand-crafted items.
Nearby: Old Wilkes Jail Museum, Ben Long Frescoes

Directions: From Asheville, take I-40 East to Exit 131 just beyond Hickory. Take NC 16 North to Wilkesboro and continue through, crossing the Yadkin River. Once you cross the river, take a left onto 6th Street and follow it across the railroad tracks and up a big hill. Look for a cemetery on your right and then bear sharply to the left onto Hinshaw Street. Go two blocks and look for the art gallery on your left at the juncture of Hinshaw, Trodgon, and Elizabeth streets.

West of Asheville

Allison-Deaver House

The Allison-Deaver house is one of Western North Carolina's finest surviving examples of early 19th-century architecture. Located in Transylvania County in Brevard, NC, the superbly restored house and farmstead are open to the public. The main house—a two story, wood timber structure with a full two-tiered porch—sits atop a steep sided hill overlooking an old Indian trail which later became a main road for settlers into the Davidson River region of what was Old Buncombe County. The house built by Benjamin Allison in 1815, was added onto by William Deaver in 1840.

Location: Brevard, NC
Distance: 45 minutes from Asheville
Address: Hwy. 280, Brevard, NC 28712
Telephone: 884-5137, Transylvania Historical Society
Hours: April-October: Friday-Saturday 10 a.m.-4 p.m., Sunday 1-5 p.m.
Fees: Donations accepted
Allow: 1 hour
Of Note: Still a work in progress, the restoration is being sponsored by the Transylvania County Historical Society. It is being operated as a house restoration museum at this time where visitors can see various stages of restoration. Listed in the National Register of Historic Places. The oldest frame house in Western North Carolina
Nearby: Brevard Music Center, Spiers Gallery, Brevard Area Waterfalls, Pisgah National Forest
Directions: From Asheville, take I-26 East or US 25 South to Airport Rd. Follow Airport Rd. south towards Brevard. The Allison-Deaver House is on a hill just before you reach the intersection of NC 64. From Hendersonville, take Hwy. 64 West to the intersection of NC 280. Turn right. The Allison-Deaver House will be a short distance on your left.

Brevard Music Center

In operation for more than 60 years, the Brevard Music Center is known for its premiere festivals, pleasant setting and the highest standards in music education. With more than fifty concert events scheduled each year, the Music Center provides not only wonderful entertainment but a unique training environment for over 400 gifted students from across the nation.

Location: Brevard, NC
Distance: 45 minutes from Asheville
Address: 1000 Probart St. (PO Box 312), Brevard, NC 28712
Telephone: 884-2011
FAX: 884-2036
Website: www.brevardmusic.org
Hours: Box Office: Monday-Wednesday noon-4:30 p.m. Other days noon-
             show intermission. Performances June 26-August 10.
Fees: Vary with performances
Allow: Performances average two hours.
Tips: Contact Box Office for schedule brochure.
Nearby: Pisgah National Forest, Brevard Area Waterfalls.
Directions: From Asheville, take NC 280 South to Brevard. From downtown
             Brevard follow Probart Street to the Brevard Music Center. Street
             signs mark the way.

Canton Area Historical Museum

The Canton Area Historical Museum is a history heritage museum focusing
on the culture and history of Canton and Haywood County. The museum has
extensive photo archives, exhibits, as well as coverage of Champion Mill and the
area's early logging railroads.

Location: Canton, NC
Distance: 30 minutes from Asheville
Address: 58 Park St., Canton, NC 28716
Telephone: 646-3412
Hours: Monday-Friday 10 a.m.-noon, 1-4 p.m.; weekends by appointment
             only
Fees: None
Allow: 1 hour
Nearby: Pressley Sapphire Mine
Directions: From Asheville, take I-40 West to East Canton, Exit 37. Take 19/23
             South to Park Street in Canton.

Cherokee County Historical Museum

Housed in the old Carnegie Library in downtown Murphy, the Cherokee
County Historical Museum has a collection of more than two thousand artifacts
from the time of the infamous Trail of Tears. Many of the artifacts were collected
in Cherokee County, excavated from Indian mounds, or purchased from area
citizens over the past seventy years. For the most part, the museum reflects the
lifestyle of the Cherokee Indians, although some exhibits also focus on the early
white settlers as well as the 16th century Spanish explorers who passed through
the area in search of gold and other precious metals.

Location: Murphy, NC
Distance: 2 hours from Asheville
Address: 87 Peachtree St., Murphy, NC 28906
Telephone: 837-6792
FAX: 837-6792
Hours: Monday-Friday 9 a.m.-5 p.m.; Closed national holidays.
Fees: None
Allow: 1-2 hours
Of Note: Museum building listed in National Register of Historic Places
Tips: The museum also has an exhibit of antique dolls.
Directions: From Asheville, take I-40 West. Take Exit 27 to 74 West. Follow 74 West to NC 19. Follow 19 into Murphy. The Museum is right behind the courthouse in the center of town.

Cherokee Indian Reservation

The 56,000-acre Cherokee Indian Reservation is home to more than 10,000 Eastern Band of the Cherokee members. Each year, thousands of visitors from across the country come to discover this enchanted land and to share the natural mountain beauty the Cherokee have treasured for centuries.

A visit to Cherokee is like stepping into the past. You'll find a nation still linked to ancient customs and traditions that enable them to live in harmony with nature as their ancestors did. The Reservation, known as the Qualla Boundary, has a number of outstanding attractions. Among them is the Museum of the Cherokee Indian, Qualla Arts & Crafts Mutual (the most outstanding Indian-owned and operated arts & crafts co-op in the country), "Unto These Hills" Outdoor Drama, Oconaluftee Indian Village, Cherokee Heritage Museum and Gallery, and Tribal Bingo and Gaming Casino.

There are 28 campgrounds on the Reservation, and many motels and cabins. Be sure and visit the Cherokee Visitor Center on Main Street in downtown Cherokee. They have information available about accommodations, dining and attractions.

The Reservation also boasts more than 30 miles of regularly stocked trout streams. The fishing is excellent, and every year trophy rainbow and brown trout are caught.

Location: Cherokee, NC
Distance: 2 hours from Asheville
Address: Cherokee Visitor Center, Main St. (PO Box 460), Cherokee, NC 28719
Telephone: General Information (800) 438-1601, 497-9195
Tribal Bingo (800) 410-1254
Casino Information (800) 438-1601
Unto These Hills 497-2111
Qualla Arts & Crafts Mutual 497-3103
Museum of the Cherokee Indian 497-3481

FAX:	497-3220
E-mail:	chero@dnet.net
Websites:	www.cherokee-nc.com
	www.cherokeesmokies.com
	www.cherokeemuseu,.org
	www.oconalufteevillage.com
Hours:	Museum open June-August 9 a.m.-8 p.m. Monday-Saturday, 9 a.m.-5 p.m. Sunday; September-June: 9 a.m.-5 p.m. daily.
	Qualla Arts & Crafts Mutual open daily June-August: 8 a.m.-8 p.m.; September-October: 8 a.m.-6 p.m.; November-May: 8 a.m.-4:30 p.m.
	Oconaluftee Village open daily May 15-October 25 9 a.m.-5:30 p.m.
	Cherokee Heritage Museum: April-November: 9 a.m.-5 p.m. daily; May-October: 9 a.m.-10 p.m. daily
	Unto These Hills open nightly, except Sundays, mid-June through August
	Harrah's Cherokee Casino open all year, 24 hours a day
	Cherokee Tribal Bingo open daily at 4 p.m. year-round
	Trout Fishing last Saturday in March-February
Fees:	Museum: $6 adults, $4 children 6-12, Under 6 free.
	Qualla Arts & Crafts Mutual: (Free)
	Oconaluftee Village: $12 adults, $5 children 6-13, under 6 free
	Cherokee Heritage Museum: $8 adults, $4 children 6-10, under 6 free
	Unto These Hills: $11 adults, $5 children 12 and under; $14 reserved seats, all ages
	Trout Fishing: $5/day
	Campgrounds (Rates vary)
Allow:	Plan to spend the whole day
Nearby:	Great Smoky Mountains National Park, Nantahala National Forest
Directions:	From Asheville, take I-40 West to Exit 27. Follow signs to Cherokee on Hwy. 19 South (may be congested in summer).

Cradle of Forestry

The Cradle of Forestry, a National Historic Site, is located in Pisgah National Forest. It is the site where scientific forestry was first practiced in America over 85 years ago. In 1889, George Vanderbilt began buying land southwest of Asheville to build a country estate. His plans included a palatial home surrounded by a large game preserve. To manage the forest property, Vanderbilt hired Gifford Pinchot, father of American forestry. Pinchot's management proved profitable through the sale of wood products, so Vanderbilt purchased an additional 100,000 acres in the mountains surrounding Mt. Pisgah. Pisgah Forest, as it became known, was the first large tract of managed forest land in America. It later became the nucleus of the Pisgah National Forest.

In 1895, a German forester, Dr. Carl Schenck, succeeded Pinchot as manager of Pisgah Forest. Schenck intensified forest operations and three years later launched the first forestry school in America, the Biltmore Forest School. The school lasted until 1914.

In 1968, Congress passed the Cradle of Forestry in America Act, establishing 6,400 acres of the Pisgah National Forest to preserve and make available to the public the birthplace of forestry and forestry education in America.

Public facilities at the Cradle of Forestry provide visitors with exciting programs and displays on the rich history of American forestry. The Forest Discovery Center, two paved interpretative trails, and living history exhibits are major attractions at the historic site. A 1900 portable steam powered sawmill and a restored 1915 Climax locomotive are also on exhibit.

Location: Pisgah District of the Pisgah National Forest
Distance: 1 hour from Asheville
Address: Cradle of Forestry, Pisgah National Forest, 1001 Pisgah Hwy., Pisgah Forest, NC 28768
Telephone: 877-3130
FAX: 884-5823
Website: www.cradleofforestry.com
Hours: Open April to October, 9 a.m.-5 p.m.
Fees: $4 adults, $2 children 6-17, under 6 free
Allow: 3 hours
Of Note: National Historic Site
Nearby: Brevard Area Waterfalls, Sliding Rock, Looking Glass Falls, Pisgah Forest State Fish Hatchery, Pisgah Center for Wildlife Education
Directions: From Asheville: Take Airport Rd. (NC 280) off of Hendersonville Hwy. in Arden. Continue on 280 past Asheville Airport to Wal-Mart Shopping Plaza just before Brevard. Turn right onto US 276 into Pisgah Forest to Cradle of Forestry. From Hendersonville: Take US 64 West from Hendersonville to intersection of Hwy. 280 and US 276 at the Wal-Mart Shopping Plaza. Continue straight through light to US 276 into Pisgah Forest and Cradle of Forestry.

Franklin Gem & Mineral Museum

Housed in the historic old jail (circa 1850) of Macon County, the Franklin Gem and Mineral Museum has many fascinating exhibits concerning North Carolina gems and minerals. On display is a 2¼ pound ruby along with other fascinating stones.

Location: Downtown Franklin, NC
Distance: 1½ to 2 hours from Asheville
Address: 25 Phillips St., Franklin, NC 28734
Telephone: 369-7831
Hours: May 1-Oct. 31 10 a.m.-4 p.m. Monday-Saturday

Fees: None
Allow: ½-1 hour
Directions: From Asheville, take I-40 West to Exit 27. Take Hwy. 74 West to Hwy. 441 South (Exit 81). Follow 441 South to Franklin.

Great Smoky Mountains Railroad

The Great Smoky Mountains Railroad gives passengers a chance to recapture the thrills and romance of early trains with its excursions through the mountain countryside. Steam and diesel locomotives pull authentic passenger cars on half-day excursions through the mountains and valleys of Western North Carolina.

There are open cars, coaches and club cars to choose from, as well as a popular weekly dinner train. Excursions leave from a number of sites: Dillsboro, Bryson City and Andrews. The trains run on passenger schedules for half-day round trips. Passengers ride in comfortable, reconditioned coaches, crown coaches, club cars, cabooses and even open cars. The club cars and dining cars have historic pasts and have been lovingly restored, as have the cabooses.

A full excursion schedule is offered, including summer season "Raft and Rail" trips that combine a train ride and whitewater rafting experience into one package, Gourmet Dinner Trains, and many other special events. The Caboose is available for group rental.

Location: Dillsboro, Bryson City and Andrews, NC
Distance: 1½-3 hours depending upon destination
Address: Great Smoky Mountains Railroad, 1 Front St., Box 397, Dillsboro, NC 28752
Telephone: (800) 872-4681, 586-8811
FAX: 586-8806
Website: www.gsmr.com
Hours: March-December, times vary. Train schedules are available at Asheville and Hendersonville Visitor Centers.
Fees: In-Season Standard Excursions: Adult fares range from $28 diesel-$40 steam; Children 3-12 $13 diesel-$15 steam. Off-season discounts available. Prices vary on special events.
Allow: 3½ to 4½ hours round trip.
Tips: Very popular attraction. Make reservations well in advance if you wish to go during the leaf season. Reservations suggested at all times. Write for or pick up a brochure at Visitor Centers.
Directions: From Asheville, take I-40 West to Exit 27. Take 19/23 Hwy. 74 West to Exit 81 (Dillsboro). Go to first red light and turn left on Haywood Street. Proceed to post office and turn right onto Depot Street.

Harrah's Cherokee Casino & Hotel

Located on a site that was known as the "Magic Waters" in Cherokee is the visually stunning complex of Harrah's Cherokee Great Smoky Mountains Casino.

Superbly designed to blend in with the breathtaking natural surroundings beside a sparkling trout stream, the huge 175,000 square-foot casino building is barely visible from Hwy. 19. The approach drive features landscaping highlighting native plants and trees and nearing the casino, one is greeted by massive stone columns and a waterfall. The overall effect upon first seeing the building in its natural setting is that of a remote mountain lodge nestled deep in some immense wilderness.

The casino cost $85 million to build and is situated on 37 acres, tucked tightly between two mountains that reflect the bluish haze that gives the Great Smoky Mountains their name, featuring virgin forest and a stunning panoramic backdrop. Designed by one of the nation's leading casino and destination resort design firms, the Minneapolis-based Cunningham Group, Harrah's Cherokee Casino is an architectural triumph. Inside, the mountain lodge theme is continued, with colorful Native American art and artifacts, the use of natural materials indigenous to the area and a truly spectacular display of neon lightning in the ceiling that comes to life, complete with rolling bursts of thunder whenever a jackpot is won at one of the 1,800 video gaming machines.

In the 60,000 square-foot gaming area, guests can play at the video gaming machines, which include the innovative "Lock-n-Roll," which has a second-spin feature on all or some of the reels. Additional video gaming options include the popular favorites such as Poker, Blackjack, Craps and Keno. Guests can also take in a variety of shows and performances highlighting nationally famous entertainers at the 20,000 square-foot entertainment area complete with a 1,500-seat concert hall and space for special events and festivals, or select from three full-scale restaurants: the 400-seat Fresh market Square Buffet, the 125-seat Seven Sisters Restaurant, and a 35-seat sports-themed Winning Steaks Deli, complete with an actual race car coming through a wall.

Located conveniently adjacent to the main gaming hall is a retail shop featuring not only Harrah's line of gifts but also top quality crafts from Cherokee crafters. Guests who park in the 1,800-space parking lot are provided with shuttle bus service. Harrah's Casino also boasts a world-class 252-room hotel that is connected to the casino via the Sky Bridge walkway.

Open seven days a week, 24 hours a day, Harrah's Cherokee Casino is owned by the Eastern Band of Cherokee Indians and managed by Harrah's Entertainment, Inc., the premier name in the casino entertainment industry. The Cherokee Casino is the newest addition to a company that has been in business since 1937, when William Fisk Harrah opened the doors to his first bingo parlor in Reno, Nevada. Harrah's Entertainment, Inc., has evolved over the years into a company with more than $1.6 billion in revenues and more than 23,000 employees at casinos in nine states entertaining some 28 million guests a year. The casino at Cherokee alone employs more than 1,000 people, the majority from the surrounding Cherokee community. It is the third tribal-owned gaming facility managed by Harrah's and the only facility of its kind between Tunica, Miss., and Atlantic City, N.J. Harrah's Entertainment, Inc., besides being one of the biggest companies of its type, also boasts a reputation as a very community-minded group, the best in the gaming industry.

While gaming is strictly for adults in the alcohol-free casino, Harrah's has provided for the safety and entertainment of children in the Planet-4-Kidz section. The Mississippi-based child-care center specialists, Planet-4-Kidz, operate the 6,200 square-foot center away from the casino floor. Amenities range from toys to games to art supplies, a video wall with a karaoke stage and activities that teach something of the Cherokee culture and heritage, to a 3,000 square-foot video arcade for teenagers. Planet-4-Kidz also features its own restaurant, Perky's Pizza, completely contained within the child-care center. The center's features and activities are geared to the safety, well-being and entertainment of family members from six weeks to teenagers. At peak operation it can accommodate about 75 children, and uses a ratio of one staff member per three children under the age of 3, and an approximate ratio of one to five for children ages 3-12. As a security measure, the facility uses a Sensormatic system which requires both parents and children to wear non-removable wristbands. Children are released only to the adults with corresponding wristbands. Harrah's maintains a zero-tolerance policy regarding underage gambling (18 is the legal age in North Carolina), and was awarded the first corporate award by the National Council on Problem Gaming for its leadership role in fighting the problem of underage gaming.

Harrah's also offers their Total Gold Card, a player benefit card, free of charge. The Gold Card secures, with use, valuable rewards, complimentary gifts and benefits at Harrah's casinos across the country. The Cherokee Casino also offers valet parking, meeting space rooms, free sodas, coffee and tea and a specialty coffee bar. The casino had a grand opening to the public on Nov. 13, 1997.

Location: Cherokee, NC
Distance: 1½ to 2 hours from Asheville; may take longer during the peak summer tourist season because Hwy. 19 leading into Cherokee through Maggie Valley from Asheville is a two-lane mountain road.
Address: Harrah's Cherokee Smoky Mountains Casino, Intersection of Hwy. 19 and Business Rte. 441, P.O. Box 1959, Cherokee, NC 28719
Telephone: (800) 427-7247, 497-7777
Hotel: (800) 427-7247, 497-7777
FAX: 497-5076
E-mail: (Addressee)@ harrahs.cherokee.com
Website: www.harrahs.com/tour/tour_cherokee.html
Hours: Casino: 24 hours a day, seven days a week, all year
Seven Sisters Restaurant: Wednesday, Thursday & Sunday 5-10 p.m.; Friday & Saturday 5-11 p.m.
Fresh Market Square Buffet: 10:30 a.m.-10 p.m. Sunday-Thursday; 10:30 a.m.-11 p.m. Friday and Saturday
Winning Steaks Deli: Open daily, noon-2 a.m.
Hotel: Harrah's Casino Hotel: 252-room world-class hotel located next to the casino. Connects to casino through Sky Bridge walkway. Indoor pool, hot tub and exercise facility. 5-story parking garage with valet service. Shelu Restaurant in hotel offering room service. Harrah's

Casino, Intersection of Hwy. 19 and Business Rte. 441, Cherokee, NC 28719. 497-7777. $129-$199, discount for Player's Card members. www.harrahs.com

Fees: None to enter casino, parking is free. Childcare at Planet 4 Kidz: $5/hour under 3 years; $3.50/hour over 3 years.

Of Note: 2,400 video gaming machines, no dealers. Casino has 50,000 square feet of Class III gaming space. Class III games are those that require "skill or dexterity." Jackpot limit is $25,000.

Games include video re-spin (Lock-n-Roll) with Wild Cherry, Double Diamonds, and more; Video Blackjack; Video Poker; Video Craps and Video Keno.

Harrah's Cherokee Casino is alcohol-free, as is the Cherokee Reservation on which it is located.

Nearby: Cherokee Indian Reservation, Great Smoky Mountains National Park, Nantahala National Forest, Great Smoky Mountains Railway

Directions: From Asheville take I-40 West to Exit 27. Follow US-74 West through Waynesville. Take Hwy. 441 North to Cherokee. Take right at first light. Harrah's is at the next intersection.

Highlands Nature Center

Live animal exhibits, garden tours, and children's programs are all facets of this excellent nature center. Their emphasis is on Southern Appalachian biodiversity and geology. They also have exhibitions of Native American artifacts and culture

Location: Highlands, NC
Distance: 1-1½ hours from Asheville
Address: 930 Horse Cove Rd. (PO Box 580), Highlands, NC 28741
Telephone: 526-2623
FAX: 526-2797
Hours: March-October: Monday-Saturday 10 a.m.-5 p.m.
Fees: General Admission: Free; Children's Programs: usually $5 per child
Allow: 1-2 hours
Nearby: Pisgah National Forest, Brevard area waterfalls
Directions: From Asheville, take NC 280 West to Brevard (280 begins as Airport Rd., accessible from US 25 or I-26). NC 280 joins NC 64 just before reaching Brevard. Follow 64 West to Highlands. In Highlands, turn left at the first light onto Main Street. Proceed through the next light (Main Street turns into Horse Cove Rd.) and look for the Nature Center on your left.

Jackson County Museum

Exhibits offer insights into the events and people of the Western North Carolina Mountains, especially focusing on Jackson County from prehistoric times to the present. Exhibits change every six weeks.

Location: Sylva, NC
Distance: 1 1/2 hours
Address: 773 West Main Street, Sylva, NC 28779
Telephone: 586-1447
Admission: None
Directions: Take I-40 West from Asheville to Exit 27, then Hwy. 23 South to Sylva.

John C. Campbell Folk School

Established in 1925, the John C. Campbell Folk School is one of America's premier folk art schools. Listed on the National Register of Historic Places, the school offers a wide range of instruction in traditional and contemporary art, crafts, music, dance, nature studies, gardening and cooking.

Location: Brasstown, NC
Distance: 2 hours from Asheville
Address: One Folk School Rd., Brasstown, NC 28902
Telephone: (800) 365-5724, 837-2775
Admission: Free
Website: www.folkschool.org
Directions: I-40 West to Exit 27, US 19/23/74. Take 23/74 to Waynesville/ Sylva. At Exit 81 take US 23/441 South to Franklin. In Franklin, the US 441 bypass merges with US 64 West. Follow 64 West from Franklin towards Hayesville. Eight miles west of Hayesville, turn left on Settawig Rd. Follow the signs to the Folk School.

Macon County Historical Society & Museum

Housed in the historic Pendergrass Building (circa 1904), the Macon County Museum collection including clothing, antiques, photographs, textiles, documents, and other artifacts pertaining to the history and culture of Macon County and other areas of Western North Carolina. They also have extensive genealogy files and archives relating to local history.

Location: Franklin, NC
Distance: 1½-2 hours from Asheville
Address: 36 West Main St., Franklin, NC 28734
Telephone: 524-9758
Hours: Monday-Friday 10 a.m.-4 p.m.
Fees: Donations accepted
Allow: 1 hour
Of Note: The Pendergrass Building is listed in the National Register of Historic Places.
Nearby: Franklin Gem and Mineral Museum
Directions: From Asheville, take I-40 West to Exit 27. Take Hwy. 74 West to Hwy. 441 South (Exit 81). Follow 441 South to Franklin.

Mountain Heritage Center

This museum highlights Southern Appalachian history through exhibitions, publications, educational programs and demonstrations and promotes the rich mountain traditions. The "Migration of the Scotch Irish People" is the center's permanent exhibit. The center also produces temporary exhibits highlighting blacksmithing, mountain trout, the southern handicraft movement, the enduring popularity of handwoven coverlets and other subjects.

Location: Campus of Western Carolina University in Cullowee, NC
Distance: 1 hours from Asheville
Address: H.F. Robinson Building, Western Carolina University, Cullowee, NC 28723
Telephone: 227-7129
Website: www.wcu.edu/mhc
Hours: 8 a.m.-5 p.m. Monday through Friday; 2-5 p.m. Sundays June through October only.
Fees: None
Allow: 1 to 2 hours
Directions: From Asheville, take I-40 West to Exit 27 and follow Hwy. 19/23, Hwy. 74 to Exit 85 for Western Carolina University.

Mountain Museum

Local history from mountain men to the 1920s. On display are horse-drawn farming equipment, quilts, area photographs, tools, Civil War artifacts and mountain lore.

Location: Waynesville, NC
Distance: 1/2 hour
Address: 1856 Dellwood Rd., Waynesville, NC 28786
Telephone: 926-1901
Admission: None
Directions: Take I-40 West to Waynesville.

Museum of North Carolina Handicrafts

Located in the historic 1875 Shelton House, the Museum of North Carolina Handicrafts features a unique the works of some of the state's most renowned artisans. Special collections of pottery are exhibited in nearly every room of the Shelton House including examples from Seagrove and rare pieces from Jugtown Potteries and Pisgah Potteries. There is also an extensive collection of native American artifacts as well. Other rooms house collections of coverlets, quilts, china painting, jewelry, period furniture and musical instruments.

Location: Downtown Waynesville, NC
Distance: 1 hour from Asheville
Address: 307 Shelton St., Waynesville, NC 28786

Telephone: 452-1551
Hours: May-October: 10 a.m.-4 p.m. Tuesday through Friday. Call to confirm.
Fees: $4 adults, $1 children under 12
Allow: 1 hour
Of Note: Located in 1875 Shelton House which is listed in the National Register of Historic Places.
Directions: From Asheville take I-40 West to Exit 27 and follow NC 19/23 South to Waynesville onto Hwy. 276. This road turns into Main Street. Past the 1st Baptist Church bear left 2 blocks to intersection of 276 and Shelton Street. Museum is on corner.

Perry's Water Garden

Located in Franklin, Perry's Water Garden has the country's largest collection of aquatic gardens. Owner Perry Slocum has created over 147 ponds on 13 acres featuring exotic sunken gardens highlighted with old fashioned antique rose beds and other above-ground flowers. Naturalized grass and dirt paths meander throughout. In addition to the multitude of iris, water lilies, and lotus, the gardens are home to thousands of brightly colored koi and goldfish. If you love flowers and gardens, this center is a must! Also, their outstanding retail center offers fish, plants, and other water garden-related items.

Location: Franklin, NC
Distance: 2 hours from Asheville
Address: Gibson Aquatic Farm Rd., Franklin, NC 28734
Telephone: 524-3264
FAX: 369-2050
Hours: May-September 9 a.m.-5 p.m.
Fees: None
Allow: 2 hours
Tips: Wear comfortable walking shoes.
Nearby: Franklin Gem and Mineral Museum, Cherokee Indian Reservation
Directions: From Asheville, take I-40 West to Exit 27. Take Hwy. 74 West to Hwy. 441 South (Exit 81). Follow 441 for 14 miles and turn right on Sanders Town Rd., then right on Bryson City Rd. for 2 miles. Turn right on Cowee Creek for 1 mile, then left on Leatherman Gap Rd. ¼ mile. Turn right onto Gibson Aquatic Farm Rd.

Pisgah Center for Wildlife Education

Located in the Pisgah National Forest at the site of the Pisgah Forest State Fish Hatchery, the Pisgah Center for Wildlife Education features a reception and orientation area the includes aquarium exhibits, the NC Wild Store gift shop, and wildlife exhibits. Run by the NC Wildlife Resources Commission, this facility is a wonderful place to become acquainted with the diverse wildlife and habitats of the Blue Ridge and Appalachian mountains.

Besides the fascinating dish hatchery, with thousands of trout both large and small, informative exhibits strung along an interpretive trail are another of the Center's popular aspects. The outdoor exhibits on the trail include stations that focus on wildlife conservation, the geology of the Blue Ridge Mountains, unique NC habitats, preservation of streams and wetlands, responsibility and safety in the woods, the science of wildlife management, NC Wild Education Sites, the ecology of wetlands, and ways to get involved in wildlife conservation.

Location: Pisgah District of the Pisgah National Forest
Distance: 1 hour from Asheville
Address: 475-C Fish Hatchery Rd. (PO Box 1600), Pisgah Forest, NC 28768
Telephone: 877-4423
Website: www.wildlife.state.nc.us/ConservationEd/pisgah
Hours: 8 a.m.-5 p.m. daily except Thanksgiving, Christmas, & New Year's Day; Fish raceways are open daily 8 a.m.-4 p.m.
Fees: None
Allow: 2-3 hours
Tips: Great place to take the kids. A perfect blend of education and fun. The trout at the hatchery will be a vacation highlight!
Nearby: Brevard area waterfalls, Sliding Rock, Looking Glass Falls, Cradle of Forestry
Directions: From Asheville: Take I-26 East or US 25 South to Airport Rd. (NC 280). Follow 280 past the airport to the Wal-Mart Shopping Plaza just before Brevard. Turn right onto US 276 into Pisgah Forest. Turn left onto Forest Service Rd. 475.   From Hendersonville: Take US 64 West to the intersection of Hwy. 280 and US 276 at the Wal-Mart. Take US 276 into Pisgah Forest. Turn left onto Forest Service Rd. 475.

Scottish Tartans Museum & Heritage Center

Located in Franklin, NC, this establishment focuses on the history of Scottish Tartans—how they were woven and used in dress over the centuries since 325. Cultural programs of weaving, music, and dance are also provided at the Center throughout the year by Friends of the Museum and volunteers. Ongoing educational programs and exhibits interpret Scottish history and culture, including migrations of the Scots, concentrating on the Scots who settled in Western North Carolina. The museum is over 2,200 square feet and contains the official registry of all publicly known tartans and is the only American extension of the Scottish Tartans Society in Pitlochry, Scotland. Visitors are invited to view their family tartan on computer and trace their Scottish heritage in the tartan research library.

Location: Franklin, NC
Distance: 1½-2 hours from Asheville
Address: 86 East Main St., Franklin, NC 28734

Telephone: 524-7472
FAX: 5241092
Website: www.scottishtartans.org
Hours: Monday-Saturday 10 a.m.-5 p.m., Sunday 1-5 p.m.
Fees: $1 Adults, 10 & under free
Allow: 1-2 hours
Tips: The Center has a great gift shop offering a large selection of Scottish and Celtic treasures. All tartan items imported from Scotland. The Highlands Pipes and Drums are the official band of the Scottish Tartans Museum and perform at numerous events regionally. Contact the museum for their schedule.
Nearby: Franklin Gem and Mineral Museum, Cherokee Indian Reservation
Directions: From Asheville, take I-40 West to Exit 27. Hwy. 74 West to Hwy. 441 South (Exit 81). Take the first Franklin exit at the Days Inn, and go straight into town to Main Street.

Spiers Gallery

The Spiers Gallery, located at Brevard College's Sims Art Center, offers eight rotating exhibits of visiting or local artists' work. They also feature a modest collection of American art prints, paintings, sculpture, and ceramics.

Location: Brevard, NC
Distance: 40 minutes from Asheville
Address: Brevard College, 400 N. Broad St., Brevard, NC 25712
Telephone: 883-8292
FAX: 884-3790
Website: http://tornado.brevard.edu/art/Galleries.html
Hours: Monday-Friday 10 a.m.-5:30 p.m.
Fees: None
Allow: 1 hour
Nearby: Brevard Area Waterfalls, Pisgah National Forest, Brevard Music Center
Directions: From Asheville, take NC 280 South to Brevard. The College will be on your left. Turn through the main gate. Turn left at the "T" intersection. At the next intersection take another left. Sims Art Center will be the first building on your right.

Unto These Hills

One of America's most popular outdoor dramas, "Unto These Hills" is the tragic and triumphant story of the Cherokee Indians. Set against the backdrop of the Great Smoky Mountains, the drama is presented under the stars on three stages in the beautiful Mountainside Theatre. Since opening in 1950, "Unto These Hills" has been seen by over five million people. The outdoor theatre is located on the Cherokee Indian Reservation in Cherokee, North Carolina. (SEE Section Five, Chapter 2 "Cherokee Indian Reservation")

Location:	Cherokee, NC
Distance:	2 hours from Asheville
Address:	Hwy. 441 (PO Box 398), Cherokee, NC 28719
Telephone:	497-2111
FAX:	497-6987
Website:	www.cherokee-nc.com or www.dnet.net/~cheratt
Hours:	Box Office in-season: 9 a.m.-10 p.m.; otherwise 9 a.m.-4:30 p.m. Performances: 8:45 p.m. June 14-July 27; 8:30 p.m. July 29-August 24. No performance on Sundays.
Fees:	$11 adults, $5 children, $14 reserved seating
Allow:	Drama takes about 2 hours. Pre-show entertainment begins 40 minutes before show times.
Nearby:	Museum of the Cherokee Indian, Oconaluftee Indian Village, Qualla Arts & Craft Mutual, Cherokee Heritage Museum, Great Smoky Mountains National Park, Nantahala National Forest.
Directions:	From Asheville, take I-40 West to Exit 27. Take Hwy. 19/23, Hwy. 74 West to Cherokee.

Wheels Through Time Museum

Museum houses a collection of over 250 rare antique motorcycles and automobiles, accompanied by an outstanding collection of memorabilia.

Location:	Maggie Valley, NC
Distance:	1½ hours from Asheville
Address:	62 Vintage Ln., Maggie Valley, NC 28751
Telephone:	926-6266
Admission:	Yes
Website:	www.wheelsthroughtime.com
Directions:	Take I-40 West to Exit 27 (Maggie Valley). Exit on to U.S. 19/74 North to Maggie Valley on Soco Rd. The museum is located 6.5 miles on the right in Maggie Valley.

World Methodist Museum

Located at beautiful Lake Junaluska, The World Methodist Museum includes the largest collection in America of artifacts and memorabilia of John Wesley and the Wesley family. The collection includes displays of antique Wedgewood pottery and oil portraits of John Wesley and other Methodist church founders.

Location:	Lake Junaluska, NC
Distance:	1 hour from Asheville
Address:	575 Lakeshore Dr. (PO Box 518), Lake Junaluska, NC 28745
Telephone:	456-9432
FAX:	456-9433
Hours:	Monday-Friday 9 a.m.-5 p.m. year-round, June-August also open 9 a.m.-5 p.m. on Saturdays

Fees:	None
Allow:	1-2 hours
Nearby:	Lake Junaluska Assembly, Cherokee Indian Reservation
Directions:	From Asheville, take I-40 West to Exit 27. Take Hwy. 19/23 South to Lakeshore Dr., which circles the lake.

Zachary-Tolbert House Museum

Built by Mordecai Zachary in 1842, the Greek Revival Zachary-Tolbert House remains in its original state along with the world's largest collection of plain style furniture made by one craftsman where the craftsman's identity is known.

Location:	Cashiers, NC
Distance:	1½ hours from Asheville
Address:	Hwy. 107 (2 miles south of the crossroads), Cashiers, NC 28771
Telephone:	743-4002
Admission:	Yes
Directions:	From Asheville take NC 280 South to Brevard. Continue on through Brevard on NC 64 to Cashiers.

Chapter Three
Retreat & Conference Centers

W estern North Carolina, due in part to its overwhelming natural beauty, is home to a number of religious retreat and conference centers. These are included in this book since you may be interested in visiting one or more during your stay. As would be expected, all are in breathtaking settings and immaculately maintained. The administration at each center has indicated that they welcome all visitors.

Billy Graham Training Center at The Cove

Located in a lovely mountain cove just east of Asheville, the Billy Graham Training Center holds year-round seminars and retreats for those seeking in-depth Bible studies, and a deeper experience of God's love. The Cove features two inns: Shepherd's Inn and Pilgrim's Inn. The facilities and grounds at the Cove are especially beautiful in design and landscaping.

Location: Asheville
Address: The Cove
PO Box 19223, Asheville, NC 28815
Telephone: 298-2092, (800) 950-2092
FAX: 299-0276
Website: www.thecove.org
Directions: From Asheville take I-40 East. Get off at Exit 55 Porters Cove Rd. Center entrance is on immediate right.

Chatlos Chapel at The Cove

Bonclarken

Located in historic Flat Rock in the Blue Ridge Mountains of Western North Carolina, Bonclarken is nestled among acres of tall white pines, hemlocks, spruce and rhododendron. At an elevation of 2,221 feet and located just off US Hwy. 25, Bonclarken is only 4 miles from Hendersonville. Bonclarken is owned by the Associate Reformed

Bonclarken, a haven for birds and others

Presbyterian Church and is available for use year-round by any groups desiring to rent the facilities and agreeing to live within the rules and regulations governing its use. Rich in history and tradition, Bonclarken has served the Associate Reformed Presbyterian Church and others since 1922. The beautiful hotel on the grounds was built in 1886 as a private home Dr. Arthur Rose Guerard, a Charlestonian who came to Flat Rock to build a home for his German bride. He used only the finest materials in the parquet floors and the wainscoting and the mantels were carved in Germany of rosewood, ebony and cherry. Bonclarken today offers a variety of facilities to individuals and groups. Complete dining, meeting, recreational and camping facilities round out the total service offering at Bonclarken.

Location: Flat Rock, NC
Distance: 45 minutes from Asheville
Address: 500 Pine Dr., Flat Rock, NC 28731
Telephone: 692-2223
FAX: 697-1735
Website: www.arpsynod.org/bonclarken.html
Of Note: Listed in the National Register of Historic Places.
Directions: From Main Street in Hendersonville go south on Hwy. 25 four miles to Pine Dr. Look for Bonclarken sign on left.

Christmount

Christmount, an agency of the Christian Church (Disciples of Christ), is located one mile south of Black Mountain. The Christmount conference center occupies one square mile of mountain land, cooled by numerous springs and creeks, at an elevation of just under 3,000 feet. Christmount is open year-round with a variety of accommodations including the Gaines M. Cook Guest House, the Guest House East, Davis Hall, Holly Park, and camp cabins. Most camps and conferences are related to the Christian Church (Disciples of Christ).

Location: Black Mountain, NC
Distance: 30 minutes from Asheville
Address: 222 Fern Way, Black Mountain, NC 28711
Telephone: 669-8977
FAX: 669-6301
Website: http://home.
earthlink.
net/~christmount/
Directions: Exit from I-40 in Black Mountain onto Hwy. 9 (Exit 54). Go south one mile to gate on left.

Prayer garden at Christmount

Kanuga

Kanuga is a year-round conference facility, closely affiliated with the Episcopal Church. Kanuga maintains the following programs: Kanuga-sponsored conferences, two summer camps for young people, parish family weekends, guest accommodations, Mountain Trail Outdoor School, retreats, national and regional programs sponsored by the Episcopal Church, and a special camp session for homeless, abused, and disadvantaged children.

Kanuga Lake

Located near Hendersonville, Kanuga's extensive conference center and camp facilities are situated on 1,400 acres of woodland, crisscrossed by streams, ridges and valleys. There is an 30-acre lake, ponds and complete outdoor recreational facilities and accommodations that range from rustic cottages to the spacious and modern Kanuga Inn.

Location: Hendersonville, NC
Distance: 1 hour from Asheville
Address: Kanuga Lake Rd. (PO Box 250), Hendersonville, NC 28793
Telephone: 692-9136
FAX: 696-3589
Website: www.kanuga.org
Directions: From I-26, take Exit 18 onto US 64 West into Hendersonville. Turn left on Hwy. 25 South (Church Street) and drive 9 blocks. Turn right onto Kanuga Street, go 4 miles to Kanuga triangular sign. Turn right, drive 1½ miles to Kanuga Entrance Park. Turn right and go ½ mile.

Lake Junaluska Assembly

Nestled in the mountains of Western North Carolina west of Asheville, Lake Junaluska Assembly is the conference and retreat center for the Southeastern Jurisdiction of the United Methodist Church, and home of the SEJ Administrative Council. The Assembly provides a wide variety of accommodations and con-

Lake Junaluska

ference facilities which will comfortably support groups ranging in size from 5 to 2,000. The Assembly welcomes individuals, families, church groups, educational organizations and many other groups. The 200-acre Lake Junaluska is surrounded by 1,200 acres of beautiful rolling hills and valleys. Located on the lake is the Cokesbury Gift Shop, which carries gifts, books and crafts.

Location: Lake Junaluska, NC
Distance: 1 hour from Asheville
Address: PO Box 67, Lake Junaluska, NC 28745.
Telephone: 452-2881, (800) 222-4930
FAX: 456-4040
Website: www.lakejunaluska.com
Directions: From Asheville, take I-40 West to Exit 27 to 19/23. Lake Junaluska is a few miles on the right.

Lutheridge Conference Center & Camp

Lutheridge is a 160-acre conference center and camp atop scenic Crescent Hill just south of Asheville. The Center offers an intimate setting that boasts a mix of comfortable adult lodging and rustic cabins for youth, modern conveniences, and beautiful year-round scenery.

Entrance gate at Lutheridge

Lutheridge is owned and operated by the North Carolina, South Carolina, Southeastern and Florida-Bahamas synods of the Evangelical Lutheran Church in America (ELCA).

Location: Just south of Asheville
Address: 2511 Hendersonville Rd., Arden, NC 28704
Telephone: 684-2361
FAX: 687-1600
Website: www.lutheridge.com
Directions: Take Exit 9 Airport Rd. off I-26 South. Proceed to Rt. 25, Hendersonville Rd. Lutheridge is located south on Hendersonville Rd.

Montreat Conference Center

Montreat Conference Center, a conference center of the Presbyterian Church (U.S.A.) is located 15 miles east of Asheville, just outside Black Mountain. Montreat is a special place to meet and enjoy the refreshing sights and sounds of the Blue Ridge Mountains. With 29 meeting facilities, Montreat offers a comfortable environment for conferences, retreats seminars or other special gatherings. Year-round facilities include a number of options available for housing, dining, classrooms, and recreation. Montreat's beautiful setting makes it the perfect place for all types of outdoor recreation. Hiking on marked trails in the surrounding mountains, swimming in the outdoor Olympic-size pool, and boating and canoeing on Lake Susan are among the many options. Montreat also has superb guest accommodations including Assembly Inn, and the Winnsborough.

Location: Montreat, NC
Distance: 45 minutes
Address: 401 Assembly Dr. (PO Box 969), Montreat, NC 28757
Telephone: 669-2911, (800) 572-2257
FAX: 669-2779
Website: www.montreat.org

Left Bank Building on Lake Susan at Montreat Conference Center

Directions: Take I-40 West from Asheville. Get off at Exit 64, Black Mountain. Go north on Route 9 through Black Mountain, two miles to the Montreat Gate.

Ridgecrest Conference Center

Ridgecrest Conference Center began in 1907 as a summer retreat for Southern Baptists. Today Ridgecrest thrives as a year-round conference center, attracting over 60,000 guests a year. While the Sunday School Board of the Southern Baptist Convention owns and operates the conference center, Ridgecrest attracts Christian groups from diverse backgrounds, as well as nonprofit organizations, school groups, and

Ridgecrest Confernce Center

government groups. Ridgecrest offers over 52,000 square feet of conference space, eighty-one conference rooms, and three auditoriums of various sizes. Outstanding dining and recreational facilities are also available to guests.

Location: Ridgecrest (17 miles east of Asheville)
Distance: 30 minutes Asheville
Address: PO Box 128, Old Hwy. 70, Ridgecrest, NC 28770.
Telephone: 669-8022, (800) 588-7222
FAX: 669-9721
Website: www.lifeway.com/ridgcrst.htm
Directions: From Asheville, take I-40 East and get off at Exit 66. At top of ramp, turn left. At the first junction, turn right onto Old US 70 and continue a short distance to Ridgecrest.

YMCA Blue Ridge Assembly

Located in Black Mountain, 15 miles east of Asheville, is the YMCA Blue Ridge Assembly. Founded in 1906 as a YMCA student conference center, the Assembly has hosted over half a million people in its rich history. Blue Ridge serves a diverse mix of not-for-profit religious, social, educational and family groups. Nestled on over 1,200 acres of woodlands, YMCA Blue Ridge Assem-

Robert E. Lee Hall at YMCA Blue Ridge Assembly

bly provides restful surroundings for groups large and small and a variety of comfortable accommodations that range from hotel-style to cottages. Blue Ridge also offers a diverse range of meeting facilities, and numerous recreational options. In the summer, Blue Ridge is known for its plentiful and delicious food served family style.

Location: Black Mountain, NC
Distance: 30 minutes from Asheville
Address: 84 Blue Ridge Circle, Black Mountain, NC 28711
Telephone: 669-8422
FAX: 669-8497
Website: www.blueridgeassembly.org
Directions: From Asheville take I-40 East. Get off at Exit 64 and go south on Hwy. 9. Proceed less than ½ mile and bear right on Blue Ridge Rd. Turn left at the small Blue Ridge Assembly sign.

Chapter Four
Western North Carolina
Cities & Towns

hile in-depth presentation of cities and towns in Western North Carolina other than Asheville, Hendersonville and Flat Rock is beyond the scope of this book, the following list is included should you be interested in obtaining further information on outlying areas. Beyond individual listings, two websites (www.highcountryhost.com and www.smokymtnhost.com) are all-in-one stops for various regional information. Since restaurants can come and go, please visit my book's web site—ashevilleguidebook.com—for the most up-to-date restaurant listings.

Andrews
Websites: www.andrewschambercommerce.com
www.cherokeecountychamber.com
Phone: Andrews Chamber of Commerce: (877) 558-0005
Andrews Town Manager: (828) 321-3113
Elevation: 2,350 feet
County: Cherokee
Population: 1,600+
Attractions: Great Smoky Mountains Railroad, Nantahala National Forest, Nantahala River

Nestled in a scenic valley at the far western end of the North Carolina mountains, Andrews is a small town virtually untouched by large-city influences and remains a place to enjoy a more leisurely pace of life.

Dining
Chestnuts Café ($): A great spot for a light meal. Main St., Andrews, NC 28901. (828) 321-4566. Call for hours.
Elsie's Steak and Seafood ($-$$): Steak, seafood and more served in a casual, friendly atmosphere. 358 Main St., Andrews, NC 28901. (828) 321-4915. Call for hours.

Accommodations

Andrews Valley Inn: 50 spacious guest rooms with panoramic mountain views. Complimentary breakfast. 138 Country Hearth Ln., Andrews, NC 28901. (888) 777-7901 or (828) 321-2176. $77. www.andrewesvalleyinn.com

Cozad-Cover House Bed & Breakfast: The Cozad-Cover House, built circa 1905, is an imposing two-and-a-half-story gable-roof frame home. They have expansive manicured grounds to enjoy and also have a cottage and studio apartment. 1194 Main St., Andrews, NC 28901. (828) 321-1017. $8-$115. www.coverhousebandb.com

Hawsdene House B&B Inn and Cottages: Mountain getaway retreat on 20 acres located about 10 minutes from downtown Andrews. 381 Phillips Creek Rd., Andrews, NC 28901. (800) 447-9549, (828) 321-6027. $85-$125. www.hawkesdene.com

Bakersville

Website: www.bakersville.com
Phone: Bakersville Town Hall: (800) 227-3912
Elevation: 2,460 feet
County: Mitchell
Population: 350+
Attractions: North Carolina Rhododendron Festival, Mount Mitchell

Bakersville, located to the northeast of Asheville, is the home of the famous North Carolina Rhododendron Festival held every spring during the height of the blooming season. The county seat of Mitchell County, Bakersville still retains the charm of a small mountain community, and is a convenient jumping-off point to explore the surrounding mountains.

Dining

Bogie's ($): Fast, friendly service, homemade pies, fresh home cooking. Daily specials, known for their pinto beans, cornbread and onions. View of the Roan, Home of the Rhododendron Festival. 624 Hwy. 226, Bakersville, NC 28705. 688-7272. Call for hours.

Accommodations

Bicycle Inn: Located in a quiet countryside setting, the Bicycle Inn offers accommodations for cyclists. If you are into biking, either road or mountain, this is the place for you. Great food, expert advice and guided tours. 319 Dallas Young Rd., Bakersville, NC 28705. 688-9333. $59-$69. www.bicycleinn.com.

Laurel Oaks Farm: Charming log house and secluded chalet, fully equipped for vacation rentals. Accommodate 5-7 and 4 persons, respectively. 7334 Hwy. 80, Bakersville, NC 28705. 688-2652, (800) 528-7356. $85-$130. www.virtualcities.com/vacation/nc/b/ncbb6v1.htm

Saylor Lake RV Park: Privately owned RV park located on beautiful 5-acre stocked lake. Electronic security gate, covered picnic table, electric, water, sewer, phone and cable TV hookup at each site. No restrooms or bathhouse. 1022 Saylor Lake Rd., Bakersville, NC 28705. (877) 688-4411, 688-4411. $20. http://hometown.aol.com/saylorlake/index.htm

Banner Elk

Website:	www.townofbannerelk.org, www.banner-elk.com
Phone:	Town of Banner Elk: (828) 898-5398
	Banner Elk Chamber of Commerce: (828) 898-5605, (800) 972-2183
County:	Avery
Elevation:	3,739 feet
Population:	937
Attractions:	Sugar Mountain Ski Resort

Located in the northeast section of the mountains, Banner Elk is a quaint mountain community that offers tourist activities including skiing, golf, hiking, horseback riding, whitewater rafting and fishing. Surrounded by high peaks and rugged ridges, Banner Elk has stronger historic and cultural ties with the neighboring mountainous regions of Tennessee and Virginia than all of the other regions of North Carolina. Lees-McRae College has been located in the area for over 100 years and the College Drama Department presents theatrical productions during the summer months. Banner Elk is also host every October to the famous Wooly Worm Festival.

Dining

Banner Elk Café ($$): Noted for their burgers! Gourmet Coffee Shop & Pizzeria associated with the Café. Varied menu, seafood, chicken, shrimp scampi, country fried steak. Kid's menu. Hwy. 194, Banner Elk, NC 28604. 898-4040. Winter: Sunday-Thursday 7 a.m.-9 p.m., Friday-Saturday 7 a.m.-10 p.m.; Summer: open daily 7 a.m.-10 p.m.

Corner Palate ($$): Steaks, pastas, sushi, seafood. Daily blue plate specials. 500 Yonahlasse Ln., Banner Elk, NC 28694. 898-8668. Open daily 11 a.m.-10 p.m.

Louisiana Purchase ($$$): A great Cajun Creole menu with seasonal chef selections as well. Northern Italian and French influences. Award-winning wine list, over 850 bottles! 537 Shawnee Haw Ave., Banner Elk, 28604. 963-5087. Reservations suggested. Winter: Tuesday-Saturday 5:30-10 p.m., May-November, Monday-Saturday 6-11 p.m. www.louisianapurchase.net

Sorrento's ($$): Genuine homemade Italian cuisine. Steaks, chops, eggplant and chicken dishes and authentic Italian desserts. Elegant decor. Suite 107 Village Shops of Banner Elk, Hwy. 184 & 194, Banner Elk, NC 28604. 898-5214. Winter: Thursday & Monday 4-10 p.m., Friday 4-11 p.m., Saturday 4 p.m.-2 am., Sunday 4-10 p.m. Summer: Lunch: Thursday-Monday 11 a.m.-3 p.m., Dinner: Monday, Thursday-Sunday 4-10 p.m. Closed Tuesday & Wednesday all year.

Stonewalls ($$): Great steaks, prime rib, daily fish specials, crab legs, Maryland crab cakes, salad bar. Hwy. 194, Banner Elk, NC 28604. 898-5550. Sunday-Thursday 5-10 p.m., Friday-Saturday 5-11 p.m.

Accommodations

Archer's Mountain Inn Bed & Breakfast: Archer's Mountain Inn, perched at 5,000 feet elevation, is a cozy 15-room inn and log home featuring fireplace suites, Jacuzzi suites, fabulous mountain views and full breakfast daily. The dining room, Jackalope's View, has an eclectic menu and award-winning wine list, and panoramic mountain views. Enjoy downhill skiing, hiking, mountain biking, white water rafting, golf and cool mountain temperatures. 2489 Beech Mountain Parkway, Banner Elk, NC 28604. (888) 827-6155, 898-9004. $70-$175. www.archersinn.com

The Inn at Elk River: Williamsburg-style colonial inn and restaurant offering eight gracious rooms with private baths, TVs, and four with fireplaces. Rooms are furnished with queen-size beds, as well as two with king-size beds. All open out to decks that run the full length of the inn and offer beautiful panoramic views of the surrounding mountains and the Elk River Golf and Country Club. 875 Main St. W., Banner Elk, NC 28604. 898-9669. $95-$145. www.elkriverinn.com

The Perry House Bed & Breakfast: The Perry House was built in 1903 and recently restored into a beautiful country inn complete with custom-designed furnishings by master craftsmen Carl and Jim Stanton of Linville, North Carolina. Guests will enjoy the ambiance of a turn-of-the-century getaway while being pampered with all the modern conveniences. Each beautifully decorated bedroom offers luxury with a warm, cozy feeling and rates include a delicious, full breakfast. Refreshments are always available. 153 Klonteska Dr., Banner Elk, NC 28604. 898-3535, 877 806-4280. $79-$129. www.perryhouse.com

The Pinnacle Inn: Condominium rentals by the day, weekend, week, month or season. Indoor heated pool with sundecks, sauna, steam room, hot tubs and exercise room. Tennis and shuffleboard complex, and golf privileges at local courses. 301 Pinnacle Inn Rd., Banner Elk, NC 28604. (800) 405-7888, 387-2231. $60-4115. www.pinnacleinn.com

1902 Turnpike House: A distinctly grand country house, offering great breakfasts served each morning around the large farm table in the dining room. The freshest fruits and home-baked breads begin the breakfast feast served on fine china with heirloom crystal and silver. Open year-round, and the only B&B with an outdoor hot tub! 317 Old Turnpike Rd., Banner Elk, NC 28694. (888) 802-4487, 898-5611. $85-$109. www.1902turnpikehouse.com

Beech Mountain
Website: www.beechmtn.com
Phone: Chamber of Commerce: (800) 468-5506, (828) 387-9283
Town Hall: (828) 387-4236

Elevation: 5,506 feet
County: Avery
Population: 350
Attractions: Beech Ski Resort

The town of Beech Mountain is known for its world-famous ski resort as well as its cool summer weather—temperatures rarely get above 72 degrees. Located in the northeast section of the mountains, Beech Mountain is the highest in elevation of all towns in the northeastern United States. Offering a nice selection of quaint stores and restaurants, as well as a large choice of outdoor sports, Beech Mountain is a year-round destination.

Dining

Brick Oven Pizzeria and Pasta: Dough made fresh daily. Cheesesteak sandwiches, meatball subs and other great sandwiches. Cappuccino and desserts. 402 Beech Mountain Parkway, Beech Mountain, NC 28604. 387-4209 or 387-4000.

Fred's Backside Deli ($): Hot and cold deli sandwiches, pizza, salads, burgers, fresh-baked desserts and ice cream. Breakfast, lunch and dinner. Located in Fred's General Mercantile Store. 501 Beech Mountain Parkway, Beech Mountain, NC 28604. 387-9331. 7:30 a.m.-8 p.m. seven days a week. (qinter hours may vary). www.FredsGeneral.com

Jackalope's View ($$): Gourmet dining with great mountain views. Live jazz and music from local artists, wine tastings and patio dining during summer months. Jackalope's View holds the coveted Wine Spectator award of excellence. Located in Archer's Inn. Reservations suggested. 2489 Beech Mountain Parkway, Beech Mountain, NC 28604. 898-9004. Dinner only: Tuesday-Sunday 5-9:30 p.m. www.archersinn.com

Jordan's Restaurant ($$): Fine dining known for fresh mountain trout, rack of lamb, wild game duck and more. International cuisine. Full-service bar and fireside lounge. Live music on weekends. 608 Beech Mountain Parkway, Beech Mountain, NC 28604. 387-9449. Open May 12th. Wednesday-Sunday 5-10 p.m. Reservations suggested.

O'Shaughnessy's Restaurant & Pub ($$): Irish restaurant and pub located just 100 yards from the entrance to Beech Mountain Ski Resort. American food with an Irish flair. 1001 Beech Mountain Parkway, Beech Mountain, NC 28604. 387-2266. June until October. 4 p.m. until closing, usually seven days a week. Call for reservations. www.oshaughnessys.com

Accommodations

4 Seasons at Beech: Located at the top of Beech Mountains, 4 Seasons at Beech is an English Tudor-style lodge that offers unspoiled wilderness beauty, friendly service and comfortable accommodations. Efficiency units and one-bedroom suites. Game room, exercise room and on-site restaurant. 608 Beech Mountain Parkway, Beech Mountain, NC 28604. 387-4211. $65-$110. www.4seasons.beech.net

Archer's Mountain Inn: Country inn offering 15 rooms, each with fireplace, private bath and great views. Breakfast included. Jacuzzis available in some units. 2489 Beech Mountain Parkway, Beech Mountain, NC 28604. (888) 827-6155, 898-9004. $70-$195. www.archersinn.com

Beech Alpen Inn: This rustic country inn offers 25 guest rooms, some with fireplaces. Amenities include a complimentary continental breakfast each morning, color cable television and a private bath in each room. Nestled in a curve of the Beech Mountain Parkway, the Beech Alpen complements its mountain setting with an old-world charm that recalls the rustic inns of Europe. Restaurant on premises. 700 Beech Mountain Parkway, Beech Mountain, NC 28604. 387-2252, (866) 284-2770. $69-$89. www.beechalpen.com

Top of the Beech Inn: Swiss-style lodge with 23 guest rooms. Huge sitting area with stone fireplace. Complimentary continental breakfast each morning. Most rooms have view of ski slopes. 700 Beech Mountain Parkway, Beech Mountain, NC 28604. 387-2252. $69-$89. www.beechalpen.com

Black Mountain

Website: www.blackmountain.org

Phone: Chamber of Commerce: (800) 669-2301, (828) 669-2300
Town Hall: (828) 669-8732

Elevation: 2,400 feet

County: Buncombe

Population: 7,511

Attractions: Christmount, YMCA Blue Ridge Assembly, Historic Montreat, Montreat College, Lake Tomahawk, Swannanoa Valley Museum, Black Mountain Center for the Arts, Old Depot Art & Craft Gallery

Located about 15 minutes east of Asheville, the charming village of Black Mountain has long been known as the "Front Porch of Western North Carolina." Filled with distinctive shops, restaurants and craft galleries, Black Mountain has become a tourist destination in its own right, and has stepped out of the shadow of larger neighboring Asheville. There is a wonderful historic district including an antique railroad depot. The community also offers a diverse program of outdoor recreation including golf on the Black Mountain Public Golf Course, public tennis, ballfields, croquet, walking paths and a picturesque Lake Tomahawk. The backdrop for this great little town is the Black Mountain range with Mount Mitchell and the Seven Sisters soaring in the distance. In the late summer, the town also is host to the famous Sourwood Festival.

Dining

Berliner Kindl German Restaurant & Deli ($$): Authentic German cuisine, unique Bavarian decor and a full deli offering cold cuts, breads, spices, teas, coffee, chocolates and cookies. Smoke-free dining. 20 Ball St., Black Mountain, NC 28711. 669-5255. Tuesday-Saturday: Lunch and dinner 10 a.m.-9 p.m.

Cherry Tree Corner Ice Cream & Soda Shoppe ($): '50s-style soda shop offering malts, floats, shakes, sodas, cherry cokes, free lemonade pie, cookies, candy and more. 100 Cherry St., Black Mountain, NC 28711. 669-0555. Monday-Saturday 11 a.m.-11 p.m., Sunday 1-9 p.m.

Coach House Seafood & Steak ($$): Steaks and seafood, known for their seafood platters and grilled dishes. 508 West State St., Black Mountain, NC 28711. 669-4223. Tuesday-Thursday 11 a.m.-9 p.m., Friday 11 a.m.-9:30 p.m., Saturday 3-9 p.m., Sunday 11:30 a.m.-9 p.m.

French Quarter Café ($$): Cajun seafood from Louisiana. Outdoor seating during the summer. 203 East State St., Black Mountain, NC 28711. 669-1989. Tuesday-Saturday 11:30 a.m.-9 p.m., Sunday 11:30 a.m.-3 p.m. Closed Monday.

Monte Vista Hotel: Delicious homestyle cooking, specialty dishes. Meals are usually served buffet-style, but a menu is also available. The breakfast buffet on Saturday and Sunday morning consists of fresh fruits, cereal, milk, oatmeal, grits, eggs, bacon, sausage, biscuits, gravy, waffles, hotcakes, french toast, juice, and coffee. Third-generation ownership. 308 West State, Black Mountain, NC 28711. 669-2119. Breakfast seven days a week year-round, 7-10 a.m. Winter season: Lunch: call for hours, Dinner: Friday seafood buffet, Saturday night prime rib buffet 5-7 p.m. Summer season: Lunch noon-2 p.m., Dinner: Monday-Saturday 5-7 p.m. www.montevistahotel.com

Red Rocker Inn ($$): A meticulously restored, award-winning bed and breakfast inn serving great food. Candlelit tables, fireplace and spectacular garden porch for summer dining. Homemade specialties and great desserts. Dinner beginning at 6 p.m. Monday-Thursday and 6:30 Friday and Saturday. Grandma's Sunday Dinner at 1:00 (reservations required) and country breakfasts daily at 8:30 a.m. 136 N. Dougherty St., Black Mountain, NC 28711. 669-5991, (888) 669-5991. www.redrockerinn.com

My Father's Pizza & Pasta ($): Known for their great pizza! Italian-American specialties with full-service menu. Garden dining, dine-in or take-out. 133 Cherry St., Black Mountain, NC 28711. 669-4944. Monday-Thursday 11 a.m.-9 p.m., Friday and Saturday 11 a.m.-11 p.m., Sunday noon-8 p.m.

Verandah Café ($): Gourmet sandwiches, salads, homemade soups and desserts. English cottage garden interior. 119 Cherry St., Black Mountain, NC 28711. 669-8864.

Accommodations

Bella Luna Inn: Six-bedroom inn serving full gourmet breakfasts. Complimentary wine in the afternoons. Cape Cod house about three blocks walking distance to downtown. 99 Terry Estate Dr., Black Mountain, NC 28711. 664-9714. $95-$150.

Inn on Mill Creek: Located on seven acres that include pond, waterfall, forests and fields. Four large guest rooms each with private baths. Fireplaces, hot tubs and full country breakfast. Mill Creek Rd., (PO Box 185) Ridgecrest, NC 28770 (near Black Mountain). 668-1115, (887) 668-1115. www.inn-on-mill-creek.com

Monte Vista Hotel: Old-fashioned hotel with touches of the past that has graced Black Mountain since 1919. Cable television in a few rooms instead of TVs in every room, a payphone and message board instead of room phones, and old oak trees instead of air-conditioning. Porches feature wicker rockers, plants and a swing. Third-generation ownership. 308 West State, Black Mountain, NC 28711. 669-2119. $65-$75. www.montevistahotel.com

Red Rocker Inn: A meticulously restored, award-winning bed and breakfast inn serving great food. Seventeen elegant guest rooms, each with private bath. Central air conditioning. Great front porch with rockers of course! 136 N. Dougherty St., Black Mountain, NC 28711. 669-5991, (888) 669-5991. $95-$145. www.redrockerinn.com

The Black Mountain Inn: A restored stagecoach stop and former artist's retreat, The Black Mountain Inn offers eight comfortable rooms and suites, each with their own private bath. Located on three wooded acres. Full home-cooked breakfasts. 718 Old Hwy. 70, Black Mountain, NC 28711. (800) 735-6128, 669-6528. $88-$135. www.blackmountaininn.com

The Inn Around the Corner: 1915 four-square Victorian inn. Closest inn to the historic downtown section of Black Mountain. Five large guest rooms with two suites with private baths and gourmet breakfast. 109 Church St., Black Mountain, NC 28711. 669-6005, (800) 393-6005. $110-$160. www.innaroundthecorner.com

Tree Haven Bed & Breakfast: Beautifully restored 1908 farmhouse with five guest rooms each with private bath. Healthy gourmet breakfasts, non-smoking and air-conditioned rooms, 1.3 acres with gardens and stream and convenient to downtown and Montreat. 1114 Montreat Rd., Black Mountain, NC 28711. 669-3841, (888) 448-3841. $75-$95.

Blowing Rock
Website: www.blowingrock.com
Phone: Chamber of Commerce: (800) 295-7851, (828) 295-7851
Elevation: 4,000 feet
County: Watauga
Population: 1,500
Attractions: The Blowing Rock, Appalachian Heritage Museum, Mystery Hill, The Frank T. Williams Railroad Museum

The historic village of Blowing Rock sits aside the Eastern Continental Divide and is centrally located to most of the major area attractions. There is a professional summer stock theatre (the Blowing Rock Stage Company), horseshoes, Scottish Highland games, Christmas and 4th of July celebrations in the park and abundant outdoor recreational opportunities. Its rich history stretches back to the 1500s, when the great explorer Desoto supposedly looked for gold in the area. The town is named after its main attraction, The Blowing Rock.

Dining

Best Cellar Restaurant ($$): Fine dining in a 60-year-old authentic log cabin. Nightly menu includes raw oyster bar, Angus beef, fresh seafood and delicious homemade desserts. Open year-round with all ABC permits. 276 Little Springs Rd., Blowing Rock, NC 28605. 295-3466. Dinner only, reservations suggested. December-May: Thursday-Monday 5:30-9:30 p.m. May-December: Monday-Saturday 5:30-9 p.m.

Canyons of the Blue Ridge ($$): Mexican-Southwestern favorites including burritos, chimichangas, enchiladas, quesadillas, Asian specialties, and old favorites that include steaks, fish & chips and garden burgers. Live music on most nights. Lunch: 11 a.m.-5 p.m. Dinner: 5 p.m. until. Sunday brunch: 11 a.m.-2:30 p.m. Reservations suggested for parties of five or more. 8960 Valley Boulevard (Hwy. 321), Blowing Rock, NC 28605. www.canyonsbr.com

Crippen's Restaurant ($$$): Located in an elegant country inn with fireplace and parlor. Honors include "Best Restaurant in North Carolina," Greensboro News & Record and Certificate of Honor from James Beard Foundation. Menu changes daily. Full bar and extensive wine list. Creative appetizers, fresh meats and game, homemade pastas and desserts and seafood. Dinner only, reservations suggested. Crippen's Country Inn, 239 Sunset Dr., Blowing Rock, NC 28605. 295-3487. May-November: seven days a week, 5-9:30 p.m., November-May: Friday & Saturday, 6-9 p.m. www.crippens.com

Elliott's Restaurant ($$$$): Located in a historic mansion, the Westglow Spa, Elliott's Restaurant offers fine dining with an emphasis on healthy foods. 2845 Hwy. 221, South, Blowing Rock, NC 28605. 295-4463, (800) 526-0807. Reservations required. Dinner: 6-8:30 p.m. seven days a week. www.westglow.com

Manor House Restaurant and Pub at Chetola Resort ($$$): Located in the historic 1846 Estate House at Chetola Resort, the Manor House Restaurant and Pub is a step back to another era. Fine dining in three vintage dining rooms, a lakeside veranda and in the pub. Continental cuisine with mountain specialties. North Main St., Blowing Rock, NC 28605. 295-5505. (800) 243-8652. Reservations recommended. Breakfast: beginning at 8 a.m. Lunch: 11 a.m.-2 p.m. Dinner: 5:30-10 p.m. www.chetola.com

Speckled Trout Café & Oyster Bar ($$): Fresh seafood since 1986 including local rainbow trout. Specialty sandwiches, chicken pot pie, baby back ribs, vegetarian strudel and more. 922 Main St., Blowing Rock, NC 28605. 295-9819. Dinner reservations suggested. Open seven days a week year-round. Breakfast and lunch: 9 a.m.-3 p.m. Dinner: 5-9 p.m.

Accommodations

Crippen's Country Inn: A newly restored early 1900s country inn with parlor and living room with fireplace. Nine luxurious and spacious guest rooms, each with private bath. 239 Sunset Dr. (PO Box 528), Blowing Rock, NC 28605. $99-159. www.crippens.com

Gideon Ridge Inn: A secluded bed and breakfast inn with ten guest rooms, each with private bath. Views of the Blue Ridge Mountains. Full hot breakfast and afternoon tea. 6148 Gideon Ridge Rd., (PO Box 1929), Blowing Rock, NC 28605. $150-280. www.ridge-inn.com

Maple Lodge Bed & Breakfast Inn: A historic village inn, located near shops, galleries and restaurants. Eleven guest rooms and suites, private baths, hand-made quilts, goose-down comforters and country antiques throughout. Stone fireplace, two parlors and library and game tables. Smoke-free. 152 Sunset Dr. (PO Box 1236), Blowing Rock, NC 28605, 295-3331. $100-180. www.maplelodge.net

The Inn at Ragged Gardens: Located in downtown Blowing Rock just off Main Street, the 100-year old manor building is surrounded by an acre of lawn and gardens. Twelve guest suites and rooms all have private baths and fireplaces. Full gourmet breakfast and afternoon wine and hors d'oeuvres. 203 Sunset Dr. (PO Box 1927), Blowing Rock, NC 28605. 295-9703. $170-310. www.ragged-gardens.com

Chetola Mountain Resort: Situated on 87 acres just a short walk from downtown, Chetola Resort was established in 1846 as a way station for horse-drawn mail carriages. First-class luxury accommodations in the lodge and condominiums. Fine dining in the Manor House and Pub, and large guest rooms, full-service spa and indoor recreation center with pool, whirlpools and exercise rooms. North Main St., Blowing Rock, NC 28605. (800) 243-8652, 295-5500. Lodge: $124-138. www.chetola.com

Roaring River Chalets: Located two miles from Blowing Rock, the Roaring River Chalets offer chalets with cable TV, kitchen, separate bedrooms and private decks overlooking the Roaring River. 408 Roaring River Rd., Blowing Rock, NC 28605. 295-3695. $79-$185 per chalet. www.rrchalets.com

The Green Park Inn & Resort (NRHP): Historic 1882 grand Victorian hotel features 85 beautifully appointed guest rooms. Championship golf, tennis, swimming and hiking. Elegant dining in the Green Park dining room. US Hwy. 321 South, Blowing Rock, NC 28605. (800) 852-2462, 295-3141. $99-$169.

Boone

Websites: www.visitBooneNC.com
www.boonechamber.com

Phone: Boone Area Chamber of Commerce: (828) 264-2225, (800) 852-9506
Boone Convention & Visitors Bureau: (888) 251-9867, (828) 262-3516
Boone City Hall: (828) 262-4530

Elevation: 3,500 feet

County: Watauga

Population: 13,900

Attractions: Mast General Store, Appalachian State University, Appalachian Cultural Museum, Horn in the West, Hickory Ridge Homesite, Turchin Center for the Visual Arts, Tweetsie Railroad

Located just off the Blue Ridge Parkway in the northeast section of the mountains, Boone has much to offer the visitor. Really a small city, Boone is a destination in much the same way Asheville is. Dominated by Appalachian State University and located in the "Heart of the High Country," Boone has a wide array of stores, restaurants, galleries and things to do. It is even know as the "Firefly Capital of America!" Golf courses, skiing and outdoor sports abound.

Dining

Casa Rustica ($$): Northern Italian/American cuisine. 1348 Hwy. 105 South, Boone, NC 28607. 262-5128. Reservations suggested. Open daily, 5-9 p.m.

Mike's Inland Seafood ($$): Great seafood, wide variety of dishes. They also have a similar restaurant in nearby Banner Elk. 174 Jefferson Rd., Boone, NC 28607. 262-5605. Lunch and dinner: Tuesday-Thursday 11 a.m.-2 p.m., 5-9 p.m.; Friday 11 a.m.-2 p.m., 4-10 p.m.; Saturday 4-10 p.m.; Sunday noon-8 p.m.

Red Onion Café ($$): A little bit of everything, including Mexican, Italian and vegetarian dishes. Soups, pizza, beer, wine and homemade desserts. 227 Hardin St., Boone, NC 28607. 264-5470. Lunch and dinner, seven days a week, 11 a.m.-9:30 p.m., Friday & Saturday until 10 p.m.

Pepper's ($$): Wide-ranging menu with Cajun night on Tuesdays and Thursdays and Italian night on Mondays and Wednesdays. Shadowline Dr., Boone, NC 28607. 262-1815. 11 a.m.-9 p.m., Friday-Saturday until 10 p.m.

Wildflower ($$): Casually eclectic fine dining in a relaxed atmosphere. Great service and renowned presentation of food. 831 West King St., Boone, NC 28697. 264-3463. Dinner only. Reservations suggested. Seven days a week, 5-10 p.m., but call during the winter as hours will change seasonally.

Accommodations

Lovill House Inn Bed & Breakfast: Built in 1875 by Captain E.F. Lovill, a Civil War hero and state senator, the Lovill House Inn is rich in family and community history. Careful restoration has preserved the charm of this historic farm house. Each of six large and airy guest rooms has been totally updated with private baths, cable televisions and telephones. Guest room walls have been double built and insulated to ensure privacy. 404 Old Bristol Rd., Boone, NC 28607. (800) 849-9466, 264-4204. $145-$185. www.lovillhouseinn.com

Fall Creek Cabins: Private log cabins set on a 54 secluded mountain acres. Great views, trails and rushing mountain trout streams. Two-story log cabins nestled privately in the woods. Each cabin features cathedral ceilings, two bedrooms, two full baths, reading/sleeping loft, woodburning fireplace and covered porch with hot tub, swing, rocking chairs and gas grill. PO Box 190, Fleetwood, NC 28626. (336) 877-3131. Cabin rentals from $165-$190 per night. www.fall-creek-cabins.com

High Country Inn: Country inn located in a peaceful wooded setting near downtown Boone. 120 rooms, indoor/outdoor heated pool, hot tub, sauna, fitness center, Geno's Sport's Restaurant and Lounge. King rooms with fireplaces, suites with Jacuzzi, two 3-bedroom log cabins with kitchens, living rooms and stone fireplaces. Cable TV with Showtime. 1785 Hwy. 105, Boone, NC 28607. (800) 334-5605, 264-1000. $40-$89.

Hound Ears Lodge & Club: A 900-acre luxury resort and residential community tucked away in the mountains near Boone. Mobile Four-Star resort with golf, tennis, hiking and swimming facilities. Among the lodge, clubhouse suites, an executive suite and a penthouse honeymoon suite, there is a total of 29 guest rooms. Two different plans are offered: a modified American plan (with breakfast and dinner included) or, during the winter, a European plan (with no meals included). Hwy. 105 South, Boone, NC 28607. 963-4321. $135-$180. www.houndears.com

The Inn at Yonahlossee: The Inn at Yonahlossee is located at the Yonahlossee Resort & Club, a year-round residential resort community. Conveniently located between Boone and Blowing Rock, the 300-acre Yonahlossee Resort & Club is bordered by Moses Cone Memorial Park at an elevation of 4,800 feet. This setting boasts splendid views of nearby mountain ranges and lush green valleys. Full range of guest accommodations including inn rooms and cozy studio cottages. Continental breakfast includes both hot and cold cereals, selections of bagels and danishes, yogurt, orange juice, milk, coffee, teas and hot chocolate. 226 Oakley Green, Boone, NC 28607. (800) 962-1986, 963-6400. $99-$435. www.yonahlossee.com/

Brevard

Website: www.visitwaterfalls.com
Phone: Transylvania County Tourism: (800) 648-4523, (828) 883-3700
City Hall: (828) 884-4123
Elevation: 2,200 feet
County: Transylvania
Population: 6,800
Attractions: Over 250 waterfalls, Brevard College, White Squirrels, Pisgah National Forest, Cradle of Forestry, Pisgah Center for Wildlife Education, Gorges State Park, Dupont State Forest, Sliding Rock

Located in the heart of Transylvania County about 45 minutes southwest of Asheville, Brevard is a wonderful little city that is not only a great place to live but also a renowned tourist destination. Nearby state and national forests beckon, and Brevard is right at the center of one of the most famous waterfall regions in America. Over 250 are located within a short drive of downtown. Brevard is also home to a colony of white squirrels that even have their own festival and to the Brevard Music Festival, one of the best music festivals in America.

Dining

Chianti's Italian Café & Bar ($$): Located in nearby Pisgah Forest, Chianti's Italian Café has been awarded the Circle Sticker for Low Fat Dinners by the NC Division of Public Health. They offer a wide menu, with specialties that include ravioli marinara, chicken parmigiana, mussels modena and pasta primavera in tomato basil sauce. 10 New Hendersonville Hwy., Pisgah Forest, NC 28768. 862-5683.

Hobnob ($$$): European-American fine dining in downtown Brevard. Full bar and extensive wine list. 226 West Main St., Brevard, NC 28712. 966-4662. Reservations suggested. Open seven days a week. Lunch: 11:30 a.m.-2:30 p.m. Dinner: 5:30-9 p.m. Live music on Friday, Saturday and Sunday nights. Sunday Brunch: 11 a.m.-2:30 p.m.

Old Hickory House ($): Specialties include barbeque, steaks, chicken and seafood. 842 Country Club Rd., Brevard, NC 28712. 884-7270. Monday-Saturday, 5-9 p.m. Sunday lunch 11 a.m.-3 p.m.

Jordan Street Café ($$$): Non-smoking restaurant offering fine American cuisine. Outdoor patio. 30 West Jordan St., Brevard, NC 28712. 883-2558. Reservations suggested. Dinner: Monday, Wednesday, Thursday and Sunday: 5-9 p.m., Saturday 5-10 p.m., Sunday brunch 10 a.m.-2 p.m.

Pisgah Fish Camp ($): Located near the entrance to the Pisgah National Forest, they offer a wide array of seafood, chicken and steaks. Family-oriented with children's specials. In business since 1967. Hwy. 64 and Hwy. 276, Pisgah Forest, NC 28768. 877-3129. Open daily 11 a.m. until closing. Lunch buffet 11 a.m.-2 p.m. Monday-Friday.

Accommodations

Chestnut Hill Bed & Breakfast (NRHP): Originally known as the Hanckel-Barclay House, it was built in 1856 and is one of the rare remaining examples of mid-nineteenth century Greek Revival-style frame houses. Chestnut Hill offers imposing views overlooking the French Broad River Valley and is reached by a long winding drive up the hillside through woods and rhododendron groves. Spacious rooms with working fireplaces, private baths, TVs, VCRs and central air and heat. 400 Barclay Rd., Brevard, NC 28712. 862-3540. $125-$185. www.bbonline.com/nc/chestnuthill

Earthshine Mountain Lodge: Located between Brevard and Cashiers, in the famed Toxaway resort area, Earthshine Mountain Lodge is a 75-acre "grandmother's farm" built upon a 100 year-old homestead. Adventure and hospitality are their hallmarks. Horseback riding, high ropes course, picnicking, hiking, barnyard animals... Earthshine offers it all for those who want to experience the natural side of the mountains. The main lodge is a 1 ½-story hand-built cedar log home with rock fireplaces, handmade quilts and log beds and rockers. Ten guest rooms in addition to the "Sunrise Cottage" with its three suites. Rt 1, Box 216-C, Lake Toxaway, NC 28747. 862-4207. $150. www.earthshinemtnlodge.com

The Greystone Inn (NRHP): Situated on beautiful Lake Toxaway near Brevard, the Greystone Inn offers fine cuisine and accommodations in a charming historic mansion. Golf, tennis, hiking, skiing, canoeing and fishing are only steps away from the Hillmont Inn, the mansion and the lakeside suites. Daily champagne cruises! AAA Four-Diamond award recipient. Greystone Ln., Lake Toxaway, NC 28747. 966-4700, (800) 824-5766. $350-$595. www.greystoneinn.com

The Inn at Brevard (NRHP): Built in 1885, the inn offers gracious accommodations, great service and fine dining. Furnished with period antiques, it is located in downtown Brevard. 410 East Main St., Brevard, NC 28712. 884-2105. $95-$130. www.InnatBrevard.8M.com

The Womble Inn: Located two blocks from the center of Brevard, The Womble Inn offers five guest rooms furnished in antiques with private baths. The inn's café serves great breakfasts and lunch. 310 West Main St., Brevard, NC 28712. 884-4770. $65-$75. www.thewombleinn.com

Bryson City

Website: www.brysoncity.com, www.greatsomkies.com
Phone: Swain County Chamber of Commerce: (828) 488-3681, (800) 867-9246
Bryson City Town Hall: (828) 488-3335
Elevation: 2,000 feet
County: Swain
Population: 1,400
Attractions: Great Smoky Mountains Railroad, Great Smoky Mountains National Park

Unique among mountain communities, Bryson City is located right next to the Great Smoky Mountains National Park. Over 40 percent of this great national park is located in Swain County, and the park sets the tone for this lovely mountain city. There are a large number of accommodations for such a small city, largely because of the number of visitors who wish to visit the park.

Dining

Everett Street Diner ($): Country breakfast with homemade biscuits, Belgian waffles, fresh omelets. Children's menu. All non-smoking restaurant. 52 Everett St., Bryon City, NC 28713. 488-0123. Breakfast and lunch only. Daily lunch specials. Monday-Friday 7 a.m.-2 p.m., Sunday 10 a.m.-2 p.m. (brunch menu), noon-2 p.m. (Sunday dinner).

Mountain Steak House ($$): Steaks, seafood and chicken over live charcoal, candlelight dining and causal dress. Known for their prime ribs. 4041 Hwy. 19/74 West, Bryson City, 28713. 488-4399. Dinner only. Monday-Thursday 4-9 p.m., Friday-Saturday 4-10 p.m.

Anthony's Pizzeria ($): Great homemade, hand-tossed pizza, extensive menu offering various specialty Italian dishes. By far the best pizza in the area! Beer, wine and mixed drinks. 103 Depot St., Bryson City, NC 28713. 488-8898. Monday-Sunday 11 a.m.-9 p.m.

Fryemont Inn ($$): The Fryemont Inn's dining room features gleaming hardwood floors, a huge stone fireplace, brass and wood paddle fans and vaulted ceiling fans. All dinners include soup of the day, mixed green salad, entrée, family-style side dishes and dessert. They also offer an extensive wine list and a full-service bar. Fryemont Rd., Bryson City, NC 28713. (800) 845-4879. April 19 until December 1. www.fryemontinn.com

Relia's Garden Restaurant ($$): Located on the nearby Nantahala River in a spectacular setting, Relia's offers great food in a wonderful, casual outdoor atmosphere. The restaurant overlooks its own organic gardens that provide some of the greens for the meals. Guests may dine on the porch and enjoy views of the mountains and the magnificent Nantahala River. 13077 Hwy. 19/74 West at the Nantahala Outdoor Center, Bryson City, NC 28713. 488-2175. April through September. Dinner. Sunday-Thursday 5-9 p.m., Friday & Saturday 5-10 p.m. www.nco.com

Accommodations

Calhoun Country Inn: Fifteen rooms with private baths offering porch rocking chairs, antiques and period furniture, handmade quilts. Great homemade breakfasts featuring teas, fresh yeast breads, homemade jams and jellies, cobblers, churned butter, sourwood honey and hot biscuits. Children welcome. L135 Everett St., Bryson City, 28713. 488-1234. $65-$135. www.calhouncountryinn.com

Charleston Inn Bed & Breakfast: Twenty rooms, five traditional B&B rooms and 14 larger, more modern rooms. "My Smoky Mountain Home" cabin. Beautifully landscaped gardens. Full country breakfast and dinner on Thursday, Friday and Saturday. 208 Arlington Avenue, Bryson City, NC 28713. 888 285-1555, 488-4644. $95-$135, $155 cabin. www.charlestoninn.com

Folkestone Inn Bed & Breakfast: A 1920s farmhouse, the Folkestone Inn is located in a grove of giant Norway spruces, beside a mountain brook, at the Deep Creek area of the Great Smoky Mountains National Park, on the quieter, softer side of the Smokies. 101 Folkestone Rd., Bryson City, NC 28713. (888) 812-3385, 488-2730. $88-$119. www.folkestone.com

Fryemont Inn ((NRHP): Situated on a mountain shelf overlooking the quiet village of Bryson City and the Great Smoky Mountains National Park, the Fryemont Inn offers secluded comfort and excellent dining in the atmosphere of a bygone era. Casual elegance and rustic beauty are hallmarks of this outstanding county inn. Fryemont Rd., Bryson City, NC 28713. (800) 845-4879. April 19 until December 1. $133-$220. www.fryemontinn.com

Randolph House: Listed in the National Register of Historic Places, the Randolph House (circa 1895) is known for its tradition of friendly mountain hospitality in a turn-of-the-century setting. 223 Fryemont St., Bryson City, NC 28713. (800) 480-3472, 488-3472; off season, call (770) 938-2268. Closed November through March. Call for rates. www.randolphhouse.com

Falling Waters Adventure Resort: Located 12 miles west of Bryson City, Falling Waters Adventure Resort is a 22-acre retreat for outdoor lovers. Surrounded by hardwood forests and situated high on a cliff complete with waterfall, Falling Waters has hiking trails, spectacular views, outdoor charcoal grills and modern restroom facilities along with accommodations in the Group Lodge (44 bunks) and the Yurt Village. Operated by Wildwater Ltd. Rafting, one of WNC's premier rafting companies. Open from March through November. (800) 451-9972, 488-2384. Yurt rental: $56-76, Lodge: $14 per person. www.fallingwatersresort.com

Burnsville
Website: www.yanceychamber.com
Phone: Yancey County Chamber of Commerce: (800) 948-1632, (828) 682-7413
Burnsville City Hall: (828) 682-2420
Elevation: 2,815 feet
County: Yancey
Population: 7,000
Attractions: Mount Mitchell State Park, Rush Wray Museum of Yancy County History, The Historic Nu Wray Inn

Located about halfway between Asheville and Boone, Burnsville is nestled among 19 of the highest mountains in the east. Nearby Mount Mitchell, at 6,684 feet, is the highest peak east of the Mississippi River, and it is accompanied by 18 other peaks over 6,300 feet. The county seat of Yancey County, Burnsville was established in 1833, and has probably as many artisans and craftspersons per capita as any town in the United States.

Dining
China Garden ($): Chinese cuisine. Crab leg buffet All-You-Can-Eat on weekends. 409 West Main St., Burnsville, NC 28714. Tuesday, Wednesday, Thursday & Sunday: 11:30 a.m.-9 p.m., Friday & Saturday: 11:30 a.m.-10 p.m.

Garden Deli ($): Deli fare with specialties that include flounder filet, cordon bleu and a great selection of sandwiches. 107 Town Square, Burnsville, NC 28714. 682-3946. Lunch only: 11 a.m.-2 p.m. www.garden-deli.com

Nu Wray Inn ($$): The Fireside dining room in the Nu Wray Inn offers breakfasts and dinners that have attracted visitors and local folk for years. Specialties include English roast beef dinner, fried chicken, ham and roast turkey. With each main course there are a variety of fresh vegetables, homemade biscuits, homemade dessert and a choice of coffee or tea. Breakfast is a treat with a choice of an authentic English breakfast or regional Southern cooking. A continental breakfast is also available. Dinner menus include several regional dishes and upscale daily specials. Specialty nights feature Italian cuisine, southern barbecue and English fish and chips. Town Square, P.O. Box 156, Burnsville, NC 28714. (828) 682-2329, (800) 368-9729. Breakfast: 8-9:30 a.m. Monday-Friday, 7:30-9:30 a.m.; Dinner Monday-Thursday 5:30-8 p.m., Friday & Saturday 5:30-10 p.m.; Sunday Lunch 11:30 a.m.-2:30 p.m. www.nuwrayinn.com

Sally's Kitchen ($): Southern country cooking featuring crisp fresh salads, sandwiches, country dinners, South Toe dogs, fresh baked pies and pizza. 5735 Hwy. 80 South, Burnsville, NC 28714. 675-1881. Monday, Wednesday, Thursday & Friday: 11 a.m.-2 p.m. (lunch), 5-8 p.m. (dinner). Saturday & Sunday noon-7 p.m.

Accommodations

Clear Creek Ranch: A full-service dude ranch patterned after western ranches. Great secluded mountainside location surrounded by the Pisgah National Forest. Views, horseback riding, great trout fishing in nearby South Toe River and in private pond hayrides, cookouts, campfires, line dancing, whitewater rafting and much more. Season is April through Thanksgiving. 100 Clear Creek Dr., Burnsville, NC 28714. (800) 651-4510. Adults $195, Children 6-15 $125, Children 2-5 $40. www.clearcreekranch.com/main.html

Nu Wray Inn: Opened in 1833, the Nu Wray Inn is the oldest continuously operating inn in western North Carolina. Its two-tiered porch is a favorite place for guests to relax and enjoy the rocking chairs. 26 guest rooms and six suites, landscaped grounds, garden fountain and large deck. Town Square, P.O. Box 156, Burnsville, NC 28714. (828) 682-2329, (800) 368-9729. $80-$100. www.nuwrayinn.com

Terrell House Bed & Breakfast: Located in a nice, quiet neighborhood within walking distance of town square, shops and restaurants. A restored 1900s colonial built as a girl's dormitory for the Stanley McCormick School. Six guest rooms with private bath, sitting area and queen or twin beds. Full breakfast served on fine china in the formal dining room. 109 Robertson St., Burnsville, NC 28714. 682-4505. $65-$80.

Wray House Bed & Breakfast: Located just off the town square, the Wray House, built in 1902, offers a combination of gourmet and country. Each guest room offers a different and very appealing decor with queen-size bed and well-appointed private bath. 2 South Main St., P.O. Box 546, Burnsville, NC 28714-2929. (877) 258-8222, 682-0445. $65-$125. www.wrayhouse.net

Canton & Clyde

Website: www.cantonnc.com, www.haywood-nc.com
Phone: Haywood County Chamber of Commerce: (828) 456-3021
Canton City Hall: (828) 648-2363
Clyde City Hall: (828) 627-2566
Elevation: Canton: 2,589 feet, Clyde: 2,460 feet
County: Haywood

Population: Canton: 2,500, Clyde: 1,336
Attractions: Canton Area Historical Museum, Old Pressley Sapphire Mine (Canton)

Located just to the west of Asheville, the two small towns of Canton and Clyde are situated next to each other along the Pigeon River, and are grouped together because of that in my guidebook. Both are great little towns that are mainly light industrial, with the major industry, Blue Ridge Papers, formerly the Champion Paper Mill, dominating the scene in Canton.

Dining

Corner Sandwich Shoppe ($): Favorite local restaurant featuring a wide menu of delicious sandwiches, hotdogs, burgers and salads. 127 Park St., Canton, NC 28716. 648-5757. Monday-Saturday, 11 a.m.-9 p.m.

Skeeter's Park Street Café & Barbecue House ($): Another local favorite specializing in Eastern Carolina barbeque. Southern country breakfasts also. 79 Park St., Canton, NC 28716. 648-8595. Monday-Saturday 7 a.m.-9 p.m.

Accommodations

Earthbound Lodging: A wilderness resort located on 70 acres of riverfront and mountainside property near the Blue Ridge Parkway. Offering hiking and biking trails, tubing, campfires, fishing and movies. Secluded and riverfront tent/RV sites, unique camping cabins and a furnished lodge suite. Pets welcome. 22 Water Way, Canton, NC 28716. 648-8867, (877) 789-4770. $33-$78. www.earthboundlodging.com

WindDancers Lodging & Llama Treks: New B&B nestled in a peaceful mountain cove of woodlands, streams and pastures of llamas! Nine bright spacious guest rooms in three contemporary log buildings offer a choice of exotic, ethnic decors. Tubs for two, kitchens, fireplaces, VCR, decks, patios, trails and great views. Wind-Dancers is also a llama ranch and trekking company. On their surrounding 270 trail-filled mountain acres, or in the nearby Pisgah National Forest, their wonderful, wooly llamas work for a living. WindDancers guides have selected beautiful trails and the llamas carry the gear, supplies and fresh food for an exciting, gourmet adventure. Meet these gentle creatures and explore the ancient Smoky Mountains. 1966 Martins Creek Rd., Clyde, NC 28721. 627-6986. $115.

Cashiers

Website: www.cashiers-nc.com
Phone: Chamber of Commerce: (828) 743-5941, (828) 743-5191
Elevation: 3,486 feet
County: Jackson
Population: 1,500; second-home families and part-time residents: 10,000
Attractions: Zachary-Tolbert House Museum, Waterfalls

Nestled in the southwestern section of the mountains, Cashiers is a beautiful, upscale little town that has welcomed visitors for over 150 years. Nineteen easily accessible pristine waterfalls in the immediate area are one of the main attractions as well as the excellent restaurants and numerous gift, antique and craft shops.

Dining

Brown Trout Mountain Grille ($$): Specializing in Fresh Mountain Cuisine and Chef Daniel's specialty of the day featuring trout, steak, seafood, lamb, pasta and pizza cooked to perfection. Delicious appetizers, wines, spirits and live music. Children's menu. Reservations required. 35 Hwy. 281 North, Lake Toxaway, NC 28747. 877-3474. Seven days a week. Dinner beginning at 5:30 p.m. until closing.

Horacio's Restaurante ($$): Haute cuisine. Wide variety of dishes, everything prepared fresh daily. Seafood, Italian, lamb specials, pizzas, shrimp dishes and more. Hwy. 64 East, Cashiers, NC 28717. 743-2792. Reservations suggested. Dinner only. 5 p.m. until closing, Monday through Saturday.

Lightwater Grille ($$): Specializing in fresh fish, quality steaks and featuring daily chef specialties. Dine inside or outside on the porch overlooking the pond. Reservations suggested. Hwy. 107 North, ½ mile from the crossroads on the left. 743-5410. March-November. Lunch: Tuesday-Saturday 11:30 a.m.-2 p.m. Dinner: 5:30 p.m. until closing.

The Orchard ($$): American cuisine with southern flavor, wide-ranging menu. Fresh mountain trout, fresh seafood, beef, lamp, pork, chicken. Known for their "Menninger lamb chops" and macadamia nut. salmon dishes. Brown-bagging policy. 905 Hwy. 107 South, Cashiers, NC 28717. 743-7614. Reservations suggested. Summer-Fall: Tuesday-Sunday, 5:30 p.m. until closing. During off-season, call for dinner hours.

Wild Thyme Gourmet Continental Café ($$): Gourmet sandwiches on freshly baked breads, great homemade soups and pastries. Village Walk, Unit A, Cashiers, NC 28717. 743-1065. Summer: Monday-Saturday, 9:30 a.m.–9:30 p.m. Winter season, call for hours.

Accommodations

Innisfree Victorian Inn: 11 luxuriously appointed rooms and suites, some with four-poster canopied beds, private garden tubs, fireplaces and verandahs. Overlooking Lake Glenville. Candlelit breakfast in tower, afternoon and evening refreshments, AAA Four-Diamond Aware. Hwy. 107 North (PO Box 469), Glenville, NC 28736. Call for directions. 743-2946. $119-$300. www.innisfreeinn.com

Fairfield Sapphire Valley Resort: A true four-season resort offering golf, tennis, horseback riding, indoor and outdoor pools, canoes, paddle boats, fishing boats, hiking and skiing in winter. Two restaurants, hotel rooms, efficiencies, 1- to 3-bedroom condos. 70 Sapphire Valley Rd., Sapphire, NC 28744. (800) 533-8268, 743-3441. $90-$245.

High Hampton Inn & Country Club (NRHP): 116 rooms, 18-hole golf course with bent grass greens, six clay tennis courts, private lake, fishing, sailing, swimming. Children's programs. Fitness and hiking trails. Open April through November. American plan, inn and cottages. Also 2-, 3-, and 4-bedroom colony homes with daily maid service. 1525 Hwy. 107 South, Cashiers, NC 28717. (800) 334-2551, 743-2411. $89-$120. www.HighHamptonInn.com

Millstone Inn: Spectacular mountain views from the 11 elegantly furnished rooms and suites. Lovely sitting room with large fireplace, antiques and exposed beams. Peace and tranquility in eight acres with hiking trails to the Nantahala Forest and Silverslip Falls. Hwy. 64 (PO Box 949), Cashiers, NC 28717. (888) 645-5786, 743-2737. $131-$198. www.millstoneinn.com

Singing Water Camping Resort: Sixty-four campsites (42 full hookup, 20 W/E; 32 sites on stream) fire rings, grills and picnic tables on all sites. Swimming pond, campstore, two playgrounds, tenter's kitchen, laundry, rustic cabins. All facilities open May 1 through October 31. Call for rates. 1006 Trout Creek Rd., Tuckaseegee, NC 28783. 293-5872. www.gocampingamerica.com/singingwaterc

Cherokee

SEE: Section on Cherokee Indian Reservation in Cultural Attractions
Websites: www.cherokee-nc.com
www.cherokeecountychamber.com
Phone: Cherokee County Chamber of Commerce: (828) 837-2242
Cherokee Welcome Center: (800) 438-1601, (828) 497-9195
Elevation: 3,000 feet
County: Cherokee
Population: 13,079
Attractions: Harrah's Cherokee Casino, Mountain Farm Museum, Museum of the Cherokee Indian, Oconaluftee Indian Village, Unto These Hills Outdoor Drama of the Cherokee, Qualla Arts & Crafts Mutual

Located in the heart of the Cherokee Indian Reservation, the village of Cherokee is a major destination. Offering a wide range of accommodations, restaurants and things to do, Cherokee is host to hundreds of thousands of visitors each year. The main attraction in the area is Harrah's Cherokee Casino, but other more historical attractions are also very popular, especially the Oconaluftee Indian Village and Unto These Hills Outdoor Drama.

Dining

Fresh Market Square at Harrah's Casino ($): 400-seat capacity buffet located in the casino. All you can eat. Breakfast: 11:15 p.m. to 9 a.m. Lunch: 11 a.m.–4 p.m. Dinner: 4-10 p.m. Harrah's Casino, Intersection of Hwy. 19 and Business Rte. 441, Cherokee, NC 28719. 497-7777.

Grandma's Country Buffet ($): All you can eat dining, featuring selections of fried chicken, seafood, beef, hickory smoked ribs, home-cooked vegetables, baked beans, hush puppies, salad bar and fresh-made desserts. Intersection of

Hwy. US 19 and US 441, Cherokee, NC 28719. 497-4504. Breakfast, lunch and dinner: 7 a.m.-closing (9-10 p.m.).

Granny's Kitchen ($): Locally known for great country cooking. Specialties include roast beef, steak, southern fried chicken, ham, soups and fresh trout on Friday nights. Full salad bar. 1058 Paint Town Rd. (Hwy. 19), Cherokee, NC 28719. 497-5010. Summer hours: 7-9 p.m. Closed Monday.

Seven Sisters Restaurant at Harrah's Casino ($$): Fine dining in the casino. Dinner: Wednesday, Thursday and Sunday 5-10 p.m., Friday & Saturday 5-11 p.m. Harrah's Casino, Intersection of Hwy. 19 and Business Rte. 441, Cherokee, NC 28719. 497-7777.

Tee Pee Restaurant ($$): Wide menu featuring a full buffet, country cooking, fresh trout and more. Open seven days a week serving breakfast, lunch and dinner. 7 a.m.-9 p.m. 516 Tsali Boulevard, Cherokee, NC 28719. 497-5141.

Accommodations

Cherokee KOA Resort Campground: Top-rated KOA resort offering 420 sites on 25 acres. Primitive tent sites, paved sites with full hook-ups and everything in-between. Swimming, tennis, huge Jacuzzi, movies, trout fishing, playground, volleyball, kennels, rental cars, dataports, game room and entertainment. 113 cozy Kamping Kabins and seven Kamping Kottages on the river and by the trout ponds. 92 KOA Kamping Rd., Cherokee, NC 28719. (800) 825-8352, 497-9711. Tent sites: $23.25-$29.25, Kabins: $49.95-$84.95, Kottages: $139. www.cherokeekoa.com

Harrah's Casino Hotel: 252-room world-class hotel located adjacent to the casino and connected by the Sky Bridge Walkway. Indoor pool, hot tub and exercise facility. Five-story parking garage with valet service. Shelu Restaurant in hotel offering room service. Harrah's Casino, Intersection of Hwy. 19 and Business Rte. 441, Cherokee, NC 28719. 497-7777. $129-$199, Discount for Player's Card members. www.harrahs.com

Newfound Lodge: 75 units available, private balconies on the Oconaluftee River, swimming pool with in-ground heated spa, access to trout fishing on the river, A/C, cable TV, phones, two miles from Harrah's Cherokee Casino. Big Boy restaurant on premises. 1192 Tsali Blvd (441 North), Cherokee, NC 28719. 497-2746. $54-$88.

Panther Creek Lodge & Cabins: Offering premier creekside cabins. Fireplaces and Jacuzzis, antiques and Native American decor, full kitchens and baths, linens and firewood provided. Wrights Creek Rd., Cherokee, NC 28719. 926-2613. $57 economy cabin per night, $497 per week, 3-night and weekend specials. www.panthercreekresort.com

Riverside Motel and Campground: 34 waterfront rooms looking out on the Soco River. A/C, cable TV, queen-size beds, sheltered picnic area with grills, swimming pool, campground with 30 shady waterfront hookup sites, tube rafting, one mile to Harrah's Cherokee Casino. 441 South at Old 441, Cherokee, NC 28719. 497-9311. www.riversidemotelnc.com

Chimney Rock

Websites: www.thehickorynutgorge.com
www.lake-lure.com
Phone: Hickory Nut Gorge Chamber of Commerce: (828) 625-2725
Elevation: 1,000 feet
County: Rutherford
Population: 200+
Attractions: Chimney Rock, Hickory Nut Gorge, Lake Lure

Located in the beautiful Hickory Nut Gorge area south of Asheville, the village of Chimney Rock sits at the base of the famous Chimney Rock and along the Rocky Broad River. Primarily catering to tourists who are visiting the Rock and nearby Lake Lure, the village is a convenient stopping spot for lunch or some souvenir shopping.

Dining

Duncan's Bar-B-Que ($): Duncan's Bar-B-Que has been serving great barbeque since 1967. They specialize in hickory-smoked barbeque pork, both sliced and minced, hickory-smoked ribs, sold by the portion, pound, or rack, and all-beef jumbo hotdogs. Dinners include great homemade slaw and baked beans. Located along the river in Chimney Rock Village, they offer riverside picnic tables with a beautiful view of the Rocky Broad River and surrounding mountains. Main St., Chimney Rock, NC 28720. 625-1578. Open Wednesday-Sunday and weekends only during the winter.

Esmeralda Inn Restaurant ($$): Fine dining in a historic inn with great views and beautiful gardens. Specializing in "Southern Fine Dining Cuisine" and known for their shrimp and grits, coastal seafood, mountain trout, beef, pork, duck and quail. From the soup to the desserts, all dishes are made to order in-house from scratch. A children's menu is available. PO Box 57, Chimney Rock, NC 28720, 625-9105. Open April-November for lunch and dinner. Thursday-Saturday 5:30 8:30. Reservations required. www.esmeraldainn.com

Genny's Family Restaurant ($): Genny's Family Restaurant is a totally smoke-free and alcohol-free restaurant that has been open since 1976. They specialize in homestyle cooking with a wide variety of vegetables and side orders such as real mashed potatoes, pinto beans, grandma's green beans, homemade coleslaw, potato salad, rice and gravy, hushpuppies and cornbread. Lunch and dinner specials include homemade chicken and dumplings, country-style steak, and locally raised fresh mountain trout. Desserts include homemade apple pie and hot blackberry cobbler. Dine inside or on the deck overlooking the Rocky Broad River. 451 Hwy. 74A, Chimney Rock, NC 28720. 625-2171. Open year-round Monday through Saturday 8 a.m.-8 p.m. during summer season. Call for hours November-March.

Laura's House ($): Family-style home cooking served with Southern hospitality. Located across the street from the entrance to Chimney Rock Park, it serves "all you can eat" Southern family-style meals. Completely renovated in 2001, the restaurant has a 130-year tradition of serving meals on this property. Fine food, great views and Southern hospitality! 390 Main St., Chimney Rock, NC 28720. (828) 625-9125. Monday-Thursday 11 a.m.-8 p.m., Friday 11 a.m.-9 p.m., Saturday-Sunday 8 a.m.-8 p.m.

The Cajun Pig ($): Serving award-winning hickory-smoked barbeque, mesquite-smoked ribs, beef brisket and chicken in distinctive log cabin setting. Other specialties include Cajun gumbo jambalaya, and red beans and rice. 496 Main St., Chimney Rock, NC 28720. 625-0701. Friday 5-8 p.m., Saturday 11 a.m.-8 p.m., Sunday 11 a.m.-4 p.m. www.cajunpig.com

Accommodations

Esmeralda Inn: 14 guest rooms with private baths in a historic 20,000 sq.ft. inn. Great views and beautiful gardens. Continental breakfast. Excellent in-house restaurant. Open February-December. PO Box 57, Hwy. 74A, Chimney Rock, NC 28720. 625-9105. $99-$129. www.esmeraldainn.com

The Carter Lodge on the River: Located next to the Rocky Broad River, The Carter Lodge offers 16 rooms with balconies overlooking the river, including a honeymoon suite. Trout fishing, picnicking and great views. 273 Main St., Chimney Rock, NC 28720. 625-8844. $65-$125. www.carterlodge.com

Columbus

Website: www.nc-mountains.org
Phone: Polk County Visitor Center: (800) 440-7848
Elevation: 1,131 feet
County: Polk
Population: 992
Attractions: Polk County Courthouse, FENCE

Columbus is the Polk County seat where the government offices and the historic courthouse are located. The beautiful Polk County Courthouse is one of the oldest still in use in North Carolina and has been fully restored to its original grandeur.

Dining

Calvert's Kitchen ($): Family dining in a cozy atmosphere. Mills St., Columbus, NC 28722. (828) 894-0268. Monday, Tuesday, Thursday & Friday: 11 a.m.-8 p.m., Wednesday: 11 a.m.-2 p.m.

El Sureno ($): Mexican food. 205 East Mills St., Columbus, NC 28722. (828) 894-0541. Sunday-Thursday: 11 a.m.-10 p.m., Friday & Saturday: 11 a.m.-11 p.m.

The Brick ($): International cuisine. Mill St., Columbus, NC 28722. (828) 894-2299. Monday-Friday: 11:30 a.m.-9 p.m., Sat: 4-9 p.m.

Accommodations

Butterfly Creek Inn: Tucked next to a mountain creek, complete with waterfall, the Butterfly Creek Inn offers great breakfasts, bedside treats, flowers and candlelight desserts. The also offer spa services and other amenities. 780 Smith Dairy Rd., Columbus, NC 28722. (828) 894-6393. www.butterflycreek.net

Cullowhee

Website: www.mountainlovers.com
Phone: Jackson County Travel & Tourism: (800) 962-1911, (828) 586-2155
Elevation: 2,400 feet
County: Jackson
Population: 4,000
Attractions: Western Carolina University, Mountain Heritage Center

The community of Cullowhee is home to Western Carolina University, a member of the University of North Carolina system, and is located in a scenic valley about 45 minutes west of Asheville. A college town, Cullowhee is also a stopping point for the millions of visitors who are drawn to this mid-mountain region for its spectacular landscapes and vast array of outdoor recreational opportunities, including world-class mountain biking, backpacking and whitewater rafting.

Dining

The Blue Squirrel ($): Burgers, soups, salads, pizzas and more. Live entertainment evenings. Old Cullohwee Rd., Cullowhee, NC 28723. 293-7472. Monday-Sunday 11 a.m.–3 p.m.

Accommodations

Fox Den Cottages: Three cottages with elegant interiors that include light oak floors, complete kitchens, wood-burning fireplaces and washers and dryers. Linens, dishes, split and stacked firewood, satellite TV, covered decks with country rockers and barbeque grills with each cottage also. 46 Redtail Ln. (PO Box 129), Cullowhee, NC 28723. 293-0828, (800) 721-9847. $75-$100. www.cat2.com/foxden/

The River Lodge Bed & Breakfast: Tucked in the Blue Ridge Mountains on a river bend, the River Lodge was built with 100-year-old hand-hewn logs taken from old barns and cabins from the Smoky Mountains and sits on six acres of manicured fields with several streams that flow into the Tuckaseegee River. A cascading waterfall runs alongside the inn and a standing forest of 100-year-old pines are the backdrop. Rhododendrons, hemlocks and ferns line a long driveway that winds its way to the entrance. Complimentary full breakfast. 619 Roy Tritt Rd., Cullowhee, NC 28723. 293-5431, (877) 384-4400. $115-$220. www.bbonline.com/nc/riverlodge/index.html

Dillsboro

Websites: www.visitdillsboro.org
www.dillsboromerchants.com
Phone: Jackson County Travel & Tourism: (800) 962-1911, (828) 586-2155
Elevation: 1,800 feet

County: Jackson
Population: 200+
Attractions: Great Smoky Mountains Railroad

Founded by Williams Dills in 1884 just after the coming of the Western North Carolina Railroad, Dillsboro was incorporated in 1889. An early destination stop not only because of its abundance of scenic mountain location and railroad, this quaint mountain village had many popular restaurants and tourist hotels, one of which, the historic Jarrett House, is still serving great meals. Today Dillsboro is well-known as one of the best places to board the Great Smoky Mountain Railroad, a very popular tourist excursion train.

Dining

Dillsboro Smokehouse ($$): A full-service restaurant specializing in hickory-smoked barbecue: pork, chicken, beef, ribs and turkey. Rated "Best in USA" by the Houston Chronicle in 1994. 403 Haywood St., Dillsboro, NC 28725. 586-9556. April-November: Monday-Thursday 11 a.m.-9 p.m., Friday-Saturday 11 a.m.-10 p.m., Sunday 11 a.m-8 p.m. December-March: Monday-Thursday 11 a.m.-8 p.m., Friday 11 a.m.-9 p.m., Sunday 11 a.m.-3 p.m.

Dillsboro Steak & Seafood ($$): Family-owned and -operated restaurant serving fresh seafood and the finest steaks. Seafood specialties served broiled, blackened, stuffed or lightly hand-breaded for deep frying perfection. 489 Haywood Rd., Dillsboro, NC 28725. 586-8934, FAX (828) 586-0123. Lunch: Tuesday-Sunday 11:00 a.m.-4 p.m. Dinner: Tuesday-Saturday 4-9 p.m., Sunday 4-8 p.m. www.dillsborosteak-seafood.com

Jarrett House ($$): Traditional country cooking served family-style in an inn that dates back to 1884. Dine in a historic setting. 100 Haywood St., Dillsboro, NC 28725. (800) 972-5623, 586-0265. April-December: Lunch: Monday-Saturday 11:30 a.m.-2:30 p.m. Dinner: 4-8 p.m. Sunday traditional dinner served family-style: 11:30 a.m.-2:30 p.m. and 4-8 p.m.

New Horizons Café ($): Daily "soup 'n' sandwich" special. Sandwiches, salads, vegetarian selections, fresh baked pies and cakes. 16 Dills St., Dillsboro, NC 28725. 631-0088. Open daily from 7:30 a.m. until 4 p.m. Dinner: Friday 5-8 p.m.

The Well House ($$): Serving gourmet deli sandwiches since 1977. Homemade soups, their own smoked barbeque and delicious desserts. Dine-in, take-out, picnic box lunches. Craft Circle, Dillsboro, NC 28725. 586-8588. Monday-Wednesday 11 a.m.-3 p.m. Thursday-Friday 11 a.m.-8 p.m. Saturday 11 a.m.-3 p.m. Closed Sunday.

Accommodations

Applegate Inn Bed & Breakfast: Located within walking distance of dining, shopping, fishing and the Great Smoky Mountains Railroad, this one-level bed and breakfast offers full breakfast, private entrances, whirlpool tubs and fireplaces. 163 Hemlock St., Dillsboro, NC 28725. 586-2397, FAX 828 586-2397. $80-160. www.applegatebed-breakfast.com

Dillsboro Inn: Riverfront bed and breakfast next to waterfall on whitewater river adjacent to Riverfront Shops. Four bedrooms and two suites, three fireplaces, hot tub, private baths. 146 New River Rd., Dillsboro, NC 28725. 586-3998. $80-$120. www.earthplaza.com/dillsboro

Jarrett House: Built in 1884, this refurbished inn features guest rooms in the style of that period. Step back in history! Acclaimed restaurant on premises features country cooking served family-style. 100 Haywood St., Dillsboro, NC 28725. (800) 972-5623, 586-0265. $80-$120. www.jarretthouse.com

Olde Towne Inn: Comfortable country charm and cooking in historic 1878 farmhouse across the street from the Great Smoky Mountains Railroad and shops. 300 Haywood St., Dillsboro, NC 28725. (888) 528-8840, 586-3461. $80-$160. www.dillsboro-oldtowne.com

Squire Watkins Inn: Located in downtown Dillsboro near the shops. Great shady porch for reading and watching! 657 Haywood St., Dillsboro, NC 28725. (800) 586-2429, 586-5244. $80-$120.

Forest City

Websites: www.townofforestcity.com
www.rutherfordtourism.com

Phone: Forest City Manager: (828) 245-4747
Rutherford County Tourism Development Authority: (800) 849-5998, (828) 245-1492

Elevation: 1,100 feet

County: Rutherford

Population: 7,450

Attractions: Lake Lure, Chimney Rock, Rutherford County Farm Museum, Rutherford County Museum

Located on the far eastern edge of the mountains, Forest City was incorporated in 1877 as Burnt Chimney, with the name changed to Forest City in 1887. This small city in the foothills has much to offer visitors, including a nice selection of stores. Forest City is also known for the great display of Christmas lights that brighten the downtown area every holiday season.

Dining

Caulfield's Restaurant ($): Italian-American cuisine, casual atmosphere with piano entertainment nightly. Known for Philly steak and cheese subs. Full line of Italian classic dishes. 220 Oak St. Extension, Forest City, NC 28043. 286-0707. Lunch and dinner: Thursday, Friday, Saturday and Sunday 11 a.m.-9 p.m.

Daily Grind Neighborhood Espresso Bar & Eatery ($): Great coffee and espresso, muffins, bagels, danishes baked fresh daily. Known for brownies. Soups and bread bowls. Wide variety of sandwiches and specialty desserts, including their famous sour cream coconut cake. Outdoor dining in the summer, and jazz and blues music on Friday and Saturday nights. 106 West Main St., Forest City, NC 28043. 248-2700. Tuesday-Friday 7 a.m.-5 p.m., Saturday 8 a.m.-3 p.m.

Accommodations

Comfort Inn: A/C, cable TV, phones, in-room coffee, hair dryers, micro fridges, dataports, whirlpool tubs, non-smoking rooms, meeting/banquet room (50 persons) golf packages, outdoor pool, FREE deluxe continental breakfast. 205 Commercial Dr., Forest City, NC 28043. 248-3400.

Jameson Inn: A/C, cable TV, phones, pool, non-smoking rooms, handicap rooms, exercise equipment, deluxe continental breakfast. Hwy. 74A next to Tri-City Mall. (800) 526-3766, 287-8788.

Ramada Limited: A/C, cable TV, phones, pool, non-smoking and handicap rooms, complimentary breakfast. No pets. Business services. 2600 US Hwy. 74-A Bypass near Tri-City Mall. (800) 232-8574.

Franklin

Website: www.franklin-chamber.com
Phone: Franklin Chamber of Commerce: (800) 336-7829, (828) 524-3161
Elevation: 1,900 feet
County: Macon
Population: 3,024
Attractions: Franklin Gem & Mineral Museum, Macon County Historical Museum, Scottish Tartans Museum, Perry's Water Garden

Know as the "Gem of the Smokies," Franklin is the county seat of Macon County and is next to the Little Tennessee River. Much of the land around Franklin is unspoiled national forest, making the town an excellent stopping-off point if your destination is the wilderness. The Franklin area is also known for many gem mines, with rubies, sapphires and garnets the major gemstones found. In September, the Macon County Fair, the state's only true agricultural fair, is held here and in October, Scottish Heritage Week brings to life traditional concerts, lectures and highland games.

Dining

BJ's Ribs & Bar-B-Que ($): Southern-style ribs and barbecue. 549 Highlands Rd., Franklin, NC 28734. 349-9784. Seven days a week, 11 a.m.-7 p.m.

Talent's Stage Stop ($$): Great little lunch spot located downtown. 130 Palmer St., Franklin, NC 28734. 524-2064. Tuesday-Friday: 11 a.m.-3 p.m. for lunch and Friday 5-8:30 p.m. for dinner.

The Chef & His Wife ($$): Known for their fine steaks and seafood. In business since 1995. 15 Courthouse Plaza, Franklin, NC 28734. 369-0575. Monday-Friday Lunch: 11 a.m.-2:30 p.m. Dinner: Tuesday-Saturday 5-9 p.m.

The Summit Inn Restaurant ($$): American cuisine: shrimp, steak, chicken, with vegetarian meals as well. Mountain trout a specialty of the house. 210 E. Roger St., Franklin, NC 29734. 524-2006. Open March through December.

Willy's Bar-B-Que ($): Southern style barbecue. 240 Cunningham Rd., Franklin, NC 28734. 524-0414. Monday-Thursday 11 a.m.-2:30 p.m., 5-8:30 p.m. Friday-Saturday 11 a.m.-2 p.m., 5-9 p.m. Closed Sunday.

Accommodations
Buttonwood Inn Bed & Breakfast: A small, four-room bed and breakfast adjacent to the public Franklin Golf Course, Buttonwood Inn is decorated in a delightful country-home motif, featuring antiques, handmade-family quilts, collectibles and country crafts. 50 Admiral Dr., Franklin, NC 28734. 369-8985, (888) 368-8985. $55-$82.

Hummingbird Lodge: Located on a mountaintop setting, Hummingbird Lodge offers three guest suites and gourmet breakfast! Their breakfast menu includes french toast sundaes with fresh fruit and whipped cream (topped with a cherry, of course), popovers with ham gravy and asparagus, a down-to-earth farmer's breakfast, or pancakes with ice cream. You will find an accompaniment of homemade granola, muffins, breads, seasonal fruit, assorted teas, and Gevalia coffee. 1101 Hickory Knoll Ridge Rd., Franklin, NC 28734. 369-0430. $85-$95. www.hummingbirdlodge.com/index.html

Mountainside Vacation Lodging: Small, privately owned and operated five-unit vacation suites facility that offers private porches, great views and cozy immaculate rooms. Excellent AAA ratings. All units have front porches with rocking chairs and swings overlooking the Watauga Vista Valley. 8356 Sylva Hwy., Franklin, NC 28734. 524-6209. $60-$70. www.franklin-chamber.com/mtsidevacationlodging/

The Franklin Terrace (NRHP): The Franklin Terrace, built as a school in 1887, is a lovely two-story bed and breakfast that offers nostalgic charm and comfortable accommodations. Its wide porches and large guest rooms filled with period antiques return to a time gone by when Southern hospitality was at its best. 159 Harrison Avenue, Franklin, NC 28734. 524-7907. $52-$69. www.franklinterrace.com/

The Snow Hill Bed & Breakfast (NRHP): The Snow Hill Inn bed and breakfast is located eight miles north of downtown Franklin on 14 acres of quiet seclusion. Croquet or badminton available in the summer on the lawn, or just relax on the shaded porch. Full breakfast. 531 Snow Hill Rd., Franklin, NC, 28734. 369-2100, (800) 598-8136. $69-$99. www.bbonline.com/nc/snowhill/rooms.html

Hayesville
Website: www.claycounty-nc-chamber.com
Phone: Clay County Chamber of Commerce: 828 389-3704
Elevation: 2,200 feet
County: Clay
Population: 400

Attractions: Historic Clay County Courthouse, nearby Lake Chatuge, John C. Campbell Folk School, Peacock Playhouse (Home of the Licklog Players Theatrical Group)

Hayesville is a tiny village located at the heart of Clay County in the far western reaches of the mountains. The focal point of the town is the historic county seat courthouse, built in 1888 where many of the county's festivities are held. Clay County is one of the least populated counties in Western North Carolina and offers the visitors an abundance of outdoor activities. Hayesville is also home to the famous John C. Campbell Folk School. Expect to meet really friendly folks on your visit to Hayesville!

Dining

Country Cottage Restaurant ($): Casual dining in a friendly, homey atmosphere. Home-cooked food and homemade desserts. Affordable prices and a wide menu. Very popular restaurant with local folks. Hwy. 69 South, Hayesville, NC 28904. 389-8621. Breakfast, lunch and dinner: Monday-Thursday 6 a.m.-8 p.m., Friday & Saturday 6 a.m.-9 p.m., Sunday 6 a.m.-3 p.m.

Rib Country West ($): Delicious smoked baby back barbecue ribs and sliced meat with a great choice of fixin's. Dine in or carry out. 495 Hwy. 64 Business, Hayesville, NC 28904. 389-9597. Open daily: Monday-Friday, Lunch: 11 a.m.-2 p.m., Dinner: Monday, Tuesday, Thursday, Friday 5 p.m.-closing; Saturday & Sunday, Lunch: noon-3 p.m., Dinner: 5 p.m.-closing.

The Yellow Jacket Café ($): Hamburgers, French fries, foot-long hotdogs, onion rings, salads, beverages and homemade desserts in a friendly atmosphere. 4 Hwy. 69 at Four Points, Hayesville, NC 28904. 389-1144. Breakfast and lunch, Monday-Friday 6 a.m.-4 p.m.

Accommodations

Lakeview Cottages & Marina: Chalet-style cottages nestled on Lake Chatuge. Private decks, fully equipped kitchens, A/C, cable TV. Launching ramp, barbecue hut and grills, pontoon and fishing boat rentals. Six miles east of Hayesville. 17 Cottage Court, Hayesville, NC 28904. 389-6314. $49-$75.

Deerfield Inn: Motel-style inn located on scenic Lake Chatuge with lakeviews from all rooms. Pets allowed. Spacious air-conditioned rooms with two queen-size beds and cable TV. Free continental breakfast. 40 Chatuge Ln., Hayesville, NC 28904. 389-8272. (866) 389-8272. $60-$70. www.deerfield-inn.com

Tusquittee Campground & Cabins: RV and tent camping sites with full hookups, picnic tables and grills. Heated bathhouse, pavilion, playground and nature trails. Pets allowed. In scenic, secluded Tusquittee area of Hayesville. 9594 Tusquittee Rd., Hayesville, NC 28904. 389-8520, (877) 315-6148. Open year-round. Cabins $29-$79, Campground: RV $14, Tent $12.

Highlands

Websites: www.main.nc.us/highlands
               www.highlandschamber.org
Phone: Highlands: (828) 526-2118, (828) 526-5266
               Highlands Chamber of Commerce: 828 526 2112
Elevation: 4,118
County: Macon
Population: Year-round: 3,000, second-home families and part-time residents: 25,000
Attractions: Highlands Nature Center, Waterfalls, Nantahala National Forest

Highlands is located in the heart of the beautiful Nantahala National Forest, about a two-hour drive west of Asheville. An affluent and quaint resort town with an annual influx of families that own second homes, Highlands has an abundance of fine restaurants, shops, accommodations and upscale stores. Outdoor recreational opportunities abound, including hiking, fishing, boating, horseback riding and rock climbing. Highlands is also home to the Highlands Playhouse, which for over 50 years has provided great summer stock theatre. Another great local resource is the Highlands Nature Center and Biological Station located on Horse Cove Rd.

Dining

Lakeside Restaurant ($$): A casual restaurant serving fresh seafood, beef, lamb, chicken and pasta entrees. Generous portions, delicious flavors and a lovely wine list. Daily specials. Smallwood Ave., Highlands, NC 28741. 526-9419. April-December. Reservations suggested. Dinner: Tuesday-Saturday 5:30-9 p.m.

On the Verandah ($$): Contemporary cuisine in one of Highlands' most scenic dining settings overlooking Lake Sequoyah. The owner is particularly interested in chile peppers, which appear in many dishes, as well as in a hot sauce collection, which now numbers 1,300. The hot sauces are displayed on a wall of the dining room, and are available for use by customers. 1536 Franklin Rd., Highlands, NC 28741. 526-2338. March 15-November, March: Friday & Saturday, April to Thanksgiving: Dinner seven nights a week beginning at 6 p.m. Reservations suggested. Sunday brunch from 11 a.m.-2 p.m., www. ontheverandah.com

Ristorante Paoletti ($$): Serving superb Italian cuisine for over 16 years in Highlands. Prime chops, Colorado lamb, homemade pastas and seafood. Extensive and award-winning wine list. East Main St., Highlands, NC 28741. 526-4906. Dinner 5:30-10 p.m., April: Tuesday-Saturday; May-November: Monday-Sunday; December: Saturday & Sunday only. Reservations suggested.

The Log Cabin Steakhouse ($$): Specializing in steaks, Mexican fare and Highlands' own "Cabin Onion." Located in an authentic Joe Webb cabin. Reviewed in Southern Living. Located behind the Hampton Inn in Highlands just off Hwy. 106. 526-3380. Dinner only, beginning at 5:30 p.m. seven days a week. Reservations suggested.

Wolfgang's on Main ($$$): New Orleans specialties, steaks, pastas and Bavarian food. Dining in the Garden Pavilion, outside deck or by the fireplace inside. 474 East Main St., Highlands, NC 28741. 526-3807. Closed February and March. Dinner only beginning at 5:30 p.m. Closed Wednesday. Sunday New Orleans Brunch 11:30 a.m.-2 p.m. Hours and days of operation change seasonally. Call for reservations. www.wolfgangs.net

Accommodations

4½ Street Inn: Fully restored 100-year-old house offering 10 antique-filled guest rooms with private baths, some with fireplaces. Tranquil 1.3-acre setting in town. Gourmet breakfast, wine and hors d'oeuvres, home-baked cookies. Morning paper, fluffy robes, bicycles, outdoor hot tub, wrap-around porch, gardens and sundeck. 55 4½ St., Highlands, NC 28741. (888) 799-4464, 526-4464. $110-$140. www.4andahalfstinn.com

Highlands Inn (NRHP): A cornerstone of Highlands, the Highlands Inn has been welcoming guests since 1880. Each room with private bath is individually decorated in period furnishings. Lovely extended continental breakfast included. The inn features antique furnishings, colonial paints, wallcoverings and stenciling by a master stenciling artist. 420 Main St., Highlands, NC 28741. (800) 964-6955, 526-9380. $79-$179. April-November. www.highlandsinn-nc.com

Highlands Suite Hotel: Immaculate modern two-room suites, with whirlpool spa, fireplace, cable TV with VCR, kitchenette with refrigerator, microwave and coffee maker. Private balconies and continental breakfast served daily. 200 Main St., Highlands, NC 28741. (800) 221-5078, 526-4502. $80-$155. www.highlandssuitehotel.com

Inn at Half-Mile Farm: Country inn located one half-mile from Highlands. Surrounded by 17 acres of woodlands, pastures, streams and a great pond. Guest rooms are all individually decorated and feature king- or queen-size beds, many with fireplaces, baths with jetted tubs, separate showers and private decks. Full hot breakfast and early evening hors d'oeuvres and wine. Half-Mile Rd., Highlands, NC 28741. 526-8170. (800) 946 6822. $160-$285. www.innathalfmilefarm.com

Main Street Inn: The Main Street Inn has been welcoming guests for over 100 years. The inn's architecture is of the federal farmhouse style and was restored to its original circa-1885 luster during the winter of 1998 by New York architect and designer Christopher E. Dubs. The inn offers 20 rooms with private baths, individual heating and air-conditioning, telephones, cable TV and afternoon tea. 270 Main St., Highlands, NC 28741. (800) 213-9142, 526-2590. $115-$185. www.mainstreet-inn.com

Hot Springs

Websites: www.hotspringsnc.org
www.madisoncounty-nc.com
Phone: Hot Springs Visitor Center: (828) 622-7611, (888) 446-8777
Madison County Chamber of Commerce: (828) 689-9351
Madison County Visitors Center: (828) 680 9031
Elevation: 1,330 feet
County: Madison
Population: 700+
Attractions: Whitewater Rafting on the French Broad River, Hot Mineral
Springs

Hot Springs, located on the French Broad River about 40 minutes north of
Asheville, was started when hot mineral springs were discovered in 1792. In the
early 1800s it was a famous resort town that catered to folks looking for relaxation
in the mountains as well as healing in the mineral springs. Today, Hot Springs still
welcomes visitors who wish to explore and play in the surrounding mountains, and
the naturally occurring hot springs are still an attraction as well.

Dining

Bridge Street Café ($$): The famous Bridge Street Café features elegant yet
earthy dining with the centerpiece of the kitchen the traditional Italian wood-
fired brick oven. The menu makes extensive use of fresh, locally grown organic
vegetable, organic flours and grains and has a distinctive Mediterranean flavor,
including home-baked breads, pasta dishes, seafood, chicken and duck specials,
Italian desserts and fine wines from Italy, California, Washington and Oregon.
145 Bridge St., Hot Springs, NC 28743. 622-0002. Reservations suggested.
Thursday-Sunday, dinner beginning at 5:30 p.m., Sunday brunch 11 a.m.-2
p.m. www.bridgestreetcafe.com

Mountain Magnolia Inn & Retreat ($$): Located in the historic James H. Rumbough House, this inn serves fine dining by reservation only. 204 Lawson St.
(PO Box 6), Hot Springs, NC 28743. 622-3543. Dinner served nightly 5:30-9
p.m. during the late spring to early fall season. www.mountainmagnoliainn.
com

The Paddlers Pub ($$): Upscale dining offering the freshest of foods, and even
herbs from their own gardens. Specialties include their great Maryland-style
crab cake appetizer, garlic-parmesan roasted oysters or the house favorite: local
pan-fried trout. Live entertainment. Bridge St., Hot Springs, NC 28743. 622-
0001 11:30 a.m.-9:00 p.m. seven days a week.

Accommodations

Bridge Street Café & Inn: The inn features four bright, high-ceiling rooms
overlooking Spring Creek, each furnished with antiques and with ceiling fans
and original wood floors. Two shared baths have showers. One of them boasts

an antique clawfoot tub. Guests enjoy a continental breakfast of fresh pastries, cereal, juices, organic coffee and teas served downstairs in the café. 145 Bridge St., Hot Springs, NC 28743. 622-0002. $55-75. Open through October. www.bridgestreetcafe.com

Duckett House Inn: Duckett House Inn, a turn-of-the-century farmhouse, is nestled in a lovely valley surrounded by the Pisgah National Forest. Gourmet breakfasts. State Rd. 209, Hot Springs, NC 28743. (828) 622-7621. $58-$120. www.duckethouseinn.com

Lippard House Bed & Breakfast: Built in 1875, the Lippard House is one of the oldest remaining structures in Hot Springs. Spring Creek, a lively year-round stream, meanders though the yard below the house. Breakfast included. Located three blocks from downtown. 112 Walnut St., Hot Springs, NC 28743. 622-7507. $90.

Mountain Magnolia Inn & Retreat: Located in the historic James H. Rumbough House, this inn features private baths, fireplaces, balcony and beautiful gardens. There is also a garden house with three bedrooms and two baths. Fine dining by reservation. 204 Lawson St. (PO Box 6), Hot Springs, NC 28743. 622-3543. $100-185. www.mountainmagnoliainn.com

Mountain Side Cabins: Secluded, efficient, romantic cabins that offer informal living in an atmosphere that is cozy and homey. Each cabin is private and set apart from the others, each with a backyard complete with picnic table, campfire site and barbecue pit. Great mountain views. 441 Rebel Dr., Hot Springs, NC 28743. 622-7647, 877-331-1311. $60. www.mountainsidecabins.com

Jefferson & West Jefferson

Website: www.ashechamber.com
Phone: Ashe County Chamber of Commerce: (336) 246-9550
Elevation: Jefferson: 3,000 feet, West Jefferson: 3,200 feet
County: Ashe
Population: Jefferson: 1418, West Jefferson: 1107
Attractions: Mount Jefferson State Natural Area, New River State Park, Ben Long Frescoes

Located in the heart of Ashe County, Jefferson and West Jefferson are two small mountain villages that offer convenient stopping-off points to visit the surrounding mountains and attractions, especially the Mount Jefferson State Natural Area and New River State Park.

Dining

Frasers Restaurant ($$): A full-service restaurant serving lunch and dinner. Lunch menu consists of freshly made soups, salads, sandwiches and specialties. Dinner features fresh seafood, steaks, pasta and regional favorites. 108 South Jefferson Avenue, West Jefferson, NC 28694. (336) 246-5222. Call for hours.

Glendale Springs Inn & Restaurant: Elegant French-American cuisine, also you may chose to dine on their wrap-around porch for a more casual setting. (336) 982-2103, (800) 287-1206. 7414 Hwy. 16, Glendale Springs, NC 28629. Breakfast: 8:30-9:30 a.m. (reservations required for breakfast). Lunch: 11 a.m.-2 p.m. Dinner: 5-9 p.m. Open Thursday-Tuesday, closed Wednesday. www. glendalespringsinn.com

Accommodations

Buffalo Tavern Bed & Breakfast: Located in a beautiful colonial home built in 1872 that originally was a tavern. Features three guest rooms with private baths, queen-size beds, fireplaces with gas logs and clawfoot tubs. Candlelight gourmet breakfast served on antique china with crystal and silver. 985 West Buffalo Rd., West Jefferson, NC 28694. (877) 615-9678, (336) 877-2873. $115-$135. www.buffalotavern.com

Fall Creek Cabins: Private log cabins set on 54 secluded mountain acres. Great views, trails and rushing mountain trout streams. Two-story log cabins nestled privately in the woods. Each cabin features cathedral ceilings, two bedrooms, two full baths, reading/sleeping loft, wood-burning fireplace and covered porch with hot tub, swing, rocking chairs and gas grill. PO Box 190, Fleetwood, NC 28626. (336) 877-3131. Cabin rentals from $165-$190 per night. www. fall-creek-cabins.com

Glendale Springs Inn & Restaurant: Nine guest rooms, some with fireplaces and Jacuzzis. Full breakfast with room. On Blue Ridge Parkway at Milepost 258. (336) 982-2103, (800) 287-1206. 7414 Hwy. 16, Glendale Springs, NC 28629. Breakfast: 8:30-9:30 a.m. (reservations required for breakfast). Lunch: 11 a.m.-2 p.m. Dinner: 5-9 p.m. Open Thursday-Tuesday, closed Wednesday. Open Thursday-Tuesday, closed Wednesday. www.glendalespringsinn.com

The River House: Nestled in a natural bowl of the Blue Ridge Mountains, River House is an 1870s farmhouse with rooms and cabins open year-round. It overlooks the North Fork of the ironically named New River, one of the most ancient in North America. 1896 Old Field Creek Rd., Grassy Creek, NC 28631. (336) 982-2109. www.riverhousenc.com

Lake Lure

Websites: www.lake-lure.com
http://ci.lake-lure.nc.us/
www.thehickorynutgorge.com
Phone: Town of Lake Lure Administration: (828) 625-9983
Hickory Nut Gorge Chamber of Commerce: (828) 625-2725
Elevation: 1,000 feet
County: Rutherford
Population: 1,400
Attractions: Lake Lure, Chimney Rock, Bottomless Pools

Located on the 725-acre Lake Lure, considered one of the most beautiful man-made lakes in America by *National Geographic*, the village of Lake Lure offers a good selection of shops, restaurants and accommodations.

Dining

Azaleas Restaurant at Lake Lure Golf and Beach Resort ($): American cuisine. 112 Mountains Blvd., Lake Lure, NC 28746. 625-9882. Breakfast, lunch and dinner from 8 a.m.-9 p.m. April-November. Call for hours during winter. www.lakeluregolf.com

BayFront Bar and Grill ($): BayFront Grill offers great ribs and burgers. Beer and margaritas! On the water at the junction of Hwy. 64/74A and Hwy. 9 in Lake Lure. PO Box 681, Lake Lure, NC 28746. 625-4075. Lunch starting at 11:30 a.m. Dinner starting at 5 p.m.

Lakeview Restaurant at Lake Lure Golf and Beach Resort ($$): Fine dining by candlelight. 112 Mountains Blvd., Lake Lure, NC 28746. 625-3045. Open April-November 5-9 p.m. Reservations suggested. www.lakelure golf.com

Das Kaffeehaus at Gaestehaus Salzburg ($$): Authentic German/Austrian cuisine. Homemade Austrian pastries, German beers and wines. Das Kaffeehaus began as an Austrian pastry and coffee shop, but now has become a full German restaurant that still serves fantastic pastries! Austrian music! 1491 Memorial Hwy., Lake Lure, NC 28746. 625-0093. Lunch: Wednesday-Saturday 11:30 a.m.-2 p.m. Dinner: Wednesday-Saturday 6-8 p.m. Dinner reservations required. www.gaestehaussalzburg.com

Larkin's on the Lake ($$): Larkin's serves fine steaks, seafood, mountain trout, prime rib and more. Located on the water at the junction of Hwy. 64/74A and Hwy. 9 in Lake Lure. PO Box 681, Lake Lure, NC 28746. 625-4075. Lunch starting at 11:30 a.m. Dinner starting at 5 p.m.

Accommodations

Chimney Rock Inn: Cozy rooms, cottages and kitchens, Jacuzzis, fireplaces and decks. Located between Chimney Rock and Lake Lure. 3207 Memorial Hwy., Lake Lure, NC 28746. (800) 625-2003, 625-1429. Rooms: $75-$100, Cabins: $100-$210. www.chimneyrockinn.net

Fairfield Mountains Resort: Vacation homes, condominiums and efficiency units located on Lake Lure. Resort amenities include golf, tennis, hiking, fishing, boating and swimming. 747 Buffalo Creek Rd., Lake Lure, NC 28746. 625-9111, (800) 829-3149. $170-$700 per night, 2-night minimum stay for vacation homes, $155-$295 per night, some with 2-night minimum, for condos, and $90 per night for efficiency units. www.fairfieldmountains.com

Lake Lure Golf and Beach Resort: Resort villas, homes and condos on Lake Lure. Two championship golf courses, resort amenities, three restaurants, tennis, boating, hiking, activity center, swimming pools, marina and beach. 112 Mountains Boulevard, Lake Lure, NC 28746. 625-3000. $100-$245. www.lakeluregolf.com

Lake Lure Inn and Conference Center: Historic inn that is located right across from the beach in Lake Lure. Presidents Franklin D. Roosevelt and Calvin Coolidge, Emily Post, and F. Scott Fitzgerald all have stayed at this elegant 50-room hotel. 2771 US Hwy. 64/74A. PO Box 101, Lake Lure, NC 28746. (888) 434-4970, 625-2525. $95-105. www.lakelureinn.com.

The Chalet Club: Secluded mountainside resort with lodge and seven spacious cottages. Great views, fireplaces, balconies, fishing, boating, hiking, seven miles of private trails, tennis courts and swimming pools. 532 Washburn Rd., Lake Lure, NC 28746. (800) 336-3309, 625-9315. Rooms in lodge: $210-$222, Cottages; $226-$678. www.chaletclub.com

The Lodge on Lake Lure: Elegant 12-room bed and breakfast on the lake. Boating, swimming, fishing, golf and hiking. Great views, stone fireplaces, terraces, distinctive dining and beautiful lakeside dock. PO Box 519, Lake Lure, NC 28746. (800) 733-2785, 625-2789. $149-$250. www.lodgeonlakelure.com

Lenoir

Website: www.caldwellcochamber.org
Phone: Caldwell County Chamber of Commerce: (828) 726-0616
Elevation: 1,182
County: Caldwell
Population: 16,793
Attractions: Caldwell Arts Council, Caldwell County Historical Society Heritage Museum, Fort Defiance

The county seat of Caldwell County, the city of Lenoir was named for the Revolutionary War hero General William Lenoir. Known for its furniture industry and numerous outlets, Caldwell County and Lenoir offer much to the visitor in the way of shopping and true southern hospitality.

Dining

Acapulco Mexican Restaurant ($): Lunch specials, known locally for excellent Mexican food. 110 Valencia Place NE, Lenoir, NC 28645. 754-1879. Saturday & Sunday 11 a.m.-8:30 p.m., Monday-Friday 11 a.m.-8:30 p.m.

Giovanni's of Lenoir ($): Italian cuisine; pizzas are one of their specialties. 925 Wilkesboro Blvd NE, Lenoir, NC 28645. 754-1000. 11 a.m.-9 p.m. Monday-Saturday, closed Sunday.

Village Inn Pizza Parlor ($): All-you-can-eat pizza buffet, largest salad bar in Lenoir area at 55 items. 1234 Morganton Blvd, Lenoir, NC 28645. 758-8900. Monday-Saturday 11 a.m.-10 p.m., Sunday noon-10 p.m.

Accommodations

Comfort Inn of Lenoir: 78 rooms, complimentary breakfast. 970 Blowing Rock Blvd. NE, Lenoir, NC 28645.

Jameson Inn: 350 W. Wilkesboro Rd., Lenoir, NC 28645. (828) 758-1200.

Summer Hill Bed & Breakfast: Built in 1913, Summer Hill's English-style ambiance features warm oak woodwork and fine heart pine floors. Outside there are sweeping lawns, large old oaks and a majestic vista of the Blue Ridge Mountains. A full, hot breakfast of your choice is served along with a daily newspaper. 1248 Harrisburg Dr. SW, Lenoir, NC 28645. (800) 757-0204 (Reservations), 757-0204. $75-$105.

Red Carpet Inn: 100-room hotel with comfortable guest rooms, complimentary breakfast bar and courtyard complete with swimming pool. 142 Wilkesboro Blvd., Lenoir, NC 28645. (828) 758-4403.

Linville

Website: www.averycounty.com
Phone: Avery/Banner Elk Chamber of Commerce: (828) 898-5605, (800) 972-2193
Elevation: 3,500 feet
County: Avery
Population: No information available; small unincorporated community
Attractions: Linville Caverns, Grandfather Mountain, Linville Gorge, Linville Falls

The little community of Linville, located at the foot of Grandfather Mountain, takes its name from the Linville River. Linville was originally developed as a summer resort where families from the North Carolina piedmont could escape the heat and mosquitoes that characterize summers in the south.

Dining

Eseeloa Lodge and Restaurant ($$-$$$): Fine dining in this historic country inn. Entrees at the restaurant usually include free-range chicken and rainbow trout. Jacket and tie required at dinner. 175 Linville Ave., off 221, Linville, NC 28646. (800) 742-6717, (828) 733-4311. www.eseeola.com

Accommodations

Eseeloa Lodge and Restaurant: Recently renovated, the Eseeloa Lodge is one of Western North Carolina's finest mountain getaways. Rebuilt in 1936, this lakeside lodge sits 3,800 feet above sea level and offers many outdoor activities, including golf. All rooms overlook the manicured gardens and grounds. 175 Linville Ave., off 221, Linville, NC 28646. (800) 742-6717, (828) 733-4311. www.eseeola.com

High Hampton Inn: A luxurious resort with over 1,400 acres of tall hemlocks, mixed hardwoods and mountain laurel. Besides the inn itself, High Hampton offers quaint cottages that blend into the quiet landscape. Golf, tennis, children's activities and hiking are only a few of the activities available. 1525 Hwy. 107 South, Cashiers, NC 28717. (800) 334-2551. $92-$126. www.high hamptoninn.com

Linville Falls

Website: www.averycounty.com
Phone: Avery/Banner Elk Chamber of Commerce: (828) 898-5605, (800) 972-2193
Elevation: 3,500 feet
County: Avery
Population: No information available; small unincorporated community
Attractions: Linville Caverns, Grandfather Mountain, Linville Gorge, Linville Falls

Nestled at the confluence of Highways 221 and 183, Linville Falls is a convenient stopping point for travelers from all directions. Linville Falls is named after a beautiful two-tiered waterfall located nearby. The actual Linville Falls can be reached by going one mile north on the parkway to reach the designated parking area. From there it is less than a mile hike to view the falls.

Dining

Spear's BBQ & Grill ($$): Specializing in smoked pork, trout and steaks. Providing outdoor dining. Extensive beer and wine beer. Located next to Linville Falls Lodge and Cottages, Highways US 221 and NC 183 Intersection, Linville Falls, NC 765-2658. Mid-April to October, seven days a week: 11:30 a.m.-9 p.m. November to Mid-April, Friday: 5-9 p.m., Saturday: 11 30 a.m.-9 p.m., Sunday: 11:30 a.m.-7 p.m. www.linvillefallslodge.com

Accommodations

Linville Falls Lodge and Cottages: Tall evergreens, waterfalls, peaceful walks surround this country lodge and cottages. Located at the intersection of Highways US 221 and NC 183, Linville Falls, NC 28647. (800) 634-4421, 765-2658. $60-$70, Cottages $105-$125. www.linvillefallslodge.com

Little Switzerland

Website: www.mitchell-county.com
Phone: Mitchell County Chamber of Commerce: (828) 765-9483
Elevation: 3,500 feet
County: Mitchell
Population: 200+, varies seasonally
Attractions: North Carolina Mining Museum, Emerald Village

Dining

Big Lynn Lodge Restaurant ($$): Dining with scenic mountain vistas, breakfast and dinner menus serving home cooking! NC Hwy. 226-A, Little Switzerland, NC 28749. (800) 654-5232. Reservations required. April-October, open daily 7:30-9 a.m., 6-7:30 p.m.

Chalet Restaurant at The Switzerland Inn ($$): Breakfast, lunch and dinner. Blue Ridge Parkway at NC Hwy. 226-A (Milepost 334) Little Switzerland, NC 28749. 765-2153. Call for hours. May through October.

Crabtree Meadows Coffee Shop ($): Breakfast, lunch and dinner. Eclectic menu. Milepost 340, Blue Ridge Parkway, Little Switzerland, NC 28749. 675-4236. 10 am.-6 p.m. seven days a week. May through October.

The Skyline Café ($$): Located in the Skyline Inn, the Cafe is best known for its great country breakfasts, offered daily year-round. Lunch and dinner menus offer a full selection ranging from their unique "Cheeseburger in Paradise," to rainbow trout, steaks, chicken, seafood, sandwiches, appetizers, and desserts. A wide variety of beverages is available, including a large selection of beer and wine. Located at the intersection of NC 226 and NC 226A at Milepost 331 Blue Ridge Parkway, Little Switzerland, NC 28749, 765-9394. Hours vary seasonally; call for hours. www.the-skyline.com/skyline4.htm

Mountain View Restaurant ($$): Breakfast, lunch and dinner. Full menu, Blue Ridge Parkway at NC 226 (Milepost 331), Little Switzerland, NC 28749. 765-4645. Daily breakfast, lunch and dinner. Winter: only breakfast and lunch. Call for hours.

Accommodations

Alpine Inn: Rustic mountain inn established in 1929. Great views, balconies available in some rooms and full breakfast. All rooms have private baths. Hwy. 226A, Little Switzerland, NC 28749. 765-5380. $44-$75. Open May-October. www.insidenc.com/alpineinn.htm.

Big Lynn Lodge: Restful mountain-top lodge perched on the Eastern Continental Divide next to the Blue Ridge Parkway. Relaxed atmosphere and breathtaking vistas. Modified American Plan (breakfast/dinner) included in rate. On-site game room, library, player piano, horseshoes, shuffleboard and hiking. Full-service restaurant with beer/wine permit. NC Hwy. 226-A, Little Switzerland, NC 28749. (800) 654-5232. Open Mid-April through early November. $87-$135. www.biglynnlodge.com

Skyline Inn: The historic three-story inn offers lodging on the second and third floors, with ground-level entrance to each floor. Seventeen guest rooms Each room has color cable TV and A/C. No in-room phones. Located at the intersection of NC 226 and NC 226A at Milepost 331 Blue Ridge Parkway, Little Switzerland, NC 28749. 765-9394. $45-$55. www.the-skyline.com/skyline3.htm

Switzerland Inn: Established in 1910, this historic mountain-top lodge provides "a little of Switzerland" in decor and scenic views. Full breakfast included. Great views of rolling grounds and surrounding mountains. Lodge, suites, cabins, cottages and chalets. Full-service restaurant with beer/wine permit on premises. Blue Ridge Parkway at NC Hwy. 226-A (Milepost 334), Little Switzerland, NC 28749. 765-2153. $80-$135.

Maggie Valley

Website: www.visitmaggie.com
Phone: Maggie Valley Convention & Visitors Bureau: (828) 926-1686, (800) 624-4431
Elevation: 3,020
County: Haywood
Population: 600+
Attractions: Wheels Through Time Museum, Cataloochee Ski Area

Maggie Valley is a tourist-oriented village that occupies a lush green valley in the middle of the Western North Carolina mountains. The main street though town is lined with craft, antique and gift shops, campgrounds, motels and restaurants. Whitewater rafting to horseback rides, antique motorcycles to snowboarding jumps, Maggie Valley really does have a lot to offer. The Great Smoky Mountains National Park and the Blue Ridge Parkway are both at their doorstep and the surrounding National Forests also offer many choices for exploring the wonderful setting that makes up Western North Carolina.

Dining

J. Arthur's Restaurant ($$): American cuisine. Full ABC permit. 2843 Soco Rd., Maggie Valley, NC 28751. 926-1817. Reservations suggested. November-April: Closed Sunday-Tuesday; May-October: Open seven days a week. Dinner only beginning at 5:30 p.m.

Joey's Pancake House ($): Great pancakes! 4309 Soco Rd., Maggie Valley, NC 28751. 926-0212. Open April-October. Closed Thursday. Breakfast only.

Valley Room at the Maggie Valley Resort ($$$): Fine dining, American cuisine in relaxed, luxurious setting. 1819 Country Club Dr., Maggie Valley, NC 28751. 926-1616. November-March (call for hours); April 1st-October 31st open seven days a week. Breakfast: 6:30-9:30 a.m. Lunch: 11:30 a.m.-5 p.m. Dinner: 5:30-9 p.m. Reservations suggested. www.maggievalleyresort.com

Snappy's Italian Restaurant & Pizzeria ($): Pizzas, subs, Italian dishes. 2769 Soco Rd., Maggie Valley, NC 28751. 926-6126. Open seven days a week for lunch and dinner, Sunday 5-9 p.m., Monday-Thursday 11 a.m.-10 p.m., Friday & Saturday 11 a.m.-11 p.m.

Arf's ($$): American cuisine. 4352 Soco Rd., Maggie Valley, NC 28751. 926-1566. January-April: Closed Monday-Wednesday; summer season: open seven days a week. Dinner only. 5:30 until closing.

Accommodations

Jonathan Creek Inn & Maggie Valley Villas: Jonathan Creek Inn & Maggie Valley Villas is a resort motel with a difference. All of their rooms are beautifully decorated and are full of "homey" touches and country charms. Most of the rooms feature hand-stenciling and all are decorated with handmade wreaths. Indoor heated pool, creekside hot tub, mountain-view villas, creekside villas, children's play area, creekside grill and pavilion, stocked trout stream. Three Diamond AAA rating. 4324 Soco Rd., Maggie Valley, NC 28751. (800) 577-7812, 926-1232. $69-$109. www.jonathancreekinn.com

Maggie Valley Resort: Golf resort offering lodge and villa accommodations. Swimming pool and spectacular gardens. 1819 Country Club Dr., Maggie Valley, NC 28751. 926-1616. $109-$129. www.maggievalleyresort.com

Mountain Joy Cottages: Mountain Joy Cottages are located at the historic homestead of Maggie Setzer, for whom Maggie Valley was named. All of the cottages have wood-burning fireplaces, cable TV with HBO, fully equipped kitchens, barbeque grills, picnic tables and open onto great views. The cottages feature an indoor pool and hot tub. 121 Setzer Cove Rd., Maggie Valley, NC 28751. (888) 926-1257. $130-$185 (subject to change). www.mountainjoy-cottages.com

Pioneer Village: Cozy cabins located beside Campbell Creek in Maggie Valley. Originally built over 175 years ago, the one- and two-bedroom cabins have been renovated for modern comfort and convenience. There is also a rustic four-bedroom lodge. 219 Campbell Creek Rd., Maggie Valley, NC 28751. 926-1881. $90-$125. www.geocities.com/sandilday

Smokey Shadows Lodge: Situated on a bluff at 4,500 feet, the 1953 rustic native stone and hand-hewn log Smokey Shadows Lodge features feather beds under handmade quilts and country furnishings. The long front porch offers a magnificent view. They also offer a 100-year-old chestnut log cabin with stone fireplace. Smokey Shadows Ln., Maggie Valley, NC 28751. 926-0001. $80 Lodge, $125 Cabin. www.smokeyshadows.com

The Chalet: Located in a secure and relaxing setting 150 feet above US Hwy. 19 in Maggie Valley, The Chalet offers one- and two-bedroom apartments with kitchenettes or full kitchens, studios, hot tub suites, fireplaces, cable TV, full baths and laundry facilities. Each room opens in this European setting onto a vast manicured lawn. Gas barbecues, putting green, horseshoes and a gazebo tub with deck. PO Box 1415, Maggie Valley, NC 28751. (800) 371-8587, 926-2811. April-January. $69-$179. www.visitthechalet.com

Marion

Website: www.mountaintreasures.net
Phone: McDowell County Chamber of Commerce: (828) 652-4240
Elevation: 1,395 feet
County: McDowell
Population: 5000
Attractions: Historic Carson House

Marion is the county seat of McDowell County. It is a thriving small city located on the eastern edge of the mountains and is home to many small industries including those that manufacture medical supplies, lumber and paper products, electronics and transportation equipment, tools, apparel, textiles and furniture.

Dining

Carolina Chocolatiers ($): Specialties are great chicken salad and homemade hand-dipped chocolates. 8 N. Main St., Marion, NC 28752. 652-4496. Open daily 10:30 a.m.-3 p.m., Thursday and Friday, 5-9 p.m.

Countryside Barbeque ($): Features home-cooking and weekend breakfast buffet. Rutherford Rd. near intersection of NC 226 and US 221, Marion, NC 28752. 652-4885. Tuesday-Thursday 7 a.m.-8 p.m., Friday-Saturday 7 a.m.-8:30 p.m.

Hook & Anchor Family Seafood ($): Seafood specials, spacious quarters. 950 Rutherford Rd., Marion, NC 28752. 652-9467. Wednesday-Saturday, 4-10 p.m., Sunday, noon-9 p.m.

Ivan's ($$): Full menu, specialty entrees, full-service bar. 80 Finley Rd., Marion, NC 28752. 659-9151. Sunday-Thursday 11 a.m.-9 p.m., Friday-Saturday 11a.m.-10 p.m.

Little Siena ($): Italian entrees, large fresh-cooked American lunch buffet. Intersection of US 70 West and NC 80, Marion, NC 28752. 724-9451. Monday-Thursday 11 a.m.-2 p.m., 5-9 p.m., Friday 11a.m.-2 p.m., 5-9 p.m., Saturday 5-10 p.m., Sunday 11 a.m.-9 p.m.

Accommodations

Cottages at Spring House Farm: The Cottages at Spring House Farm offer first-class accommodations in a secluded mountain environment. Spring House Farm encompasses 92 acres of hills and valleys, woodlands, meadows, fields, trails, trout ponds, creeks and streams. The original homeplace, built in 1826, is listed in the National Register of Historic Places. The four newly built resort cottages feature fully equipped kitchens, queen- or king-size beds, fireplaces, hot tubs, decks and grill. Sugar Hill Rd., Marion, NC 28752. (877) 738-9798, 738-9798. $210-$265; 2-night minimum stay. www.springhousefarm.com.

Shamrock Inn: Shamrock Inn is a restored home of the early 1900s located in downtown Marion. Five rooms including a two-room suite downstairs and four upstairs rooms. Unique stained glass and period art work. 10 West Henderson St., Marion, NC 28752. 652-5773. $65-$150. http://home.wnclink.com/shamrock

Mars Hill

Website: www.madisoncounty-nc.com
Phone: Madison County Chamber of Commerce: (828) 689-9351
Elevation: 2,325 feet
County: Madison
Population: 2,000+
Attractions: Rural Life Museum, Mars Hill College, Wolf Laurel Ski Resort

Mars Hill is a small college town perched on a hill 18 miles north of Asheville. Dominated by the gorgeous Mars Hill College campus, this quaint village is surrounded by picturesque rolling mountains and valleys. The college, a Christian liberal arts school, is the oldest educational institution in North Carolina and attracts students from all across America.

Dining

Little Creek Café ($): Since 1951 offering simple, hearty, home-cooked food seasoned with a true touch of country. Known for great homemade pies! 11660 Hwy. 23, Mars Hill, NC 28754. 689-2374. Monday-Friday 6 a.m.-8 p.m., Saturday 6 a.m.-3 p.m., Sunday 7 a.m.-3 p.m.

Main Street Deli ($): Dine in or take out. Subs, salads, sandwiches, barbeque and daily specials. North Main St., Mars Hill, NC 28754. 689-9849. Monday-Friday, (lunch) 11:30 a.m.-2:30 p.m., (dinner) 5-7 p.m., Saturday (lunch only).

Pizza Roma ($): All-you-can-eat buffet. Great white pizza with spinach. Yum! 126 Carl Eller Rd., Mars Hill, NC 28754. 689-5542. Sunday-Friday (lunch buffet) 11 a.m.-2 p.m., Tuesday-Wednesday (dinner buffet) 5-8 p.m.

Wagon Wheel Restaurant ($): Country cooking with homemade daily specials. Burgers, fries and root beer floats. Delicious homemade pies. 89 Carl Eller Rd., Mars Hill, NC 28754. 689-4755. Monday-Friday 6 a.m.-8 p.m., Saturday 6-3 p.m.

Accommodations

Comfort Inn: Award-winning property, spectacular mountain views created with the guest in mind. Many features to accommodate all types of travelers, pool, deluxe continental breakfast. 167 J.F. Robinson Ln., Mars Hill, NC 28754 (Exit 11 on Hwy. 19/23 North). 689-9000. $65-$90.

Wolf Laurel Lodge & Retreat: New lodge in the Wolf Laurel Ski Resort area, just north of Mars Hill off I-26. Large kitchen, meeting space and game room. 41 Beauty Spot Cove Rd., Mars Hill, NC 28754. 680-9173. Call for rates.

Marshall

Website: www.madisoncounty-nc.com
Phone: Madison County Chamber of Commerce: (828) 689-9351
Elevation: 1,920 feet
County: Madison
Population: 900+
Attractions: French Broad River

Located right on the beautiful French Broad River, Marshall, the county seat of Madison County, is one of the most picturesque villages in all of Western North Carolina. A fun place to visit, Marshall, like Dillsboro and other true mountain towns, retains much of its past and is like stepping back into time. There are a good selection of stores and restaurants, and of course Marshall's location along the river is a great jumping-off place to further adventures in the surrounding hills or on the river.

Dining

Rock Café ($): Full-service restaurant. Grill items, home-cooked buffet with dessert. 18 Main St., Marshall, NC 28753. 649-1566. Call for hours.

The Café ($): Great homemade pies, steaks, fish. 1650 Hayes Run Plaza, Marshall, NC 28753. 649-1033. Open seven days a week. Breakfast, lunch and dinner. Monday-Friday 6-8 p.m., Saturday-Sunday 7 a.m.-3 p.m.

Accommodations

Marshall House Bed & Breakfast: Built in 1903, with eight guest rooms. Children, smoking and pets allowed. 100 Hill St., Marshall, NC 28753. 649-9205. $40-85. www.marshallhouse.org

Morganton

Websites: www.ci.morganton.nc.us
www.burkecounty.org
www.burkecounty.com
www.hci.net/~bcttc

Phone: Morganton City Managers Office: (828) 438-5228
Burke County Chamber of Commerce: (828) 437-3021
Burke County Visitor Information Center: (828) 433-6793

Elevation: 1,182 feet

County: Burke

Population: 17,310

Attractions: Old Burke County Courthouse and Heritage Museum, Quaker Meadows Plantation, Senator Sam J. Irvin Jr. Library, Brown Mountain Lights, Lake James, South Mountains State Park, Catawba River Greenway Park

Morganton, North Carolina, the county seat of Burke County, offers the unique charms of a small city yet embraces technology, new development and progressive thinking. The heart of Morganton is its vibrant downtown filled with restaurants, galleries, clothiers and antique shops. The city is surrounded by rich natural resources that provide not only pristine water and picturesque mountain ranges but invite a host of recreation activities. Located in the foothills to the east of Asheville, Morganton also is home to the Historic Morganton Festival and the entire city celebrates children with SunFest each summer, a festival designed for children!

Dining

Judge's Riverside BBQ ($): Specializing in smoked pork, beef and chicken barbeque. Also a wide variety of other dishes. Located on the beautiful Catawba River. Outside seating on four decks. 128 Greenlea Ford Rd., Morganton, NC 28655. 433-5798. Summer hours: seven days a week, 11 a.m.-10 p.m., winter hours: Sunday-Thursday, 11 a.m.-9 p.m., Friday 11a.m.-10 p.m.

King Street Café ($$): In a 100-year old Victorian home, French cuisine dining, white tablecloth. Known for food and service. Specials nightly. 207 S. King St., Morganton, NC 28655. 437-4477. Reservations suggested. Dinner only. Wednesday-Saturday 5-9 p.m.

The Original Emporium ($): Varied menu, family-oriented. Noted for their golden harvest grill, chicken fingers and appetizers. Full bar. 1101 North Green St., Morganton, NC 28680. 433-9275. Lunch and dinner: Sunday-Wednesday 11 a.m.-9 p.m., Thursday-Saturday 11 a.m.-10 p.m.

Yianni's ($$): Mediterranean cuisine with an upscale twist. Full bar and excellent wine selection. 112 West Union St., Morganton, NC 28655. 430-8700. Lunch and dinner: seven days a week, 11 a.m.-10 p.m.

Accommodations

College Street Inn: The College Street Inn is a corporate bed and breakfast. It is a private cottage that caters to the business traveler with spacious living accommodations, private conference facilities and customized gourmet meals. 204 S. College St., Morganton, NC 28655. 430-8911. $69-$79. www.thecollegestreetinn.com

Fairway Oaks Bed & Breakfast: Located adjacent to the 5th green and 6th tee box of Silver Creek Plantation Golf Course, Fairway Oaks bed and breakfast is a four-room facility that caters to the discriminating visitor/golfer. Our rooms have king or queen beds and private baths, with telephone and cable TV. Jamestown Rd., Morganton, NC 28655. 584-7677. (888) 584-7611. $65. www.fairwayoaksbandb.com

Robardajen Woods Bed & Breakfast: Their slogan is "Back to the slower days of front-porch living" and it rings true for the cabins of this country bed and breakfast. Country breakfast served at the main lodge, four cabins with porches and rocking chairs, each completely furnished. Very close to Lake James. 5640 Robardajen Woods, Nebo, NC 28761. 584-3191. $100 per cabin nightly.

Murphy

Website: www.cherokeecountychamber.com
Phone: Murphy City Hall: (828) 837-2510
Cherokee County Chamber of Commerce: (828) 837-2242
Elevation: 1,583
County: Cherokee
Population: 2,000+
Attractions: Cherokee County Historical Museum, The John C. Campbell Folk School, Cherokee National Forest

Situated at the most western tip of North Carolina, Murphy occupies a serene corner of the mountains highlighted by hundreds of creeks, waterfalls and deep lush forests. The county seat, Murphy, offers a quaint downtown for shopping, a historic courthouse, a public library and a county historical museum.

Dining

AKATA Japanese Steak House ($$): Offers Japanese selections and open hibachi grill for family entertainment, cooking the food in front of you. 86 Hiawassee St., Murphy, NC 28906. (828) 835-3435.

Bledsoe's Mountain View Restaurant ($-$$): Located inside Mountain Vista Inn. Home cooking, serving full menu, also full buffet bar. 78 Terrace Avenue, Murphy, NC 28906. (828) 835-8912. Closed on Wednesday.

Doyle's Cedar Hill Restaurant ($$): Fine dining, relaxed atmosphere. Eclectic mix of contemporary southern, seasonal, vegetarian, international and traditional favorite dishes. Terrific wine list and brown bag. 925 Andrews Rd., Murphy, NC 28906. (828) 837-3400.

Shoebooties Café ($$): Distinctive downtown dining! Dinner entrees feature signature chef specialties a well as steak, seafood, chicken and pasta dishes. Lunches include homemade soups and quiches, fresh salads and classic deli sandwiches. Live music and baby back ribs on Friday nights; a special gourmet menu, white linen and live dinner music on Saturday nights. Distinctive imported and domestic wines; brown bagging permitted. 25 Peachtree St., Murphy, NC 28906. (828) 837-4589. Open Tuesday through Saturday for lunch and dinner, closed Sundays and Mondays.

Slow-to-Go ($): Slow-to-Go is an order-ahead, pick-up food service offering lunch and ready-to-bake meal replacement entrees. Their emphasis is on "local foods to local people," serving "slow food," made with quality, sustainable products. 945 Conaheeta St., Murphy, NC 28906. (828) 835-8646.

Accommodations

A Gathering of Angels B&B: As a mountain retreat inn and bed and breakfast they offer 12 guest rooms with private baths in a secluded mountain retreat with 50 acres, hiking trails, mountain streams, waterfalls, pond, flower gardens. Breakfast is included and massage is available. Open year-round. 181 Alf Branch Dr., Murphy, NC 28906. (828) 837-3202, (888) 837-2643. www.a-gathering-of-angels.com

Angels Landing Inn: Step back in time and enjoy old-fashioned southern living with a touch of Victorian charm. Relax on the veranda or stroll downtown or to a nearby park. 94 Campbell St., Murphy NC 28906. (828) 835-8877. www.bbonline.com/nc/angelslanding

Huntington Hall Bed & Breakfast: Each of the five spacious guest rooms, one of which is a separate cottage, has a personality of its own with period furnishings. Individual heating and air-conditioning unit, color TV and private bath are part of each room. A full breakfast, afternoon refreshments and nightly turn-down services are a part of a guest's day. 272 Valley River Ave., Murphy NC 28906. (828) 837-9567, (800) 824-6189. www.bed-breakfast-inn.com

The Eagle Ranch on Ice Mountain: A scenic destination offering cabin lodging, hiking, whitewater rafting and horseback trail riding. Located on the most western mountain range in North Carolina. 13950 US Hwy. 64 West, Murphy, NC 28906. (423) 496-1843, (800) 288-3245.

Newland

Website: www.banner-elk.com
Phone: Avery/Banner Elk Chamber of Commerce: (828) 898-5605, (800) 972-2183
Elevation: 3,621
County: Avery
Population: 706
Attractions: Avery County Museum

Newland is the county seat of Avery County and was incorporated in 1913, beating out three other areas for that honor. It also has the distinction of being the highest county seat east of the Mississippi. A recently remodeled classical courthouse overlooks a quaint town square, bordered by shops and churches and a memorial to Avery County veterans. The square is home to the annual Heritagefest on the first weekend in July and the Avery Arts Council's Art on the Square celebration on the third weekend in July.

North Wilkesboro

Websites: www.wilkesnc.org
www.north-wilkesboro.com
Phone: Town of North Wilkesboro: 336) 667-7129
Wilkes County Chamber of Commerce: (336) 838-8662
Elevation: 1,016
County: Wilkes
Population: 4,200+
Attractions: W. Kerr Scott Dam and Reservoir, Stone Mountain State Park

Each year the first weekend in October, thousands of visitors come to North Wilkesboro for the Brushy Mountain Apple Festival. This event, sponsored and organized by the Brushy Mountain Ruritan Club and the Town of North Wilkesboro, is one of the oldest and most celebrated festivals in the southeastern United States. The nearby Blue Ridge Parkway, Stone Mountain State Park and W. Kerr Scott Dam and Reservoir make North Wilkesboro a perfect spot to visit while enjoying these great outdoor attractions.

Dining

E & J Restaurant ($): 313 Wilkesboro Ave., North Wilkesboro, NC 28659. (336) 838-8112. Call for hours.

Elk Creek Inn ($$): Located outside of North Wilkesboro in nearby Ferguson, the Elk Creek Inn offers fine dining in a country (and equestrian-centered) setting. 512 Meadow Valley Rd., Ferguson, NC 28659. (336) 973-5706. Reservations recommended. Call for hours.

Sixth and Main ($$): Dinner restaurant offering a varied menu that includes great steaks and fish, specialty appetizers and exotic entrees that include grilled buffalo rib eye, Chilean seabass, elk steaks, and arctic char. Six individual dining rooms and full-service bar. 210 6th St., North Wilkesboro, NC 28659. (336) 903-1166. April-December: Tuesday-Saturday 6-10 p.m. January-March: 5:30-9:30 p.m.

The Coffee Tavern ($): Offering specialty drinks, fresh pastries and gourmet deli sandwiches in a warm, relaxing atmosphere. 1401 Willow Ln., North Wilkesboro, NC 28659. (336) 838-6900. Monday-Saturday 8 a.m.-evenings (call for closing hours).

The Cottage House ($-$$): 306 Elkin Hwy., North Wilkesboro, NC 28659. (336) 667-5564. Call for hours.

Accommodations

Addison Inn: In operation since 1983, the Addison Inn offers 115 professionally appointed rooms, complimentary continental breakfast, evening cappuccino and outdoor swimming pool. AAA Triple Diamond Award Winner. US Hwy. 421 North, Wilkesboro, NC 28697. (336) 838-1000. $61.99. www.Addisoninn.com

Elk Creek Inn: Located outside of North Wilkesboro in nearby Ferguson, the Elk Creek Inn is an equestrian-centered country resort. 512 Meadow Valley Rd., Ferguson, NC 28659. (336) 973-5706. www.goleatherwood.com

Old Traphill Mill Resort: A 200-year grist mill, with a 16-foot waterwheel on Little Sandy Creek, rooms in mill, and 240 sq. ft. cabins, great campground with larger than average campsites on the creek, horseback, hiking trails, fishing. Located one mile from Stone Mountain State Park and convenient to North Wilkesboro. They also rescue animals and have some exotic animals on the premises, including an emu, wild ponies and a white-tailed deer! 452 Traphill Mill Rd., Traphill, NC 28685. (336) 957-3713. $75-$150, Cabins $50-$125.

Old Fort

Websites: www.oldfort.org
www.mcdowellnc.org
Phone: Old Fort Chamber of Commerce: (828) 668-7223
Old Fort Mayor's Office: (828) 668-4244
Elevation: 1,438 feet
County: McDowell
Population: 1,000+
Attractions: Historic Carson House, Mountain Gateway Museum, Old Fort Railroad Museum

In existence as a village since 1869 and originally a fort built by the colonial militia before the Declaration of Independence, the settlement served for many years as the western outpost of the early United States. Just over the railroad tracks on the right is the town square; on the left next to the arrowhead is the old yellow depot, which also serves as a small railroad museum and houses the Chamber of Commerce. Amtrack Railroad service is planned to be restored by 2008 and the old depot is being prepared for that day.

Dining

D&B Café ($): Great light breakfast and lunches, specializing in unique herb bread sandwiches and gourmet soups. Their tuna delight sandwich is a must. A well-known local gathering place. 25 East Main St., Old Fort, NC 28762. 668-7786. Breakfast and lunch, Tuesday-Friday, 9 a.m.-4 p.m., Saturday 9 a.m.-3 p.m.

Four Oaks ($): Family-style seafood restaurant that has been around for over 30 years! Steaks, chicken and great hamburgers cooked homestyle. Hearty and large servings. Specialties include flounder filet, rainbow trout and their favorite "sea flower" appetizer. Located on Bat Cave Rd. 300 yards from Exit 73 off I-26, Old Fort, NC 28762. 668-4929. Lunch and dinner, Tuesday-Sunday 10 a.m.-10 p.m.

Mustard's Last Stand ($): Hearty southern cooking with daily specials. Home-cooked meals and delicious subs. One of the house specialties is the mini-burger. 186 Catawba River Rd., Old Fort, NC 28762. 668-4737. Lunch and dinner, Monday-Friday 10 a.m.-7 p.m., Saturday 10 a.m.-3 p.m.

Old Fort Connection ($): Country homestyle cooking, delicious homemade desserts and pastries. Breakfast served all day Saturday. 1259 Hwy. 70 West, Old Fort, NC 28762. 668-4752. Breakfast and lunch, Monday-Friday 6 a.m.-2 p.m., Saturday 6 a.m.-noon.

Whistle Stop ($): Family run pizzeria and sub-shop. Made-from-scratch pizzas. 27 Main St., Old Fort, NC 28762. 668-7676. Tuesday-Friday 11 a.m.-9 p.m., Saturday 4-9 p.m.

Accommodations

Catawba Falls Campground: Offering full RV hookup camping, cabin rental, and tent camping for over 20 years. 35 Peggy Loop, Old Fort, NC 28762. (828) 668-4831.

Inn on Mill Creek: Seven guest room bed and breakfast inn with four spacious rooms and suites in main house and three new suites in lake house. Rooms with fireplaces and hot tubs available. Full country breakfast with fresh fruit from inn's orchards. Two-story greatroom, piano, fishing, hiking, biking and massage available. 3895 Mill Creek Rd., Old Fort, NC 28762 (PO Box 185, Ridgecrest, NC 28770). (877) 735-2964, 668-1115. $100-160. www.inn-on-mill-creek.com

Robbinsville

Website: www.grahamchamber.com
Phone: Graham County Chamber of Commerce: (828) 497-3790, (800) 470-3790
Elevation: 2,064 feet
County: Graham
Population: 700+
Attractions: Joyce Kilmer Memorial Forest, Nantahala National Forest

Located at the far western end of the state, Robbinsville, the Graham County seat, was incorporated in 1893. A delightful small town that is a welcome stop for visitors seeking recreation in the wonderful wilderness areas surrounding it, especially the old-growth Joyce Kilmer Memorial Forest and the Nantahala National Forest, Robbinsville is small on size but large on mountain hospitality.

Dining

Tapoco Lodge Restaurant ($$): Cuisine in the lodge restaurant is traditional southern cooking, with a different dinner served each night. Full American Plan with hearty breakfast, light lunch and hearty dinner. Rt. 72 (Box A-1), Tapoco, NC 28771. (800) 822-5083, 498-2435. Open March-November. www.tapocolodge.com

Tootie's Café ($): Southern country cooking offering wide-ranging menu. Everything from burgers to seafood. Bluegrass singing Saturday evenings beginning at 7 p.m. during the summer season. 1235 Hwy. 28, Stecoah, NC 28771. 479-8430. Winter hours: Monday-Saturday 7 a.m.-7 p.m., Summer: Monday-Saturday 7 a.m.-9 p.m.

Accommodations

Beech Creek Cabins: Located just minutes away from white rafting and canoeing on the Nantahala River, hiking on the Appalachian Trail and the best mountain bike trails at "Tsali." Beech Creek offers spacious two-bedroom cabins with full kitchen, living room, dining room and bath. 568 Left Fork Beech Creek Rd., Robbinsville, NC 28771. (888) 525-9650, 479-2225. $65-$75. www.beechcreekcabins.com

Mountain Hollow Bed & Breakfast: Situated on 35 wooded acres in a pristine mountain valley. Featuring the Catherine Ann Suite, the Cottage Room, the Heart to Heart Room, and the Serenity Woods Room. Rte. 2 (Box 176 E5), Robbinsville, NC 28711. 479-3608. $55-$125. www.kikos.com/mountainhollow

Snowbird Mountain Lodge: Two-story lodge listed in the National Register of Historic Places. Built in 1941, Snowbird Mountain is nestled on almost 100 acres of undisturbed mountaintop. The Main Lodge is distinguished by a cathedral ceiling with hand-cut chestnut beams, butternut paneling, a 2,500-volume library and two massive stone fireplaces. Snowbird Mountain also offers accommodations in the charming Wolfe Cottage and the newly constructed Chestnut Lodge. Rates include breakfast, picnic lunch and gourmet dinner. 4633 Santeetlah Rd., Robbinsville, NC 28771. 479-3433. March-November. $175-$320. www.Snowbirdlodge.com

Tapoco Lodge Resort: Built in 1930 by the Aluminum Company of America, Tapoco Lodge offers all the fine amenities of a great country resort. Main lodge and spacious cottages, all with air-conditioning. Cuisine in the lodge restaurant is traditional southern cooking, with a different dinner served each night. Full American Plan with hearty breakfast, light lunch and hearty dinner. Rt. 72

(Box A-1), Tapoco, NC 28771. (800) 822-5083, 498-2435. Open March-November. $69-$149. www.tapocolodge.com

The Blue Boar Inn: A renovated country house hotel located just a short walk from Lake Santeetlah offering exceptional accommodations, including eight spacious, elegant guest rooms, each with private porch, sitting area, king- or queen-size beds, large bath, central heat and air-conditioning, television, telephone and refrigerator. The inn offers canoes, kayaks and pontoon boats for rent at the Blue Boar's Lake Santeetlah landing. 1283 Blue Boar Rd., Robbinsville, NC 28711. 479-8126. Open April 5-November 3. $95-$135. www.blueboarinn.com

Rutherfordton

Websites: www.rutherfordtourism.com
www.rutherfordcoc.org
Phones: Rutherford County Tourism Development Authority: (800) 849-5998, (828) 245-1492
Rutherfordton Chamber of Commerce: (828) 287-3090
Elevation: 929 feet
County: Rutherford
Population: 4,100+
Attractions: Lake Lure, Chimney Rock, Rutherford County Farm Museum, Rutherford County Museum

Rutherfordton, the county seat, offers an attractive courthouse square on a vibrant, easy-going all-American Main Street. Nearby are restaurants, shops, banks, offices, the Rutherford Hospital, clothing outlets, golf and lodgings. Pleasant homes line shady, rolling neighborhood streets in this charming town to the east of Asheville.

Dining

Vineyard Restaurant ($$): Great Italian cuisine. 151 Central St., Rutherfordton, NC 28139. 288-0240. Monday-Saturday 11 a.m.-9 p.m., Sunday noon-4 p.m.

Mi Pueblito ($): Mexican cuisine, excellent fajitas: chicken, beef, shrimp. 139 South Washington St., Rutherfordton, NC 28139. 286-2860. Monday-Friday: 11 a.m.-2 p.m., 5-10 p.m. Saturday: noon-10 p.m., Sunday: noon-9 p.m.

Accommodations

Carrier Houses Bed & Breakfasts (NRHP): Two elegantly restored Victorian homes located side by side in the heart of downtown Rutherfordton. Experience the charm of a bygone era gracefully enhanced by the comfort of all modern conveniences. Private bathroom in every bedroom. Full breakfast is included. Cable TV, phones, non-smoking rooms, no pets. 255 North Main St., Rutherfordton, NC 28139. (828) 287-4222, (800) 835-7071. $60. www.carrierhouses.com

Green River Plantation: Built in 1804, the Green River Plantation is a magnificent 42-room mansion offering bed and breakfast accommodations. It is also open for weddings, tours and events. Some rooms have kitchens and the ones without are supplied with refrigerators and coffee pots. Three rooms have queen-size beds, the fourth has a double. All have private entrances and bathrooms. Breakfast is served in the Tea Room which overlooks the swimming pool The home rests on 366 acres of land that reflect all of the gentility and refinement of the old pre-Civil War South. Coxe Rd., Rutherfordton, NC 29139. 286-1461. $80-$125. www.green-river.net/

Pinebrae Manor Bed & Breakfast: A country estate with beautiful and relaxing views. Nature trail, four rooms with private baths and large gathering room. The guest bedrooms all have private baths, telephones, TVs and are individually temperature-controlled. Breakfast served each morning in the dining room with beautiful table settings include sausage, bacon or ham with eggs, grits and homemade biscuits. There are also fresh fruits and fruit juices. 1286 NC 108, Rutherfordton, NC 28139. 286-1543. $52-$69. www.pinebrae.blueridge. net/manor.html

River Creek Campground: Rustic cabins. Riverside with scenic view of mountains. Campground with full amenities. All waterfront sites. Open year-round. 217 River Creek Dr., Rutherfordton, NC 28139. 287-3915. Cabins: $30-$70, RV: $22-$25, Campsites: $20-$25. www.nccamping.com/

Saluda

Websites: www.saluda.com
              www.nc-mountains.org
Phone: Polk County Visitor Center: (800) 440-7848
              Saluda City Office: (828) 749-2581
Elevation: 2,060 feet
County: Polk
Population: 575
Attractions: FENCE, Saluda's Historic Railroad Depot District

Saluda, situated in the foothills to the south of Asheville, is a town of old-fashioned charm and beauty, with 16 of its buildings listed on the National Register. Nestled peacefully in the mountains, their Main Street is also a National Historic District and offers restaurants, galleries and a variety of small shops. Saluda used to be a railroad stop on the way to Asheville from the lowlands and, to this day, the steep climb up the mountains is called the "Saluda Grade." The historic railroad district allows visitors a chance to catch a glimpse of local railroad history.

Dining

Green River Bar-B-Q ($): Great southern barbeque. 176 Main St., Saluda, NC 28773. 749-9892. Tuesday-Thursday 11 a.m.-8 p.m., Friday-Saturday 11 a.m.-9 p.m., Sunday noon-3 p.m.

Orchard Inn ($$$$): Tryon establishment for elegant, fine dining, Dinner served in four courses. Hwy. 176, Saluda, NC 28773. 749-5471. Tuesday-Saturday: One seating at 7 p.m.

The Purple Onion Café & Coffee House ($$): American bistro-style cooking: Mediterranean French, Italian dishes. Live music on the weekends. 16 Main St., Saluda, NC 28773. 749-1179. Closed Wednesday and Sunday. Lunch 11 a.m.-3 p.m., dinner 5-8 p.m. (Friday and Saturday until 9 p.m.). www. purpleonionsaluda.com

Good Thyme Café ($): Great breads from Wildflower Bakery on premises. Sandwiches, quiche, all homemade soups and fresh bakery items. Breakfast and lunch. 173 East Main St., Saluda, NC 28773. 749-9224. Wednesday-Saturday 8:30 a.m.-4:30 p.m., Sunday brunch 10 a.m.-3 p.m.

Accommodations

Charles Street Garden Suite: Guest accommodation in a suite that offers a tranquil garden setting with delightful outdoor sitting areas, including a swing at the entrance. Charles Street Garden has been featured in the HGTV network series "A Gardener's Diary." 76 Charles St., Saluda, NC 28773. 749-5846. $85.

Orchard Lake Campground: Two private lakes, wooded campsites with fire rings for tents, RVs and trailers (full hook-up), A-frame cottages for rent, lodge with kitchen facilities, restrooms with hot showers. Open April through October. 460 Orchard Lake Rd., Saluda, NC 28733. 749-3901. $25 per campsite.

The Oaks Bed & Breakfast: Victorian bed and breakfast furnished with American and Oriental antiques and original artwork in an atmosphere of easy elegance. Wrap-around porch and decks, croquet. Four bedrooms, each with private bath in main and two guest suites. 339 Greenville St., Saluda, NC 28773. (800) 893-6091, 749-9613. $115-$250. www.theoaksbedand breakfast.com

The Orchard Inn: Built in 1900 as a Southern Railroad destination, the Orchard Inn sits on a 12-acre crest of the Warrior Range in the Blue Ridge Mountains. A grand country inn, it offers nine guest rooms and four cottages, all comfortably furnished with period pieces and antiques. Full breakfast included. Hwy. 176, PO Box 128, Saluda, NC 28773. (800) 581-3800, 749-5471. $119-$245. www.orchardinn.com

Sparta

Website: www.sparta-nc.com
Phone: Alleghany Chamber of Commerce: (800) 372-5473
Elevation: 2,939 feet
County: Alleghany
Population: 1,800+
Attractions: Alleghany County Courthouse

Located at the center of Alleghany County to the northeast of Asheville, and at the confluence of highways US 21 and NC 18, Sparta is a classic southern small mountain town, with a great courthouse as the major building. There is an older business district with overtones of years gone by and two shopping centers, a satellite campus of Wilkes Community College and Alleghany Memorial Hospital.

Dining
Inn of the Red Thread ($$): Fine dining offering a variable gourmet menu and an eclectic collection of wines and beers. Friday evenings only. Reservations required. 110 Mountain Hearth Rd., Sparta, NC 28675. (336) 372-8743.

Mountain House ($$): Fresh seafood and homemade cooking. Also known for their chicken and dumplings which is offered on Wednesdays only. Homemade desserts. Hwy. 113, Piney Creek, NC 28663 (just north of Sparta). (336) 359-2580. Breakfast, lunch and dinner. Monday-Wednesday 6 a.m.-8 p.m., Thursday-Saturday 6 a.m.-9 p.m. Closed Sundays.

Sparta Restaurant ($): Home cooking with emphasis on seafood. 41 North Main, Sparta, NC 28675. (336) 372-8016. Monday: 6 a.m.-2 p.m., Tuesday-Saturday: 6 a.m.-8 p.m.

Accommodations
Inn of the Red Thread Bed & Breakfast: The Inn of the Red Thread is a rustic bed and breakfast getaway in a forest setting. Grounds include a mountain creek, two ponds, trails and marked meditation walks. Full breakfasts, labyrinth, main lodge with three guest rooms, and three spacious cabins with cathedral ceilings, fireplaces and whirlpool tubs for two. 110 Mountain Hearth Rd., Sparta, NC 28675. (336) 372-8743. $95-$140, Cabins $140. www.innofthered thread.com

Harmony Hill Bed & Breakfast: A restored 1890 Queen Anne residence, Harmony Inn offers six bedrooms with private baths. Gourmet breakfast in the dining room, in the gazebo, on the deck or on the wicker-furnished porch. 1740 Halsey Knob Rd., Sparta, NC 28675. (336) 372-6868. $125-$145.

Doughton-Hall Bed & Breakfast: The historic former residence of Congressman Robert L. Doughton, Doughton-Hall is an 1890s Queen Anne-style house. Four rooms, each with private bath. Buffet breakfast with everything from traditional ham, eggs and grits to soufflé and croissants. NC Hwy. 18 South, Laurel Springs, NC 28644. (336) 359-2341. $80.

Bald Knob Farm House: Nestled among a Christmas tree farm and surrounded by flowers and shrubs, Bald Knob Farm House offers country living in a relaxing atmosphere. Whole-house rental with four large bedrooms with antique furnishings. PO Box 491, Sparta, NC 28675. (336) 372-4191. $75. www.sparta-nc.com/aur

River Bend: River Bend is a custom-made, two-story (1,700 sq.ft) log home on 42 secluded acres bordering the Little River. Great river views, trout fishing and wildlife. 1602 White Pine Dr., Ennice, NC 28623. (336) 657-8838. $125-$140.

Tranquility Unlimited: A log vacation home on the Little River surrounded by Blue Ridge Mountains forest. Two-stories with living/dining room, kitchen, bedroom, bath and laundry on first floor. Second floor has loft with futon, bedroom with bath. Gated road for complete privacy. 87 Pine River Ln., Sparta, NC 28675. (336) 372-8260. $135. www.sparta-nc.com/tranquility

Spindale

Website: www.rutherfordtourism.com
Phone: Rutherford County Tourism Development Authority: (800) 849-5998, (828) 245-1492
Elevation: 1,094 feet
County: Rutherford
Population: 4,000+
Attractions: Lake Lure, Chimney Rock, Rutherford County Farm Museum, Rutherford County Museum

Located midway between Forest City and Rutherfordton, Spindale is home to Isothermal Community College which is the cultural and learning center for the entire area. Concerts at the Foundation, the college's new convention and performance facility, are among the best of the cultural season, and WNCW, the campus radio station, airs the best in regional and alternative music to the world. Spindale also offers a stretch of the Thermal Belt Walking Trail, following an old railroad right of way, and also has a very nice Farmer's Market.

Dining

Carolina Café ($): Down-home country cooking. 1026 East Main St., Spindale, NC 28160. 286-2411. Breakfast and lunch: Monday-Friday 6 a.m.-3 p.m., Saturday and Sunday 6 a.m.-2 p.m.

Spindale Drug ($): Step back in time for great sandwiches, soups, salads. Noted for their old-fashioned soda fountain service. 101 West Main St., Spindale, NC 28160. 286-3746. Monday-Friday 8:30 a.m.-7 p.m.; Saturday; 8:30 a.m.-4 p.m., Sunday 1:30-3 p.m.

The Shakes Shop ($): Known for their hamburgers and dinner plates. Breakfast, lunch and dinner. 612 West Main St., Spindale, NC 28160. 286-4792. Monday-Friday: 7 a.m.-2 p.m., Saturday 7 a.m.-11:30 p.m., Sunday 7 a.m.-9 p.m.

Spindale Restaurant ($): Daily specials, sandwiches, salads, soups, dinner plates. Breakfast, lunch and dinner. 411 West Main, Spindale, NC 28160. 287-2215. Monday 11 a.m.-8 p.m., Sunday 11 a.m.-2 p.m. Closed Saturdays.

Spruce Pine

Websites: www.sprucepine.org
www.mitchell-county.com

Phone: Spruce Pine Town Hall: (828) 765-3000
Mitchell County Chamber of Commerce: (828) 765-9483, (800)
227-3912
Elevation: 2,517 feet
County: Mitchell
Population: 2,500+
Attractions: North Carolina Museum of Minerals, Orchard at Altapass

Located northeast of Asheville on the banks of the Toe River, Spruce Pine is
in a region of the mountains that is famous for its gem mines. World-class rubies
and sapphires have been found nearby and the gem-mining culture has its roots
deep in Spruce Pine history.

Dining

Afternoon Delight ($): Delicious food, hometown hospitality, specialty items
of different foods, along with delicious homemade desserts and breads. Lunch
and supper specials everyday. 14701 Hwy. 226 South, Spruce Pine, NC 28777.
765-7164. Open Monday-Saturday 8:00 a.m. to 9:00 p.m. Closed Tuesday.
Sunday brunch 9:00 a.m.-3:00 p.m.

Chez Lien ($): Chinese cuisine and Oriental specialties. 424 Summit Ave., Spruce
Pine, NC 28777. 765-9767, seven days week: 11 a.m.-10 p.m.

Grassy Creek Country Club Restaurant ($$): Everything from burgers to
chicken florentine. Hwy. 226 at the Grassy Creek Golf Course, 2360 Swiss
Pine Lake Dr., Spruce Pine, NC 28777. 765-6589. Lunch: Monday-Friday 11
a.m.-2 a.m. Dinner: Friday-Saturday 5-9 p.m.

Papas Pizza-To-Go ($): Well-known local pizza restaurant. 665 Commons Shop-
ping Center, Spruce Pine, NC 28777. 765-6565. Weekdays: 11a.m.-9 p.m.,
Weekends: 10 a.m.-10 p.m.

Accommodations

Bear Den Creek Side Cabins: 400 private wooded acres adjacent to the Blue Ridge
Parkway. 144 campsites for tents, pop-ups and all types of recreational vehicles.
Water, electricity, fire-rings and picnic tables at each site. Sites with full hook-
ups. Modern bath houses; each with hot showers, coin-operated washers and
dryers. Also custom-built white pine cabins with oak floors nestled alongside a
mountain stream. Cabins furnished with all amenities, including a fireplace and
Jacuzzi. Year-round availability. 600 Bear Den Mountain Rd., Spruce Pine, NC
28777. 765-2888. Cabins $60-$200, Campsites $29-$58. www.bear-den.com/

Pinebridge Inn & Executive Center: Unique hotel that was once Spruce Pine's
only schoolhouse. Early 1920s brick building with 44 spacious and beauti-
fully appointed rooms. High ceilings, tall windows and a touch of classroom
memorabilia. Apartment and cottage available. Deluxe breakfast served daily.
101 Pinebridge Avenue, Spruce Pine, NC 28777. (800) 356-5059, 765-5543.
$59-$139. www.pinebridgeinn.com/

Springmaid Mountain: Secluded 400-acre retreat located on the North Toe
River. Cabins, bunkhouse, campsites. 2171 Henredon Rd., Spruce Pine, NC
28777. 765-2353, (888) 297-0725. Cabins $47-$74, Campsites $6-$21. www.
appnetsite.com/springmaid/

Sylva

Websites: www.townofsylva.org
www.mountainlovers.com
Phone: Sylva Town Offices: (828) 586-2719
Jackson County Chamber of Commerce: (828) 586-2155, (800)
962-1911
Elevation: 2,036 feet
County: Jackson
Population: 2,450
Attractions: Jackson County Museum

Sylva is a quaint town in Western North Carolina surrounded by the beautiful
mountains and has a delightful downtown area has many restaurants and shops
along tree-lined streets. To their credit, the citizens of Sylva have also provided
for the children of the community a wonderful, home-built state-of-the-art playground that is as good as any in the state!

Dining

Alan's on Main Street ($$): Classic innovative cuisine, fresh seafood from
Florida, wide-ranging menu including vegetarian dishes. 553 West Main St.,
Sylva, NC 28779. 631-4545. Reservations suggested. Tuesday-Saturday: 5 p.m.
to closing.

Bella Roma Pizzeria ($): Pizzas, Italian and Greek dishes, pastas, subs. 1070
Skyland Dr., Sylva, NC 28779. 631-3355. Monday-Thursday 5-9 p.m., Friday-
Saturday 5-10 p.m.

Lulu's on Main ($$): Acclaimed restaurant offering a varied and imaginatively
prepared menu. Featured in Southern Living and acclaimed as one of their
regional favorites. 612 West Main St., Sylva, NC 28779. 586-8989, Monday-
Saturday: 11:30 a.m.-9 p.m. www.lulusonmain.com

Soul Infusion Tea House & Bistro ($): Unique teahouse experience. Deli
sandwiches, soups, salads, chilis and more. Live music on the weekends. Teas,
fresh fruit juices, smoothies and great selection of beer and wine. 628 E. Main
St., Sylva, NC 28779. 586-1717. Tuesday-Thursday 11:30 a.m.-8 p.m., Friday
noon-midnight and Saturday 5 p.m.-midnight. www.soulinfusion.com/

Sweet Dreams Bakery & Deli ($): Great local bakery. Fresh homemade soups
and sandwiches. Wonderful specialty cakes including Italian Crème, Hershey's
Bar and Chocolate Mouse Raspberry Torte. 894 E. Main St., Sylva, NC 28779.
586-0939. Lunch: Monday-Friday 7:30 a.m.-5:30 p.m., Saturday 9 a.m.-2 p.m.
(bakery only open).

Accommodations

Balsam Mountain Inn (NRHP): The inn, located in nearby Balsam, is among the oldest in the North Carolina mountains. Construction began in 1905. It was modeled after the Saratoga Inn in New York and features Neoclassical architecture. A hallmark of the inn is its 100-foot-long, two-tier porch dotted by restored oak rockers. The porch offers splendid views of the Great Balsam Mountains. Seven Springs Dr., Balsam, NC 28707. (800) 224-9498. www.balsaminn.com.

Freeze House: Overlooking downtown Sylva, the Freeze House offers four rooms with private baths. Full breakfast. 71 Sylvan Heights, Sylva, NC 28779. 586-8161. $65-$100. www.bbonline.com/nc/freeze/index.html

Mountain Brook: A collection of quaint fireplace cottages sprinkled on a mountainside! AAA-approved, Mountain Brook has been operating for over 20 years. The cottages were constructed in the 1930s and are nestled in woodlands with rushing streams nearby. Picnic area, game room, nature trail, charcoal barbeque grills, stocked trout pond, spa and sauna. 208 Mountain Brook Rd., Sylva, NC 28799. 586-4329. $90-$140. www.mountainbrook.com

Mountain Creek Cabins: Completely furnished cabins, cottages and deluxe mountain homes. All units have full kitchens, TV with DSS satellite, fireplaces, grills and linens. Some units have telephones and some allow pets. Located just outside Sylva. PO Box 178, Dillsboro, NC 28725. 586 6042, (877) 525-4933. $78-$86. www.mountaincreekcottages.com

Tryon

Websites:	www.tryon-nc.com
	www.nc-mountains.org
Phone:	Town of Tryon: (828) 859-6654
	Polk County Visitor Center: (800) 440-7848
Elevation:	1,100 feet
County:	Polk
Population:	1,760
Attractions:	Polk County Historical Museum, FENCE

The small mountain town of Tryon, located southeast of Asheville, is well-known for the equestrian events held at the Foothills Equestrian Nature Center (FENCE) almost every weekend from April through October. The village also has a number of art and craft galleries, and a nice selection of restaurants and accommodations, and over the years, Tryon has earned the reputation as one of the friendliest towns in the south.

Dining

Isaac's at Melrose Inn ($$): Located in the Melrose Inn, Isaac's offers American cuisine and selected Peruvian dishes. 55 Melrose Avenue, Tryon, NC 28782. 859-7014. Breakfast: Monday-Saturday 7:30-11 a.m.; Lunch: Monday,

Tuesday, Thursday and Friday 11 a.m.-2 p.m.; Dinner: Thursday and Friday 5:30-8:30 p.m.; Sunday Brunch 11 a.m.-2 p.m.

Pine Crest Inn ($$$): Once a favorite of F. Scott Fitzgerald and Ernest Hemingway, the inn is listed in the National Register of Historic Places. Their extensive dinner menu combines the tastes of the region with the flair of contemporary American cuisine. 200 Pine Crest Ln., Tryon, NC 28782. (800) 633-3001, 859-9135. Monday-Thursday: 8.-10 a.m.; Monday-Thursday 6-9 p.m., Friday and Saturday 6-9:30 p.m.; Sunday 11 A.M-2 p.m. Reservations requested.

Ruth's ($): Southern-style home cooking! 100 North Trade St., Tryon, NC 28782. 859-6336. Breakfast daily beginning at 9 a.m. and lunch from 11 a.m.-2:30 p.m.

Sidestreet Pizza & Pasta ($): A Tryon institution, they are known for their great Italian food and pizzas. 201 South Trade St., Tryon, NC 28782. 859-5325. Monday, Thursday and Friday: 11 a.m.-9 p.m.; Saturday 11 a.m.-10 p.m.; Sunday 3-9 p.m.

Stone Hedge Inn ($$$): Their menu offers an eclectic mix of contemporary specials and traditional favorites including angus beef filet, North Carolina mountain trout, fresh fish and jumbo shrimp, chicken and much more. Sunday brunch features eggs benedict, omelets and quiche. 222 Stone Hedge Ln., PO Box 366, Tryon, NC 28782. 859-9114. Dinner: Wednesday-Saturday, 6-9 p.m. Reservations required. Sunday brunch: noon-2:30 p.m.

The European Bistro ($): Greek cuisine offering homemade specialties and fresh seafood. 246 North Trade St., Tryon, NC 28782. 859-6155. Monday-Friday 10 a.m.-8 p.m.; Saturday 8 a.m.-8 p.m.

Accommodations

Melrose Inn: Built in 1889, the Melrose Inn offers a wide variety of rooms to choose from, each is beautifully decorated with its own unique motif, ranging from roses to angels to the sea. Full breakfast. Located in Tryon, NC 28782. 859-7014. $65-$120. www.tryon-melrose-inn.com

Mimosa Inn: Situated on the site of the original Mills Plantation, the Mimosa Inn offers ten restored guest rooms with private baths and a guest house. Large common areas and antiques throughout. Full breakfast included. White columns, southern hospitality! One Mimosa Inn Ln., Tryon, NC 28782. 859-7688, (877) 646-6724. Rates start at $95. www.carolina-foothills.com

Stone Hedge Inn: Located three miles from Tryon town center, the Stone Hedge Inn includes a main house, guest house and a pool-side cottage all surrounded by gardens, wooded walks and rolling meadows. Each building is a unique fieldstone structure, constructed in the 1930s from local stone. Known also for their fine dining. 222 Stone Hedge Ln., PO Box 366, Tryon, NC 28782. 859-9114. $110-$145. www.stone-hedge-inn.com

Tryon Old South Bed & Breakfast: Built in 1910 and restored to its former Colonial Revival elegance, the Tryon Old South Bed & Breakfast is located two block from downtown Tryon. 107 Markham Rd., Tryon, NC 28782. (800) 288-7966, 859-6965. Rates start at $55. www.tryonoldsouth.com

Pine Crest Inn (NRHP): Once a favorite of F. Scott Fitzgerald and Ernest Hemingway, the Pine Crest Inn offers individually decorated rooms, suites and cottages with private baths. Their Fox and Hounds Bar creates an intimate library setting, and they are known for fine dining and great breakfasts. AAA Four-Diamond Award. 200 Pine Crest Ln., Tryon, NC 28782. (800) 633-3001, 859-9135. $95-$190. www.pinecrestinn.com.

Valdese

Websites: www.ci.valdese.nc.us
                www.burkecounty.org
Phone: City of Valdese: (828) 879-2120
                Burke County Chamber of Commerce: (828) 437-3021
                Burke County Travel & Tourism Center: (888) 462-2921
Elevation: 1,203 feet
County: Burke
Population: 4,485
Attractions: Museum of Waldensian History, Trail of Faith, From This Day Forward, Waldensian Heritage Winery

A city rich in history, Valdese has a heritage that dates back to the middle ages. Its settlers, known as "The People of the Valleys" came originally from the Waldensian communities located in the Alpine Valleys of northern Italy and settled in the area around Valdese. Founded in 1893, Valdese remains a town still linked by its roots to Italy.

Dining

Myra's Little Italy ($$): Enjoy a great Italian meal. Offering pizza, pasta and wide variety of Italian cooking. 155 Bobo St., Valdese, NC 28690.

Myra's Ice Cream and Sandwich Shop ($): Unique 1950s atmosphere complete with jukeboxes and period decorations. Wide selections of sandwiches and delicious cream treats. 212 Main St. West, Valdese, NC 28690. 879-8049. Seven days a week, 9 a.m.-11 p.m.

Valle Crucis

Websites: www.vallecrucis.com
                www.boonechamber.com
Phone: Boone Area Chamber of Commerce: (828) 264-2225, (800) 852-9506
Elevation: 2,800 feet
County: Watauga
Population: No information available; small unincorporated community

Attractions: Original Mast General Store

Located high in the mountains near Boone, Valle Crucis (The Vale of the Cross) is a historic community that has been around for 200 years. It is home to the original Mast General Store, the Holy Cross Episcopal Church and the Valle Crucis Conference Center, as well as many other shops, galleries and studios featuring handmade crafts and art, rustic furniture and pottery.

Dining

Mast Farm Inn Restaurant ($$): Located in the historic Mast Farm Inn, this great restaurant serves fresh, organic contemporary regional cuisine. Fireside or terrace dining. Aunt Josie's Espresso and Wine Bar also serves appetizer portions of their entree menu. 2543 Broadstone Rd., Valle Crucis, NC 28691. (888) 963-5857, 963-5857. Reservations suggested. Dining schedule varies with season. Call for hours. www.mastfarminn.com

Accommodations

Mast Farm Inn Bed & Breakfast: The Mast Farm Inn is a full-service country inn that has been welcoming guests with both rooms in the farmhouse and getaway cottages for couples and families. A hot country breakfast is served to inn guests, included with lodging. Renowned restaurant and bar features fresh, organic contemporary regional cuisine. 2543 Broadstone Rd., Valle Crucis, NC 28691. (888) 963-5857, 963-5857. $155-$195, cottages $225-255/ www.mastfarminn.com

Waynesville

Websites: www.waynesville.com
www.downtownwaynesville.com
www.haywood-nc.com
www.smokeymountains.net

Phone: Haywood County Chamber of Commerce: (828) 456-3021, (877) 456-3073

Elevation: 3,600 feet

County: Haywood

Population: 10,000+

Attractions: Museum of North Carolina Handicrafts, Mountain Museum, Haywood Arts Repertory Theatre

Haywood County's largest and oldest town, Waynesville is located about 40 miles west of Asheville. Rich in history dating back almost 200 years and known for its true southern hospitality, Waynesville has a wealth of unique shops, arts and crafts galleries, restaurants and accommodations. Shade trees, brick sidewalks, benches, water fountains, art and iron sculpture adorn the vibrant downtown area and make this lovely street a destination in its own right.

Dining

Clyde's Restaurant ($): Located in nearby Hazelwood, Clyde's Restaurant is perhaps the most famous in Haywood County, and deservedly so. A true country restaurant with a full menu, Clyde's has been known for their absolutely fabulous homemade pies since the 1930s! Specialties include coconut cream, lemon, chocolate and banana, all topped with rich sugar meringue. Not to be missed. 2107 S. Main St., Hazelwood, NC. 456-9135. Open Tuesday-Sunday from 6 a.m.-10 p.m. Closed Mondays.

Lomo Grill Café ($$): Italian Mediterranean Cuisine and Argentine Grill. The main dining room has recently been renovated, and new granite-topped tables in the wine bar allow diners who arrive early to nibble on one of the restaurant's acclaimed appetizers and have a drink before dinner. The Lomo Grill is good enough to have been featured in Southern Living magazine. Award-winning food and wine. 44 Church St., Waynesville, NC 28786, 452-5222. Lunch: Monday-Saturday 11a.m.-3 p.m. Dinner: Monday-Saturday 5:30-9 p.m. (hours for dinner vary during winter season). www.lomogrill.com

O'Malley's on Main Pub & Grill ($): Traditional pub fare. Their slogan is "A Little Piece of Ireland." 172 N. Main St., Waynesville, NC 28786. 452-4228. Monday-Wednesday 11 a.m.-10 p.m. Thursday-Saturday 11 a.m.-11 p.m. (bar stays open). Closed Sunday.

Stefano's Mediterranean Grill ($$): Regional Mediterranean specialties and American favorites offered in a casual atmosphere. 111 North Main St., Waynesville, NC 28786. 452-0027. Lunch: Monday-Saturday, 10:30 a.m.-2:30 p.m. Dinner: Monday-Saturday 5-10 p.m. (hours for dinner vary during winter season).

The Patio ($): Light lunch fare, wine and beer, specialty cheese shop. 24 Church St., Waynesville, NC 28786. 454-0070. Summer hours: Monday-Thursday 11 a.m.-7 p.m., Friday 11 a.m.-10 p.m., Saturday and Sunday 11a.m.-4 p.m.

Whitman's Bakery & Sandwich Shoppe ($): Great bakery that has been in business since 1945. Wide selection of sandwiches, salads and deli dishes. 18 N. Main St., Waynesville, NC 28786. 456-8271. Bakery: Tuesday-Saturday 6 a.m.-5:30 p.m. Sandwich Shoppe: Tuesday-Saturday 11 a.m.-3 p.m.

Accommodations

Balsam Mountain Inn: Balsam Mountain Inn, nestled in the mountains near Waynesville, is one of the south's grand old inns. Built at the turn of the century, this lovingly restored romantic inn features a casual elegance that's lured travelers for decades. Visitors find 50 comfortable, spacious guest rooms and suites, each with its own unique decor. Peace and quiet is guaranteed as rooms come without phones or televisions. The inn's amenities include Seven Springs restaurant, a 2,000-volume library, two meeting rooms, card/puzzle room, sitting parlor, hiking trails, gift shop and two 100-foot porches, perfect for rocking and relaxing. Balsam Mountain Inn, Balsam, NC. (800) 224-9498. www.balsaminn.com

Mountain Creek Bed & Breakfast: Retro-style 1950s decor. Full gourmet breakfast, pet-friendly, whirlpool suites, tree-top balcony rooms, creeks, paths, and woods! Owners are avid cyclists and hikers. Knowledgeable about area hikes and trails. (800) 557-9766, 456-5509. 146 Chestnut Walk Dr., Waynesville, NC 28786. $85-$125. www.mountaincreekbb.com

Pisgah Inn: Located at an elevation of 5,000 feet above sea level on top of Mount Pisgah on the Blue Ridge Parkway, the Pisgah Inn not only offers visitors truly spectacular vistas but also great food in their on-site restaurant. Blue Ridge Parkway, Milepost 408, (828) 235-8228. www.pisgahinn.com

Rivermont Cabins: Nine rustic and contemporary hand-hewn log cabins by the Pigeon River. A waterfront retreat nestled on 70 acres offering fireplaces, swimming, hiking, barn game room, old-fashioned porches with rockers and golf privileges. 126 Deer Run Dr., Waynesville, NC 28786. 648-3066. $415-$985, 2 persons weekly rental of cabin. www.rivermont.com

Swag Country Inn: The Swag is a place for rest, rejuvenation, discovery and creation. Built out of century-old hand-hewn logs and located atop a 5,000-foot mountain, the Swag Country Inn is an award-winning refuge surrounded by 250 acres. Great views and hospitality. 2300 Swag Rd., Waynesville, NC. (800) 789-7672. www.theswag.com

The Old Stone Inn: Wonderful hillside setting surrounded with 100-year-old trees, The Old Stone Inn offers easy access to town, bountiful breakfasts and award-winning candlelight dining. Rooms and cottages. 109 Dolan Rd., Waynesville, NC 28786. (800) 432-8499, 456-3333. March-November. $104-$184. www.oldstoneinn.com

Treasure Cove Cabins: Cabins complete with fireplaces, Jacuzzis, massage table, central heat and A/C, full kitchen, TV, gas grill, washer/dryer and covered porch. Ten minutes from the Blue Ridge Parkway, just across the road from Little East Fork River, fishing, hiking, mountain biking trails all nearby. 388 Little East Fork Rd., Canton, NC 28786. 627-6037. Two-night minimum, $125-$150 per night. www.treasurecovecabins.com

Weaverville

Website: www.weaverville.net
Phone: Town of Weaverville: (828) 645-7116
Elevation: 2,176
County: Buncombe
Population: 2,600+
Attractions: Zebulon B Vance Birthplace, Dry Ridge Historical Museum, Gourmet Gardens Herb Farm

Located just north of Asheville about 12 miles, Weaverville was the birthplace of Zebulon T. Vance, governor of North Carolina in 1862-65 and 1877-79, who was born in the beautiful Reems Creek Valley to the east of the eventual town center. Incorporated in 1874, Weaverville today is a welcoming community with many great little shops, fine restaurants and places to stay for the night. A must-see if you do visit is the Vance Birthplace, a restored colonial homesite run by the State of North Carolina.

Dining

Asheville Pizza Café ($): Great pizzas, salads and exotic sandwiches. Live entertainment on Thursday and other days during summer season. 55 North Main St., Weaverville, NC 28787. 658-8778. Monday-Saturday 11a.m.-9 p.m., Sunday 4-9 p.m.

Stoney Knob Café ($-$$): Dining alfresco, wine bar and live music. 337 Merrimon Ave., Weaverville, NC 28787. 645-3309. Call for hours.

Sunnyside Café ($$): Wonderful fine dining. Wide menu with entrees ranging from almond-crusted local mountain trout to roasted herb-crusted pork loin. Luncheon menu of soups and salads. 18 N. Main St., Weaverville, NC 28787. 658-2660. Lunch: Monday-Friday 11:30 a.m.-2 p.m. Dinner: Tuesday-Saturday 5:30-9 p.m.

The Weaverville Milling Company ($$): The Milling Company is a comfortable and homey restaurant located in a former mill. Homemade food with mountain trout a specialty. Reems Creek Rd., Weaverville, NC 28787. 645-4700. Reservations suggested. Dinner 5-9 p.m. Closed Wednesday.

Accommodations

Inn on Main Street: A 100-year-old Victorian inn furnished in turn-of-the-century antiques. This romantic air-conditioned bed and breakfast features great breakfasts and whirlpool tubs. 88 S. Main St., Weaverville, NC 28787. (877) 873-6074, 645-4935. $115-$145. www.innonmain.com

The Hawk and Ivy Bed & Breakfast: A holistic country B&B retreat located in nearby Barnardsville on 24 acres. The main house was built in 1910 and features a wrap-around porch and private guest rooms. The guest cottage has two stories, each with its own entrance, bath and full kitchen. The houses are surrounded by wildflower meadows with wonderful views, a small swimming pool, woods and the Ivy River. 133 North Fork Rd., Barnardsville, NC 28709. (888) 395-7254, 626-3486. $90-$125. www.hawkandivy.com

Dry Ridge Inn: Built in 1849, the Dry Ridge Inn features eight rooms with private baths, some with fireplaces. 26 Brown St., Weaverville, NC 28787. (800) 839-3899, 658-3899. $95-$155. www.dryridgeinn.com

Freedom Escape Lodge: Great country lodge offering luxurious accommodations. Private lake, fishing, swimming, outdoor sports. 530 Upper Flat Creek Rd., Weaverville, NC 28787. 658-0814, (888) 658-0814. $119-$169. www.freedomescapelodge.com.

Secret Garden Bed & Breakfast: The Secret Garden stands as a beautiful circa-1904 low-country Charleston-style Victorian home. Surrounded by a giant hemlock hedge, the house features a 60-foot verandah as well as a large outdoor yard and gardens. A full gourmet breakfast is served each morning, offering original recipes along with afternoon hors d'oeuvres, evening refreshments and nightly turndown service. 56 North Main St. (P.O. Box 2226), Weaverville, NC 28787. 658-9317, (800) 797-8211. $125-$145. www.virtualcities.com/ons/nc/m/ncm50010.htm

Wilkesboro

Website: www.wilkesnc.org
Phone: Wilkes County Chamber of Commerce: (336) 838-8662
Elevation: 1,042 feet
County: Wilkes
Population: 3,200+
Attractions: Wilkes Art Gallery, Old Wilkes County Jail Museum, Old Wilkes Walking Tour, Stone Mountain State Park, W. Scott Kerr Dam & Reservoir, John C. Walker Community Center Theatre, Wilkes Community College Gardens

Home to the celebrated MerleFest, an internationally acclaimed acoustic and bluegrass music festival, Wilkesboro has much to offer visitors. Nearby outdoor attractions, the many downtown shops and galleries and the multifaceted cultural life in this charming mountain town ensure a great visit. Wilkesboro has been in existence for over 200 years as a village, and is also the county seat of Wilkes County.

Dining

Amalfi's Italian Restaurant ($-$$): Italian cuisine. 1919-G Hwy. 421, Wilkesboro, NC 28697. (336) 838-3188. Call for hours.

Chile Verde ($): Mexican and American cuisine. 1502 Mal Square, Wilkesboro, NC 28697. (336) 838-1999. Monday-Thursday: 11a.m.-10 p.m., Friday: 11a.m.-10 30 p.m., Saturday: 12 a.m.-10:30 p.m., Sunday: 12 a.m.-9 p.m.

Don's Seafood ($$): Excellent seafood served in a casual atmosphere. 1200 River St. Wilkesboro, NC 28697. (336) 667-3331. Dinner only. Tuesday-Thursday 4:30-8:30 p.m., Friday and Saturday 4:30-9 p.m., Sunday 11:45 a.m.-2:30 p.m. (lunch only).

Hadley's ($): Homestyle country cooking. Specialty of the house is homemade apple pie. 328 Wilkesboro Ave., Wilkesboro, NC 28697. (336) 838-8351.

McAlister's Deli ($): 1840 Winkler St., Wilkesboro, NC 28697. (336) 667-0669.

Accommodations

Old Traphill Mill Resort: A 200-year grist mill, with a 16-foot waterwheel on Little Sandy Creek, rooms in mill, and 240 sq. ft. cabins, great campground with larger than average campsites on the creek, horseback, hiking trails, fishing. Located one mile from Stone Mountain State Park. They also rescue animals and have some exotic animals on the premises, including an emu, wild ponies and a white-tailed deer! 452 Traphill Mill Rd., Traphill, NC 28685. (336) 957-3713. $75-$150, Cabins $50-$125.

Chapter Five
Western North Carolina Wineries

A complete list of all wineries in the state of North Carolina can be found at the NC Wine website: www.ncwine.org. The wineries listed below are only those found in the mountains.

Biltmore Estate Winery
Location: Asheville
Address: Biltmore Estate, Asheville, NC
Phone: (800) 543-2961
Hours: Monday-Saturday 11-7, Sunday noon-7
Wine List: Chardonnay Sur Lies, Riesling, White Zinfandel, Sauvignon Blanc, Chenin Blanc, Cardinal's Crest, Cabernet Sauvignon, Cabernet Franc, Merlot, Chateau Biltmore Chardonnay, Chateau Biltmore Cabernet Sauvignon, Vanderbilt Claret, Brut Sparkling

Cerminaro Vineyard
Location: Boomer
Address: 4399 Wilkesboro Blvd, Boomer, NC 28606
Phone: (828) 754-9306
Hours: By appointment only
Wine List: DeChaunac, Chancellor, Leon-Millot, Merlot, Seyval Blanc, Vignoles, Cayuga White

Cerminaro Vineyard
Location: Rhona
Address: 837 Pardue Farm Rd., Rhona, NC 28670
Phone: (336) 984-3296
Hours: Thursday-Saturday: noon-6, Sunday; 1-6, other times by appointment only
Wine List: Cabernet Franc, Chambourcin, Viognier, Chardonel, Melody

Chateau Laurinda
Location: Sparta
Address: 690 Reeves Ridge Rd., Sparta, NC 28675
Phone: (828) 650-3236
Hours: Tuesday-Saturday: 10-7, Sunday 10-5
Wine List: Merlot, Cabernet Sauvignon, Cabernet Franc, Syrah, Chambourcin, Seyval Blanc, Riesling, Pinot Gris, Viognier Apple, Blackberry, Plum, Muscadine

Ritler Ridge Vineyards
Location: Candler
Address: 5 Piney Mountain Church Rd., Candler, NC 28715
Phone: (828) 665-7405
Hours: Wednesday-Sat: 11-5
Wine List: Red Table Wine, White Table Wine, Pinot Gris, Cabernet Sauvignon, Cabernet Franc

Silohouse Vineyard and Winery
Location: Haywood County
Address: Rte. 1, Walker Rd., Waynesville, NC 28786
Phone: (828) 456-5408
Hours: By appointment only
Wine List: Cabernet Sauvignon, Chardonnay

The Teensy Winery
Location: Union Mills
Address: 3661 Painters Gap Rd., Union Mills, NC 28167
Phone: (828) 287-7763
Hours: By appointment only
Wine List: Chardonnay, cabernet Sauvignon

Waldensian Heritage Wines
Location: Valdese
Address: 4940 Villar Ln. NE, Valdese, NC 28690
Phone: (828) 879-3202
Hours: Thursday-Sunday: 1-6, Monday-Wednesday: by appointment only
Wine List: Heritage Burgundy Valdese, Burgundy Valdese, Blanc Royale, Waldensian White, Piedmont Rose, Blush Regale, Villar Rouge

Index

Subject Index

Other publications from R. Brent and Company

The Synoptic Gospels:
A Journey Into the Kingdom
Volume I: From Bethlehem to the River Jordan

by Edward L. Bleynat, Jr.

In this first volume of *The Synoptic Gospels: A Journey Into the Kingdom*, Ed Bleynat has created a much needed guide for those seeking to better understand the stories of Jesus as told in the Gospels of Matthew, Mark and Luke.

The Synoptic Gospels:
A Journey Into the Kingdom
Volume II: From the Desert to the Mount

by Edward L. Bleynat, Jr.

In the second volume of *The Synoptic Gospels: A Journey Into the Kingdom*, Bleynat continues the unfolding story, which takes us from the barren desert wilderness near the River Jordan to the fertile mount of God's revelation. This series makes teaching adult Christian education easy for everyone. Comes with everything needed, including discussion questions, detailed maps, illustrations, scripture, a comprehensive biblical and historical timeline, extensive index, and additional reading resources.

Called to Honor
Memoirs of a Three-War Veteran
World War II • Korea • Vietnam

By Colonel John Edward Gray, USA, Retired

A gripping TRUE *story that reads like an action adventure!*
This is the remarkable story of Col. Gray's life and 30-year career as a serviceman.

Souvenirs
From the Life of a Renegade Priest

by Rev. James S. Petty, M. Div.

This memoir of unforgettable stories is an oustanding collection of wonderful vignettes. You may laugh, you may cry. Yet one thing is certain: your life will not be left unchanged by this powerful and sometimes painfully honest tribute to life, relationships, love, sickness and death.

I Am Not Ready To Die Just Yet
Stories of Healing

by The Reverend Anne C. Brower, M.D.

Through insights gained from her vast research and the heart-warming stories of determined survivors, Brower describes how to move beyond and through disease to live a whole and vibrant life.

Feasting on Food and the Enneagram
a book of recipes and insights

compiled and edited by Holy Ground

For those who work the land, set the table, and savor the feast with a grateful heart

Call 828-350-9898 or visit rbrent.com to order your copies today.